The Sleep Lady®'s
Good Night,
Sleep Tight

Gentle Proven Solutions to Help Your Child Sleep
Without Leaving Them to Cry It Out

The Sleep Lady®'s
GOOD NIGHT, SLEEP TIGHT

KIM WEST, LCSW-C
with JOANNE KENEN

hachette
BOOKS

New York

Copyright © 2020 by Kim West and Joanne Kenen
Cover design by Terri Sirma
Cover photograph copyright © LightField Studios / Shutterstock
Cover copyright © 2020 Hachette Book Group, Inc.

Excerpt from *Good Night Yoga* © 2015 Mariam Gates, Illustrated by Sarah Jane Hinder (http://www.sarahjanehinder.com) used with permission from the publisher, Sounds True, Inc.

Text from "7 Signs Your Child Has Developed a Healthy Attachment" is reprinted by permission of Mark Loewen, licensed professional counselor and founder of LaunchPad Counseling in Richmond, VA (launchpadcounseling.com).

Hachette Books
Hachette Book Group
1290 Avenue of the Americas, New York, NY 10104
HachetteBooks.com
Twitter.com/HachetteBooks
Instagram.com/HachetteBooks

Printed in the United States of America

Revised and updated edition: March 2020

First edition: 2005, 2006; revised edition 2009

Hachette Books is a division of Hachette Book Group, Inc.

The Hachette Books name and logo are trademarks of Hachette Book Group, Inc.

The Hachette Speakers Bureau provides a wide range of authors for speaking events. To find out more, go to www.hachettespeakersbureau.com or call (866) 376-6591.

The publisher is not responsible for websites (or their content) that are not owned by the publisher.

Library of Congress Cataloging-in-Publication Data has been applied for.

ISBNs: 978-0-7382-8613-6 (trade paperback); 978-0-7382-8614-3 (e-book); 978-1-5491-2391-7 (audiobook)

LSC-C

Printing 2, 2020

CONTENTS

Chapter 1

WHAT I BELIEVE AND WHY

"How is the baby sleeping?" It's one of the first questions parents of a new baby face, after "Boy or girl?" or "How much did she weigh?" If the baby sleeps well, the answer all too often is "Oh, she's a good baby." By implication, those who don't sleep are bad babies, which to me is a ludicrous notion. These parents, already overwhelmed by exhaustion, now must also deal with feelings of inadequacy that they are failing their first duty as parents: to teach their babies to sleep.

Of course, the millions of babies who don't initially sleep through the night are not moral failures. They are just new little people who have not yet learned to put themselves to sleep. *Learn* is the key word. We all know that the need for sleep is biological, but we don't always realize that the ability to sleep is a learned skill. All children can learn it. All parents can teach them. But like everything else in life, some just need a little more help than others.

Parents around the world know me as The Sleep Lady. I'm a licensed child and family therapist—and the mother of two daughters—and for over two decades, I've focused my practice on helping tens of thousands of weary and bleary-eyed families all around the world find solutions to their children's sleep problems. I've worked with parents of babies who are old enough to sleep through the night but aren't yet doing so, nap-resistant toddlers, older children who won't stay in their beds (or who sneak into their parents' beds uninvited). I won't promise you no tears, but I do aim for fewer tears, and I never tell you to just shut the door and let your baby bawl alone in the dark. Part of the mission of the Sleep Lady Shuffle and this book is to ease your concern about your baby's crying and help you see that it's a way your baby communicates with you. Once you understand how your child is communicating and what she is trying to tell you, sleep coaching naturally becomes gentler and less overwhelming for the whole family. The Sleep Lady Shuffle is my method to help sleep-coach babies from six months old and older. It isn't a drastic, cry-it-out approach; I guide parents through step-by-step changes in bedtime, napping, and overnight routines that haven't been working. It is gentle and family-centric, allowing parents to consider their values, philosophies, lifestyles, goals, and temperaments, instead of being a one-size-fits-all concept. It is also gentle because it is centered on finding balance between what parents can instinctually teach their child and what a child is innately capable of doing. It encourages responsive parenting, as our babies and children have not yet mastered self-soothing and need us to teach them, gradually and gently. I believe this approach fosters a more synchronistic parent-child relationship, helping them learn to communicate with one another from day 1: to be responsive but not enabling, to be interpretive and not overly anxious, to be confident and not inconsistent. We are here to be available to our children and to give them tools. We can't do all the work for them, but we can support them and reinforce those tools until they learn for themselves. That kind of responsive parenting is at the core of the Sleep Lady Shuffle.

MY PERSONAL JOURNEY THROUGH
SLEEP DEPRIVATION

It was twenty-five years ago when I had my daughter Carleigh, and she became my first guinea pig (she probably wouldn't want me calling her a guinea pig, as she's much prettier). As a newborn, Carleigh had mild jaundice. She was a "bird feeder," and breastfeeding was a big learning curve for the two of us. I was given *well-intended* advice from a lactation consultant to wake Carleigh during the night every hour and a half to feed her. I would try to wake her and feed her, only to have her wake for a moment and then fall right back asleep. And then I would be awake for hours trying to wake her to feed her. I started to have hallucinations from sleep deprivation . . . really!

All alone at 2:00 a.m., crying, with a sleeping baby in my arms who I couldn't get to eat and a sleeping cat curled up by my side (I had never been jealous of a cat before!), I reached my breaking point. I woke the next morning from what was basically a nap with the realization that doing the same thing over again was not going to help Carleigh or me. There had to be a better—less insane—way.

I went against the social norm at the time—which was feed on demand (i.e., whenever a baby cried and according to no schedule). Culling from what I knew about child development, attachment, and reading nonverbal cues, I put Carleigh on a flexible, gentle eating and sleeping routine during the day. Eventually, I started to put her down awake at bedtime, staying with her as she fell asleep and never letting her cry alone. I only fed her when she woke up at night—no more waking her up to try to feed her. I tweaked, I experimented, I still breastfed her, but I was following my intuition that told me how I wanted to care for her and, more importantly, how Carleigh needed to be cared for. Carleigh was growing, happy, and sleeping through the night early on. I was blossoming in my role as a mother.

I had the naysayers who would tell me, "Oh, that's a stage . . . it will change," or "Oh, you were lucky," and I would have my moments of doubt.

But I remember a nurse telling me, "That's not luck, Kim, it's you." And I put that thought in my back pocket. I started to help my family, and then my friends, when they had babies.

Somewhere in between this and working as a therapist, I had another baby. Gretchen had horrible reflux and was—and still is—one of those alert kids! (We'll talk much more about alert children in Chapter 3.) Gretchen put me in my place by showing me that sleep coaching is not a cookie-cutter activity; what worked for her sister did not work for her. And that ultimately helped me become a better Sleep Lady.

Friends and friends of friends began calling me for sleep help. As word spread and more and more people reached out, I added this specialty to my family therapy practice. At that time, there weren't any baby and toddler sleep coaches or parenting coaches, and we didn't have the Internet as we know it now, let alone Alexa. However, there was a book out there by Richard Ferber, a doctor in Boston who popularized the "cry-it-out" method, which bore his name—Ferberizing. Ferber was the first one to stick his neck out there on what was and still is a controversial topic: graduated extinction (i.e., checking in on a child at gradually increasing time intervals—five minutes, then ten minutes, etc.). Then came the other prominent pediatricians who recommended and popularized "full extinction," which meant letting the child cry it out with no parental response or intervention. To me, that provides little empathy for the plight of the sleepless new parent as well as the physical and emotional pain parents feel when their child is screaming. These doctors weren't in the trenches like I was. They conducted onetime consults with no follow-up. They were not coaching a parent through the process and didn't really understand the toll. My instincts were clear: letting my child cry it out all alone wasn't how I wanted to sleep coach *or* how I wanted to raise my own children.

I tried to find someone to mentor me or supervise me or even to brainstorm with me about a gentle approach—one that was more realistic and less emotionally painful for us all. But there were no peers in my field to speak to or who were accessible. There were no training programs, and sleep consulting or coaching wasn't considered a field. So I researched and read and talked to my friends and did more research and reading. I taught myself, I built on my knowledge of child development and attachment theory, I honed my skills and defined my method. And I listened to the parents. With each family I assisted, I grew and learned and modified. I wasn't sure how to structure or build my practice. I knew I wanted families to be happy and well rested, to be empowered, and most of all, to know they had choices when it came to sleep coaching. That it wasn't just cry it out or do nothing or hold the baby all day and night.

My passion (obsession at times) for the topic of sleep and development, for helping others (I am a therapist, after all), and the rewards of sleeping parents are what kept me going. In the end, and after some work, my determination and honing the program worked. I never dreamed that I would have a trademarked name, the Sleep Lady (which a three-year-old client gave me), and create a gentle method for sleep coaching known as the Sleep Lady Shuffle, or SLS. And with each passing day, *I find again and again that the need for gentle sleep coaching is so much bigger than I could ever fill in a thousand lifetimes. In a nutshell, I'm saying it's not just you.*

And if you are starting out with any uncertainty about sleep coaching, as many parents do, I hope you take solace in the tens of thousands of people who have had success with my approach. The success rate, I truly believe, is based on the philosophy and approach I have built and refined over twenty-plus years. That means if you and your child are struggling with the uphill battle of learning to sleep, it's only going to get better from here.

THE SLEEP LADY'S PROCLAMATION

Because I want this book to mimic what it's like to work with one of the Gentle Sleep Coaches® I have trained in the Sleep Lady method, so you can reap all the benefits of the Sleep Lady system, I would like to share the ideas and beliefs that have become the bedrock of my gentle system. As I mentioned, you can only adopt a set of ideas and make it your own if there is a transparency and understanding of the philosophy that lies behind it. That's the only way you can know if it is right for you. I believe parents need to know the method behind my madness if they are to quickly grasp and implement the strategies set forth in this book. So with that said, here is the short list of what I believe makes for a successful sleep-coaching strategy.

I believe sleep coaching is subjective: To the extent that you get advice, whether from doctors or well-meaning friends or relatives, it usually falls into one of two categories. On one hand are the variants of cry-it-out. On the other are the attachment parenting theorists, who promote co-sleeping and nursing on demand well past the early months of infancy. Either of those approaches is fine—*if* they feel right for you and right for your kids. They aren't fine if they don't feel right, if they strain your marriage, if they don't fit into your adult needs—or if they don't help your child learn to put himself to sleep and stay asleep. Your subjective needs and beliefs count. You can get creative, you can be more responsive and less reactive, and there is definitely an opportunity for more balance. My Sleep Lady approach is a gentler alternative for families who emotionally or philosophically resist letting their babies cry it out, feel judged for their ideas on how to sleep coach and raise their children, tried "Ferberizing" with no success, and let their child cry it out completely but found it didn't help. I have also worked with families who believe in co-sleeping but find that their children aren't really sleeping all that well, even nestled snugly with Mom and Dad. And I've helped guide many families who did bed share for a few months or a few years but now want the family bed to revert to a marital one.

I believe sleep is highly personal, and therefore, so is sleep coaching: Anyone who has ever shared a bed or a room with someone—a sibling, a college roommate, a partner—can attest that there isn't just one way to sleep. Some of us kick off the blankets in our sleep, while others have the thermostat down to arctic temperatures. Some fall asleep at the drop of a hat (I hate them), while others—like me—need to quiet the mind before even thinking about sleep. Some like the room as dark as an Alaskan winter, while others prefer to wake up to natural sunlight. Sleep preferences and styles range widely and affect everything from the kind of mattress we prefer to whether we have the talent of being able to sleep on a plane (I wish I had that talent) or the kinds of aesthetics we would like in our sleep space. If this sleep subjectivity is a fact for us, then why should sleep be any different for our babies?

Some families want their children to sleep on Montessori floor beds, while others have siblings sharing rooms. Other families are passionate about co-sleeping, but still need advice on sleep training, and the preferences vary in infinite measure. Therefore, when I work with families, I explore their values, lifestyles, and approaches to parenting as I develop an individual sleep plan. In this book, you will have the opportunity to do the same exploration, which will help you feel in control of how you sleep coach your child. I never suggest anything that would make anyone feel like a horrible parent, nor do I believe in miracle cures and no-cry techniques, simply because they unfortunately don't exist. When we go to change a pattern or behavior and our babies are nonverbal, they will cry and not understand the change—and if they are verbal, they will cry and have words of protest. Changing sleep patterns can take time, and it definitely takes consistency. Most families solve their bedtime problems within two weeks, even if poor napping, early rising, and occasional night awakenings take a little longer. The bottom line is I believe parents should have choices in sleep coaching. The choices shouldn't be simply between cry-it-out or suffer for months or years.

I believe that, generally, six months is the optimal time to start sleep coaching. Don't worry if you didn't start at six months or you yourself weren't ready to stick to it. As you can see, my book gives age-by-age instructions on bedtime, nap time, early rising, and sleep-related developmental changes all the way to age five.

But with very rare exceptions, we don't sleep coach before six months because babies just aren't ready. That doesn't mean we don't start very gentle "sleep shaping" with newborns. We'll learn about that in Chapter 2.

Babies have intricate, delicate, and rapidly changing development patterns that cannot be dismissed when considering how they learn to sleep. In the chapters that follow, you will find a milestones chart that explains what is happening developmentally and how each stage can cause nighttime sleep and nap regressions. Milestones are skills, like self-regulation and soothing, and the things babies learn to do by a certain age—like focusing their vision, reaching out, exploring, and learning about the things around them. For now, here are a few things to consider about infant sleep before the age of six months.

* Infant sleep cycles do not yet resemble those of adults, so making allowances for our babies makes sense.
* Babies before the age of four months have not yet established a circadian rhythm (i.e., their internal clock).
* Before three or four months, babies do not produce melatonin, a hormone that promotes sleep by relaxing our muscles and making us drowsy. Secretion levels of serotonin are linked to darkness, another aspect of our circadian rhythm.
* As a family therapist, I do not recommend extinction (the cry-it-out method) or gradual extinction with newly adopted children, children in foster care or placed in new homes, and children with special needs. I find the parental fading of the Sleep Lady Shuffle to be more effective with these children who may have challenges self-regulating.

I believe in empowering parents to be confident: Douglas Teti, professor of human development and psychology at Penn State, has led a study about a parent's state of mind, published in the *Journal of Family Psychology*, based on videotaped footage of families in their own homes. It revealed that a parent's emotional state may be a hugely important contributor to healthy infant sleep. "What parents do at bedtime doesn't seem to matter as much as how they do it. . . . So you can decide to co-sleep or not co-sleep or you can decide whatever bedtime routine you want to follow. That seems secondary to whether or not parents are feeling good and comfortable with what they're doing."

Though Teti's study of mothers was small, his findings suggest that even if I give you every sleep trick in the book and you devour the pages of this one, it is your confidence in yourself as a parent, combined with your faith that your child can learn the skills vital to falling asleep, that will help you succeed. We'll discuss more on what Teti says about "emotional availability" of parents during bedtime routines (and frankly at all times) in Chapter 3.

I believe in making friends with your baby's tears (and toddler's tantrums): We've all heard the adages "Make friends with your fear" or "Understand your enemy," and we can put these to good use when our babies cry or our toddlers throw a tantrum. So many parents are frightened by those cries, and when they can't stop them, those tears do indeed feel like their hearts are shattering into a million little pieces. However, it's easier for us as parents to tolerate the tears if we understand that they are a form of communication—just in a preverbal language we are not versed in.

I believe in responsive parenting: Responsive parenting allows for the balance between assisting your baby and letting your baby figure it out for himself: responding to a child's cry is, in my opinion, nonnegotiable when sleep coaching, both for his sake and for your own peace of mind. As parents, we need to be sure they are okay, that they haven't spit up or gotten tangled in something, that their diapers haven't leaked, or that they weren't spooked by a sound or shadow. But I also believe that balance between comforting our children and allowing them to learn to comfort themselves is an essential component of sleep coaching. The Sleep Lady Shuffle is designed to *minimize frustration and maximize reassurance.* By being present and emotionally available, by confidently offering physical and verbal caresses and reassurances, we reduce stress on ourselves and on our children. And where there is stress, there is cortisol (a hormone), and cortisol is no good for sleep!

I believe that setting limits and boundaries makes for happy and securely attached children (who also sleep better): Parents tell me that they are hesitant about providing structure and direction; they are nervous about enforcing rules or confronting negative behaviors. I often hear a parent say, "I don't want my child to feel bad about himself," or "I don't want to crush her spirit," or "I don't want my child to not like me." As my colleague Peter Grube, a clinical social worker, notes to me, "Parents want to be loving, but unfortunately, the term *loving* is often interpreted as meaning no boundaries for the child or parent."

Countless studies tell us that our children do need structure, consistency, and clear boundaries, at bedtime and during the day. Setting limits does not mean that we don't give our children some choice or autonomy. Rather, it means giving age-appropriate choices within healthy boundaries—boundaries that actually make children feel safe and protected. In the age-specific chapters in Phase 2 of this book, I will give you advice and strategies for your child's sleep to do just this. As a family therapist who has counseled parents on an array of issues, I cannot stress enough how learning to set boundaries and limits during sleep coaching will come in handy later when child-rearing extends into other areas of life. When children get a little older, boundary setting and setting limits throughout the day—and not just at bedtime—will be essential to sleep coaching.

I believe in informed choice: Parenting isn't a one-size-fits-all job, nor is it something we do solely based on blind recommendations, marketing campaigns, or opinions of professionals we've never met, myself included. We can of course gather the information at hand, weigh its potential benefits, relevance, risks, and lifestyle implications related to our family's needs, and make an informed choice that is consistent with our own values. This couldn't be truer when it comes to sleep coaching. All the research, proven theories, product reviews, and sage advice in the world will not match what your instincts say to you about what is right for the needs of your child and your family. Informed choice coupled with your unique parenting philosophies equals a consistently happy, well-rested, and thriving family. If something works for you, even if it isn't the most popular or glamorous approach to parenting—you will likely stick with it, and that is the key to sleep coaching.

CONSISTENCY IS YOUR SECRET TO SUCCESS

Once you have a sleep-coaching plan in place, it's absolutely crucial to be consistent—even in the middle of the night when you're tired and not thinking clearly. Sending mixed messages—which behavioral scientists call *intermittent reinforcement*—to your child throughout the day (and night!) will only frustrate him. He won't be able to decipher what type of behavior merits rewards and what type of behavior doesn't. Inconsistently reinforced behavior is the hardest type of behavior to modify or extinguish. It takes longer to change, and it always gets worse before it gets better. This is particularly true of a child who's more than one year old.

Here are three examples of intermittent reinforcement with children and sleep that I want to help you avoid:

* "Sometimes I feed you to sleep, and sometimes I don't." For example, you may nurse your baby to sleep, feed him if he wakes after 10:00 p.m., rock him to sleep if he wakes again before 1:00 a.m., and then finally bring him into your bed out of desperation. This causes confusion. I want you to work toward putting your child down to bed drowsy but awake (we will discuss this thoroughly in Chapter 4) and responding to him consistently the same way throughout the night.
* "Sometimes I've let you cry for fifteen or thirty minutes because I was desperate and heard this approach might work—but then I couldn't take it anymore and went in, picked you up, and rocked you to sleep." This is an example of how you can train your child to cry until you put him to sleep—any way you can!
* "Sometimes I bring you in to my bed—but only after 5:00 a.m." Please remember that your child can't tell time. Why wouldn't he expect to come to your bed at 2:00 a.m. if you bring him in after 5:00?

Keep in mind, too, that children actually crave consistency at bedtime (and all the time, for that matter). When they know what to expect, and what's expected of them, it reassures them and helps them feel safe and sound.

I believe in being kind to yourself: It has become common today to compare ourselves and our families to idyllic snapshots posted on social media. I cannot tell you how many people have confided to me that they believe themselves to be among the minority when it comes to having a baby who just won't sleep. Trust me—this is not the case, and you are not alone. Just because your friends are posting pictures of blissfully sleeping infants does not mean that their kids aren't fussing and waking just as much as yours are—in the photos that don't make it onto social media. My experience working with parents all around the world tells me that more parents than not struggle. They don't know that things can be better or know where to turn for help . . . or feel they will be judged for wanting to sleep coach their child because they are barely hanging on. I understand how desperate exhausted parents can feel—and luckily, the Sleep Lady Shuffle can offer you non-desperate solutions. But please try to understand that you didn't do anything "wrong." Be kind to yourself— we are all doing the best we can as parents. And have faith that you can improve your family's sleep!

YOUR CHILD'S SLEEP SUCCESS

You will see progress quickly, but give it a few weeks to consolidate the gains, to see the old patterns fade away. Sometimes you'll accomplish 90 percent of your goals in a matter of days, meaning your life should be much more bearable. But it can then take longer for you to get that last 10 percent in place. Be patient and remember that learning a skill—whether sleeping, walking, handling a fork, or using the potty—takes time. Disruptions of routines, including illness, moving, travel, or a parent away on business, can also cause temporary setbacks. If you stick to the routine, your child should absorb those minor shocks and get back to his normal schedule in a reasonable period of time. Eventually, his sleep skills will be so secure that he can take them anywhere—on vacation, to his grandparents' house, later to slumber parties, summer camp, and even off to college.

Before you turn to the chapter on your child's age group, please read the chapters included in Phase I of this book, as they contain the foundational information and concepts that will make sleep coaching a lot more effective and efficient in the long run. The extra time you spend reading now will save you lots of sleepless nights later.

SINGLE MOMS, SINGLE DADS, AND SAME-SEX COUPLES

I know that there are many ways to make a family—and my Sleep Lady system can work for all of you. I can say that with confidence because I've seen it. You may have to make some adaptations here and there, particularly if you are the only parent around at bedtime and the only one dealing with middle-of-the-night wakenings and early risings. Get as much support as you can from friends and family and other new moms and dads. Check out my advice on divorce or widowhood on page 410. For families with two dads, since neither of you is nursing, you have a little more flexibility in dividing bedtime and nighttime feeding responsibilities. No matter what your circumstances, be kind to yourself—and get as much rest as you can, whenever you can.

AN IMPORTANT NOTE ABOUT HOW TO USE THIS BOOK

The Sleep Lady Shuffle has two distinct phases plus what I call *maintenance*, where we troubleshoot or deal with regressions during sleep coaching. In the first few months of life, which are addressed in Phase 1: Sleep Shaping, we concentrate on bringing home and bonding with your newborn, getting to know your baby, learning appropriate soothing techniques, and establishing basic rhythms and routines that will help babies learn to sleep. It's subtle but effective. For many newborns, this foundation will enable them to start going to sleep by themselves and staying asleep all night between ages four and six months. Other babies may need more intervention, and my Sleep Lady Shuffle, which is taught in Phase 2: Sleep Coaching, provides an action plan that is structured but gentle.

The Shuffle is not designed for newborns, and in Phase 1 of this new edition, I offer information that will explain why newborns are not ready for sleep coaching. But I do include a robust primer for parents who want to prep and begin right away to build their and their baby's confidence. This framework will allow for successful sleep coaching when the time is right. Typically, I do not introduce sleep coaching until about six months—which is also the time when most of my clients seek me out as well. It's as if a baby's internal clock goes off at around six months and signals he is ready for sleep coaching. This is not to say some parents haven't had success with the Sleep Lady Shuffle with a healthy baby as early as four and a half months. But not all infants are ready for that; indeed, the science tells us that many of them are not. Always check with your baby's doctor before beginning any sleep-coaching system.

Parenting is all about consistency, consistency, consistency. That's especially true for sleep. I hope you will take a little bit of time to familiarize yourself with my philosophy and the various elements and recurring themes of my system in Phase 1 of this book (Chapters 2–6). And when you are ready to put it into action, please remind yourself (and your spouse or partner, or anyone else who shares childcare) of that need for consistency. Research has shown that whatever sleep system you choose—and I am so honored you have chosen mine—consistency is the single biggest factor in success.

I've included in the appendix valuable information regarding safe sleep recommendations and postpartum mood disorder. From a practical standpoint, knowing how to create conditions for safe sleep will set you up for sleep-coaching success. But equally important is learning self-care, and checking in on how you are feeling emotionally—especially while experiencing all the changes that parenthood (and exhaustion) bring— will help you tend to your health while gauging the right time to start (and sometimes pause) sleep coaching.

It is my pleasure to offer this book to you. It holds the information you would receive if you were working directly with me or one of my certified Gentle Sleep Coaches. Thank you for entrusting the Sleep Lady method with the well-being of your child and family. You can do this, and so can your baby. Together, you will *gently* sleep tight.

Phase I

SLEEP SHAPING

A coach is a person who teaches, directs, and supports those who need assistance with their development. A coach doesn't play the game or do the work for the players. Even when the team loses, the coach can give strategies for doing better next time, but still can't play the game for them. It's the same with sleep.

Our children need us first and foremost to support their developmental milestones and to achieve healthy habits. This is why I believe we don't "train" our children to sleep but coach them. We follow their lead, understand their biological and emotional capacities at each age or stage of their lives, and work in tandem with their natural rhythms. We can help our children learn how to fall asleep, but we can't keep doing so much of it for them, not beyond the newborn stage. When they have trouble sleeping, we can empathize, we can reassure, we can guide, we can support—and like the coach, we can help them acquire the skills to do it better next time. But then we have to begin to let them do it themselves.

A great athlete is only as great as his or her coach. It is my life's work and passion to help your child become an excellent sleeper, but that first requires my helping you become an even more excellent coach. Phase 1 of the Sleep Lady Shuffle is your training manual to understand your role as your child's sleep shaper, no matter how old your child is when you choose to get started. Many foundational concepts will be repeated throughout the book because they are important to know before you begin formal sleep coaching. I've planted most of them in the chapters that follow with the hope that once you know the ground rules, the expectations, and the nature of sleep, your age-specific sleep coaching will be that much more effective and efficient. For now, let's consider this portion of the program—sleep shaping from newborn to age five months—as the prelude for formal coaching later.

Chapter 2

WHEN YOUR NEWBORN
COMES HOME

"Get your sleep now" was a piece of advice that Erika received from her older sister as together they dressed new baby Kaeden in his "homecoming" outfit. After two days of bonding and recovery time at the hospital where Erika delivered Kaeden, it was time to bring baby home. "For the first three weeks, all Kaeden did was sleep," Erika remembers. "So when people asked me, 'How is he sleeping?' I couldn't help but think it was an odd question."

Bringing home baby may not be a milestone for your child, but for parents, it certainly is a milestone for the record books! Nothing says, *You're a parent now,* like finding yourself sitting in the back seat of your car (probably for the first time) with a little human being facing backward in a car seat. It's surreal and it's memorable, and there's nothing better! Ninety-nine percent of the time, the baby makes the car ride home with her eyes closed in a sweet slumber. Just like Erika, Kaeden's mom, you might think, *Sleep training? Easy peasy, lemon squeezy.*

That's because newborns (birth to three months) sleep a lot—around sixteen hours a day! Which is why sleep coaching, also called *sleep teaching* or *sleep learning*, isn't typical or even necessary for a newborn. I have built my practice on helping babies learn to sleep anywhere between the ages of six months and six years. It is my belief that while it is never too late to start teaching a child to sleep, it could be too early. In fact, while some experts tout the efficacy of "extinction," or the cry-it-out method, in very young infants, there's no research supporting that practice, according to Macall Gordon, a researcher at Antioch University–Seattle and one of my Gentle Sleep Coaches (who has scoured the scientific literature on this point). In fact, there has been scant research on what happens in babies, even a few months older, for whom extinction or cry-it-out methods don't work. Gordon further notes that the success rate of extinction methods is wrongly skewed; it does not work for some 40 percent of infants. And even if you do try to sleep train your young infant, babies commonly go through sleep regressions at around four months (i.e., their sleep gets worse) that may make early sleep intervention counterproductive. That's why I feel so strongly about creating options that are gentler on both parent and child and giving families more choices in how to approach such a vexing but important part of parenting.

So when you are bringing home baby, I want you to focus less on behavioral sleep interventions and more on setting yourself up for success. There is plenty you can do for your little sleepyhead now, even if she isn't developmentally ready to be coached to sleep—no matter the sleep intervention you choose.

That is why I like to call this time Phase 1—the precursor to sleep coaching. Naturally, we are very gentle at first, just nudging babies to start distinguishing between day and night, light and dark. Later, we'll start teaching them to fall asleep with less assistance from us, to sleep longer intervals at night, to lengthen their naps. Those naps, as we'll see, will be important for several years because overtired children who don't sleep enough during the day actually have a harder time sleeping well at night. Many parents are ambivalent about sleep coaching in these first months. On one hand, the moms and dads want to sleep and know that their babies need to sleep, too. On the other hand, infants fuss and cry enough as it is. Parents wonder why they should endure any more tears or force the child to shed them. In fact, there are a lot fewer tears than you would imagine. In these first few months, we shape sleep ever so gently, and your baby will get plenty of soothing, holding, and snuggling.

In the first months of life (typically zero to three months), we concentrate on establishing basic rhythms and routines that will help babies learn to sleep better. You can gently shape some newborns' sleep habits early on and hopefully prevent future sleep problems. We also learn a repertoire of soothing techniques that will help us become more confident parents, able to help our babies feel calm and secure, without relying exclusively or constantly on the breast or a bottle. Consider this precious time a sleep-shaping phase and less a sleep-coaching phase. Cherish these first few months—which will fly by—as your gift of time to bond with your baby. There will be plenty of opportunities soon enough to worry about sleep.

BONDING WITH YOUR BABY

Some of us feel an intense bond the minute our babies are born. For many other parents, that passionate connection isn't that immediate—and they feel guilty. Be kind to yourself; it often takes days or weeks for those feelings to well up, and it can even take a few months, an ongoing process of positive give-and-take, for parents and babies to form a secure attachment. If persistent sadness interferes with the bonding, please seek an evaluation for postpartum mood disorder (see Appendix B, "Postpartum Mood Disorder, Baby Blues, and Daddy Depression").

You don't have to be a supermom or superdad to create the bond as you get acquainted with your baby. But here are some ways you can nudge the attachment along. Some may be intuitive for you.

* Create routines that your child can expect and count on—not just at bedtime, mealtime, and bath time. Have a special toy for diaper changes or a favorite song as you start your daily walks.
* Respond to his needs quickly. If he cries because he's wet, change him. If he makes hungry noises, feed him. If you can't address his need immediately, acknowledge him clearly and let him know you heard him and will be there as soon as you can. If possible, give him a toy to hold and talk to him while you finish up whatever you're do-ing (such as taking care of another child!). You can't spoil a child by being "too responsive" in the first nine months or so of life.
* Cultivate predictability. To feel safe and secure, babies need to know they can count on you. Your routines and prompt responses will help meet this need for predictability.
* Hold him! Physical skin-to-skin contact is vital. Strap him onto your chest or use a sling rather than a stroller. Hug him, cuddle him, look into his eyes, and when he coos at you, coo back! On the other hand, you don't have to "wear" your baby every minute, and it's not a crime to use a stroller some of the time. Remember that babies need and enjoy stimulation from playing on mats, baby gyms, tummy time, and the like, too, so you don't need to hold him all the time. For more on bonding and attachment, I highly recom-mend the Circle of Security website (www.circleofsecurity.org) and their free handout, "Building a Secure Attachment for Your Baby."

These early sleep-shaping techniques are subtle but effective. But they won't have your baby sleeping through the night at two, four, or (in most cases) even twelve or fourteen weeks. Babies just aren't wired to sleep all night in the first few months, although some will sleep six or eight hours at a stretch after the newborn period, around the end of the third month. But these early sleep-shaping steps do lay a foundation, and for many infants, that will be enough. Some babies will start going to sleep by themselves and staying asleep all night between four and six months. Other babies may need more help from you to learn to sleep. We'll talk more about my Sleep Lady Shuffle and other aspects of sleep coaching in subsequent chapters.

GETTING SET UP FOR SUCCESS: FIVE HEALTHY SLEEP HABITS THAT ARE INFANT-APPROPRIATE

Let's get your baby off to the right start. If you follow these simple practices, your baby will have an easier time learning to sleep and will sleep longer, either figuring it out on his own or when you begin sleep coaching him at six months. If you learn nothing from me except these steps, your life will be simpler. You will discover during the next few years that babies and children go through numerous sleep stages—learning to sleep through the night, changing nap schedules, separation anxiety, and the like—and laying a good foundation will help your baby and your entire family travel down these developmental paths.

THE SLEEP LADY'S TOP FIVE SLEEP-START TIPS

1. Experiment with a variety of soothing techniques to avoid crutches. (We'll talk more about sleep crutches in Chapter 4.)
2. Offer a pacifier for soothing and sucking after breastfeeding has been established, usually between four and six weeks.
3. Feed your baby when he wakes up on occasion so you are not always feeding your baby to sleep.
4. Occasionally put your baby down a bit more awake than normal at bedtime or naps. Stay with her and soothe her to sleep. When she is older and you are both ready, you can start putting her down more and more awake. We'll discuss more about the concept of drowsy but awake in Chapter 4.
5. Create a peaceful sleep environment.

SLEEP LADY SLUMBER SUGGESTION #1: EXPERIMENT WITH A VARIETY OF SOOTHING TECHNIQUES

If you give babies a chance, they will develop a host of ways to soothe themselves, but in the first few months, they do need your help. Our challenge is to find soothing techniques other than nonstop breastfeeding or bottle-feeding, which can risk becoming a sleep crutch if the child can't fall asleep without feeding. However, as I mentioned in the Sleep Lady's Proclamation, I am a firm believer in a mother following her own instincts, so if nursing your baby is what you are committed to doing, even if the baby isn't necessarily feeding, you should be empowered to do what's right for you and your child.

Regardless of how you approach soothing your baby, Dr. Harvey Karp's helpful book, *The Happiest Baby on the Block: The New Way to Calm Crying and Help Your Newborn Baby Sleep Longer* (2002), recommends the "5 S's"—swaddling, side holding, "sh-sh-sh," swinging, and sucking—to get the baby through the first few months, sometimes called the *fourth trimester.*

Swaddling

The pressure of swaddling, similar to what babies felt in utero, comforts them and lengthens their sleep—and it often works well along with white noise. Wrap him snugly in a thin receiving blanket, making sure the blanket is not near his face, and his ears and toes are not too hot. Usually, babies like their hips to be slightly bent. For the first three months, they usually like having their arms inside the blanket. There are lots of great swaddling products to choose from!

Occasionally, a baby just doesn't like being swaddled. Don't force it; it's not a requirement. Babies often send clear signals that they don't like being constrained anymore as they get more mobile, and you can just stop it. Or it stops working when they begin rolling around. But if your baby hasn't sent such a signal, stop the swaddling sometime between four and six months.

Side Holding and *Sh-sh-sh*

Babies should sleep on their backs to reduce the risk of sudden infant death syndrome, or SIDS, but not all of them like it. It's not a position they experienced in utero, and it may trigger their *Moro*, or *falling*, *reflex*. To ward off that falling sensation, it may help if you hold the baby at a little bit of an angle as you put him down, so his feet are a bit lower than his head.

Babies don't have to be on their backs when they are awake or when you are holding them. Many find it comforting to be on their sides, particularly their left side if they have reflux. You can hold him on his side in your arms or on your lap, swaddled if you like, and make a gentle, rhythmic *sh-sh-sh* noise to remind him of your heartbeat in utero. Swing or sway your body a little for comfort. Holding him on his side helps with that fussy evening period or with colicky babies who cry more than average—which, believe it or not, is a total of three hours a day. The swing or sway should be in a slightly upright position, which lessens reflux and allows a burp to jiggle out, according to Dr. Karp. However, remember that there's a difference between holding a baby on his side and putting him to sleep on his side. Side holding is wonderful; side sleeping is dangerous.

The American Academy of Pediatrics advises against side sleeping for young babies. If you think your baby is more comfortable on his side, do not make a change without discussing side-sleeping safety with your pediatrician. When he gets old enough to sleep safely on his stomach or side, usually when he can roll over consistently in both directions, you may find that your baby suddenly begins to sleep more soundly if that's naturally more comfortable for him.

Swinging

Gently rocking and swinging our babies is so instinctive that I scarcely have to mention it, but it does calm newborns. It's also fine to let your baby nap in a swing during the day for the first two months. After that, he'll still like being in the swing, and you can use it for fun and comfort or those stubborn afternoon naps, but don't use it for sleeping in all night long. Please be cautious; the swing has a scoop shape that can cause the baby's head to fall forward to the chest, which is a hazard, as it can block his airway. Reposition his head in an upright position.

SLEEP LADY SLUMBER SUGGESTION #2: OFFER A PACIFIER FOR SOOTHING AND SUCKING

The final *S* of Dr. Karp's 5 S's is the sucking reflex. Sucking is a natural instinct for babies and is part of their soothing reflex, so for parents who are worried that pacifiers are bad or that they are the start of a hard-to-quit habit, take solace. Babies do need to suck, especially during the first few weeks. It's not just about food; babies suck on their fingers, their hands, their pacifiers. Research suggests that pacifiers may also help protect babies against SIDS, but the medical advice on pacifiers has changed frequently over the years, and it may well change again. Please check with your doctor, and check in again as your baby gets a little older.

If your baby spits out the pacifier, don't automatically replug it! If you keep plugging up his mouth all the time, you may be hampering his early attempt to communicate with you and interfering with your ability to differentiate between his cries. Sometimes he will want the pacifier back—and he'll let you know it. But if you don't assume it's the pacifier he wants, you may realize he's trying to tell you something else. You'll be surprised how many times babies spit out the pacifier, parents stick it in, babies spit it out, the parents stick it back in, never stopping to think that maybe the baby is spitting it out for a reason. If, after the first few months, he's taking the pacifier more than you would like, try other soothing techniques and assess the reasons he might be fussing (e.g., how long has he been awake, when did he last feed, is the environment too stimulating, is his diaper wet?). Also, pacifiers don't help very gassy babies, because they tend to swallow more air as they suck it.

Why pacifiers may protect against SIDS isn't completely clear. First Candle, an organization dedicated to preventing infant deaths, cites several possible explanations, among them that pacifiers may discourage babies from turning over onto their tummies during sleep. The sucking reflex may also keep them from falling into a deep sleep, or it may position the tongue to keep the airways open.

Even if you use the pacifier when the baby sleeps, you may choose not to use it all the time when he is awake and fussy. You can reconsider how and when you want him to continue with the pacifier at about six months. When babies get older, they may start sucking their thumbs, which is a perfectly good way of self-soothing and satisfying that instinct to suck. Some parents prefer it. Unlike a pacifier, you can't lose a thumb, you don't have to worry about it falling on the floor, and you can't forget to pack it in the diaper bag!

A lot of children outgrow thumb sucking on their own, but my daughter Carleigh didn't. When she was five, we found the perfect behavioral modification technique, although it meant we had to adopt her kindergarten class's hamster! You'll hear about that adventure when we get to preschoolers.

SLEEP LADY SLUMBER SUGGESTION #3: FEED YOUR BABY WHEN HE WAKES UP ON OCCASION AND SLEEP LADY SUGGESTION #4: PUT YOUR BABY DOWN A BIT MORE AWAKE THAN NORMAL

In the first weeks, we usually do feed our babies to sleep at bedtime and when they are hungry during the night. But once he is about twelve weeks old, consider trying to put him down a tad bit more awake at least once a day. He doesn't have to be wide awake, just a little bit more awake than usual. Stay and offer physical and verbal reassurance. You can even try patting and shushing him to sleep. If he just ends up crying more than you feel comfortable with . . . stop and try again on another day or even in a few weeks! However, if all goes well, slowly over the next few weeks or months, try to make this the norm at bedtime.

Sometimes he will fall asleep feeding, and then of course you shouldn't wake him. What you want to aim for is feeding him until he has had enough to eat and is getting drowsy. Then unlatch him from the bottle or breast gently before he falls fully asleep. It may take a little practice, but you'll figure it out within a few days, and if it doesn't work one night, just try again another time when you feel you both are ready. (See Chapter 4 for a more detailed explanation of drowsy but awake, which is the cornerstone of the Sleep Lady Shuffle.)

SLEEP LADY SLUMBER SUGGESTION #5: CREATE A SLEEP-FRIENDLY ENVIRONMENT

The American Academy of Pediatrics recommends room sharing with your baby for at least the first six months of life and ideally the first year. I strongly believe that the baby's environment affects his sleep. I like room-darkening shades and calm, soothing colors in the baby's bedroom. Even if you choose to have the baby in your room initially, it is good to get started quieting down for sleep in a cozy, sleep-friendly room. I don't like bright or stimulating mobiles in the crib. Let him enjoy the mobile somewhere else, where he spends awake time. At bedtime, the message to the brain is *Slow down,* not *Stay up and watch your bright-colored mobile spin.* I also want the crib to be a place for sleep and maybe for a few minutes of quiet play right after waking as he gets a little older. Here are some ideas on how to make your child's sleep space peaceful, even if he is room sharing with you.

White Noise and Music

White-noise machines, fans, or sound screens can be useful during the first few months, or even longer for naps. Babies who are extremely alert also do well with white noise, because it helps them shut the world out. I have found that a white-noise machine or app or a fan is more effective than music in screening out sounds, but many parents understandably prefer lullabies, and that's fine.

By around two to three months, take care to use the music only to set the mood before you put her down. Play music as she gets ready for bed, but don't keep it running as she is falling asleep, and don't keep putting it back on during the night when she wakes up. Let it wind down at bed time, or turn it off or turn the volume down very, very low. When it goes off, it goes off—that's it.

Motion Sleep

Motion sleep can trip up parents. Newborns are very portable. They can sleep wherever you put them—car seats, strollers, swings, bouncy chairs, noisy cafés, the mall, at your best friend's house when her three kids are all bouncing off the playroom walls. But even though they can do this, it doesn't mean they should do this. It's okay some of the time (like in the late afternoon and early evening), but try to have them nap in a nice, quiet crib or bassinet most of the time, starting at about six to eight weeks. At around three to four months old, you may notice that your baby no longer sleeps as easily on the go and instead needs to be home and in her crib or bassinet.

In the first few months, motion sleep is helpful, especially for naps. Day sleep develops after night sleep. So feel free to use motion to fill that daytime sleep tank! A well-napped baby will sleep better at night.

At five months, Nina's daughter, Lydia, was still on the same schedule—or nonschedule—she'd had as a newborn. Nina and Lydia were often on the go, feeding on the run, with Lydia grabbing a nap in a car seat or stroller. But Lydia didn't eat well, and she didn't nap well. Nina learned that Lydia needed more structure and less stimulation. She needed to nap in her own home, in a quiet place, with no lights, no noise, no distractions. "She became more aware of her surroundings; she couldn't just nurse anywhere, sleep anywhere," Nina said. "I realized I needed to be home for naps."

Bedtime Routine

If there's one thing that just about every sleep-coaching professional agrees on, it's that all children need a comforting and predictable bedtime routine. They need it from early infancy (typically at the six-week mark) right up through the school years. A few quiet activities like books, songs, or prayers help the baby throw that switch in his brain from alert to sleepy. There are also terrific guided meditation apps and YouTube videos that are pleasant for children of any age. Simply search online for *kid-friendly meditation* or *meditation for kids* and you'll see some ingenious options! Meditation that focuses on breathing is a great skill to learn as early as possible and will help children learn tools for self-regulation. A great, simple method is called *Take 5 Breathing*, which you can learn about at Childhood101.com.

Your routine will be very simple at first until you learn more about your child, and then modify it as she grows. In the infant stage, you'll probably start with a warm bath, then move into her dimly lit room. Maybe you'll do a few minutes of infant yoga (see Chapter 17). Nurse her or maybe have the other parent or caregiver give her a bottle. Swaddle, snuggle, or rock her, and then lay her in her crib or bassinet. And then what? Don't worry about not knowing what to do after that. In Phase 2, we will cover this in depth, age by age.

YOUR BABY'S SENSES: NATURE'S GUIDE TO THE INNER CLOCK

As you spend time shaping your child's sleep habits and helping him adapt his circadian rhythm, you'll notice how your baby's senses naturally guide him. Here are a few interesting things to keep in mind about how schedules and senses intersect.

* Daylight keeps a person's internal clock aligned with the environment. It's that alignment that helps with sleep coaching!
* Studies show that babies exposed to bright lights in the early afternoon often sleep better at night.
* Some researchers recommend avoiding exposure to light at night— both for babies and parents, because it is said to interfere with

melatonin and the biology of sleep. But when sleep coaching, many parents like a dim night-light so they aren't bumping into things in the middle of the night. I generally endorse that dim night-light, but I have worked with children who responded better to coaching in complete darkness. You'll discover rather quickly if your child is one of them. Lights that are amber, orange, or red (check out https://lowbluelights.com) may be less disruptive than conventional white light bulbs that emit blue rays (also called *the glow*). In fact, according to experts at Harvard Medical School, blue light emitted from your smartphone or tablet and your energy-efficient LED lights at bedtime are detrimental to a good night's sleep. If you live in an active household or a noisy neighborhood, consider using a white-noise machine or a fan. A white-noise machine not only drowns out sounds of activity so you don't have to tiptoe around a sleeping baby but promotes relaxation prior to sleep by providing a constant, soothing sound for the brain. Once your baby is asleep, white noise works all night long to drown out the random noises that can cause partial awakenings (see Chapter 4). That means that sleep is more solid and deep, and everyone can rise feeling more rested and restored. Babies can learn to sleep through routine household sounds, but some places are just really loud, and some children are sensitive. Go ahead and block the noise from heavy traffic, rumbling trucks, nearby construction, barking dogs, noisy neighbors, siblings, or your own social hour.

* Many people say they prefer to use their television as background sound to help themselves and their children fall asleep. However, this is not considered white noise, and the glow of the television itself is not great for sleep. I, as well as most pediatric experts, highly discourage any child having a television or other electronic device in his room, especially when sleep coaching (see the sidebar "Say No to the Glow" on page 30). Install room-darkening shades if your child is an early riser or if your child does not want to sleep

at his usual bedtime during summer nights. The shades are also great for naps. Visit my website (https://sleeplady.com/products) for a list of products I find helpful for sleep coaching, like room-darkening shades and white-noise machines.

* Some children go through phases where they get soaking wet and their diapers just can't withstand it. Luckily, diaper companies have gotten on board to provide superabsorbent diapers for "overnight." If you need to change your child's diaper just as you are putting her to bed at night or nap time, change her quietly and keep the lights as low as you can. If you can manage it, slip a travel changing pad under her in the crib or bed and change her there instead of picking her up, taking her out, and having to get her back into bed all over again, which could become overstimulating for her. After nine months, babies may learn to vomit or poop on demand, tripping up sleep and nap coaching. We will discuss this "dirty" little trick and what to do about it in Chapter 8, "Nine to Twelve Months."

SAY NO TO THE GLOW

Dr. Nicholas Kardaras, an addiction expert, coined the term *Glow Kids* to describe the generation of children who are put into a trance when handed a digital device—pads, tablets, smartphones, laptops. He contends in his book *Glow Kids: How Screen Addiction Is Hijacking Our Kids—and How to Break the Trance* that children who do not have a fully developed frontal cortex—the executive function of the brain—should stay off digital screens. He says technology is not at all bad, but like a movie that is rated PG-13, technology also needs to be age appropriate because children's brains are more fragile developmentally. This generation of screen media is different from how, say, television is and was back in my day. TV is a passive visual, but the images and activities on newer screen devices can be overly stimulating and create hyperarousal. That's certainly not good for sleep routines and circadian rhythms.

Dr. Kardaras says an abundance of research shows that screens are affecting the frontal cortex in a child's brain—just as a cocaine addiction would. Further, he contends the screens impede brain development, ADHD diagnoses have increased, and dopamine levels are raised. Before age ten, children do not have the same neurological apparatus that adults do (frontal cortex development) to handle stimulation. He says, for instance, adults can engage in a stimulating experience like drinking coffee or watching a movie and walk away afterward. Children before the age of ten cannot self-regulate in the same way; they simply don't have a braking mechanism in their brains that says, *Let's stop.*

I talk about developmental milestones in this book as they relate to your child's sleep patterns and needs as she grows. One milestone is learning social interaction and cues to develop social intelligence, empathy, and how to make eye contact and listen intently. Dr. Kardaras posits that children under ten who are hitting the various milestones of social interaction but who are "very digitally immersed" are missing out.

"Interpersonal skills is a developmental window just like learning language and if they are not socially interacting, they suffer interpersonally," Kardaras says in a Yahoo! News feature. Experts say we should have eye contact in our daily lives at least 70 percent of the time. Today's children, sadly, have eye contact less than 20 percent of the time.

"Develop the brain first," Dr. Kardaras suggests. Then when the developmental window opens so that children can engage their own cutoff switch, introduce devices for no more than an hour a day.

The bottom line: from age zero to ten, a child's development is the most fragile. Most pediatricians and child development experts recommend keeping children off *habitual* use of digital screens from the age of zero to ten.

If you are interested in learning more about the effects of the glow as you are developing your sleep-coaching plan, I recommend Dr. Kardaras's insightful and thought-provoking book.

Chapter 3

GETTING TO KNOW YOUR CHILD

Phase 1, sleep shaping, depends on meeting your child where he is. That means understanding him as he grows and develops preferences while he begins to understand and learn about you right back! This chapter demystifies the nature of our bond with our children—from how we form attachments to how their temperaments affect sleep—so we become more in tune with their personal preferences and needs. Your child's unique preferences will become guideposts when you begin formal sleep coaching.

ATTACHMENT PARENTING
AND SLEEP COACHING

You've likely come across the concept of attachment parenting, popularized by Dr. William Sears in his many parenting books. Naturally, your choices about how you want to raise your child reflect your desire to encourage a secure attachment. That's a cornerstone of emotional health. But exactly what does *attachment* mean? And how does it affect sleep coaching?

Attachment is a deep and enduring emotional bond that connects one person to another across time and space. The renowned psychologists Mary Ainsworth and John Bowlby were onto this attachment thing back in the 1960s and '70s—a lot earlier than you might have expected. Since those two landmark researchers, subsequent attachment theorists have added to the definition of attachment parenting (i.e., the methods we use to foster the parent-child bond). The word *attachment*, though, is tricky because it elicits an image of literal attachment. And that has led to a strong connection between attachment and co-sleeping, the idea that you should sleep attached to your child. And that image seems at odds with sleep coaching. Indeed, many proponents of attachment parenting argue against sleep training, saying it undermines that secure attachment that we seek. I agree that sleep coaching is not appropriate for newborns. I'm also very supportive of co-sleeping for parents who choose that. I devote all of Chapter 12, "Making Choices About Co-Sleeping, Bed Sharing, and Room Sharing," to how to co-sleep or share a room with your baby and how to incorporate the Sleep Lady Shuffle so you can co-sleep and still teach your child to sleep well and independently. (That chapter also helps you gently stop co-sleeping if it's not right for you.) But I am here to tell you that co-sleeping (and breastfeeding into toddlerhood if you choose) and gentle sleep coaching are not mutually exclusive.

I agree with Dr. Sears in that it's all about building a strong parent-child bond, giving your child that solid emotional foundation that will allow her to have healthy, emotionally fulfilling relationships in her life. But you can have a securely attached child and still help your children acquire the tools they need to be independent and grow. Numerous studies show children need some very simple things along with plenty of love and nurturance: structure, clear boundaries, and consistency. As Dr. Sears himself wrote, *"Attachment Parenting is an approach, rather than a strict set of rules. It's actually the style that many parents use instinctively. Parenting is too individual and baby too complex for there to be only one way."* Attachment parenting also urges you to "strive for balance in personal and family life," which you can't do if you are exhausted to the point of desperation.

Sometimes I wonder if perhaps those who practice attachment parenting don't truly understand what *sleep training* means. Most people who think of sleep training automatically conjure images of screaming babies crying it out (Ferberizing), but it can be far gentler. This is exactly why I prefer the term *sleep coaching*.

Attachment is a balance between security and support, confidence and freedom. It's all about allowing our babies and later children to learn how to deal with their emotions (including anger, frustration, and excitement) constructively. This includes helping your baby learn to self-regulate behaviors; for example, sleep. When you turn to your age-specific chapter and begin the Sleep Lady Shuffle, you will see my techniques absolutely foster reassurance, response, and respect for your child's needs, communication, and temperament—all of which signal to your child that she is safe and loved and never abandoned or left to figure sleep out all on her own.

THE EIGHT CORE PRINCIPLES OF ATTACHMENT PARENTING

Attachment Parenting International outlines eight core principles. Not only do I agree with them, but they have deeply influenced my sleep-coaching philosophy and methodology that have helped countless parents and children.

1. Preparing for pregnancy, birth, and parenting
2. Feeding with love and respect
3. Responding with sensitivity
4. Using nurturing touch (such as skin-to-skin contact and baby wearing)
5. Ensuring safe sleep (primarily when co-sleeping), physically and emotionally
6. Providing consistent and loving care
7. Practicing positive discipline
8. Striving for balance in personal and family life

LaunchPad Counseling in Richmond, Virginia, which specializes in helping families overcome stressful circumstances, explains healthy attachment like this: "Attachment is emotional communication without words. It represents a relationship that is more than just bonding or feeling close to your child. Ideally, *attachment* becomes healthier and stronger the more your child experiences safe emotional connections. As your child's needs were met before he could convey his needs, wants, and emotions verbally, *attachment* developed over time."

When we dive more deeply into the Sleep Lady Shuffle in Phase 2: Sleep Coaching, you will see how my method fits the idea of healthy attachment—a parental offering of gradual transitions, consistent responses, and a sense of security all while allowing the baby to do the work of falling asleep on her own.

How can you tell if your baby is healthily attached? On its website, LaunchPad offers the following seven signs.

1. **Your child prefers your company to that of strangers.** Your child seeks you out with eye contact, gestures, or physical relocation. While your child can spend time with other people without much anxiety, he looks to you for support, a good indicator that he will have the ability to seek out appropriate social support later in life.

2. **Your child looks to you to be comforted.** Your child trusts that you know and understand his needs intuitively. He is secure in the knowledge that you are available and willing to be there when a need arises or life becomes scary or uncomfortable.

3. **Your child welcomes and engages you after an absence.** The mood is positive and accepting when you and your child are reunited after a period of separation. Your child's disposition is warm, relaxed. He greets you openly.

4. **Your child gives, takes, and shares.** The ability to complete these actions habitually, with little upset, is a key sign that social skills are well developed. Your child is generally not concerned with or worried by the presence of other children. He is empathetic and able to remain relatively balanced emotionally throughout social interactions.

5. **Your child delays gratification.** A child with a healthy *attachment* is also able to wait without becoming anxious, overwrought, or upset. He feels secure that a toy will be returned, his turn will come, or a promise will be honored, though this does not mean that it will always be easy for him.

6. **Your child is responsive to discipline.** Healthy *attachment* facilitates trust. Your child's ability to receive firm direction and willingly allow you to guide him is a strong indicator that he trusts you to teach him how to behave properly. Over time, your child's choices are wiser and more careful.

7. **Your child is confidently independent.** The beauty of a healthy attachment is that it promotes feelings of safety and trust between you and your child. At the same time, *attachment* supports the development of a confident, secure child, ready to explore and adapt to new situations. A securely attached child investigates neighborhoods, schools, and communities without much fear, secure in the knowledge that he has a safe place waiting for him.

EMOTIONAL AVAILABILITY

Emotional availability is a research-based, scientifically driven way of understanding the quality of communication and connection between a parent (or caregiver/educator) and child.

What exactly is *emotional availability*? "Simply put, it means 'being there for your children,'" says the International Center for Excellence in Emotional Availability website, "but it entails much more than helping them with their homework, picking them up from school, putting dinner on the table, taking an occasional day off to spend 'quality time' with them." Robert Emde, emeritus professor of psychiatry at the University of Colorado School of Medicine, describes it as being able to signal emotionally—both sending and receiving signals. "It's about 'attunement' to someone else's needs and goals. And for a parent, it means responding to a wide range of emotions, not just a child's distress," he wrote in his 1980 article "Emotional Availability (EA)."

In her book *Raising a Secure Child,* psychologist and researcher Zeynep Biringen talks about parents' ability to "read" their children. She says that when parents are emotionally reachable and "able to read the emotional signals (through body and verbal language based on attachment and EA principles)" of their kids, the children will perform better in a wide variety of situations. Learning how to read our children, even in infancy, discerning their preferences and making adjustments based on our observations of their behaviors, gestures, responses, and patterns, is a major part of my gentle sleep-coaching approach.

Dr. Douglas Teti, the Penn State psychology professor I mentioned earlier in my Sleep Lady Proclamation, has done a lot of work on the direct correlation between emotional availability and sleep. He's been conducting a fascinating longitudinal study as part of the Study of Infants' Emergent Sleep Trajectories (yes, it's known as the SIESTA study), looking at data from thirty-five families with infants from one month to two years in age. He used the Emotional Availability Scales (1998), which measure parents' sensitivity, their ability to set appropriate limits, or conversely, whether they exhibited hostility and intrusiveness when interacting with their child. It's probably not surprising that he found "the infants of mothers with high emotional availability had fewer bedtime disruptions and woke up less during the night." Examples of emotional availability were mothers cuddling and talking softly to their infants, giving them reassurance by using phrases such as *It's okay* as they prepare them for sleep. At the other extreme of low emotional availability was the mother who threatened to take her two-year-old's toys away if he didn't lie down and close his eyes.

Dr. Teti's work has broader implications than bedtime cuddling equals happy babies, because emotional availability is about more than putting the baby to bed; it's about how we relate to our children overall. Creating a sense of security in our children by being truly focused on our children (I'll remind you in every single age-specific chapter about this focus—for instance, by putting down your phone during bedtime stories!) is one of the building blocks that children—and their parents—need to fall asleep and stay asleep.

BEDTIME IS AN OPPORTUNITY TO BE
EMOTIONALLY AVAILABLE

The bedtime routine is an opportunity to emotionally connect and bond deeply with your child. This is especially true as our little ones become more aware of the world, are exposed to more people, and become more verbally responsive. The quiet time you spend together during the bedtime routine can be a chance to check in with your child, without distractions, about her emotions, questions, curiosities, confusion, dilemmas, and so on. It's a time to be fully emotionally available.

"Findings demonstrate that parents' emotional availability at bedtimes may be as important, if not more important, than bedtime practices in predicting infant sleep quality," Teti wrote. "Results support the theoretical premise that parents' emotional availability to children in sleep contexts promotes feelings of safety and security and, as a result, better regulated child sleep."

In a nutshell, a bedtime routine alone is not as powerful as being emotionally available while doing your bedtime routine.

Some ideas to help you build EA into your bedtime routine:

* Don't bring your phone or tablet into your child's bedroom; leave your phone in the living room (this alone may take some adjustment). You want to give the message to your child that you are fully present for her in those twenty or so minutes.
* Allow her to choose whether she wants to play quietly with a toy or puzzle with you or read a book. Allow her to choose the book. (With older children, you'll generally move toward bedtime reading, not toys.)
* Have fun when reading! Point to the pictures and connect what she sees in the book to real life.
* Kiss, hug, and lovingly touch your child during your bedtime routine.
* Ask him what he liked about his day.
* Point out something you noticed he learned or did well that day. "You were able to share your toys with Ryan when he came over to play today. He really appreciated that. You were very patient."
* Do some yoga poses together.

UNDERSTANDING TEARS

By being present, by offering physical and verbal caresses and reassurances, we reduce the stress on ourselves and on our children, but we won't eliminate every single tear. However, it's easier for us as parents to tolerate the tears if we understand that they are a form of communication and if we think about what our children are trying to tell us through their cries.

When a young baby or toddler is crying, he is telling you that he wants or needs something. And that's all his brain can concentrate on at that moment. When you calm him by helping him meet that need, his brain can focus on other things. But if you don't respond to that need, if you repeatedly ignore the cries, it can lead to overstimulation and lay the groundwork for later difficulties. Some research suggests that a pattern of unattended crying can actually affect the wiring of the brain. A baby whose brain becomes used to chaos may seek out chaotic situations later in life. Now please note that I'm talking about *a pattern of prolonged unattended crying.* I don't mean that a little bit of crying will destroy your child's psyche or prevent him from forming a secure attachment. You will not scar your child for life if he fusses (safely) in his swing while you are nearby taking a shower. Naturally, we are less willing to allow crying with a newborn than we are with an older baby. That's one reason I recommend only the gentlest of sleep-shaping techniques in the first few months of life, and I don't introduce my Sleep Lady Shuffle until a baby is six months old. (Sometimes a modified version can work after four months or in desperate situations, which is why I am working on a specific book that addresses such modification.)

Hearing those cries can be hard on parents, especially during sleep coaching. It's easier if you remind yourself that the cries are his way of saying, *Why did you put me down awake? I don't know how to go to sleep! You're supposed to put me to sleep. I am tired! What are you doing? Why have you changed things? This is frustrating, and I don't like it one little bit!* This is where you have to remember that you are the coach, not the player.

You are giving love and support and comfort and reassurance—being that secure base. But you aren't fixing, rescuing, or doing it all for him. You aren't erasing every scrap of frustration (even if your heart aches to) at the price of his learning and sleeping. And once you give him that safe and secure space from which to learn, from which to explore, sleep isn't all that different from when a child feels safe enough to take a few steps away from you on his own and venture out at a playgroup or chase after a butterfly.

Watch your baby. You will see him work through that frustration, and you get to watch him learn. You will see him discover what helps him go to sleep, what feels good, what is soothing. You will see him learn to suck his thumb, or rock his body, or rub a soft blanket against his cheek. Once children gain confidence, when they know they own this skill, going to sleep isn't so hard anymore; it isn't so mysterious. And there's no longer a need to cry. By teaching your child to sleep, you have not damaged him emotionally. You have helped him grow.

"We thought we were bad parents if our baby was crying," said Megan. "We thought crying made him feel alone and abandoned; we thought crying was torturing him. But we learned that we were hurting him by not letting him sleep. Sleep was so important to his growth and development. You have to keep telling yourself that over and over again. He needs to sleep; what you are doing is right."

Parents often ask me how long their child will cry. The answer is usually a lot less than you expect. However, older toddlers and preschoolers may cry and protest more than young babies simply because their problematic sleep patterns are more ingrained. Exceptionally aware and alert babies might cry a bit more than other children because they have a harder time shutting out the world so they can sleep. Children whose parents have been inconsistent about sleep may also cry more as you begin sleep coaching. But throughout this book, you will be able to see how more consistent parenting makes life—and sleep—easier both for ourselves and for our children.

YOUR CHILD'S TEMPERAMENT

Learning to recognize the temperament of a child is the bedrock of optimal parenting. When we discuss bonding and attachment or emotional availability or understanding tears, the heart of each topic is attunement with the temperament of a child. In my years as a sleep coach (and a mother), I've seen again and again that so much about how a child learns to sleep, what self-soothing techniques she chooses, how adept she is at regulating sleep-wake cycles, down to whether she prefers a bath before bed or at another time of day all comes down to temperament. If we learn to crack the code of our child's temperament, we can tailor sleep coaching and motivate a child much more easily. Bottom line: temperament is hugely important to note when parenting in general and particularly crucial with sleep and sleep coaching

Admittedly, most of the parents who seek me or my Gentle Sleep Coaches around the world have children who are highly alert. It isn't hard for me to relate to these parents—and children—as my second daughter, Gretchen, was certainly what I call a highly alert child. Even in her infancy, she was keenly aware of her surroundings, so enthralled by activity and engaged with the world that she didn't want to miss a beat by going to sleep. You might be nodding because this temperament might sound very familiar to you. These kids are shrewd! They know what they want (probably not the same as what *you* want), and that usually means they require you to make a bit of a pivot when sleep coaching.

One landmark study from 1956 (and after all these years, it's still the gold standard and the foundation for subsequent research on temperament) tracked people from infancy to adulthood. That helped researchers Alexander Thomas, Stella Chess, and Herbert Birch identify the nine temperament characteristics to describe a child's behavioral style:

1. **Sensory threshold:** the level of stimulation needed to evoke a response from a child.
2. **Activity level:** the level of a child's motor activity.

3. **Intensity:** the reactive energy of a response (i.e., her expressiveness of emotions).

4. **Rhythmicity:** the predictability of a child's bodily functions like appetite, sleep-wake cycles, and excretion.

5. **Adaptability:** how a child adapts to change and transitions.

6. **Mood:** a child's disposition, such as whether he is a happy-go-lucky kid, serious, cranky, and so on.

7. **Approach/withdrawal:** how the child responds to new environments, circumstances, or people.

8. **Persistence:** the ability to continue with a task despite disruptions or challenges.

9. **Distractibility:** a child's concentration or focus.

How does taking inventory of these traits in your child relate to sleep coaching? Being in tune with your child's needs prevents you from feeling as if you are using techniques that simply don't sync with your child's temperament. It helps you choose the best approach for the emotional, social, and learning needs of an individual child—and that's particularly true for the highly alert child, the ones my colleague Macall Gordon describes as having a Ferrari engine in a Prius body. They develop FOMO—fear of missing out—at a very tender age. Then they refuse to go to sleep because they are afraid they will miss out on the action.

SLEEP COACHING YOUR HIGHLY ALERT CHILD

Sleep coaching isn't impossible once you recognize that your highly alert child has her own rules about how and when she gets some sleep. These alert babies catch on to even the slightest change, so when beginning sleep coaching, we have to keep them in a zone of tolerance, which means we tread carefully, not over- or under-challenging them. The mind-set here is figuring out how much can we nudge them without blowing them out of the water. The highly alert child can be described as extremely aware and engaged, not a great napper, and very capable of going from zero to sixty in ten seconds, but then taking an hour to wind down. In fact, drowsy but awake might feel like a concept he will never grasp. They tend to reach physical milestones, like walking, early. They know what they want, when they want it—and from a young age, how to hold out until they get it.

Parents of highly alert children do experience more emotional turmoil, mostly because they are much more tired. "These children are so smart and perceptive, so you have to be quick—especially as they get older," says Macall, whose own exhausting experiences with a highly alert baby led her to dedicate her life to sleep research. "Whatever you say you are going to do, you must stick with it. If they see a chink in the armor, they will outmaneuver you."

Certain behaviors, reactions, and needs can be identified in the highly alert child. These children have filters that are open wider to the world, and it is one of our jobs as parents to be able to read them and figure out what we need to help them filter out. Once you do, you will be able to acquaint yourself with this temperament and arm yourself with the compassion, patience, and understanding that can carry you through tough rounds of sleep coaching.

When tailoring and meeting your baby's sleep-coaching standard, keep in mind the following:

1. It might be harder to read the sleepy cues of the highly alert child. For instance, some babies don't rub their eyes (they don't want to take their eyes off the world for one second), but their eyes may appear glassier. Watch the clock and go into the room, dim the lights, and pull down the shades. Once you start your presleep routine, you may suddenly see sleepy signs you didn't see in the kitchen or living room.

2. Do the Shuffle for three nights and see how she's doing—and how you are doing, too! If no progress has been made, abort the

mission—for now. You might need to wait until your baby is a little older, and that is nothing to be upset about. She just might not be ready, and maybe you aren't, either.

3. If your baby is visually alert, try removing some distractions from the walls. When you are soothing her, avoid making eye contact while you shush and pat her.

4. These babies love to be around any older siblings. Try taking the baby to a separate room when possible, away from the excitement, so she can more fully focus on your soothing bedtime or nap-time routine or even feeding.

5. Gentle massage works really well for these children, while picture books might act like catnip—or vice versa. Some babies don't like massage or are sensory sensitive. Experiment and see what works. If you notice your child perks up at the sight of *The Very Hungry Caterpillar,* find some other wind-down activity, maybe reciting a short poem instead.

6. Co-sleeping, no matter how much you are committed to it, might not be suitable to your baby's alert temperament. Many parents have told me they had to (reluctantly) go to plan B and move the baby to her own room because her alertness and curiosity were keeping everyone up at night. Sensitive to movement and smell, some children don't like the inevitable touching and crowding of personal space and literally push you away. For these babies, co-sleeping might not be their preference.

SPECIAL TIPS FOR VERY ALERT CHILDREN

Often in my practice, I've found that unusually alert, bright, and aware children tend to have a little more trouble learning to sleep. These children often reach their physical milestones—like walking—on the early side, and they tend to have slightly disturbed sleep.

Make sure you don't fall into the trap of thinking that an alert child needs less sleep than average. He needs just as much sleep as any other baby—maybe even a little *more* than average—but he has a harder time shutting out the world to get to sleep.

Room-darkening shades are essential for these babies and children; sound screens can help for naps. These babies may also need to be nursed in a dim, quiet environment because they are easily distracted. Watch your baby and the clock. Bring him into his room or into a quiet environment that is dimly lit. Wait for eye rubbing, a yawn, or other sleep cues (see Chapter 4). These children tend to be less flexible sleepers for several years, so they can be extra sensitive to disruptions of routine or travel. My suggestions in Chapter 16, "Routine Busters," can help.

DEVELOPMENTAL MILESTONES

We cannot talk about getting to know your baby without discussing developmental milestones. Each achievement brings a new opportunity to meet your child over and over again as she changes and grows. Just when you think you've got her all down pat, a milestone will occur, and likely, your little one ups the ante, becoming more equipped, independent, smarter, confident, self-aware, and faster—with you feeling proud and derailed at the same time.

What are milestones, and why must you be aware of their impact on sleep coaching? Milestones represent achievement and the performance of a new skill in a child. Physical milestones obviously mark growth in height and weight, and developmental milestones represent the kind of skill performance that we often record in our child's baby book, including rolling over, sitting up, and walking. There are also emotional milestones—when a toddler becomes a big sister, for instance, or starts preschool. What is especially key to note about cognitive, emotional, or motor developmental milestones is that they come with what Harvard pediatrician and child development pioneer T. Berry Brazelton called *sleep regressions*—when a child takes one step forward developmentally but another step back with sleep. Learning to observe milestones, and to be prepared for those changes and possible regressions, can be a game changer when it comes to managing sleep coaching.

In fact, Dr. Brazelton, in his book *Touchpoints: Your Child's Emotional and Behavioral Development, Birth to Three*, reminds us that we may see regression or a period of disorganization not just in sleep but in social, emotional, and feeding patterns as well. Dr. Brazelton explains that along with a surge of growth in brain development during a developmental milestone (like learning to walk) comes another part of development slowing down or regressing (like speaking).

I find that learning to walk brings one of the most pronounced (besides the four-month sleep regression) periods of sleep problems, though luckily, it's temporary. You may also see regressions right before your child sits up, crawls, stands, and is potty trained. I address many of these leaps in the relevant age chapters, but the key is remembering that these new skills excite children and change their view of their world, sometimes quite literally. For instance, when your child stands up in her crib for the first time, she may discover everything looks different from up there!

Of course, it's hard to know that a child is about to reach a milestone. We see the disorganization—the regression—and we may think something is wrong. We might even rush to the pediatrician. Only in hindsight do we realize that the baby was about to take her first step. "I don't know if this is true for all babies, but for both of mine, sleep got worse before they reached a new milestone. Both kids would have two or three fussy nights—it usually didn't require any intervention from me, but I could hear their disrupted sleep-squawks and whines and what seemed like fitful sleep," said Lisa, mother of Teddy and Brittany and a champion keeper of records of her children's sleep. "Then they would roll over, or stand up, or sit for the first time."

Be flexible, but stay consistent during these periods. When a child is sick, or when we travel, we do have to deviate from normal sleep rules, but with the developmental milestones, if you stay the course, the child will adapt quickly. I firmly believe that a solid understanding of how your baby grows and changes is key to sleep-coaching success. Within each age-specific chapter, I include an easy-to-read milestone chart along with detailed advice on how to handle accompanying sleep regression. This will help you apply and troubleshoot the Sleep Lady Shuffle. But even as you explore the many facets of your child—as you identify her attachment style and temperament, interpret her tears, and become aware of developmental milestones and sleep regressions—you need to also learn the actual sleep basics. In the next chapter, I'll share the science (the fun kind of science!) behind the biology and mechanics of sleep and how they interact with the Sleep Lady Shuffle.

Chapter 4

THE SCIENCE AND NATURE OF SLEEP

"Sleeping like a baby," as the saying goes, is not all it's cracked up to be. Newborns sleep a lot, about fifteen to eighteen hours a day, but their sleep is not organized, not well developed. For the first four months, about half their sleep is REM (rapid eye movement) sleep, the most active kind of sleep. That means they are sleeping lightly and are more easily aroused than an older child or an adult who spends much less time in REM. Young babies also cycle between the two sleep states, REM and non-REM, much more than adults or even older children do. Before we try to help our children sleep, it's useful to understand a little about the phases of sleep—and to understand that none of us actually "sleep through the night." But once we learn how to get ourselves back to sleep, we barely notice that we were up.

Each time a baby switches from one phase of sleep to another, they have a *partial awakening* or *partial arousal*. For us as adults, a partial awakening may last only a few seconds; we may scarcely remember it in the morning. But that brief moment of being semi-awake can startle babies—which wakes them up even more. They then cry— and we rush in and frantically try all sorts of things to rescue them from their tears.

And sometimes when we rescue them, we end up teaching them other behaviors or creating other expectations that will make it even harder for them to fall back to sleep without us. I call them sleep crutches, and we'll come back to them in a moment. As you know, I strongly believe in responding to a child's cry, both for his sake and for our own peace of mind. We need to reassure them. We need to make sure they are safe. But we shouldn't overdo it. Remember that balance between comforting our children and allowing them to learn to comfort themselves. That's an essential component of sleep shaping and coaching—or parenting overall.

WHAT'S A SLEEP CRUTCH?

We have a lot of ways to help our newborns fall asleep. We nurse them, rock them, walk them, swing them, sing to them, rub their backs, grip their tiny fingers in their cribs, take them into our beds. But as they get older—past four months, and definitely after six months—if we continue these behaviors until they fall asleep at bedtime and each time they wake up at night, they become negative associations or, as I prefer to call them, *sleep crutches*. Not because they are "negative" or bad behaviors in and of themselves. They aren't. Rocking, snuggling, and singing are all wonderful behaviors. But they become a problem, or a crutch, when they are so closely linked in the child's mind with slumber that he cannot drift off without them. Throughout this book, we'll be learning how to replace negative associations with positive ones that help babies and children go to sleep, stay asleep, and wake up happy.

SLEEP CYCLES

Sleep is divided into two basic types, REM (rapid eye movement, also known as dream sleep) and non-REM. REM sleep is both active and lighter sleep. It's when we dream and organize our memories. During REM, we have limp limbs, irregular breathing, twitching, and rapid eye movement.

Non-REM has several stages of its own. They are called *light sleep*, *true sleep*, and *deep sleep*. As we pass through them, we move from a gentle drowsiness to that state of deep, deep sleep where, if awakened, we feel groggy and a little disoriented. During non-REM sleep, our breathing is slow and regular. Our muscles are a little tense and not so floppy.

Children also have both non-REM and REM cycles, although their sleep cycles differ from adults'. For the first four months, their sleep, particularly daytime napping, is not very organized neurologically. About half of their sleep is light REM sleep, when they are quite active and easily aroused. For a newborn, that's about eight hours of REM sleep and eight hours of non-REM sleep a day. At around four months, REM sleep begins to slowly drop off, and by age two, a child's sleep cycles more closely resemble those of an adult. REM constitutes about 20–25 percent of adult sleep, or about two hours a night.

We all go through these sleep cycles, and as we switch from one phase to another, the change in our brain activity often wakes us up a little bit, that *partial arousal*. Sometimes we are more awake than at other times. For instance, about every 90–110 minutes (50 minutes for infants), while we are still in a fairly light sleep, we have a partial arousal. We don't wake up completely, but we may mumble or roll over, for example. Every three to four hours, we experience a partial wakening that is a little more pronounced. Maybe we notice that our pillow is on the floor, or we want a sip of water, or we need to adjust the blanket. Usually, we fall right back to sleep—because we know how. Babies don't—until we teach them.

When babies experience these partial arousals, they may cry out, thrash around, become startled. If they have sleep crutches, sometimes called *negative sleep associations*, the partial arousal will become a complete arousal. They are basically saying to themselves, *Hey, I'm sort of awake, and I'm in my crib. I'm tired, and I don't know how to go back to sleep without Mom nursing me or Dad walking me up and down the hallway or someone helping me find my pacifier. So now I'm going to do the only thing I can do. I'm going to cry.*

Once we help our children give up these associations, they will still have the partial awakenings, but they will no longer need to let us in on them. They can open their eyes for a second, recognize that they are safe in their own room, and then suck their thumb or reach out for their favorite stuffed animal or special blankie and get themselves back to sleep. The partial arousal stays partial.

Note: While sleep crutches are not ideal for sleep coaching, they are useful for nap-time coaching. It may sound counterintuitive, but I'll explain in the age-specific chapters how and when to use the sleep crutch during daytime sleep coaching—a necessary tool for successfully using the Sleep Lady Shuffle.

CLOCKS AND WINDOWS

We all have a circadian rhythm, an internal clock that tells us when to be awake and when to be asleep. Falling asleep when our body clocks are set to "wake" is challenging, as is staying alert when our clocks say, "sleep." Sleep is not as restorative—meaning we don't feel as rested—when we sleep off our clocks or when our clocks are on a "wake" mode. For example, people who sleep all day and work the graveyard shift, from midnight to 8:00 a.m., often don't get quality sleep because they are not in sync with their internal clocks. Or, for a two-year-old, a nap from 1:00 to 3:00 in the afternoon feels better than a nap from 4:00 to 6:00 in the evening. The clock is mostly set by light, although social cues like noise and temperature can affect it, too. (Keep in mind that blue light in our electronic devices and screens has been shown to decrease secretion of melatonin, the sleep hormone.) This is one reason that I recommend room-darkening shades for children and staying away from electronic devices, particularly for children who wake up very early or who have trouble napping.

As adults, we know how to compensate, at least in part, when our circadian clock is upset. If we have to go to sleep one night well before our usual bedtime, to catch a plane or attend an unusually early meeting,

we know how to prepare ourselves, to cue our brains to sleep at the unac-
customed hour. We try a hot bath, a good book, a relaxation recording, or
maybe just a mental image of a warm, palm-fringed beach. Babies don't
know all those tricks. They need us to protect their sleep by paying attention to the clock—both the external time and the baby's internal rhythm.

We sleep better, and we feel better, if we go to sleep at about the
same time each night and wake up at the same time each morning. To
keep ourselves "ticking" well and protect our sleep, we should regulate
our sleep. We can vary our routine on weekends, but only by an hour.

Babies are even more sensitive, especially if they are already overtired. A well-rested child can handle variations in a sleep schedule better
than an overtired child. We all know they need routines and predictability for their emotional well-being, for that sense of order and security in
their new world. But they also need routines to keep their internal clocks
correctly "wound" and to cue their brains to start preparing for sleep by
secreting melatonin. Production of melatonin, which promotes sleep by
relaxing our muscles and making us drowsy, begins sometime between
three and four months. Secretion levels are linked to darkness, another
aspect of our circadian rhythms.

WAKEFUL WINDOWS AND SLEEP WINDOWS

As you read the age-specific sleep-coaching chapters, you'll hear a lot
about "sleep windows" and "wakeful windows." *Wakeful windows* are just
what they sound like—that post-sleep, post-nap playful awake time. *Sleep
windows* refer to the internal bedtime, the natural time your baby needs
to start preparing for sleep. If you miss your child's sleep window, his
body won't be pumping out calming melatonin. Precisely the opposite
will occur. His adrenal glands will send out a rush of cortisol, a stress-
related hormone that creates a second wind. So if, by natural rhythm and
habit, he is ready for sleep at 7:00 but you keep him up until 8:00, he is
going to have a hard time getting to sleep. And even after he does get to
sleep—often with a lot more tears and resistance than normal—it will be

harder for him to stay asleep. Overtired children don't sleep better—they sleep worse (as many parents have learned the hard way)! He is more likely to wake up during the night and to wake up too early in the morning, before he is truly rested. This cycle can then lead to poor naps the next day, which will lead to an overtired baby at bedtime, which leads to poor nighttime sleep. We've all seen this pattern in our children at some time—I know I've seen it in mine. Our task is to correct this cycle before it becomes a self-perpetuating, exhausting downward spiral.

At two years old, Ilan, my coauthor's son, would rub his eyes and ask for his special songs when he got sleepy, even if he was proclaiming loudly that he didn't want to go to bed. From monitoring the eye rubbing and his general activity level, Joanne would usually know whether to speed up or slow down the bedtime routine to calibrate exactly when his head should hit the pillow. But some nights, he was able to mask his tiredness. If he began leaping up and down, shouting gleefully, "I jump on bed like monkey, Mommy!" she knew she had miscalculated and his window was slamming shut.

QUALITY AND QUANTITY

Sleep needs do vary somewhat, but the natural variations are a whole lot less than most parents think. These babies may be *getting* less sleep than average, but they *need* a lot more than they are getting. Remember, sleep begets sleep. To help you accurately gauge your child's needs, I provide average sleep requirements at the start of each age-related chapter.

Children need to get an ideal *amount* of sleep, and they need to get the ideal *kind* of sleep. Quality counts along with quantity. Good sleep should be largely uninterrupted. If your child is getting up a lot, she isn't getting all the sound sleep she needs. As we've all experienced on nights when we've slept poorly, fragmented sleep or interrupted sleep just does not make us feel rested and refreshed.

Quality sleep also means sleep that is not interrupted by medical conditions like asthma, allergies, obstructive sleep apnea, reflux, or other disorders. See Chapter 14, "Could Sleep Disturbances Be a Medical Condition?" and of course consult your pediatrician. I highly recommend keeping a sleep log to gauge the quality and quantity of sleep, as well as tracking wakeful and sleep windows. Tracking your child's sleep patterns will help you better read the cues he sends when he is tired and know when to seize a sleep opportunity and cut off challenges he might face when he hits developmental milestones.

SLEEP WINDOW SIGNS

Recognizing your child's sleep windows so that you can get him down before the cortisol rush is key. What should you look for?

* eye rubbing
* yawning
* slowed activity
* listlessness
* limpness
* zoning or staring blankly into space
* whining and fussing
* loss of interest in people and toys

Try going into a quiet, dimly lit room and engaging in a very gentle activity when you think nap time or bedtime is approaching. The signs may then appear.

DROWSY BUT AWAKE: THE SECRET SAUCE OF THE SLEEP LADY SHUFFLE

Between three and four months old, babies begin to develop their internal clocks. They begin to produce melatonin, the sleep hormone. Melatonin is triggered by sleep cues like darkness at night and bedtime routines. *Drowsy but awake* at this point really means that a child is fed, dry, warm, loved, and aware he is being placed in his crib. It might make more sense to you if you think of it as *calm but awake*. A soothing routine and an ideal bedtime are great habits to begin teaching self-soothing, even with an infant who isn't ready for more formal sleep coaching. This routine and calm behavior from parents and caregivers will set the stage for later sleep success.

If your baby falls sound asleep in your arms for every nap, every bedtime, every time he wakes up at night, he isn't going to have a clue about putting himself to sleep. I want you to put your baby down when he is drowsy but awake so he can learn to do that last part of falling asleep on his own. It's essential that we do this once we start the Sleep Lady Shuffle. Drowsy but awake takes on a different dimension as children get older. With babies, we watch for the drowsy but awake moment. With toddlers and preschoolers, we rely on a calming routine of bedtime songs and stories to prepare them for slumber.

If you have trouble visualizing what *drowsy but awake* means, think of it this way. The baby should be sleepy—but still awake enough to know that she is going into the crib. *If she falls asleep too quickly, in less than five minutes or so, she was probably too drowsy; put her to bed when she is a tad more alert the next night.*

If he's still waking up a lot at night, you may need to put him to sleep a little more awake—less drowsy—at bedtime so he gets better at resettling himself when he stirs at night. Remember, bedtime is the easiest time to learn to put yourself to sleep. He won't be able to put himself back to sleep during those partial awakenings—which can turn into full-blown, very tearful awakenings—during the night until he has mastered it at bedtime. When you start to put him down awake after his soothing bedtime routine, he will likely protest and fuss. After all, this is new for him. Don't worry, but don't get him out and start the whole routine over again. Instead, stay nearby and use your Sleep Lady comforting techniques—some of which I introduced in the opening chapters and some of which we'll delve into in the age-specific chapters—to soothe and reassure him. This is your first step in sleep coaching!

If your child just doesn't get drowsy, if he's really good at fighting sleep to keep you close by and engaged even while you are trying to stick to your calming bedtime routine, you should stop nursing, get up from the rocking chair or wherever you are, and put him into his crib or bed anyway. But spend some time thinking about your evening routine. Do you have the right bedtime—or are you putting him down too late? Are you feeding him in the dark and he is falling asleep? Do you have a really good, relaxing evening routine to help prep his mind and body for sleep? Or are you playing or interacting in ways that stir him up rather than calm him down? Once he's in bed, use your repertoire of soothing techniques to help him transition to sleep.

Chapter 5

PREPPING FOR SLEEP-COACHING SUCCESS

Teaching a baby to be an independent sleeper by gradually giving her more and more space as you do less and less for her at bedtime and in the night is much gentler than just walking away and letting her cry alone. But gentle sleep coaching requires some preparation and decision-making. **Here are eleven things to get you started—they are all essential for sleep-coaching success:**

1. Get the green light from your child's doctor. Most sleep problems are behavioral, but you should still have your pediatrician rule out any underlying medical conditions, such as reflux, asthma, allergies, ear infections, or sleep apnea. Make sure medications, including over-the-counter remedies, aren't disturbing her sleep. If you're still feeding your baby during the night, ask her doctor if, given your child's age, weight, and general health, she still needs wee-hour nourishment. Review with your pediatrician how much your child is eating during her waking hours (see suggestions below for how to keep track).

2. Choose the right time. Choose a time to start sleep coaching when you can expect about three weeks without any disruptions or major changes, including travel, moving, or having a new baby. Some families try to make these transitions during the summer or during the winter holiday season because the adults won't have to juggle so many work responsibilities. Or others begin on a Friday and take off work on Monday and agree to not travel for three weeks.

These tactics often work well, but be mindful to keep the child's schedule consistent even if yours is not. For instance, committing to a 7:30 p.m. bedtime during a holiday week or when grandparents visit might not be sustainable.

When you choose a time to begin sleep shaping, start waking up your child at a consistent time for four or five days before, preferably around 7:00 or 7:30 a.m.

3. Keep a sleep-and-feeding log. To figure out how to solve your child's sleep problem, you'll need to have a clear picture of what's happening at bedtime and during the night, what's working, what's not, how your baby is responding, and so on. Write it all down for a few days or a week, or keep track of it in my Gentle Sleep app. Having a written record, instead of relying on scrambled mental notes in your sleep-deprived brain, will give you a more accurate picture of your child's patterns and your own responses. To download a sample sleep log chart, visit my website at https://sleeplady.com/charts/.

Here are some things to note in the log:

* Where and when the baby or child goes to sleep, naps, wakes, nurses, eats, and so on.
* When, how long, and how intensely he cries (for example, is it a whimper or a scream?).
* The timing and frequency of night awakenings. How long does it take you to get him back to sleep? Do you rock him, walk him, nurse him, sing to him, rub his back, or take him into your bed?

Compare your child's daily schedule with the typical routine I suggest in the chapter corresponding to his age. If you are pretty much on track, terrific—part of your sleep-coaching work is already done. If not, don't worry, I'll walk you through it. Babies adjust pretty easily because you'll be shifting to a schedule that corresponds to what their little bodies need.

As you learn about your child's routines and body clock, pay attention to your own routines as well, particularly from about 6:00 p.m. to bedtime. Are you missing your baby's sleep cues because you are busy cooking dinner, washing dishes, checking texts or email, paying bills, or running errands? Are you focused on an older child, or children, who are also tired and need your attention in the evening? See if you can postpone some of your evening tasks until after the kids are asleep, divvy them up differently with your spouse or partner, or make some temporary modest tweaks to the older kids' routines until you get the baby sleeping.

4. Once you start my program, continue your log. Tracking your child's sleep patterns will help you figure out what's working, what's not, and what tactics you should tweak. You could use the template included here and also download my Gentle Sleep app. If you decide to work with one of my Gentle Sleep Coaches, keeping a log will be part of the program.

5. Get your child used to waking up between 6:00 and 7:30 a.m. This applies to babies over five months of age who are waking up at all different times, sometimes as late as 8:30 or 9:30 a.m., which then throws off the entire day and confuses their internal clocks. Start waking your baby by 7:30 a.m. at the latest about five days before you plan to start sleep coaching.

6. Figure out your child's ideal bedtime. This is the period of time during which she'll show signs that she's ready to sleep—yawning, rubbing her eyes, twisting her hair, fussing. Pay extra attention to how your child behaves between 6:00 and 8:00 p.m. (and make sure she's not zoning out in front of the television). As soon as she begins acting drowsy, you'll know that that's her natural bedtime—and the time at which you should be putting her down each evening going forward.

Although I usually recommend making bedtime adjustments gradually, thirty minutes or so at a time, sometimes with a child under three, you can make the changes quickly if you learn to recognize her natural patterns. For instance, if your twenty-month-old is used to going to bed at 10:00 p.m., but you can see that she's tired at 7:30 p.m., you don't need to spend days gradually adjusting. Just put her to bed at 7:30 p.m., and make sure you do so again the next night and the night after that. For this step, getting that bedtime consistency, it's okay to use any sleep crutch that works. Once you start the sleep coaching, we'll address phasing out those crutches.

If you have trouble picking up on your child's drowsy signals, you can pinpoint a reasonable bedtime for her simply by looking at when she normally wakes up in the morning and counting backward, based on how much sleep she should be getting at her age. (You'll find recommended sleep averages throughout each age chapter in Phase 2.) Let's say you have a two-year-old who tends to wake up by 7:00 every morning. The average two-year-old needs eleven hours of sleep at night, so that would mean that your child needs to have gone through her entire bedtime routine and be sound asleep by 8:00 p.m. Keep in mind that your child's cues, behaviors, and averages are what work best when customizing her bedtime.

7. Create a relaxing bedtime routine. All children, from newborns on up to school-age kids, need a set of comforting and predictable rituals to help them prepare physically and psychologically for sleep. These activities should be calm, quiet ones like reading, storytelling, or lullabies; bedtime is not the time for tickling, wrestling, scary stories, TV shows, or anything else that's distracting. Technological devices or screens are firmly prohibited when trying to get your child to sleep. Because you're preparing your little one to be separated from you for the night, the tone should be serene and reassuring. For babies over six months old, I encourage attachment to a safe *lovey*, a favorite stuffed animal or blanket that he can use to comfort himself when he wakes during the night. Also, note that depending on your child's temperament, certain rituals might not work. For instance, for highly alert babies (see Chapter 3), picture books with an active or exciting story might be overstimulating, and for more sensitive babies, a bedtime bath might pep them up instead of calm them down. And with the exception of baths and tooth brushing, the bedtime routine should take place in the child's nursery or bedroom. If your child hates some aspect of bedtime, get that part over with first. For example, if she can't stand having her teeth brushed, do it right after her bath, not after you've read two books and gotten her all snug and cozy.

CUING SLEEPY TIME

Here are some activities that work well as part of a bedtime routine, depending on a child's age. Three from this list is plenty:

* bath
* put on pajamas
* brush teeth
* go potty
* massage
* swaddle
* read books
* sing a short song
* play a quiet game
* share three things about your day
* tell a story
* listen to music
* baby or toddler yoga
* small sippy cup of water with books
* bottle or nursing
* prayers, blessings, or sending kisses and love to others
* plenty of hugs and kisses

8. **Install room-darkening shades** if your child's bedroom gets too much light, he wakes up very early, or has trouble napping. But leave a dim night-light on so that you can see him when you check on him. He'll probably sleep more soundly with that little bit of light, too, although

some children do better in total darkness. Experiment with what works for your child. His preferences might change over time.

9. Consider playing white noise or nature music if your child's room isn't very soundproof and you have a barking dog, loud neighbors, older kids, live on a busy street, and the like. Children do learn to sleep through routine household sounds (and they should to a large extent), but some places are just really loud, and some kids are really sensitive. White noise is a constant sound that helps to block out noise; you can buy a white-noise machine, or try turning on a fan.

10. Decide about the pacifier. Pacifiers can significantly reduce the risk of SIDS. They also soothe infants and are very useful tools for those caring for a fussy baby. The American Academy of Pediatrics advises using a clean pacifier when putting the infant down to sleep, although you shouldn't force the baby to take it. If you are breastfeeding, wait until breastfeeding is established—about four weeks—before introducing the pacifier.

Even if you use the pacifier when the baby sleeps and will use it during sleep coaching, I encourage you not to use it all the time. Saving it for long car rides, nap time and bedtime, as well as doctors' visits will keep the pacifier a useful sleep tool when coaching begins. I give more details on using the pacifier—as well as eventually eliminating it—in the age-specific chapters in Phase 2. It is not unusual for some children to give it up by themselves.

11. Make sure all your child's caregivers are on board. It's vital that your spouse, partner, nanny, and anyone else who frequently cares for your child understands each aspect of the sleep-training plan (and why it's important) and is willing to follow through. Remember, consistency is vital to sleep success. A baby can't learn to sleep amid constantly mixed signals. (See "How to Communicate Your Schedule to Caregivers" in Chapter 7 for what to do when you have a reluctant babysitter and also how to work around your baby's schedule if he's in day care.)

Chapter 6

THE SLEEP LADY SHUFFLE
STEP-BY-STEP

For children over six months, the Sleep Lady Shuffle embraces strategies of what is known as a *parental fading method* of sleep coaching. In fading, parents gradually diminish their role in helping their baby fall asleep, giving him room to figure out how to soothe himself. The idea is to be his coach, not his crutch. (The Sleep Lady Shuffle is also a very effective way to sleep train multiples; each age-specific chapter has a section dedicated to their unique needs.) Think of the Shuffle as a kind of weaning for sleep: you're easing your child from sleep crutches like needing to be rocked to sleep and instead establishing independent sleep practices. And you are doing this without resorting to techniques that don't align with your core parenting values (like letting your child cry it out) or that don't fit in with your lifestyle (such as bringing your baby into your bed) or—and I see this a lot—when you want to continue co-sleeping but want your family to get more sleep. The Sleep Lady Shuffle can work for children of all ages but is most often used for babies and toddlers (you'll find guidelines for using the Shuffle with older children in beds in Chapter 11, "Two and a Half to Five Years").

Briefly, the Shuffle goes something like this: After a soothing bedtime routine, you or your partner will start out seated right by your child's crib or bed, where you can easily comfort and reassure her. Every three days, you are going to move a little farther away, across the room, to the doorway, right out in the hall, where you will intervene less and less to put her to sleep, but still be able to soothe her. Sometimes I advise parents to sleep on a mattress or sleeping bag in the baby's room for a few nights as a reassuring prelude (although it may be the parents who need the reassurance as much as the child). Finally, you will be able to leave her alone for five minutes at a time so she can fall asleep on her own. This sounds like a huge leap for you, but it's not so huge for her. Through the Shuffle, you've given her nearly two weeks of preparation. As you have soothed her less, she's learned to soothe herself more, sucking a finger, twirling her hair, or nestling into her lovey. You have slowly and gently moved away at bedtime and during the night, while letting her build confidence that you are still nearby and responsive. She has learned *Mommy is there for me even though I can't see her* and *Daddy is nearby and loves me.* She will be ready to sleep on her own if you let her.

In all probability, you will still face some tears during the Shuffle, because frankly, a no-cry solution is impossible. Crying is your baby's way of communicating with you that she doesn't like change—who does? However, using the Shuffle, children generally cry much less than the hours parents commonly report in the crying-it-out and graduated extinction methods. And usually, you are close by and comforting her when she does cry, which is far less stressful for both of you.

THE SHUFFLE STEP-BY-STEP

* Start at bedtime, after a good day of napping. Go through a nice, calming bedtime routine—nursing or bottle-feeding, a song, and so on—in the child's room with a light on.
* Turn off the lights (a dim night-light is okay), and place your child in her crib drowsy but awake. For many children, this may be the first time they're put down while aware of what's happening, and they may well protest with crying and tears. Be prepared. Preverbal babies will cry, and verbal babies will cry along with offering words of protest.
* For the first three nights, position a chair beside the crib where you can sit and easily comfort and reassure your child.

GUIDELINES FOR SITTING BY THE CRIB

1. Don't try to make your child lie down (if she's old enough to sit or stand) or keep repositioning her. You won't win! Pat the mattress and encourage her to lie down. When she does, you can touch her and say soothing things like "Sh, sh," "Night-night," "It's okay," and so forth. Sit in your chair to encourage your child to sit down so she can meet you at your eye level. If she doesn't know how to sit down on her own, see Chapter 7, "Six to Eight Months," for advice on teaching her how.

2. You can stroke, *sh-sh*, pat, rub your child intermittently through the rails of the crib—but not constantly—until she falls asleep. She'll expect the same treatment when she wakes up in the middle of the night. Take your hand away when you notice your child starting to fall asleep. You don't want hand-holding to become her new crutch.

3. You must control the touch. In other words, don't let your child fall asleep holding your finger or hand, because when you move, she'll wake up and you'll have to start all over. Pat or stroke a different part of her body.

4. It's okay to pick up your child if she becomes hysterical. Stay in her room and hold her while standing until she settles down. Be careful that you don't hold your child for so long that she falls asleep in your arms. Once she's calm, give her a kiss, put her back in her crib, and sit down in the chair. One note: If you pick up your child and she immediately quiets down, then you've been had. Instead of you training her to sleep, she trained you to pick her up. Next time, wait a bit longer. You'll know within a night or two whether picking her up helps or further upsets her. If your child's crutch has been to fall asleep in your arms, please be conservative about picking her up to calm her. These babies can become hysterical, and when you pick them up to be calmed, they can conk out in about a minute or two. Hard to believe that anyone can do that! Amazing as that is, we want to avoid this when sleep coaching; otherwise, you will end up having to remove "picking up to calm" from your toolbox.

5. Stay beside her crib until she's sound asleep at bedtime and during all night awakenings for the first three days of the Shuffle. If you rush out of the room the minute your baby closes her eyes, chances are she'll wake up and you'll have to start over again. (This is especially true of children over a year old.)

6. Return to your Shuffle position, and follow these rules each time the baby wakes during the first three nights (as long as you and your pediatrician have decided to end night feeding). Go to the crib, give him a kiss, encourage him to lie down if necessary, and sit in the chair. Do this at each awakening until 6:00 a.m. "Pick up to calm" should not be the first thing you do when you enter the room.

* Every three days, you will move the chair farther from your baby's crib (see "Recommended Chair Positions," below).
* Later in the Shuffle, when you're no longer by your child's bedside but are sitting by the door, for example, and your child wakes at midnight—go over to her crib, reassure her, give her a kiss, encourage her to lie down (if she's standing), and return to your chair position by the door. You may go back over to the crib to pick her up *if* she becomes hysterical, but hold her only until she's calm, then put her back in the crib and return to your chair. Be careful not to train

her to cry until you go crib-side to "put her to sleep" by patting, rubbing, and the like, and risk creating new crutches.

RECOMMENDED CHAIR POSITIONS

These chair positions will change every three days.

Position 1: Beside the crib.

Position 2: Halfway between the crib and the door (if the room is very small or the crib is close to the door, you should instead go ahead to position 3, by the door). For children in beds, skip this chair position.

Position 3: Beside the door, inside the room.

Position 4: In the hallway, where your baby can still see you.

Position 5: In the hallway, out of your child's view but where she can still hear you.

Within a couple of weeks, you'll be able to put your baby down to sleep, say "Good night," and leave the room knowing that she'll happily and easily get herself to sleep without needing your help.

A NOTE ABOUT MULTIPLE CAREGIVERS DURING SLEEP TRAINING

As I've said, it's fine for parents to establish somewhat different bedtime routines (maybe Mom isn't into singing but Dad's a pro at lullabies, or Dad would rather tell a story than read a board book). Even so, the bedtime routines of a baby's various caregivers (including babysitters, nannies, and family members who're around regularly) should at least be similar. But while you're sleep training, it's generally a good idea to have one parent in charge each shift. If, for example, you're on day 5 of the Shuffle and Dad is sitting in a chair halfway across the room, the other parent shouldn't switch places with him after ten minutes. This just stimulates and confuses the child. That said, it's not necessary to have one person on duty all night for middle-of-the-night awakenings. Some couples split the night up or trade off because of their own sleep needs and body rhythms, one parent taking, say, midnight to 3:00 a.m. and the other parent taking 3:00 to 6:00 a.m.

GRADUATED EXTINCTION OR TIMED CHECKS

Some parents wonder whether doing graduated extinction with their child would work just as well as the Shuffle. Graduated extinction—or what I call *timed checks*—means at bedtime, after your soothing routine, you put your baby or child down drowsy but awake, leave the room, and tell them you will come check on them. Some proponents suggest leaving for five minutes and then increasing the amount of time you are out of the room, each time the child wakes up, or on each subsequent night. When you check on your child, you should go directly to his crib and give him a quick reassuring pat, but don't linger. Leave the room. Unfortunately, there's no magic number to guide you—five minutes, ten minutes—but choose one that he can tolerate and that prevents you, the parent, from rushing in too soon. Use your intuition. Sometimes going in too frequently will further upset your child. You can also extend the checks if your child is whining instead of crying or crying out very intermittently—as if you sense he may go back to sleep. If this is the case, wait by the door and listen. Do what you feel comfortable doing and what you can follow through with consistently.

The Shuffle by nature does not use timed checks; however, if this is something you would like to do—whether it is because you have to tend to another child's needs, you are concerned you may not have the patience for the Shuffle, or you feel this may be a better match for your child—it is certainly your choice. However, it is important just as it is with the Shuffle to follow through consistently. Always use your intuition and be extra aware of your child's cues and reactions so you can pivot when needed. For instance, if you decide to start off with timed checks and feel uncomfortable with the amount of crying your baby is doing, then go back to the room and sit by the crib and start the Shuffle instead. It would be better to do this than to pick him up and hold him to sleep after twenty minutes of crying.

Because the Sleep Lady Shuffle's philosophy and methodology is based on emotional availability and responsive parenting, picking up to calm is encouraged when a child is inconsolable. However, picking up to calm is done briefly, just long enough to help the child regulate and reassure him that you are by his side and supportive and loving as he learns the skill of putting himself to sleep. If you decide to use timed checks, I would encourage you to allow yourself to use "pick up to calm" during a check if your child is inconsolable—making this a gentler adaptation of Ferber's method.

In older children, sometimes parents opt to include timed checks or job checks toward the end of their sleep-coaching process, intermittently returning to the child to check on him from the doorway during early wakings, or at bedtime telling a verbal child that Mommy or Daddy has to "do something," like brush their teeth or check on the dog, and will be right back to check on them. With any sleep-coaching method, do what you feel is the right match for your parenting philosophy, your child's temperament, and what you can follow through with consistently.

Phase 2

AGE-BY-AGE SLEEP COACHING WITH THE SLEEP LADY SHUFFLE

Chapter 7

SIX TO EIGHT MONTHS

SLEEP GOALS

* *an average of eleven hours of uninterrupted nighttime sleep*
* *three and a half hours of daytime sleep spread over two to three naps*

FIRST THINGS FIRST: CREATE A SCHEDULE

Sleep coaching children six to eight months of age, in my experience, is much easier and usually quicker than coaching older children. At this age, habits developed by both parents and child during infancy haven't solidified into expected forms of behavior. Therefore, actions and responses aren't hardwired to the point where everyone is more dependent on, and emotionally attached to, bedtime habits and behaviors.

As parents, you might not yet be completely comfortable with giving up your routines—such as nursing or rocking to sleep—cold turkey. That means you might be conflicted on beginning to sleep coach. I completely understand that. *You* have to be ready. I suggest to most parents who want to sleep coach, but also want to keep certain sleep practices, to decide what is right for them. If you aren't fully ready for the Shuffle, at least begin by setting a basic daily schedule. Schedules are familiar territory for adults. We are used to doing certain expected things within a time frame. Doing the same for your baby is a terrific start to any sleep-coaching plan.

How do you want your day to begin and end? Are you an early bird? Is your partner? Have you noticed whether your child is a natural early bird while you are more of a night owl? Will you be mainly sleep coaching alone, or do you have a partner or another form of assistance available? Will you have a caregiver coming at a certain time? Do you have to drop off your child at day care? What is an ideal time for your family to turn in for the night? Do you have other children who you are also sleep training? These are just some of the questions you will ask yourself as you begin to schedule your baby's sleep, nap, and feeding routine.

We build babies' schedules around how much sleep they need, so the priority is determining how much sleep your baby requires. Everything else—his feedings, his introduction to solid food, his social engagements, his floor time or playtime—all work around his sleep needs. I opened this chapter with the average nap and nighttime sleep goals for this age group—an average of what the American Academy of Pediatrics and the National Sleep Foundation recommend. (I have found over my years working with families that those goals have worked very well for parents, but you can learn more about the two organizations' recommendations on their websites.) Sleep averages are a range, and you have to find where in that range your child fits. A chart alone can't tell you that—but watching your child's cues can. The best place to start when setting your schedule is the average amount of sleep and going from there. My recommendation is to first teach your baby the skill of falling asleep on her own, then move on to sleeping through the night, and finally to nap coaching. After a few weeks, when all of you have adjusted to your new rhythms, you will be better able to see where her sleep sweet spot is and where precisely she falls along that range. I've also seen some babies start off on the lower end of the sleep range and, as they grow, wind up on the higher end.

Below is a sample sleep schedule that parents I work with have found useful. It splits the total recommended number of hours of sleep between naps and nighttime sleep. Remember, the most important thing to do is watch your child and note how she is doing along the sleep coaching journey and ensure her sleep tank remains full.

Sample Schedule

7:00–7:30 a.m.   **Wake-up.** Upon waking, nurse or bottle-feed and give solids.

9:00–9:30 a.m.   **Morning Nap.** One and a half to two hours. Upon waking, nurse or bottle-feed and give solids.

12:30–1:00 p.m.   **Afternoon Nap.** One and a half to two hours. Upon waking, nurse or bottle-feed.

3:30–4:00 p.m.   **Optional Late-Afternoon "Bonus Nap."** About forty-five minutes to an hour. This nap is dependent upon previous nap length and/or time. Most babies this age need this nap, especially if they are not napping well or sleeping through the night yet.

5:00–5:30 p.m.   **Dinner.** Nurse or bottle-feed and give solids.

6:00–6:30 p.m.   **Bedtime Prep.** Start bath and bedtime preparations, which may include an additional bottle or nursing.

7:00–7:30 p.m.   **In Bed.** Drowsy but awake.

There is no "right" schedule for all babies, but the sample schedule above is a good framework. Some variation in the schedule is inevitable; a baby who naps for ninety minutes starting at 9:00 a.m. is not going to be on the same clock as one who naps for two hours starting at 9:30. But the starting point, between 6:00 or 7:30 a.m., and the end point, 7:00 or 7:30 p.m., should be about the same. The simplest guideline is to have about eleven to twelve hours from morning wake-up to evening sleep—and to keep it consistent. Note: It is perfectly reasonable for a child to wake up at 6:00 a.m. (even if you personally are more of a 7:30 a.m. person). If she consistently wakes up happy and well rested at 6:00 a.m., she's simply a morning bird baby. Usually a child who is an early bird has at least one parent who is one, too. If that parent can take charge of the morning routine, the 6:00 a.m. wake-up call is less of a concern. On the other hand—and this is an important distinction—if your child wakes at 6:00 a.m. but is fussy and cranky or becomes fussy and cranky an hour after she wakes, she is not an early bird but a child who is rising too early. Birds chirp, risers grunt. We will discuss how to end early rising on page 112.

That's the scheduling ideal. Let's walk through your day in more detail. Please keep in mind, this is the schedule you would like your child to follow once she is taking sufficient naps and sleeping through the night, *not* while you are sleep coaching. It's a process. Try not to have too many expectations that after a few days or even weeks your baby will be adhering to your ideal plan. But as you coach her, you will lead her closer and closer to where you would like her to be, keeping the schedule in mind.

Wake-up. A good wake-up time is anywhere from 6:00 to 7:30 a.m. Remember that one of the basic rules of sleep hygiene is to wake up and go to bed at about the same time every day.

When you are ready to start your baby's day, turn on the lights, open the blinds, and say, "Good morning." In the Sleep Lady lexicon, I call it *dramatic wake-up.* You want her to learn to distinguish between daytime awakenings and nighttime awakenings, between daytime feedings and evening ones.

Nurse or Bottle-Feed. Nurse when she wakes up and play for a while. Then get yourself some breakfast and feed her solid food. Follow your pediatrician's advice for when and how often to feed your child solids; most babies start around six months. That's her introduction to the routine of breakfast. Your child will be more open to trying new solid foods when she is well rested.

Morning Nap. About an hour and a half to two hours after she wakes up, it's time for bed again. Usually, the morning nap starts at around 9:00, a little sooner for early risers and early birds. Remember, that's the time when she should be asleep, not getting ready to sleep, so allow time to get her settled. The nap should last one and a half to two hours. A common error is starting the nap at 10:00 or 10:30. That's usually too late—and her fussing and grouching are her ways of telling you it's too late.

Awake Time and Lunch. In Phase 1, I introduced you to the term *wakeful window*. This post-nap time is her wakeful window. Plan to have two to three hours of awake time between the end of the morning nap and the start of the afternoon one. This is a nice time to play, take a walk, or practice developing motor skills like rolling over both ways.

If your agenda requires driving, try doing it at the beginning of this awake window, when she's more alert, not at the end. That way there's less chance of her dozing off in the car and throwing off her nap schedule for the rest of the day, or of getting so used to napping in the car (not as restful as sleeping in a crib) that she won't nap in a crib. Some babies will want to have a bottle and eat lunch soon after they wake from the morning nap; some can wait. It's up to you, but don't wait so long that you run into the afternoon nap. You want to build that separation between nursing or bottle-feeding and going to sleep to prevent feeding from becoming a sleep crutch or negative sleep association.

Afternoon Nap. No more than three hours should elapse between the end of the morning nap and the start of the afternoon one—and that means she should be asleep within three hours, not getting ready to sleep. Watch both the clock and your baby; she'll signal when she needs to go down. Remember to leave her a little time to unwind, to get ready to sleep. Give her a few kisses, maybe a little rocking, and put her in the crib drowsy but awake. Ideally, this nap should last one and a half to two hours.

Snack. When she wakes, she gets a snack—nursing or another bottle.

Optional Late-Afternoon "Bonus" Nap. For this particular age group during nap coaching, a third nap isn't actually optional. It's essential so the baby isn't overtired at bedtime, making it more difficult to get to sleep and stay asleep. Many babies who are sleeping through the night and even napping well will keep this bonus nap until around nine months and then outgrow it on their own. If your baby is a poor napper and her two main daily naps last an hour or less apiece, then this third nap is mandatory and might need to be encouraged beyond nine months, until she is achieving her daily sleep average. Without this nap, she'll be running on vapors. Be sure to wake your baby by 5:00 or 5:30 in order to get her to bed at 7:00 or 7:30. If she naps until 6:00, you'll have a hard time getting her to sleep at 7:00. She needs at least two hours between the end of this bonus nap and bedtime.

Dinner. Another nursing and the third solids (if advised by your pediatrician) should be around 5:00. Again, there's a little variation depending on her afternoon nap, but don't let it get too late.

Bedtime Prep. Bedtime prep is not your child's actual bedtime. Bedtime is when she is in her crib drowsy but awake, and you are in your chair position doing the Shuffle. Bedtime should be at 7:00 or 7:30, or 6:30 or 7:00 when naps are insufficient (less than the total average of three and a half hours listed above). This means that bedtime prep needs to be built into the daily schedule, at least a half hour before the baby is in her crib. Many times, parents make the mistake of considering the wind-down process or bedtime routine—whether it be running the bath, putting on pajamas, or reading stories—to be bedtime. If bedtime is 7:00, you want to bedtime prep at 6:30 or earlier, depending on what your getting-ready-for-bed routine looks like. You need time to get her ready for bed, and she needs time to get herself ready to sleep. At this age, a good rule of thumb is to allow twenty to thirty minutes, plus whatever time you need for bathing and pajamas, before she lies in her crib.

Enjoyable bedtime activities include gentle massage or baby yoga (see Chapter 17), ten minutes or so of listening to quiet music or looking at short, simple picture books. Babies at this age love singsong books—like books by Eric Carle. She may enjoy funny little caresses like having you kiss your finger and then touch it to her nose. Include her lovey, if she already has one, in any bedtime games. Have the lovey caress the baby's nose, too, or have it play peekaboo. Peekaboo and other calm and gentle games are a big hit as well, but be careful not to confuse her into thinking it is playtime.

Bedtime Feeding. It's okay to nurse or give her a bottle right before bed as long as she doesn't fall asleep or get very drowsy with this feeding. If she does depend on nursing or bottle-feeding to go to sleep, a very common pattern at this age, try to make the final nursing earlier in the bedtime routine, say, before a song or story. And make sure you feed her with the lights on. Try not to let her fall asleep sucking; put her down drowsy but awake.

In Bed. Bedtime should be between 7:00 and 7:30, and by *bedtime*, I mean in the crib, not in the bathtub or on your lap reading stories. Keep any bedtime music soft and quiet. Use music to set the mood and cue the brain for sleep, but turn it off before she gets into her crib or soon after. You don't want her so accustomed to lullabies that she can't sleep without them. If you've been playing music until after she falls asleep, slowly ease it out. Lower the volume, and try to turn it off before she's fully asleep. If you walk or rock your baby, keep it brief and stay in her room. Put her down drowsy but awake so she can learn to do that final part of falling

Sleep Lady Tip

Remember when we talked about emotional availability? (See Chapter 3, "Getting to Know Your Child.") That focused connection with your child is always important—but it's absolutely essential that we be patient and fully present at bedtime. Do your best to leave your workday behind. Forget about your to-do list for a moment. Put aside that email or phone call that upset you. Better yet, at bedtime, put aside your phone! Leave it in another room while you focus on your child. It will still be there once he's asleep. Having so many screens and devices distracting us is probably the biggest change I've seen since I started developing the Sleep Lady system. I know it's not easy to ignore your phone, but the benefits—to both you and your child—are huge.

asleep on her own. The goal of getting her down drowsy but awake is crucial (see Chapter 4). Focus your energy on getting it right at bedtime first. Once you tackle bedtime—the easiest time to learn to put oneself to sleep—the easier it will be for your baby to carry this skill over to night wakings and eventually naps.

HOW TO COMMUNICATE YOUR SCHEDULE TO CAREGIVERS

Whether you have a stay-at-home nanny, a day care center, a once-in-a-while sitter, or a grandparent taking care of your baby during the day, communicating and maintaining your new schedule can be tricky, but not futile. Even when playing by the rules of other providers and facilities, all does not have to be lost. Here are some strategies to help you all get on the same page when you become committed to sleep coaching:

1. Make a copy of your daily schedule—like the one in this chapter—and give it to your caregivers, letting them know you have begun sleep coaching and that for just a few weeks, you are asking them to be mindful of the schedule when they can.
2. Each morning when you leave your child, let the caregiver know what time your child woke up that morning, as well as how many times during the night she was up, and therefore what time she will most likely be ready for her first morning nap.
3. Ask the childcare providers if they can work toward a total of three hours of nap time no matter how they get the child to sleep. We cannot expect or presume they will be comfortable or allowed to adhere to the Shuffle or reduce the use of sleep crutches, but you can certainly ask. Sometimes that is the best we can do. Just remember that your child getting sleep throughout the day, no matter how it is accomplished, whether by rocking, in a bouncy chair, or another sleep crutch, will still help you with nighttime sleep coaching, as your child will not be overtired and will have the three hours of daytime sleep in her sleep tank.
4. If your child is napping in a crib at a day care center where toddlers share the room, ask if your baby's crib could be placed in a corner away from the action and distraction and to please use blackout shades if available. If neither is possible, ask if you can drop off your white-noise machine for her nap time.

5. Some childcare providers just won't nap train (day care centers often have their own schedules and methods). If that is the case, you can still sleep coach by adhering to your morning and evening routines, focusing on getting the child to sleep through the night. Then, on weekends, nap coach diligently. Don't worry about how that might feel inconsistent. It will take longer, but it can still work. For instructions on nap coaching your six- to eight-month-old, see the section "Much Ado About Napping" on page 116.

TAKE NOTE OF DEVELOPMENTAL CHANGES

Rolling and crawling and standing, oh my! Just when you think you have your daily schedule and coaching plan, developmental changes throw a wrench in them. These milestone moments are super exciting to witness, and they show us our children are thriving. But the developmental changes can also introduce new challenges to sleep coaching. Many times, parents come to me saying they were doing just fine with their coaching until suddenly their baby seemed to go off the rails. As we noted in Phase 1, developmental milestones often cause a sleep regression. Maybe your baby was a terrific sleeper and now suddenly refuses to go down. A baby who was taking in an average number of ounces is now voraciously feeding. Once you learn to recognize the developmental trigger, you will be able to set yourself and your baby right back on track. What follows are the most common developmental changes you can expect in the six- to eight-month age range and strategies to get through any sleep regression.

SEPARATION ANXIETY

Separation anxiety sounds scary, but it is normal. It's part of an important developmental milestone called *object permanence*, or recognizing different faces and places. Your baby suddenly understands that when you leave the room, you don't disappear like a game of peekaboo. Now, your baby is hit with the realization that you can go somewhere *without her.* The thought of being left alone can cause her to feel overwhelmed, and as a result, some anxiety may arise.

We discussed at length attachment theory and bonding in Phase 1, and believe it or not, separation anxiety is a great opportunity to secure a healthy attachment and bond even further. For instance, when your baby wakes up at night, you won't put a pillow over your head and hope his crying stops. You will respond immediately, talking to him, explaining to him that he is okay and you love him and that it is time for sleep. This will help him learn that the people he loves are close at hand and watching over him. The bond becomes stronger.

Separation anxiety has its first peak at this age, and it increases when babies are overtired. At bedtime, your baby may fight sleep to be with you. He may also wake up more often wanting to see you. So what can you do? You'll be implementing the Sleep Lady Shuffle, which promotes sleep time security in your child by using your gentle verbal and physical cues. However, there are some other tricks that can help strengthen his feeling of safety even as he learns these new self-regulating skills as part of your sleep coaching.

Use Loveys

I am a firm believer in the power of the blankie or any other soft object that catches your child's fancy and provides him with a sense of security and comfort. It must be noted that the AAP recommends having nothing in the crib until a child is one year old. If you decide you would like to introduce your child to a lovey, please discuss safety first with your pediatrician.

The technical terms for this kind of object includes *transitional object* or *security object,* but I think the term *lovey* is perfect to describe any object that your child, well . . . loves. This is what your baby turns to in the middle of the night when he wakes up, as babies often do, even for just brief moments in between sleep cycles. At this age, it usually stays in his room for sleeping time, which helps with the association with sleep. The only places that the blankie goes outside the house are to the doctor when your baby may need some extra comfort or in the carry-on bag when we go on an airplane (because it's *not* worth the risk of losing a beloved blankie if your checked luggage is lost).

If your baby has already attached himself to an object (it doesn't have to be a blankie; it can be an object like a stuffed animal—it should be something small, though, that is easy to hold in her little hand and has no removable parts like eyes that could come off), great. Go with it. If not, by the time your child is about five or six months old, it's a good idea to start thinking about what you want to become his or her lovey. For my children, it was a little security blankie—they are about twelve inches by twelve inches. Very small and not something to worry about your child having in his or her bed.

If you are concerned that your child could end up with the blankie on his face, you can tie a knot in it so it is more of an object than a blanket. If you are still nervous about having a lovey in the bed, you can lay your baby on the ground and play peekaboo with the blanket. If you put it on his face and he is able to pull it off, you may feel more comfortable with it in the bed. You know your child and his capabilities the best, so if you have concerns about introducing a lovey, wait until he is a bit older and you feel he is more capable of moving the blankie around himself. Visit my website (https://sleeplady.com/products) for an updated list of products I recommend—including loveys!

Some children don't get attached to a lovey at this age, particularly if they have another sleep crutch, such as nursing or a pacifier. If she doesn't bond, try again every now and then as she gets older. Anita, for instance, rejected the blankie her parents offered her as a baby, but when she became a toddler, she adopted Lamby. Teddy similarly spurned every plush toy he was offered but then cheerfully bonded to two plastic teethers when he was about thirteen months old, happily gripping one in each hand at bedtime.

NEW MOBILITY

Babies are like snowflakes: no two are alike. Their skills vary, so there are no definitive timetables for the emergence of developmental milestones in healthy, well-developing children, especially when it comes to new mobility. However, for the purposes of this book, my goal is to address mobility in terms of how it may affect sleep and influence sleep coaching as they typically occur for each age range. In my experience, by about six months of age, babies learn to sit up and roll, rock on their hands and knees (the precursor to crawling), and, by eight months, develop the pincer grasp and pick things up—including their pacifier.

Most children will start to crawl toward the end of this age range, at around eight months, and most pull themselves up to stand by nine months. This can disrupt sleep. You might see your baby on the monitor getting on her hands and knees in her crib and rocking. This is okay; just keep letting her do what she's doing. (If your baby is developing more quickly, such as pulling herself up to standing on her own, please turn to the next chapter, "Nine to Twelve Months.")

Rolling

Rolling is a milestone—and it can also cause sleep regressions or backsliding. It is not uncommon for babies to roll themselves over on one side—and then not be able to roll themselves back, which causes them to wake up. Imagine if you wanted to readjust yourself for comfort but couldn't. You'd wake up pretty cranky, wouldn't you? Teaching your baby to readjust her position is a good idea to prevent these sleep interruptions. Once babies learn to roll back and forth, much concern about their safety is relieved. Children learn to roll back and forth during the day before they roll at night, so be sure to offer her plenty of floor time or tummy time. If they are not rolling back and forth by six months, dramatically increase floor time. You can also physically demonstrate and teach your baby to roll rather quickly. She'll probably think rolling on the floor with a parent is a pretty fun game.

How to Teach Rolling

Place your child on her tummy, bend one leg like a frog, and position her foot so she is more on her toes. She should be using her hand as well to push herself up (same hand as the side of her bent leg). Once she is in position, gently guide her to her side with your hands. Once she is over on her back, she might be startled at first, so praise her with a "Hooray!" To teach her to roll from her back to her belly, use a toy to lure her. Touch and hold her and guide her to her side as her eyes follow the lure until she is all the way over. Please note, if your child has untreated reflux, this might be harder. Being on her belly may cause pressure, and being on her back may be painful due to reflux. Please see Chapter 14 for more on reflux.

Many of my clients tell me that the baby has begun to roll onto her belly while she is sleeping but can't roll onto her back (or vice versa), so she wakes up crying as a result. If this happens often, you will need to make practicing rolling during the day your number-one priority, because flipping her constantly in the middle of the night will be exhausting for you both.

If your child has mastered rolling during the day but she still wakes at night unable to roll herself back over, guide her onto her side and remove your hand so she can have a try at flipping the rest of the way. As she gets better at this, do less and less for her at each waking as she finally learns to flip on her own while she sleeps.

Sitting Up

It is a big deal when your child can sit up by herself without toppling over. Typically, I have seen sitting with assistance happen around the five- or six-month mark. Babies can sit solidly and hold an object in their hands by about seven months. Many times, children learn how to sit before they know how to lie back down—and you can understand why getting stuck sitting up can cause sleep disturbances. Until she learns, you will have to do it for her at nighttime. When you see this start to happen, make the entire week's priority to teach your child during the daytime how to lie down from her sitting position. At nighttime, you might find your child falls asleep literally sitting up. Leaving her asleep sitting up may mean she'll fall asleep sitting up and just plop over, but she won't hurt herself, and once asleep, she will wriggle herself into a comfortable position. Other times, the baby falling over will startle her and wake her, and that is when a sleep disturbance occurs.

If your baby wakes startled because he fell over, of course, pick him up and soothe him. And then begin the Shuffle. If he sits up again, I recommend waiting until he seems very fatigued, which I call the *magic moment*, before trying to lay him down. Many times, parents lay their babies down too early, and the babies pop back up, grabbing for their parents and protesting. Once you do lay down your tired baby, rub his back or hold him down gently with your hand, applying pressure to soothe him. Do this from a seated position, not standing. This will encourage him to stay down so he is on your level. Leave your hand on him a little longer than usual to encourage him to no longer protest the process and to keep you from using a sleep crutch like laying him down repeatedly or picking him up and holding him to sleep.

Once your child knows the skill of lying down from a sitting position, pat the mattress through the slats of the crib to encourage him to go down. At this point, you should no longer be positioning him back down.

The Pincer Grasp

You may have noticed that your baby is able to grip and maneuver a piece of cereal, pick up a small toy, or pick up the pacifier and put it in and pull it out of his mouth. He has developed what is known as the *pincer grip* (the ability to pick things up using his thumb and index finger). The average age of babies who develop the pincer grip is eight months; however, I have seen babies as early as six months do it. According to *The Portable Pediatrician*, "Babies learn to grab objects first by taking them up and holding them with thumb opposed to all fingers. From 6–9 months they perfect this grasp. Most babies learn to really 'pinch' a tiny object between nine months and a year. Babies have trouble letting go of an object at this age. If you want to keep your baby from grabbing your earrings, just give him two toys, one in each hand: he will stare at them, stymied, unable to let go to grab the forbidden object."

Many times, wakings happen in the middle of the child's sleep when the pacifier falls out of his mouth and he wakes up and can't find it; or if he finds it and hasn't developed the grasp yet, he is unable to get it back in his mouth. So the baby is put down to sleep with his pacifier in his mouth, sucking away in bliss and into a peaceful sleep. Until . . . he wakes between sleep cycles to find he no longer has the pacifier in his mouth and is unhappy and calls for assistance! This constant getting up to replug the pacifier for your baby—which one mother aptly called *rebinking*—can become a crutch to your child. What you choose to do about pacifier use—whether to wean him altogether or not—may depend on how often he's waking up and whether he needs you to find his pacifier *for him* and plug it in again and again and again. We'll talk more about the pacifier replug on page 106.

GROWTH SPURTS

Again, the timing of growth spurts cannot be pinned down, because every baby is different. However, there are some timelines you can consider. According to Happiestbaby.com, in the first year, growth spurts may occur in line with these estimates, and for the age group of six to approximately eight months, you can expect at least two!

* six months
* eight and a half months

Baby growth spurts may temporarily disrupt your carefully tended routine for about a week. Your baby will have an increased appetite and may wake more at night to feed. Even so, she may also need more sleep than usual, so she still might be clocking in extra sleep amounts.

This may not be a good time to night wean if that is what you are planning. Instead of weaning, you can build one night feeding into the sleep plan. Some babies need one feeding during the night until nine months of age (note that eight-and-a-half-month spurt).

However, be mindful as to whether your baby is consuming the bulk of her calories during the night and barely eating during the day. Some very alert babies will do this, especially those who start day care and are too excited to eat. Discuss this "mixing of days and nights" with your pediatrician, and build just one feeding during the night into your sleep-coaching plan so that when your baby wakes in the morning, she is hungry.

THE SLEEP LADY SHUFFLE

So you've created a daily schedule and taken into consideration any developmental changes that may be occurring as you begin to sleep coach. Now it's time to Shuffle! You've seen the step-by-step Sleep Lady Shuffle guide at the end of Phase 1. Here is where we put it to work for your six- to eight-month-old. As you know by now, the Sleep Lady Shuffle is a gentle behavioral modification technique that lets you be a comforting presence as your child learns to put himself to sleep in his crib. The Shuffle is used to nap coach as well, but for the purposes of this section, I will first guide you through sleep coaching at night. Tip: When you first begin day 1 of the Shuffle at bedtime, do so after you get in a day of great naps any way you can, when you know your baby has filled his daytime sleep tank.

Before beginning the Shuffle, please turn to Chapter 5: Prepping for Sleep-Coaching Success, where I lay the groundwork for sleep coaching. You are going to start out right by his side, and over a period of about two weeks, gradually move farther away until you will be able to leave the room. Often, nighttime awakenings will start to taper off because of the combination of a more structured, consistent daytime routine and this newly acquired ability to fall asleep. After the first one or two nights, crying and protesting may increase. This is called an *extinction burst*—when a behavior gets worse before it gets better. This is the time when parents want to give up—for good reason—but shouldn't. If your child were able to talk to you, he might be saying, *Hey, is this the new normal? I don't like it. Let's go back to what we used to do. I don't know how to do this.* Not too many people like change, and crying will likely be your child's way of letting you know that he isn't a big fan of change, either. Often by the fourth night, the burst subsides, and the child begins to adjust to the Shuffle as he learns his new skill. In the "Sleep Crutches and Solutions" section on page 99, I'll offer some specific reasons why babies at this age wake up (in addition to developmental milestones) and ways to address them.

When he wakes up at night during the Shuffle, as he probably will at the beginning, you will return to the same chair position you were in at bedtime earlier that night and soothe him. A few days into the Shuffle, when you are no longer sitting by the crib, you might want to go by his crib briefly to calm and caress him right before you return to that evening's position. You should follow the Shuffle schedule, moving on to the next position even if your child has had a bad night or two, fussing or waking more frequently. Don't be surprised if there's a little regression or protest the first night of each new chair position as you gradually increase your distance from his crib. If your child gets sick during the Shuffle, you might want to pause and freeze or maintain your position until he's feeling a little better. You might even have to move a little bit closer during an illness to offer more comfort, but then resume your sleep coaching when he recovers.

I would be remiss if I didn't tell you that there is no such thing as a no-cry sleep-coaching system, so expect some tears. But unlike many other sleep-coaching methods, with the Shuffle, you can pick up your baby to calm her if she gets extremely upset. However, try not to pick her up either immediately after putting her in the crib at bedtime or as the first thing you do when you go to her room during the night when she wakes. Instead, first try patting, shushing, handing her a lovey or pacifier, for example, and sitting in the chair. You will always be there to assure her that she is not alone, she is safe, and she is loved and supported as she slowly learns this new skill.

NIGHTS 1–3: NEXT TO THE CRIB

Once bath, stories, bottle or nursing, and songs are over and your baby is in his crib drowsy but awake, sit in a chair right *next to his crib*. You can sing during the get-ready-for-bed stage, but once it's time for sleep, you are better off making lulling *sh-sh* or other soothing sounds. You might want to try closing your eyes to convey a sleepy-time message and see if he mimics you. Try not to be doing anything to or for your baby the last few minutes before he goes to sleep. Let him own that last few minutes himself. Before you know it, he will own the entire process of putting himself to sleep! Stay next to his crib until he falls asleep.

On night 1, if necessary or if you are not quite comfortable, you can do more touching. But don't touch steadily; do it on and off, and know that you will need to taper off or start patting more intermittently beginning on night 2. Similarly, during your first three nights next to the crib, try to be mindful of how much touch you are offering, because on night 4, you will be positioned farther away from your baby and won't be touching as much. You will defeat moving away from the crib if you go crib-side each time to, for instance, pat him to sleep. (The no-snuggles or no-picking-up-the-baby rules, by the way, do not apply to a child who is sick, frightened, or startled.)

Many parents I work with find solace when I remind them that their baby isn't crying because she is hurt or abandoned. You are there with her in the same room, providing care and support and reassurance, teaching her a new skill and how to be independent. The baby is simply learning something new (and so are you!), and doing things for the first time can feel like hard work.

TIPS FOR THE FIRST THREE SHUFFLE NIGHTS

* *Don't get into a power struggle about laying your baby down—you won't win!* If he is sitting or standing in the crib, pat the mattress and encourage him to lie down. Stay calm and say things like "Sh-sh," "Night-night," and "It's okay, lie down." Sit down in your chair to encourage him to lie down and be closer to your level.

* *You can stroke, pat, rub, sh-sh, or sing to your child intermittently through the rails of the crib.* But don't do it constantly until he falls asleep, or it will become his new sleep crutch. Stop when he is starting to fall asleep. (Some babies don't like to be touched as they fall asleep; follow your instincts and his cues.) If you notice every time you stop patting your child that he starts crying, you are patting too much. Try to touch less and less during the first three nights, knowing that on night 4, you will be moving farther away.

* *The parent controls the touch.* Don't let the baby fall asleep grasping your finger or hand, for example, because he will wake up when you move, and it will start all over again. Pat or stroke a different part of his body or the top of his hand.

* *If the baby becomes hysterical, pick him up to calm him.* Stay in his room; don't walk around the house or sit down in the rocker. Don't let him fall asleep in your arms. When he's calm, kiss him, put him back in the crib, and sit near him in the chair. Make soothing sounds and pat or stroke him. If you pick him up and he's immediately calm, then you've been had. Instead of you training him to sleep, he trained you to pick him up! Wait a little longer next time. Trust your instincts and your knowledge of your child. You will know within a night or two whether picking him up helps or gets him more upset.

* *Stay by his crib until he is sound asleep at bedtime and during all night awakenings the first three days of the Shuffle.* If you rush out of the room the second he closes his eyes, he will wake up and be upset, and you'll have to start all over.

* *Return to your Shuffle position, and follow these rules each time the baby wakes during the first three nights* (as long as you and your pediatrician have decided to end night feeding). Go to the crib, give him a kiss, encourage him to lie down if necessary, and sit in the chair. Do this at each awakening until 6:00 a.m.

NIGHTS 4–6: HALFWAY TO THE DOOR

Move the chair *about halfway to the door*. If the room is small, move the chair to the doorway as in night 7. Continue the soothing sounds, but stay in the chair as much as you can. Get up to pat or stroke him a little if necessary, or make the same soothing sounds as you have used the past three nights. Again, try not to pick him up unless he's hysterical, and if you do pick him up, follow the technique I described for the first three nights. Stay in the chair until he falls asleep. If you allow yourself to move to the crib side and pat him almost to sleep, you will create a crutch and undo any progress you've made.

Many parents during these nights create new sleep crutches without knowing it. They will move the chair farther away from the crib, and instead of picking up their crying child (an old crutch), they will sing him to sleep (a new crutch). As you move farther away on the following nights, the child will not be able to hear the song, and then you will have a crying baby on your hands. Another trap is parents getting up and patting their child too much to soothe him. It can be easy and tempting to go to his crib side and pat him fully to sleep. Although this may seem harmless—even if it's just for thirty seconds—you can create a new sleep crutch without knowing it. Your baby will look for you to help him with these final steps of going to sleep.

NIGHTS 7–9: CHAIR AT THE DOORWAY, INSIDE THE ROOM

Continue the same soothing techniques from your chair, remembering to intervene as little as possible. If he cries a little bit, keep calmly reassuring him. He'll know that you are there, and he will fall asleep.

NIGHTS 10–12: INTO THE HALLWAY, IN VIEW

Move into the hall with the door open enough so that he can still see you. You can keep making those *sh-sh* sounds, not constantly but enough to let him know that Mom or Dad is close by and responsive. Stay until he falls asleep.

NIGHTS 13 AND ON

A significant number of babies start falling asleep and staying asleep by now. But many parents have one more step to take: giving him the opportunity to fall asleep without their visual presence. Leaving him to fall asleep without a parent in his room may seem like a huge leap for you, but it's not as big for him anymore. All that chair moving has given him nearly two weeks of preparation. He has given up some negative associations, is starting to master a new skill, and has learned that you are always nearby.

Most parents stay in the hallway or in a very nearby room, where the child cannot see them but can hear them. You can make some reassuring *sh-sh* sounds, not constantly but enough to let him know that Mom or Dad is close by and responsive. If he cries, try checking on him from his bedroom door—without going all the way into the room. Be calm and reassuring. Make some comforting sounds, conveying that you are not far away and that you know he can put himself to sleep.

Children get ritualized easily. Make the changes every three days—or less. Dragging it out makes it harder, not easier, for your baby. Give it more than three days

> ## Sleep Lady Tip
>
> When you soothe your child by going to her crib to pat or rub her back, it is important that you control the touch. Instead of having her hold your hand or finger, you should pat her. Make sure you don't caress her too steadily, or else she might cry when you stop. Do it on and off. Count to yourself if it helps—count to ten touching, then count to sixty not touching, then touch for another ten counts. You don't want to swap one negative association like rocking for another—like your constant touch for the sound of your voice.

and he'll expect you to stay exactly where you are—and get mad or upset when you try to double that distance.

Occasionally, a baby will cry or fuss a little for a few nights, but don't rush in prematurely. Let him calm down and nod off. If you check on him from the doorway, try to be fairly unobtrusive, and don't check too frequently. You want to calm him while he maintains a sleepy state. Remind yourself of how far you and your baby have come!

IF YOUR BABY IS STILL WAKING AT NIGHT

If these techniques don't eliminate those final night awakenings, you might be putting your baby to bed when he's too drowsy. It's easier for a baby to put himself to sleep at bedtime than in the middle of the night—particularly if he was 90 percent asleep before his head hit the crib mattress. Try putting him down when he's a bit more alert, even if it means backing up and doing a few more days of the Shuffle. You may find that an earlier bedtime also helps him conquer the night awakenings. Try moving bedtime a half hour earlier. If you are still nursing at bedtime, try doing that feeding a little earlier in the evening to further weaken the link between suckling and sleeping. Sometimes it helps to keep a light on while you nurse to help him break that suckle-sleep association.

NOT READY FOR THE SHUFFLE? YOU CAN TRY SWITCHING ASSOCIATIONS UNTIL YOU ARE

Some parents are more sensitive to tears and want to take sleep coaching in even slower steps if possible. *You* have to be ready to sleep coach, and often it feels like a huge leap. And if you can't take that leap, take some preparatory smaller steps before you sleep coach 100 percent.

For instance, if your child depends on you to put her to sleep by rocking, feeding, or lying down with her and you are not ready to put your child down drowsy but awake at bedtime, you can switch the crutch, or what I call *switching negative sleep associations*. If you nurse her to sleep, stop one night and instead have the other parent rock her to sleep. Yes, you are creating a new sleep crutch—from nursing to sleep to rocking to sleep—but because the behavior of the other parent rocking her is so new, the child is not as attached to it. It may be easier to stop rocking to sleep when you are ready to start sleep coaching.

Another small step you can take now is to work on gently fading out your child's current sleep crutch. For example, if you always hold your child until she's completely asleep, try holding her until she's almost asleep. Then put her in her crib and pat her all the way to sleep. You can also try patting her back to sleep during the night.

SHUFFLING WITH MULTIPLES

Your multiple babies shared a womb, and it's usually a good idea to have them share a room. Some families even put them in the same crib for a few months, until they start rolling over. Yes, they may grunt, whimper, and make all sorts of strange baby noises, but they almost always learn to sleep through each other's sounds, and you want to encourage them to do so. Be careful about responding too quickly if one makes a noise. Parents often rush in as soon as they hear a peep, fearing that one will wake up the other one. You may be reinforcing the troubled sleeper while you protect the one who is asleep. The sleeping twin may be oblivious, or she may stir but then get herself right back to sleep, or one parent might have successfully reassured her back to sleep, exactly as you want her to do. Parents of triplets or quadruplets can adapt these techniques for their children, although most don't separate them for naps simply because they don't have enough room! A parent can sit in the middle of the bedroom between the children to soothe them. The children learn quickly to sleep through their siblings' crying and fussing.

Just like with singletons, start the Sleep Lady Shuffle at bedtime after a day when your babies' daytime sleep averages have been met—which means getting naps in any way you can. Whether you need to rely on all your sleep crutches at the same time or take three car rides a day, getting the daytime sleep tank filled—even if it means taking drastic measures—is a must before beginning the Shuffle at night. If possible, move the cribs so they are at least three feet apart, and have one parent sit in a chair between the cribs. If two people are available, this will be easier to do. Each parent can sit by a crib/multiple.

After your soothing bedtime routine, place your babies in their cribs drowsy but awake, and sit in your chair position as described in the Sleep Lady Shuffle, beginning on page 90. If there is just one parent, gently move back and forth to stroke and soothe each child in turn. Follow the rules of the Shuffle for the first three nights on page 92. Make sure that by the third night, you are using your voice to soothe instead of relying too much on touch.

Both parents must be on the same page—one is not picking up more than the other, for instance. If one child is more of a problem sleeper than the other, have the parent who will be most consistent (there usually is one) sit next to that child. Or if Mom is nursing and the sleep crutch has been to nurse to sleep, have the other parent sit next to the baby since he won't expect that parent to nurse him.

If you can't move the cribs and they must remain far apart and out of your arm's reach, each parent can sit by each crib for the first three nights. By nights 4 or 5 (depending on your weaning plan), you will be sitting in the middle of the room or by the door, depending on the room size. For more on weaning and the Shuffle, see page 101. Only one parent needs to sit there. I have had both parents eager to sit in the second position—you certainly can if you want—but it's not necessary.

FREQUENTLY ASKED QUESTIONS FROM PARENTS OF MULTIPLES

Q: **I have twins, and one is a better sleeper than the other and gets woken by the other twin. How should I sleep coach them?**

A: These are the cases—when one wakes up so loudly and frequently that he does disrupt the other baby's sleep—where I do usually recommend separating them at night during sleep coaching. It's usually a good idea to leave the poorer sleeper where he is and move the sounder sleeper to another room, using a portable crib if necessary. Good sleepers tend to be more flexible and can more easily adjust to temporary new sleeping quarters, particularly if it's a little noisier or brighter than the babies' bedroom. Once the poorer sleeper is sleeping through the night (or waking for a single feeding if that's age appropriate and you're satisfied), you can return the better sleeper to the shared room.

Q: **I have triplets. How can we do the Shuffle and sit next to their cribs when there are only two parents available? And sometimes only one of us is home at bedtime?**

A: If you have triplets or quads, you can still do this, but be gentle on yourself by not expecting too much at first. You are outnumbered, after all. If you have three or four babies, each parent can't sit next to one baby, so you may have to have one parent sit between two babies or two parents tag teaming with three babies, and so on. If there is just one parent, gently move back and forth to stroke and soothe each child in turn. Follow the rules of the Shuffle for the first three nights on page 92. Make sure that by the third night, you are using your voice to soothe instead of relying too much on touch. Remember that just going through the steps of the Shuffle, you are already doing so much for your babies.

SLEEP CRUTCHES AND SOLUTIONS

Many babies have *negative associations*, or *sleep crutches*, as discussed in Chapter 4. Here are some of the most common crutches that can disrupt sleep coaching at this age.

CRUTCH: NIGHTTIME FEEDING

Example: My seven-month-old still wakes up to feed two to three times a night, even when I feed her right before bedtime! What can I do?

One of my hardest tasks is convincing parents that most healthy six- to eight-month-old babies on a normal growth curve don't need to eat at night—or at least not more than once. Even a smart, thoughtful parent who knows this in their head may still have a fear of letting their child go hungry—especially when that child is waking in the middle of the night. Check with your pediatrician to make sure your little one doesn't have a health issue that would make it necessary for her to eat during the night, but the overwhelming odds are that the main reason an older baby still gets up in search of breast or bottle is that sucking is the only way she knows how to get back to sleep. Don't be hard on yourself if your child has developed this habit. It's very common—because it works!—but it's time for your baby to learn another way to fall asleep.

Eliminating Nighttime Feeding

Families I've worked with have tried all the techniques outlined below for eliminating nighttime feedings; make the choice that best matches your child's temperament and what you can follow through with consistently. I suggest starting with the most gradual one, Method A, but if you feel confident that B or C makes more sense for you and your baby, go ahead and start with that. In any case, please read through this entire chapter; many of the tips can be applied to any of the strategies.

Whatever approach you take, it will be easier if you try to reset your baby's hunger clock so she takes in more calories by day and therefore isn't looking for more at night. I know some babies, even this young, who do a remarkable job of snacking all day so they can feast all night. Start by reviewing her daytime feeding schedule and keeping a written log of her diet for a week. Go over it with her doctor to make sure she's getting the right mix of breast milk and/or formula and solids. Try to nurse or bottle-feed her in a quiet, dim place without television, phone, or other distractions so that she can focus on taking a full feeding. This advice holds true during growth spurts, too. She may need an occasional night feeding mid-spurt, but by enhancing her daytime feedings, you'll minimize the nighttime ones.

Once you and your pediatrician have agreed that your baby does not need any feeding during an eleven-hour period at night, then choose one of the methods that follows, and decide how many nights you'll keep it up before completely eliminating the nighttime meal. Ideally, you want to be done with the process within a week, so set a specific night ahead of time as the night you will not feed her.

Three Options for Nighttime Weaning
Method A: The Taper-Off Technique

If you're nursing, gradually cut down the amount of time your baby is at the breast. For example, if she usually feeds for twenty minutes, let her go for only fifteen. Cut back every night until she's ready to give it up, or until you're down to five minutes. At that point, it's time to stop altogether. Make sure you unlatch her when she finishes eating heartily, even if it's sooner than the amount of time you've allotted; don't let her gently suckle and doze. Get her back to bed while she's drowsy but awake.

If you're bottle-feeding, you can decrease the amount of formula she gets by a few ounces every few nights. When you get to two ounces, it's time to stop. An alternative is to gradually dilute the formula until it gets so watery she decides it's not worth waking up for. I usually find reducing the total ounces in each bottle every few nights works best.

If your baby is waking to eat several times a night but only nursing for a couple of minutes or taking a couple of ounces, this method won't work for you. Choose Method B or C.

Method B: The Four-Night Phase-Out

Whether you're breastfeeding or giving a bottle, feed your baby just once during the night for three nights; it's best to *set a time* for when you'll give her that single snack, so you can either:

* feed her the first time she wakes after a set time, such as midnight, or
* the first time she wakes as long as it's been at least four hours since she's last eaten, or
* offer her a dream feed, which means you pick her up and feed her right before you go to bed. Note: Not all babies will feed well at a dream feed and then will be up an hour later. In that case, stick with a set-time approach.

WHAT'S A DREAM FEED, AND HOW DO I DO IT?

1. A *dream feed* is when you gently take your baby out of his crib at a desired set time, or after four hours from his last feeding.
2. Place your breast or the bottle on your baby's lower lip; he should start feeding, without fully waking.
3. If he is in a deep sleep, he might not feed efficiently. Rub the bottom of his feet to rouse him a bit more. Avoid talking to him or changing his diaper unless necessary, so you don't risk fully waking him.

I have found the success of dream feeds can depend on your baby's temperament. Some babies do not feed well during a dream feed, so they'll wake up hungry an hour later. If you see this happen, the dream feed might not be the right match for your baby's temperament. Consider one of the other night-time weaning options previously discussed.

Only feed her once at night and not again until at least 6:00 a.m., when you can both start your day. When she wakes at other times, sit by her crib and offer physical and verbal reassurance. On the fourth night, don't feed her at all. Remember, she has had three nights to get used to receiving fewer calories at night. Usually, parents will move their seats away from the crib on the fourth night of the Shuffle, but we're going to modify it for this night weaning. So on the fourth night when she wakes up, sit next to her crib for one more night. Comfort her from your chair as you did at bedtime. Don't pick her up unless she's hysterical, and then pick her up to calm her. If you breastfeed exclusively, it may help to put the non-nursing parent on night duty; since that parent can't nurse, your baby might adjust to the no-night-feeding routine more quickly.

Method C: Cold Turkey

You can stop offering your baby a breast or a bottle when she wakes at night. Go to her crib side as outlined in the Shuffle. Just make sure you and your partner are on the same page in this decision. If Mom has been breastfeeding, consider having the non-nursing parent handle all middle-of-the-night wake-ups, since your child knows that the other parent won't be there to nurse her.

Sleep Lady Tip

In the event you decide to feed your baby at a set time of midnight, and she wakes before her set-time feeding and stays awake fussing until the set time, do not feed her. For example, if she wakes up at 11:00 and fusses until midnight, don't pick her up and feed her just because the clock strikes 12:00. That will just teach her to fuss or cry for an hour until you feed her, and that's not the best way to minimize tears. So get her back to sleep, even if it's only for thirty minutes, until she wakes up again. So if she wakes up at 11:00, fusses until 12:00, finally falls asleep at 12:10, and wakes up at 12:45, go in and feed her. She has learned to get to sleep without food. If she is consistently waking at an hour before her set time and you think you picked the wrong time, move the set time one hour earlier the next night.

PARENTS WHO WANT TO REDUCE THE NUMBER OF FEEDINGS AT NIGHT WITHOUT ELIMINATING THEM ALTOGETHER, THIS ONE'S FOR YOU

Let's say you and your pediatrician think your baby still needs to eat at night, or you want to reduce nighttime feedings but aren't ready to cut them out altogether. Follow the first step of Method B, but don't stop feeding her on night 4. Restrict meals to once a night. Feed your child quickly, and avoid any interactions that will encourage her to stay up and try to engage you more. Coach her back to sleep for all other wakings.

CRUTCH: WALKING, HOLDING, BOUNCING, AND ROCKING TO SLEEP

Example: My child is a motion junkie. He will only fall asleep if I rock him, bounce him, or walk him when he wakes during the night. I get my ten thousand daily steps in, but my arms are about to fall off! How can I get him to stop needing all this movement?

Many of us walk, hold, bounce, or rock our newborns to sleep—or start this habit when we find that nursing doesn't get them to sleep anymore. If your child is six months or older and you are doing the Shuffle, it's time to phase these motions out. You'll know it's a problem if your child needs to be walked for more than a few minutes at bedtime, if she wakes up again as soon as you stop walking, or if she needs to be walked each time she wakes up at night. The same goes for rocking, holding, and bouncing.

Eliminating Walking, Holding, Bouncing, and Rocking to Sleep

As with so many sleep problems, the easiest time for you to institute changes is at bedtime, when you are more awake and more likely to be consistent. Before you start the Shuffle, you can begin by doing all the walking or rocking in the bedroom, not around the house, to create a positive association between the room and sleep as a precursor to sleep coaching.

Once you pick your first night of sleep coaching, have your soothing bedtime in your baby's room or near his crib. Read him a book and do a little rocking as you slowly make your way to turn off his light. Blow kisses to the moon, give him a kiss and a hug, and put him into the crib. The goal is to put him into the crib calm but awake after his soothing routine.

Sit by the crib and soothe him. If he gets overly upset, pick him up briefly and put him down as soon as he's calm. If he calms down almost instantly once you've picked him up, he didn't need to be picked up as badly as you'd thought he did.

Warning: While the Sleep Lady Shuffle encourages parents to pick up to calm their crying and distraught child, children with the crutch of being walked, held, bounced, and rocked to sleep can make this calming technique futile. For those babies, picking them up will just prolong their sleep problems and make coaching harder—with more tears, not fewer. Some babies with this crutch genuinely cry hard and then, when picked up to calm, can fall asleep in their parents' arms in under two minutes! If this happens during sleep coaching, you can inadvertently train your baby to cry hard until you pick him up. When parents are trying to eliminate this crutch, I always tell them to use "pick up to calm" as conservatively as possible. If you inadvertently train him to cry hard so he can be picked up and he falls immediately asleep, you won't be able to use the soothing technique of "pick up to calm" anymore, and you will have to endure what could be a lot of crying.

Erin needed to be walked—and walked and walked—at bedtime and for her nap. At first, her mom, Corinna, didn't mind all that much—newborns are so snuggly, and all the pacing was good post-pregnancy exercise. But Erin got heavier and heavier, and walking got harder and harder. Jeremy, Erin's dad, devoted a special pair of deck shoes to baby walking. Corinna developed pain in her arms. "I lost all my baby weight fast, but my arm was about to break!" Corinna said.

They didn't follow the phase-it-out approach. They just stopped the walking. But to prepare Erin, they first made some schedule adjustments. Her bedtime had been around 9:00 or 9:30. When they moved it up to 7:00 or 7:30, she wasn't so overtired and therefore didn't need her sleep crutch as much. They also got her up at a more consistent hour in the morning, moved her nursing and solids closer together, and rescheduled her naps so she wasn't going as long without some rest.

When they were ready to make the change, instead of making a long march around the house, they just included a brief and calming stroll around her room as part of her bedtime routine. They put her down awake, sat next to the crib, and soothed her as they did the Sleep Lady Shuffle. There were some tears, but not nearly as many as they had feared. "I thought it was going to take two hours that first night. I made Jeremy come home from work early, and we were going to order a pizza," Corinna said. "But it took a half hour, and it got easier each night after that."

If you want to go even slower than what I usually recommend regarding holding, rocking, and bouncing, you can switch associations as described on page 96. We want the baby to be aware that he is going into the crib. Even when you do this gradually, you will reach a night when your baby is more awake than usual. That's when the real coaching begins!

CRUTCH: THE PACIFIER REPLUG

Example: I've spent way too many nights on my hands and knees in the darkness of my baby's room searching for his pacifier while he wails. What can I do to get him to keep it from falling out of his mouth?

You don't have to take away the pacifier at this age. It's your choice. The pacifier itself is not a crutch; the crutch is the baby's dependence on someone replugging it when it falls out. As discussed in Phase 1, pacifiers have many benefits, including reduced risk of SIDS during the first six months of life. You can't necessarily keep the pacifier from falling out, but there are ways to address the baby replugging it by himself.

If your child does not yet have the pincer grasp and you want to keep the pacifier, you will have to wait it out, meaning you will have to replug it during your child's sleep or awakenings. Some parents try to put pacifiers in each of their child's hands and one in her mouth to increase the chances of her managing to get one of them back in her mouth. Many frustrated parents have reported that even after their child develops the pincer grasp and can replug the binky during the day, he still cries out in the middle of the night for a replug—and that's a sleep crutch. So I help parents practice with their baby during the day to master the pincer grasp (the more she does it, the faster she can master the skill) and help parents teach their already skilled baby how to do it herself during the night.

When the Pacifier Falls Out

Before babies develop the pincer grasp—the ability to pick things up using their index fingers and thumbs—you will notice they rake objects with the palms of their hands to move them. To observe your baby's skill level, place pieces of cereal or banana in front of her and watch how she tries to get them into her mouth. She might awkwardly but ambitiously move them around with her palm and then scoop them with all her curled fingers, dropping many along the journey to her mouth. Or she will be able to take one piece at a time and not miss her mouth as she eats the morsels. If she is pinching her piece of cereal or banana and picking it up, you can teach her to replug her own pacifier.

How to Teach Your Child to Replug Her Pacifier

Once she has developed the pincer grasp, she can learn how to replug her pacifier for sleep. To make it easier, leave several in her crib so one is always within easy reach.

Start by putting the pacifier in her hand, not her mouth, at bedtime and when she wakes at night. For a few nights, you might have to guide her hand to her mouth, but at this age, they learn pretty quickly. Some children want one pacifier in each hand. Then move to guiding her to one of the several pacifiers you've placed in her crib. Help her roll to her side to find one if need be. Do this for a few consecutive nights.

After about five or six days of guided practice in the crib, you are ready for the next step. At the next bedtime and during any subsequent wakings and demands for a replug, point to a pacifier for her to retrieve it. If she is having trouble finding her pacifier in the dark—even with a dim night-light—consider glow-in-the-dark pacifiers. (Yes, there is such a thing. There are several reliable brands.)

If You Decide to Wean from the Pacifier

You might be ready for this option either because she doesn't yet have the pincer grasp and you don't have the stamina to keep replugging pacifiers so many times at night *or* if she does have the pincer grasp and has learned to replug her pacifier but she's still waking up in search of it repeatedly.

> ### Sleep Lady Tip
>
> Some parents take the pacifier away at night but leave it at nap time, when it is harder for babies to settle themselves. This may not sound logical, but it really works! You will know it's time to wean the pacifier at nap time if you are going in to re-settle him multiple times during each nap.

Pick a night (or a few nights) when you are ready to cope with some unpleasantness. On the day you start, it would help if your baby had an especially nice and calming bedtime routine after a great day of naps any way you can get them. Be especially careful about getting her to bed drowsy but awake.

Don't give her the pacifier. Stroke or soothe her. Use techniques similar to those I earlier advised for parents breaking nighttime feeding or walking habits while doing the Shuffle. Every time she wakes up at night, do the Shuffle without giving her the pacifier. I understand that if she cries and protests incessantly, it's rough on you and may be for a few nights. But please stick it out. Consistency really, really matters here—and it will have its reward. Because if you give her the pacifier to get some sleep, you will risk conditioning her to cry for an hour to receive the pacifier—over and over again, indefinitely. We definitely don't want to do that. Unfortunately, there is no gradual method to weaning from the pacifier. It's either in the mouth or it's not.

CRUTCH: UNCONVENTIONAL BEDS

Example: When my daughter was a few weeks old, her reflux was terrible. The only way to ease her discomfort was to have her sleep in a swing, where the position of her body relieved the reflux. Now, at seven months with her reflux resolved, we want her in a crib of her own, and she is not having it! Have I ruined my child? Will she ever sleep well in her crib?

Some babies learn to sleep in unconventional places—swings, car seats, and the like. Maybe your baby, too, had reflux, and you placed her upright in her car seat or baby swing/chair to digest when she was very little, and she got used to dozing off while sitting upright. Maybe the soothing movement of the swing just helped relax her to sleep, but now she is outgrowing it and wants to move around more. The reliance on what I call *unconventional beds* obviously makes it tough to sleep coach. Just like the "motion junkies" discussed earlier who require bouncing, walking, holding, or rocking, there is a gentle way to transition your baby to a flat, stationary sleeping place.

Transitioning from Unconventional Beds

I worked with one little girl, nearly eight months old, who had spent every single night of her life and all her naps in a moving swing. If she woke up at night, her mother nursed her and then put her back in the swing. This child was actually quite advanced developmentally, crawling at five months and standing at six months. But she didn't have a clue as to how to sleep lying down. It took her three weeks to learn.

Her parents did the Sleep Lady Shuffle. They would lay her down in her crib after a soothing bedtime routine, and she would promptly sit up and fall asleep sitting. Then she'd fall over, which naturally would wake her up—mad. She'd sit up again, fall asleep again, topple over again, and wake up. One of her parents sat nearby, soothing her, but avoided picking her up unless she was really frustrated. They would go through this ritual several times at bedtime and several times when she woke up in the middle of the night. Eventually, she would get so tired that she would lie down and go to sleep, although she wasn't particularly happy about it. But within a few days, she was waking up less frequently and less furiously. It was taking her parents only five to ten minutes to get her back to sleep.

Initially, her mom kept the swing for naps, although she turned the swing off when the baby fell asleep, phasing out that feeling of being rocked. By the end of the first week, she had made enough progress at night that her mom felt empowered enough to start putting her in the crib for naps as well. It took another two weeks to complete nap coaching. Her parents noticed that when she began napping in the crib, she seemed better rested in general.

When you are ready to help your baby transition to a crib, keep this in mind:

* Start using the crib at bedtime, but let her stay in the swing awhile longer for nap time. But turn the swing off, fading out that rocking motion, when she falls asleep. To help her get used to the crib at night, use the Shuffle. Sit next to the crib, soothing her to sleep with *sh-sh* or with a few gentle (intermittent) pats. Follow the same rules of the Shuffle for the first three nights outlined on page 92.

* If she is still having a difficult time after the first three nights of the Shuffle, add a fourth night in your chair position. If your baby is inconsolable, of course pick her up to calm, but be mindful not to move, sway, or bounce her in your arms. It's hard to avoid that, especially when you are exhausted, because offering soothing motion

is instinctual. So just be careful. She likes motion, so you don't want to use it to get her to sleep. You might as well put her back in her unconventional bed.

* If she sits up in her crib, encourage her to lie down. If she falls asleep sitting and then falls over and cries, soothe her but don't hold her to sleep. If she starts to look like she is about to fall asleep while sitting up, gently guide her down and put your hand on her chest or back and rub her . . . encouraging her to lie down.

* If she tends to fall over and bang her head and that alone is upsetting you, then consider getting vertical crib liners. Pure Safety makes great ones!

CRUTCH: REACTIVE CO-SLEEPING

Most of the families I speak to are either co-sleeping out of desperation or they really want to continue to co-sleep but find it's not working well for their family. Families who are co-sleeping out of desperation are practicing what I call *reactive co-sleeping*. The "we didn't plan it this way" co-sleepers are reactively co-sleeping when they end up with the baby in the bed part or all of the night. This doesn't happen by choice or philosophical commitment but because it's the only way they can get their baby to sleep at bedtime or back to sleep in the middle of the night. I am not against co-sleeping if that is your choice. If you find that you are reactively co-sleeping—a "we didn't plan it this way" family—that means it has become a crutch (for both you and your baby). In Chapter 12, I address how to end reactive co-sleeping as well as how to improve safe co-sleeping, if co-sleeping is your preference.

TEMPERAMENT CHECK

By now, your baby's temperament is starting to become crystal clear. You've identified some of her cues and are beginning to know her habits, behaviors, and responses. Perhaps you've noticed that your baby likes to sleep with her head in the corner of the crib or thinks 11:00 p.m. is time to throw a party. Perhaps your baby is "fussy" or has a mind of her own.

In my experience, the *highly alert child* is the temperament that leads most of my clients to seek out my help and the help of my Gentle Sleep Coaches. In fact, about 80 percent of my clients are parents of highly alert children. If you have come to realize you have been blessed with an active, stubborn, engaged child, you might be running the risk of being more sleep deprived or frustrated—even depressed—than if you were sleep coaching a less spirited child. For more advice on sleep coaching the highly alert child, please turn to Chapter 3.

EARLY RISING

So many parents reach out to me because they started sleep coaching their child and she is sleeping a much longer stretch but waking at 4:00 or 5:00 a.m. and seemingly not wanting to go back to sleep. Or perhaps your baby was sleeping through until 6:00 or 7:00 a.m. until daylight saving time, and now, months later, she is still waking at 5:00 a.m. Early rising is such a huge and common topic. In fact, it is safe to bet that at least 90 percent of the issues my clients struggle with revolve around their babies waking up too early (before 6:00 a.m.). I have more blog articles, receive more emails, and hear from my coaches on this topic more than any other sleep-coaching topic.

Early rising is not the same as having early risers, whom I refer to as *early birds,* so as not to confuse the two. Early birds wake up earlier than many parents would like, 6:00 or 6:30 a.m., but they do so refreshed and happy. Their temperament skews more toward simply being a morning person. And in this case, you don't have to look far and wide to find that at least one parent is a morning person, too. Interestingly, research suggests there is a genetic link.

Then there are those early risers who are not happy to be up before the crack of dawn. They are tired, unrefreshed, the opposite of bright-eyed and bushy-tailed. But there they are—grouchy, awake, and not going back to sleep. This is when early rising is a problem, because the sleep tank isn't filled efficiently. And by now, we know that not getting enough nighttime sleep will affect nap quality and quantity, and nap time affects nighttime sleep—and the cycle continues.

WHAT CAUSES EARLY RISING?

While this is a very common problem, often the solution isn't one that is instant, as so many parents wish. Like any new skill, learning how to stay asleep takes time. Early rising is essentially your child having a difficult time putting himself *back to sleep* after a long stretch of sleep at night or not getting quite enough sleep to make it to his nap without being over-tired. This is more difficult than putting himself to sleep at bedtime.

For instance, I know if I get up at 5:00 or 5:30 a.m. and I'm awake a little too long, my brain starts to tick-tick-tick-tick with all the things I have to do, and I have a hard time going back to sleep. My body has gotten just enough sleep to make it hard to go back to sleep—but not enough to leave me feeling rested and restored.

Here are four factors that can cause early rising. Sometimes only one causes the early rising; for other babies, it could be all four. Note, you should first always rule out illness or undiagnosed medical conditions that can cause and contribute to sleep problems, such as obstructive sleep apnea, which we discuss more in Chapter 14, and then consider the following reasons:

1. Too drowsy at bedtime
2. Insufficient naps
3. Too long of a wakeful window between the afternoon nap and bedtime
4. Too late of a bedtime

Too Drowsy at Bedtime

The paramount lesson of helping your baby to learn to fall asleep on his own is putting him to bed drowsy but awake. You want him to be tired and ready for sleep but not falling asleep as soon as his head hits the mattress. Putting yourself to sleep is a form of self-soothing, and for him to learn, he needs to be awake enough at bedtime—the easiest time to learn the skill—so that he can master it at bedtime first and eventually apply it to night wakings as well as the early risings, which are the toughest to go back to sleep from.

Insufficient Naps

We will discuss this in the napping section, but it begs to be repeated. Short napping or not enough napping can cause increased night wakings and early rising. Quality nap time actually helps encourage quality nighttime sleep. If your child tends to take very short naps or finishes her naps early in the day, you are probably dealing with early rising. Review your child's sample schedule and the nap-coaching section and decide when you are going to start nap coaching.

Overestimating the Wakeful Window

This may seem counterintuitive, but an overtired child generally takes longer to get to sleep and will wake more often during the night, causing early rising. Review your baby's nap schedule to make sure you are not exceeding his wakeful window, and be sure there are no more than four hours between the end of his afternoon nap and his bedtime. At this age, this window will be shorter if he is not napping long enough (three to three and a half hours). More about napping in the section "Much Ado About Napping" on page 116.

Too Late of a Bedtime

Many parents are shocked when I tell them that their child's natural bedtime is likely *between 7:00 and 8:00 p.m.* And in this age group, more likely 7:00 to 7:30 p.m. If your baby's bedtime is well beyond this window, sleep in the night could be disrupted and lead to early rising! If your schedule is wildly different from the sample schedules and your child is rising early, consider adjusting bedtime earlier. Do not keep your child up too late, hoping that he will wake less often during the night and sleep later in the morning. This rarely (if ever) works. Overtired children sleep less, not more.

WHAT TO DO? RETURN TO THE SLEEP LADY SHUFFLE

While you are making adjustments based on the tips above and your child wakes before 6:00 a.m., treat it like the other night wakings and do the Shuffle. The catch is that you must use your consistent response until 6:00 a.m. If he doesn't go back to sleep, use what I like to call the *dramatic wake-up*! Leave the room for a full minute (literally, a full minute—watch the clock!). After sixty seconds, return to the room bright and cheerful with a "Good morning!" while you open the curtains and let the light flood in. This signals to your child that you are getting him up because it is morning and not because he is waking up too early!

Keep using the Shuffle in the early morning until the habit resolves. If you allow it to persist, you could be introducing a new sleep crutch that will need to be broken eventually. Keep in mind that early rising happens during the sleep-coaching process and can often take two to three weeks to fully resolve as you are working on improving naps. The two hardest or last pieces of sleep coaching to fall into place are early rising and the afternoon nap. So don't give up!

> ## Sleep Lady Tip
>
> Keep in mind that early rising happens during the sleep-coaching process and can often take two to three weeks to fully resolve as you are working on improving naps. The two hardest or last pieces of sleep coaching to fall into place are early rising and the afternoon nap. So don't give up!

MUCH ADO ABOUT NAPPING

Naps are an essential part of both baby and toddler sleep requirements. Naps allow little bodies to recharge and process the activities that have happened so far in their day. For some children, naps are a challenge, a daily struggle, and often frustrating for parents. Remember that babies from six to eight months need two naps a day, about one and a half to two hours apiece. The short third nap in late afternoon is still common at this age and is required if the earlier naps are skimpy and the child is not yet sleeping through the night. You can tackle naps at the same time you start the Sleep Lady Shuffle at night.

Once you are ready, begin with the Shuffle at night—and then tackle the first nap the next morning, then the afternoon nap (or naps). Then go on to the second night of the Shuffle. Make sure you're timing your child's naps correctly, based on his age (as indicated in this chapter). Also, be aware of his sleep cues and windows of wakefulness.

Nap coaching is hard for a plethora of reasons. The best defense is a good offense, so here are two major rules of nap coaching and preemptive strategies that will address head-on any nap-time snafus that may arise (and they will). You probably noticed I don't usually talk about "rules"; I prefer to give you a range of choices that fit your own parenting style. But after many years of working with parents of balky nappers, I have learned that these rules really help.

#1: Focus on putting your child down for a nap *in her crib, twice a day.* Go through an abbreviated version of your bedtime routine of reading a book or singing a song. Cut the rocking or swinging time in half at the beginning if you want to go slowly, or cut it more drastically if you think that will work better. Work on getting her down drowsy but awake.

Don't feel obligated to feed her before her nap; however, if nursing or bottle-feeding is your preferred way of preparing her for a nap, be careful not to let her fall asleep while eating. Remember, she has to be put in her crib awake enough that she is aware she is being put down. Draw the shades, turn on your sound machine, and watch your little one begin to demonstrate her sleepy cues of eye rubbing and yawning. Place your chair in the same place as you did the night before and follow the same steps of the Shuffle along with the same soothing techniques. Move your chair every three days, even if she didn't nap well on day 3.

#2: Spend an entire hour trying to get your child to sleep at nap time. Stay in your chair, exercising your Shuffle techniques for one whole hour. There are three possible outcomes:

1. Your baby doesn't go to sleep for the entire hour.
2. Your baby only takes a forty-five-minute nap.
3. Your baby sleeps for *less than* forty-five minutes, which is less than a sleep cycle. I call these abbreviated naps *disaster naps*.

WHAT TO DO IF YOUR BABY DOESN'T SLEEP FOR THE ENTIRE HOUR

At the end of your Shuffling hour, leave the room, count to ten, and go back into the room to do your dramatic wake-up routine: open the blinds, sing, "Nap time is over, baby!," and take your child out of bed. Since he hasn't had a morning nap, he won't be able to last (or wait) until the afternoon for his next nap. Watch his cues; if he starts yawning, dozing while you feed him, and so on—even if it's just forty-five minutes after you got him out of his crib—go ahead and try for a nap again, doing the Shuffle.

WHAT TO DO IF YOUR BABY ONLY SLEEPS FOR FORTY-FIVE MINUTES IN THE MORNING

This is the bare minimum for a nap. If he wakes up happy and seemingly refreshed, that's okay, but be aware that he might be ready for his afternoon siesta sooner rather than later (after two hours awake rather than three). Watch for drowsy cues so you don't miss his sleep window. I find that when babies wake up happy after a forty-five-minute morning nap, they often don't wake up happy and refreshed after a forty-five-minute afternoon nap. If your child naps for just forty-five minutes in the afternoon, use the Shuffle techniques to get him back to sleep. Try for at least thirty more minutes if you can.

NAP-COACHING TIPS

It's easier to get a baby to take the morning nap than the afternoon nap. Don't miss that opportunity.

Afternoon nap training is tougher. Don't get discouraged; it's normal.

Keep a sleep log during nap training.

If it's 2:00 or 3:00 p.m. and your baby has not napped well enough, you may need to resort to your backup plan, such as a nap in the stroller or car, to avoid an exhausted baby and bedtime disaster.

You will be tied to the house during nap coaching. If you feel like all you are doing all day is trying to get your baby to nap, then you are doing it right! The payoff: you'll have more freedom (and a happier, rested baby) once you have a predictable napping schedule.

If you have a nanny, babysitter, or childcare setting that can do the nap training, thank your lucky stars. If your caregiver is reluctant to do the training, see if you can win her over with a simple explanation of the sleep science. If not, explain that your child needs a full sleep tank, and if that means the sitter has to use a sleep crutch like rocking to get the child to nap or to resume a brief or interrupted nap, that's okay.

WHAT TO DO IF YOUR BABY NAPS FOR
LESS THAN FORTY-FIVE MINUTES

This is a *disaster nap*. When a child sleeps for less than forty-five minutes, he doesn't go through a complete sleep cycle and awakens at a partial arousal; it's enough to take the edge off his exhaustion but not restorative enough to make it to the next nap or bedtime without being overtired. So here's the tough message: I want you to go to him and do the Shuffle for up to an hour—what I call the *longest hour*.

Here's an example: You put your child in his crib at 9:00 a.m., he conks out at 9:30, but only sleeps until 10:00. You go in and work on getting him back to sleep—which he does, thankfully, by 10:30, after just half an hour. But he only sleeps for twenty minutes. Chances are, the negative voice in you is going to say, *I can't believe the Sleep Lady told me to do that! He cried more than he slept. What's the point of that?* But think about it: Your baby did it! He put himself back to sleep after a partial arousal from a nap—one of the hardest things to do. Going forward, he'll begin to get back to sleep more quickly and will snooze for longer if you stick with it.

DEVISE YOUR NAP-TIME BACKUP PLAN

After you have tried the nap in the crib twice during the day, you will likely need to use a backup nap plan to help fill the daytime sleep tank so your baby doesn't face bedtime even more exhausted, making it harder for him to go to sleep and stay asleep. If you check your sleep log around 2:00 or 3:00 p.m. and realize your child hasn't had enough day sleep, pull out all the stops to make sure you get that sleep tank filled. And that means forgetting the Shuffle for naps today and doing whatever it takes to get your child to nap. Remember, the priority is always having night-time sleep coaching succeed first, and that means getting sufficient daytime sleep in any way you can. This might feel like you've abandoned nap coaching (and maybe you'll even be relieved), but you haven't. By remaining aware of his daytime sleep needs and deficits, you are doing wonders for your nighttime coaching. You are not giving up. Quite the contrary.

Okay, back to the backup plan. You want to make sure that he naps one way or another for a decent interval before the afternoon is over so that you're not set up for a bad night. A backup nap can take place in the car, stroller, swing, or carrier, but try to make it different from a habit (crutch) you've been trying to break. For instance, if you've been working on ending co-sleeping at night, don't put him in your bed for your backup plan. Try a car ride or a walk in the stroller instead. If nothing else works, you may have to nap coach for a third time in the crib. I go into more detail about switching associations on page 96, if you would like more information on how it works.

Ideally, the backup nap will last at least forty-five minutes, and your child will be awake by 4:30 or 5:00 p.m. so that he's ready to sleep at his regular bedtime.

MY THREE BEST PIECES OF NAP-COACHING ADVICE

* No naps before 8:00 a.m.—even if your child has been up since 5:00! It will throw off the entire day and ingrain in him the habit of getting up too early. I realize this is a tricky dance and your child may get overtired, but it's worth it in the long run.
* Your baby's morning nap should be no longer than one and a half hours. Wake him if need be. I know this goes against the rule of "Never wake a sleeping baby," but I only want you to do it for the morning nap to help regulate your baby's sleeping times.
* Follow the same Shuffle chair positions for naps as you do at night.

If you have an older child who can't be left alone while you sit in your baby's room, you can do timed checks (see Chapter 6)—looking in on your baby at regular intervals. Base the timing on your little one's temperament, and be consistent. If you have no idea where to start, then try checking on him every seven minutes, slowly increasing the time. When you go to his crib, be reassuring but quick. You'll defeat the purpose if you pat him until he's asleep during your crib-side check.

DO I HAVE TO NAP COACH AT THE SAME TIME AS NIGHT COACH?

Don't feel guilty if you can't follow all my advice right now. Give yourself (or your babysitter) permission to let the nap coaching slide, and just do what you have to do to get your child some daytime sleep, preferably at predictable times. As nighttime sleep improves, the daytime sleep *might* fall into place on its own. If not, take a deep breath and tackle naps again in another month or two. Keep reminding yourself that good daytime sleep promotes better nighttime sleep; it helps you get through it.

If you decide not to address naps and only work on night, then do what works to help her get daytime sleep at appropriate times. But know that it will eventually stop working. Either she will wake up the minute you put her down or shortly thereafter, or you will find yourself having to hold her longer and longer to get her to sleep, only to have her nap briefly. Those will be some of your signs to say, "Okay, now it's time to start nap coaching." But if you've worked on those other pieces at night, nap coaching should be much more successful; remember, night sleep develops first, it's easier than daytime sleep, and your baby has shown you that she has started to learn the skill at night.

HOW TO NAP COACH MULTIPLES

Although I normally keep twins together at nighttime, I often recommend separating them for naps. Daytime sleep is much more challenging for most babies, and it's even harder if there's a playmate to distract or be distracted by in the next crib. Some parents keep multiples apart for naps for days or weeks, others throughout childhood. Do whichever feels best to you and seems to work for your children.

Nap coaching more than one child can be difficult. If you are lucky and one naps well, you can put him down and nap coach the other in another room (just checking as necessary on the good sleeper). More often, both will need some coaching, so separate them and do timed checks. When you calm one, leave him, then go to the other and calm him, then after ten minutes or so, go back and check on the first baby, and in another ten minutes, check on the second, and so forth. If you are struggling with both or all multiples really not napping well, then you might as well nap train them together in the same room. Instead of timed checks, follow the Shuffle along with advice on soothing and chair position in the section "Shuffling with Multiples," on page 97, for the onset of the nap.

FREQUENTLY ASKED QUESTIONS
FROM PARENTS OF MULTIPLES

Q: **I have started nap coaching my twins in the same room, but one twin is having short naps and is always waking the other. Baby B has always tended to nap longer than Baby A, and I feel like Baby A is disrupting Baby B's naps! What do I do?**

A: This is not uncommon, and often I recommend separating multiples for naps, especially if one baby is a better napper but gets woken up by the other one. Sometimes I recommend separating them temporarily, but in other cases it's indefinite and only for naps, not nighttime. If you coach both, use timed checks.

If one baby goes to sleep quicker and easier, you can put her down for naps first and then Shuffle Baby B in a separate room. Consider using a pack-and-play in another room for naps.

Use the third backup nap to even out the scales, and have both twins ready for bed between 7:00 and 7:30 p.m. This nap can be in a swing or stroller. If Baby A had two decent naps totaling around two and a half to three hours, then wake Baby A at the forty-five-minute mark, or by 5:00 p.m. Baby B might have had two forty-five-minute naps and therefore may need to go down for this third backup nap earlier or be allowed to sleep until 5:30 p.m. Baby B can still go to bed at the same time as Baby A—remember, Baby B is nap deprived.

Q: **My twins are eight months old. Baby A is sleeping through the night, and Baby B is not. Do they both need a third nap?**

A: Most babies who are sleeping through the night and napping approximately three hours a day will drop their third bonus nap by nine months. Until then, a baby needs that third bonus nap to make it to bedtime without running on fumes, which causes more crying at bedtime and more wakings during the night.

Until he is napping well and sleeping through the night, Baby B will definitely need a third nap even if he is eight months. Baby A will only need a third nap if he isn't napping well. If Baby A reached the sleep-coaching goals earlier than Baby B, he may still need that third nap, but make sure it's on the shorter side—thirty to forty-five minutes and awake by 5:00 p.m. Your end goal is to have both babies well fed and ready for bed between 7:00 and 7:30 p.m. regardless of how different their naps were during the day.

Q: **Baby A wants to start her day at 7:00 a.m., and Baby B wants to sleep until 10:00 a.m. (probably because she was up six times last night)—should I let her sleep in?**

A: No, do not let her sleep in. Wake Baby B within thirty minutes of Baby A. This will help regulate her wake-up and, more importantly, keep them on a similar schedule, which will make life oh-so-much easier!

Chapter 8

NINE TO TWELVE MONTHS

SLEEP GOALS
* *an average of eleven hours of uninterrupted nighttime sleep*
* *three and a half hours of daytime sleep spread over two to three naps*

Babies at this age on average need eleven hours of sleep at night and three during the day. At nine months, babies should nap for about an hour and a half in the morning and about one and a half to two hours in the afternoon. Most have given up that brief, third late-afternoon nap. By twelve months, the morning nap is about an hour and the afternoon nap is about an hour and a half.

Many of the problems and solutions encountered in babies from nine to twelve months old are quite similar to those found in babies from six through eight months old, but there are a few sleep-related developmental differences. At this age, babies are more mobile, crawling and standing in their cribs, and can pop up each time you put them down at bedtime. Some walk by their first birthday, a major developmental milestone that can temporarily disrupt sleep. Increased activity can tire them out, so you have to pay very close attention to their sleep windows, when they are most ready and able to fall asleep. Some can fight sleep and conceal that window. If you wean during this period, that can also alter the rhythms of bedtime.

The families in this chapter had experiences that are quite typical for this age. Many expected their babies to resist sleep changes far more fiercely than they did, and they anticipated having a lot more difficulty in coping with tears. All of them found the baby responded better than they had expected. The parents found that the tears were not as intense as they had feared, and they didn't feel so bad about letting him shed them as long as they were by his side.

"The key to success with sleep training was realizing that crying wasn't abandonment; it wasn't torture," Megan said. "We learned that sleep was so important to his growth and development that not teaching him to sleep was hurting him. We thought we would be bad parents if we let him cry. But we learned that ten minutes of crying didn't hurt him. We realized he was okay, and that made us feel so much better. You've got to just tell yourself over and over again—what you are doing is right."

FIRST THINGS FIRST: CREATE A SCHEDULE

We build babies' schedules around how much sleep they need, so determining how much sleep your baby requires is the priority. By now, you probably are well acquainted with your baby's sleep cues and temperaments, and that information is useful when formulating a daily schedule. Whether this is your first attempt at sleep coaching or you have tried in the past but found that the time wasn't right, adjusting your child's schedule according to what you have observed in the past nine or more months is a great start. I find that determining your baby's ideal bedtime and then doing the math backward takes a lot of the guesswork out of your day.

For example, your ten-month-old wakes for the day at 6:00 a.m. typically, and you've determined that he does best with eleven hours of sleep at night. That means you back up eleven hours from 6:00 a.m. to 7:00 p.m. as the ideal time for him to fall asleep each night. You can find recommended sleep averages on the websites of the American Academy of Pediatrics and the National Sleep Foundation. However, the sample schedule I provided is based on sleep averages that have worked for my clients. Feel free to adjust it as you monitor how your baby is doing with his naps, sleep, and feedings. After a few weeks of sleep coaching, you can readjust the schedule as you and your family get into a rhythm that feels right to all of you. Schedules obviously vary somewhat from one child to the next. A baby who wakes up at 6:30 a.m. will have a slightly different timetable from one who gets up at 7:30. Note: Please keep in mind this is the ideal schedule you are aiming to establish once your child is sleeping through the night. It may take a little while to get there.

Sample Schedule

7:00–7:30 a.m.	**Wake-up.** Nurse/bottle/cup and breakfast.
9:00–9:30 a.m.	**Morning Nap.** About one and a half hours. If your child is sleeping eleven to twelve hours uninterrupted at night, he might be able to stay awake until 10:00 a.m. (or three hours after waking up). Some children need a small morning snack after the nap.
12:00–12:30 p.m.	**Lunch.** Nurse/bottle/cup.
1:00–2:00 p.m.	**Afternoon Nap.** About two hours. Snack upon awakening.
5:00–6:00 p.m.	**Dinner.** Nurse/bottle/cup.
6:30–7:00 p.m.	**Bedtime Prep.** Start bath and bedtime preparations, which may include an additional bottle or nursing.
7:00–7:30 p.m.	**In Bed.** Put him down drowsy but awake, and let him fall asleep on his own.

Although I don't believe in completely rigid schedules, young children do need consistency and predictability. During the first weeks of sleep scheduling, you are better erring on the side of too much rigidity than too little.

Okay. We've taken a snapshot of the scheduling ideal. Let's walk through your day in more detail.

Wake-up. A good wake-up time is anywhere from 6:00 to 7:30. Remember that one of the basic rules of sleep hygiene is to wake up and go to bed at about the same time every day (a twelve-hour schedule). If your baby wakes up before 6:00, the "Early Rising" section on page 159 will help you teach him to sleep later.

Just like you have bedtime rituals, create morning ones. Throw open the blinds and greet the new day with special games or songs. I call this *dramatic wake-up,* and it helps your baby better define in his own mind the difference between waking time and sleeping time. This can be a good opportunity for some of those active, stimulating games—like flying baby—that dads like to play but that aren't a great idea in the last five minutes before bed. It's also nice for parents who get home from work late to start their day having fun with the baby.

Morning Nap. Give him some wind-down time to prepare for his nap. It doesn't need to be as long as the bedtime ritual, but he does need time to transition from all that revved-up morning activity to morning sleep. Try to get him down by 9:00—a little earlier, like 8:00, if he's an earlier riser, or a little later, around 9:30, if he sleeps an uninterrupted eleven or twelve hours at night. But don't let him stay up for more than a three-hour stretch. Watch for his sleep windows. Many babies yawn, suck their thumbs, or rub their eyes. Others have more idiosyncratic signals like twirling their hair or just getting a zonked-out, glassy-eyed look.

A good reference to keep at hand is "Wakeful Windows and Sleep Windows," located on page 53 in Chapter 4, in which you can find the approximate number of hours that should pass before the baby's next nap.

The morning nap should be about one and a half hours for a nine-month-old and an hour for a twelve-month-old. If your child sleeps longer but still naps well in the afternoon and makes it to bedtime, don't worry about it. If, however, he takes a long morning nap and then has trouble sleeping in the afternoon and is a wreck before bedtime, knock off fifteen to thirty minutes from the morning nap. The afternoon nap is generally a longer and more important one, and it's the one he's going to keep after he gives up the morning nap a few months from now.

The interval between the morning nap and lunch is often a good time to run some errands or go outside and play. He has just slept and is less likely to doze off in the car or stroller and throw off his afternoon nap schedule. Some kids need a small snack right after the morning nap. Others wait until lunchtime.

Lunch. Lunch is around noon or 12:30. At this age, it's usually solids, with nursing or a bottle or, even if he's closer to one year old, a cup. Try to have some playtime after lunch or take a walk. Don't have lunch so late that you go directly to the afternoon nap; you are trying to weaken associations between food, particularly the bottle, and sleep.

Afternoon Nap. The afternoon nap usually starts between 1:00 and 2:00—or around three hours after the morning nap ends. Remember to keep an eye out for that sleep window, and give him some wind-down time to transition to sleep after a period of active play and exploration. This nap should last one and a half to two hours for a nine-month-old and one and a half hours for a twelve-month-old. He'll probably want a snack when he gets up.

Dinner. Keep dinnertime early, between 5:00 and 6:00, even if both parents aren't home or aren't ready for dinner yet. Your life will be saner, and he will sleep better if you keep him on an early schedule. I find that babies have an eating window (much like a sleep window), and if you miss it, they eat poorly. Either they wake up hungry in the middle of the night, or we wake up worried that they didn't eat enough.

Bedtime Prep. Bedtime prep is not your child's actual bedtime. Bedtime is when she is in her crib, drowsy but awake, and you are in your chair position doing the Shuffle. Bedtime should be at 7:00–7:30, or 6:30–7:00 when naps are insufficient (less than a total of three hours).

Sleep Lady Tip

Remember when we talked about emotional availability? (See Chapter 3, "Getting to Know Your Child.") That focused connection with your child is always important—but it's absolutely essential that we are patient and fully present at bedtime. Try as best as possible to leave your workday behind. Forget about your to-do list for a moment. Put aside that email or phone call that upset you. Better yet, at bedtime, put aside your phone! Leave it in another room while you focus on your child. It will still be there once he's asleep. Having so many screens and devices distracting us is probably the biggest change I've seen since I started developing the Sleep Lady system. I know it's not easy to ignore your phone, but the benefits—to both you and your child—are huge.

This means that bedtime prep needs to be built into the daily schedule, at least a half hour before the baby is in her crib. Many times, parents make the mistake of considering the wind-down process or bedtime routine—whether it be running the bath, putting on pajamas, or reading stories—to be bedtime. If bedtime is 7:00, you want to bedtime prep at 6:30 or earlier, depending on what your getting-ready-for-bed-routine looks like.

Bedtime Feeding. It's okay to nurse (or give your baby a bottle) right before bed as long as she doesn't rely on it to get herself to sleep and you aren't nursing her back to sleep when she wakes up at night. If she does depend on the breast or bottle, and many babies do, try to put the final nursing earlier in the bedtime routine, say, before a song or story. Try not to let her fall asleep at the breast. Remember, drowsy but awake.

In Bed. Bedtime should be at 7:00–7:30, and by *bedtime*, I mean in the crib, not in the bathtub or on your lap reading stories. Babies this age can fight sleep much more vehemently than younger infants. I worked with one who would shake his head vigorously to stay awake at the tender age of nine months.

Keep any bedtime music soft and quiet. Use music to set the mood and cue the brain for sleep, but turn it off before she gets into her crib or soon after. You don't want her so accustomed to lullabies that she can't sleep without them. If you've been playing music until after she falls asleep, slowly ease it out. Lower the volume, and try to turn it off before she's fully asleep. If you walk or rock your baby, keep it brief and stay in her room. Put her down drowsy but awake so she can learn to do that final part of falling asleep on her own. The goal of getting her down drowsy but awake is crucial. If you or your baby has trouble with it, focus your energy first on getting it right at bedtime. It's not less important at 2:00 a.m., but it's a lot easier for parents to follow through when we are not half-asleep ourselves. Once you get it right at bedtime, it will be easier for you to carry this out consistently at other times.

On many occasions, parents who work in careers with atypical hours ask whether it is possible to keep their babies up later. My answer is always, "I can't make any promises that it will work, but you can certainly try!" A few conditions apply, however. The first is that everyone in the family has to be able to sleep later, which means the baby isn't preparing to go to day care early in the morning. The second condition is the family has to be committed to filling the daytime sleep tank and shifting the entire schedule later, including naps and meals, and so on.

Because of circadian rhythms, which are pretty sturdy by this age, there is no guarantee this could work. Use your intuition and watch your baby's sleep cues and behaviors to determine whether moving back to a more traditional schedule is best for your baby's sleep needs and overall development. For example, if your baby is now going to bed by 9:00 p.m. but continues to wake at 7:00 a.m., you should shift back to an earlier bedtime so your baby can get the sleep she needs at nighttime.

HOW TO COMMUNICATE YOUR
SCHEDULE TO CAREGIVERS

Whether you have a stay-at-home nanny, a day care center, a once-in-a-while sitter, or a grandparent taking care of your baby during the day, communicating and maintaining your new schedule can be tricky, but not futile. Even when playing by the rules of other providers and facilities, all does not have to be lost. Here are some strategies to help you all get on the same page when you become committed to sleep coaching:

1. Make a copy of your daily schedule—like the one in this chapter—and give it to your caregivers, letting them know you have begun sleep coaching and that for just a few weeks, you are asking them to be mindful of the schedule when they can.
2. Each morning when you leave your child, let the caregiver know what time your child woke up that morning, as well as how many times during the night she was up, and therefore what time she will most likely be ready for her first morning nap.
3. Ask the childcare providers if they can work toward a total of three hours of nap time no matter how they get the child to sleep. We cannot expect or presume they will be comfortable or allowed to adhere to the Shuffle or reduce the use of sleep crutches, but you can certainly ask. Sometimes that is the best we can do. Just remember that your child getting sleep throughout the day, no matter how it is accomplished, whether by rocking, in a bouncy chair, or another sleep crutch, will still help you with nighttime sleep coaching, as your child will not be overtired and will have the three hours of daytime sleep in her sleep tank.
4. If your child is napping in a crib at a day care center where toddlers share the room, ask if your baby's crib could be placed in a corner away from the action and distraction and to please use blackout shades if available. If neither is possible, ask if you can drop off your white-noise machine for her nap time.
5. Some childcare providers just won't nap train (day care centers often have their own schedules and methods). If that is the case, you can still sleep coach by adhering to your morning and evening routines, focusing on getting the child to sleep through the night. Then, on weekends, nap coach diligently. Don't worry about how that might feel inconsistent. It will take longer, but it can still work. For instructions on nap coaching your nine- to twelve-month-old, see the section "Much Ado About Napping" on page 162.

TAKE NOTE OF DEVELOPMENTAL CHANGES

Standing and crawling and cutting teeth, oh my! Just when you think you have your daily schedule and coaching plan, here come the developmental changes to throw a wrench in them. Developmental changes are those milestone moments that are super exciting to witness and indicate your child is thriving. How fast babies grow and develop is a wonder to watch, but beware of these milestones, as they can also introduce some new challenges, particularly when sleep coaching. Many times, clients come to me saying they were doing just fine with their coaching until suddenly their baby seemed to go off the rails. We discussed sleep regressions in Phase 1, and often a developmental milestone will cause a regression in your baby's sleep progress. Maybe your baby was a terrific sleeper and then suddenly refuses to go down. A baby who was clocking in an average number of ounces is now voraciously feeding. Once you learn to recognize the culprit, you will be able to set yourself and your baby back on track. What follows are the most common developmental changes you can expect in the nine- to twelve-month age range and strategies to help with sleep regressions they might cause so you all may continue your sleep journey.

SEPARATION ANXIETY

Babies have peaks of separation anxiety at about nine months, when they are crawling and sitting, and at twelve months, when they are standing, walking, and climbing. Those physical leaps often make them wake up more at night, at least temporarily, and the accompanying cognitive leaps make them more aware of strangers, places, and change. Separation anxiety sounds scary, but it is part of an important developmental milestone called *object permanence,* or recognizing different faces and places. Your baby suddenly understands that when you leave the room, you don't disappear like a game of peekaboo. Now, your baby is hit with the realization that you can go somewhere *without her.* The thought of being left alone can overwhelm, and as a result, some anxiety may arise.

Right around the first birthday, babies experiencing these anxiety peaks often start to test their parents to see what the response will be. One common test is to start bawling when the parent, particularly Mom, leaves the room at night. They are saying, *What are you going to do if I cry?*

Can I make you come back and stay with me? This can make bedtime a more wrenching time for both the child and the parent, even with babies who had been going to bed easily at a slightly younger age.

Use Loveys

If your child has not already grown attached to a lovey, encourage one now. The lovey makes the baby feel safe and secure, particularly at bedtime or when he wakes up at night. Put a few stuffed animals or blankets in his crib, and see if one has special appeal. Or try to choose one matched to his own habits and preferences.

One mom noticed that her son kneaded her fingers as she nursed him to sleep. She got him a little stuffed cow, and with a little steering from her, he gradually shifted his kneading habit from her finger to the cow's horns. After that, he was able to use his little cow to soothe himself at night.

To encourage the bond with the lovey, hold it between you and the baby when you are nursing or bottle-feeding him, and include the lovey in bedtime games like peekaboo. You may want to wear it inside your own shirt for a few hours to impart that *eau de Mom*. Play with the lovey, especially but not exclusively at bedtime. Incorporate it in peekaboo or have the lovey blow kisses or wave bye-bye to baby. If he doesn't bond despite your efforts, try a lovey again in a month or two—or maybe he'll choose one from among the presents he is sure to collect on his first birthday.

NEW MOBILITY

Standing Up

According to *The Portable Pediatrician*, "Most babies are pulling to stand by at least a year of age, often much sooner. Most babies learn to climb before they can walk, at whatever age they do walk. This can come as a major surprise. Once a baby can pull to stand, the lure of verticality becomes a major preoccupation. Babies under a year get up onto couches, low tables, anything they can pull up on and boost themselves onto. They are fearless about heights and do not understand that when you come to the end of a surface you will fall off."

The "lure of verticality" certainly goes for sleeping. Because now that they've mastered the skill of popping up, getting babies to lie back down can be a challenge—either because they don't want to, or because they don't know how to.

If your child doesn't know how to lie himself down from his newly learned standing position, sleep disturbances will understandably occur. Until he learns, you will have to do it for him at nighttime. When you see this start to happen, make it the entire week's priority to teach your child during the daytime how to lie down from his standing position. At bedtime and during the night, when your baby stands (before he has learned the skill of lying down), you will have to lay him down. I recommend waiting until he seems very fatigued, which I call the *magic moment*, before trying to lay him down. Many times, parents lay their babies down too early, and they pop back up, grabbing for them and protesting the process. Once you do lay down your tired baby, rub his back or hold him down gently with your hand, applying pressure to soothe him. Leave your hand on him a little longer than usual to encourage him to stay lying down.

How to Teach Lying Down from the Standing Position

Let your baby stand up and try to get down holding on to the coffee table—after you've babyproofed the corners and placed pillows around if necessary. This is when parents are usually grateful for the extra padding offered by diapers. Games like Ring Around the Rosy are also good for developing up-and-down motions. These practicing games should be done out of the crib, during awake time, and not at nap time or bedtime.

On your knees, so you are at eye level of your standing child, hold both of her hands and sing, "Ring around the rosy." On the cue "All fall down," fall onto your bottom, and let go of one of her hands and gently place your free hand behind one of her locked knees to bend it for her. Support her as she goes down, reinforcing with applause.

Watch your child as she pulls herself up during the day, whether it is against the couch or baby fence or wall. You might notice her knees lock. Again, gently hold her body while helping her learn to bend the knee, which will help her bring herself down softly. You can use a toy as a lure as well. If your baby has already learned to crawl, you can lure her from the standing position to her crawling position. Some children develop this skill superfast, while others are more cautious.

If your baby knows how to get down from a standing position and stands in protest shortly after you put him in the crib at bedtime, sit in your chair next to his crib and pat the mattress through the slats and encourage him to lie down. Stay sitting in your chair, which will encourage him to sit down to be on your level. Remember the rules of the Shuffle—don't get into a struggle with your baby who pops up, waiting for you to put him down. This routine will become like a game, and it will go on for hours and will end in crying for everyone. For babies who don't yet have the skill, you can apply the magic moment suggestion, waiting until your child has tired of standing and is fatigued enough that if you were to go over and help him lie down, he might be too exhausted to pop back up.

GROWTH SPURTS

The timing of growth spurts cannot be pinned down, because every baby is different. However, there are some timelines you can consider. According to Happiestbaby.com, in the first year, growth spurts may occur in line with the following estimates, and for the age group of approximately nine to twelve months, you can expect at least one!

* eight and a half months
* ten and a half months
* twelve and a half months

Growth spurts may temporarily disrupt your carefully tended routine. Your baby will have an increased appetite and may wake more at night to feed. Even so, she may also need more sleep than usual, so she still might be clocking in extra sleep amounts. This may not be a good time to night wean if that is what you are planning. Instead, you can build one night feeding into the sleep plan.

TEETHING

Teething can interfere with sleep, but far less than many parents antic ipate or believe. You have likely already encountered some cut tooth by this age, and It may seem like little white spots are appearing in your child's mouth all the time! Usually, children who sleep well will experi ence minor disruptions when they begin to teethe (except for the molars, which come in between ages one and two and can cause more pain). But children who are overtired or who don't know how to put themselves to sleep may have more trouble when teething. It's like she is saying, *I'm already tired, I'm not sure how to go to sleep, and now I have this pain in my mouth. That's going to put me over the edge, so I'm going to stay up and yell.*

To sort out how much of the sleep disruption stems from those new little teeth, compare day with night behavior. If she's her usual self all day but extra cranky or difficult at night, it is probably not the teeth. If a usually cheerful child is miserable around the clock, the trouble may well be a particularly painful tooth. The pain usually subsides as soon as the tooth comes through the gum. Ask your pediatrician about using infant acetaminophen or a similar painkiller. I also found that letting my daughters chew on cold objects by day, such as a washcloth that I had put in the freezer for a few hours, was very soothing. They also liked chomp ing on a toothbrush. Occasionally, I've worked with children who have a slew of symptoms—diaper rash, low-grade fever, diarrhea, disturbed sleep, excessive drooling, poor appetite, and crankiness—but they are a minority, and the problems usually pass as soon as the tooth pops out.

If teething problems crop up while you are in the middle of the Shuffle, progress may slow down for a few days while the tooth comes through, but stick with it. You might want to be a little more soothing, do a little more holding or patting, but don't regress to all the patterns and crutches you are trying to change. If you are just about to embark on the Sleep Lady Shuffle or are introducing new sleep manners and you suspect a tooth is about to erupt, consider delaying any changes for a day or two.

CHANGES IN EATING AND SLEEPING

The big scheduling differences between younger and older babies center on eating. Check with your pediatrician, but healthy children from nine to twelve months on a normal growth curve can usually go eleven to twelve hours at night without a feeding. Separating food time from sleep time, and creating recognizable meal and snack times instead of nonstop nibbling, helps create a sleep-friendly structure. Feed her at recognizable mealtimes: breakfast, lunch, and dinner. Many babies also have morning and afternoon snacks, but you want to get away from the idea of feeding and grazing all day (and all night). If your baby goes to bed or takes a nap right after a meal, make sure there is some time between nursing or bottle-feeding and going into the crib. You want to break that suckle-snooze association.

As babies get older, they can get emotionally attached to the bottle. It basically becomes a lovey, and that can contribute to an ingrained habit of waking up at night in search of it. Introduce a cup before the first birthday, even if you are still nursing and even if you plan on nursing for some time to come. Nurse or bottle-feed at set times, and use the cup at set times like for snack time or with solids. If you are interested in introducing the cup to your baby, turn to the next chapter, "Thirteen to Eighteen Months."

Some mothers wean their babies in the nine- to twelve-month range, and some babies basically wean themselves no matter what their mothers intended. If your baby is looking around a lot while nursing (or taking a bottle), mouthing the nipple without sucking, trying to slide off your lap before you finish feeding him, or impatiently looking like he's got better things to do, that's the signal.

Some parents find it easier to create the separation between associating sleep and nursing or bottle-feeding by no longer doing so in the baby's room. If you want to remain in his room, try keeping the light on while you nurse and turning it off when you want to signal to him that it's crib time. Otherwise, you might risk the baby falling asleep when he's feeding.

Remember, you want to place your baby, drowsy but still awake, down in the crib. This is how he will learn the skill of going to sleep on his own.

Whenever you decide to wean, it should be a natural, easy transition. But nothing is easy and natural when you are dealing with a sleep deprived, overtired baby, particularly one who hasn't learned how to fall asleep without a breast or bottle in his mouth. If you feel that it is time to stop breastfeeding for good by choice or because you believe it has become a sleep crutch to your child, turn to the "Sleep Crutches and Solutions" section on page 147 of this chapter for advice.

Introducing Milk

A significant change in diet happens at the twelve-month mark, the age at which the American Academy of Pediatrics recommends introducing milk. Experts can disagree on what your twelve-month-old should be drinking, so you should *carefully discuss this important milestone with your own pediatrician*. It is commonly agreed upon that you don't have to only use cow's milk to attain the nutrition (vitamin D, fat, DHA, and calcium) that pediatricians are after. The goal is to move from a formula bottle to—per the AAP—two to three eight-ounce glasses a day. Discuss with your pediatrician about introducing milk if you are still breastfeeding.

Milk should not be served in a bottle, as, at twelve months, he should be weaning from the bottle and using a cup. We will discuss how to introduce a cup and say goodbye to the bottle in the next chapter.

THE SLEEP LADY SHUFFLE

So you've created a daily schedule and taken into consideration any developmental changes that may be occurring as you prepare to sleep coach, and now it's time to Shuffle! You've seen the step-by-step Sleep Lady Shuffle guide at the end of Phase 1. Here is where we put it to work for your nine- to twelve-month-old. As you know by now, the Sleep Lady Shuffle is a gentle behavioral modification technique that lets you be a comforting presence as your child learns to put himself to sleep in his crib. The Shuffle is used to nap coach as well, but for the purposes of this section, I will first guide you through sleep coaching at night.

Before beginning the Shuffle, please turn to Chapter 5: Prepping for Sleep-Coaching Success, where I lay the groundwork for sleep coaching. It is best to begin sleep coaching at bedtime, after a great day of naps, getting in naps any way you can. You will have great success at nighttime if your baby's daytime sleep tank is filled. You should follow the Shuffle schedule, moving on to the next position even if your child has had a bad night or two, fussing or waking more frequently. *Don't be surprised if there's a little regression or protest the first night of each new chair position.* If your child gets sick during the Shuffle, you might want to pause and freeze or maintain your position until she's feeling a little better. You might even have to move a little bit closer during an illness to offer more comfort, but then resume your sleep coaching when she recovers.

A few things to remember: Children get ritualized easily. Make the changes every three days—or less. *Dragging it out makes it harder, not easier, for your baby.* Give it more than three days and she'll expect you to stay exactly where you are—and get mad or upset when you double that distance.

TIPS FOR THE FIRST THREE SHUFFLE NIGHTS

1. *Don't get into a power struggle about laying your toddler down—you won't win!* If he is sitting or standing in the crib, pat the mattress and encourage him to lie down. Stay calm and say things like "Sh-sh," "Night-night," and "It's okay, lie down." Sit down in your chair to encourage him to lie down and be closer to your level.

2. *You can stroke, pat, rub,* sh-sh, *or sing to your child intermittently through the rails of the crib.* But don't do it constantly until he falls asleep, or it will become his new sleep crutch. Stop when he is starting to fall asleep. (Some toddlers don't like to be touched as they fall asleep; follow your instincts and his cues.) If you notice

every time you stop patting your child that he starts crying, you are patting too much. Try to touch less and less during the first three nights, knowing that on night 4, you will be moving farther away.

3. *The parent controls the touch.* Don't let the toddler fall asleep grasping your finger or hand, for example, because he will wake up when you move, and it will start all over again. Pat or stroke a different part of his body or the top of his hand.

4. *If the toddler becomes hysterical, pick him up to calm him.* Stay in his room; don't walk around the house or sit down in the rocker. Don't let him fall asleep in your arms. Ideally, calm him while you are standing with him in your arms. When he's calm, kiss him, put him back in the crib, and sit near him in the chair. Make soothing sounds and pat or stroke him. If you pick him up and he's immediately calm, then you've been had. Instead of you training him to sleep, he trained you to pick him up! Wait a little longer next time. Trust your instincts and your knowledge of your child. You will know within a night or two whether picking him up helps or gets him more upset.

5. *Stay by his crib until he is sound asleep at bedtime and during all night awakenings the first three days of the Shuffle.* If you rush out of the room the second he closes his eyes, he will wake up and be upset, and you'll have to start all over.

6. *Return to your Shuffle position, and follow these rules each time the baby wakes during the first three nights* (as long as you and your pediatrician have decided to end night feeding). Go to the crib, give him a kiss, encourage him to lie down if necessary, and then sit in your chair. Do this at each awakening until 6:00 a.m.

NIGHTS 1–3: NEXT TO THE CRIB

Once bath, stories, and songs are over, put your baby in his crib drowsy but awake, and sit in a chair *next to your baby's crib.* You can sing during

Sleep Lady Tip

When you soothe your child by going to her crib to pat or rub her back, it is important that you control the touch. Instead of having her hold your hand or finger, you should pat her. Make sure you don't caress her too steadily, or else she might cry when you stop. Do it on and off. Count to yourself if it helps—count to ten touching, then count to sixty not touching, then touch for another ten counts. You don't want to do this so much that you swap one negative association, like rocking, for another—like your constant touch or the sound of your voice.

the get-ready-for-bed stage, but once it's time for sleep, you are better off making lulling *sh-sh* or other soothing sounds. You might want to try closing your eyes to convey a sleepy-time message and see if he mimics you. Try not to be doing anything to or for your baby the last few minutes before he goes to sleep. Let him own that last few minutes himself. Before you know it, he will own the entire process of putting himself to sleep! Stay next to his crib until he falls asleep.

On night 1, if necessary or if you are not quite comfortable, you can do more touching, but not steadily; do it on and off, and know that you will need to taper off or start patting more intermittently beginning on night 2. It's also important that the parent control the touch. Instead of having her hold your hand or finger, you should pat her. Make sure that you do not caress the child too steadily; do it on and off. You don't want to swap one negative association or sleep crutch, like rocking, for another—like your constant touch or the sound of your voice.

Unlike many other sleep-coaching methods, with the Shuffle, you can pick up your baby to calm him down when he gets extremely upset. Try not to do this either immediately after putting him in the crib at bedtime or as the first thing during the night when he wakes. If he gets really upset and you do need to pick him up, go ahead and do so, over the crib if possible. Hold him while you are standing until he's calm, but keep it brief. Try patting him, shushing him, or handing him his lovey or pacifier, for example, and sitting in the chair.

NIGHTS 4–6: HALFWAY TO THE DOOR

If the room is very small or the crib is close to the door, then move all the way to the doorway, as in night 7. Continue the soothing sounds with your voice, but stay in the chair as much as you can. Get up to pat or stroke her a little if necessary, or make some of the same soothing sounds you have used the past three nights. Be careful not to touch for too long or you'll defeat the purpose of moving away and you will find yourself constantly returning to the crib side to touch your baby to sleep.

NIGHTS 7–9: CHAIR AT THE DOORWAY, INSIDE THE ROOM

Continue the same soothing techniques, intervening as little as possible. Stay in the chair as much as you can. Don't worry if she cries a little bit; keep quietly reassuring her. She'll know that you are there, and she will fall asleep.

NIGHTS 10–12: INTO THE HALLWAY, IN VIEW

You are still *within her direct line of vision*. Make your *sh-sh* sounds, not constantly but enough to remind her that you are close by and responsive. Stay there until she falls asleep.

NIGHTS 13 AND ON

It's time to leave your baby to fall asleep on her own—if she's not sleeping already. Don't panic—it's probably harder for you than for her. She's had two weeks to prepare for this. She has surrendered some of her sleep crutches and is more secure in her sleep skills. She recognizes your support and responsiveness.

You now need to move away from your baby's room. How far away you go is up to you. You should be out of her sight, but it's fine if you want to *stay within earshot, down the hall, or in a nearby room*. If she's whimpering or crying a bit, see if you can soothe her with your voice from the doorway. But if you find you must go to her crib, do so briefly. Then return to the hallway, out of view but close enough that she can hear your soft, soothing sounds. Listen to your intuition, and check on her again from the doorway in a few minutes if you think she truly needs you. But try not to intervene too much or backtrack on all the great work you—and your baby—have done. Very rarely do babies cry for more than a few minutes after experiencing the Shuffle. Keep in mind that she has gained confidence that you are nearby and responsive. She's ready to master this skill. See "Tips for the First Three Shuffle Nights" on page 140.

IF YOUR BABY IS STILL WAKING AT NIGHT

If these techniques don't eliminate those final night awakenings, you might be putting your baby to bed when he's too drowsy. It's easier for a baby to put himself to sleep at bedtime than in the middle of the night—particularly if he was 90 percent asleep before his head hit the crib mattress. Try putting him down when he's a bit more alert, even if it means backing up and doing a few more days of the Shuffle. You may find that an earlier bedtime also helps him conquer the night awakenings. Try moving bedtime a half hour earlier. If you are still nursing at bedtime, try doing that feeding a little earlier in the evening to further weaken the link between suckling and sleeping. Sometimes it helps to keep a light on while you nurse to help him break that suckle-sleep association.

NOT READY FOR THE SHUFFLE? YOU CAN TRY SWITCHING ASSOCIATIONS UNTIL YOU ARE

I believe *you* have to be ready to sleep coach, and often it feels like a huge leap. And if you can't take that leap, take some preparatory smaller steps before you sleep coach 100 percent.

For instance, if your child depends on you to put her to sleep by rocking, feeding, or lying down with her and you are not ready to put your baby down drowsy but awake at bedtime, you can switch the crutch, or what I call *switching negative sleep associations*. If you nurse her to sleep, stop one night and instead have the other parent rock her to sleep. Yes, you are creating a new sleep crutch—from nursing to sleep to rocking to sleep—but because the behavior of the other parent rocking her is so new, the toddler is not as attached to it. It may be easier to stop rocking to sleep when you are ready to start sleep coaching.

Another small step you can take now is to work on gently fading out your child's current sleep crutch. For example, if you always hold your child until she's completely asleep, try holding her until she's almost asleep. Then put her in her crib and pat her all the way to sleep. You can also try patting her back to sleep during the night.

SHUFFLING WITH MULTIPLES

Your multiple babies shared a womb, and it's usually a good idea to have them share a room. Some families even put them in the same crib for a few months, until they start rolling over. Yes, they may grunt, whimper, and make all sorts of strange baby noises, but they almost always learn to sleep through each other's sounds, and you want to encourage them to do so. Be careful about responding too quickly if one makes a noise. Parents often rush in as soon as they hear a peep, fearing that one will wake up the other one. You may be reinforcing the troubled sleeper while you protect the one who is asleep. You may be teaching her to make noises so you'll come flying in to pick her up all the time. The sleeping twin may be oblivious, or she may stir but then get herself right back to sleep, or one parent might have successfully reassured her back to sleep, exactly as you want her to do. Parents of triplets or quadruplets can adapt these techniques for their children, although most don't separate them for naps simply because they don't have enough room! A parent can sit in the middle of the bedroom between the children to soothe them. The children learn quickly to sleep through their siblings' crying and fussing.

Just like with singletons, start the Sleep Lady Shuffle at bedtime after a day when your babies' daytime sleep averages have been met—which means getting naps in any way you can. Whether you need to rely on all your sleep crutches at the same time or take three car rides a day, getting the daytime sleep tank filled—even if it means taking drastic measures— is a must before beginning the Shuffle at night. If possible, move the cribs so they are at least three feet apart.

After your soothing bedtime routine, place your babies in their cribs drowsy but awake, and sit in your chair position as described in the Sleep Lady Shuffle beginning on page 141. If one parent is doing the Shuffle, sit in a chair between the cribs and go back and forth. If two parents or other caregivers are available, it will be easier, and each adult can sit by a child. Stroke and soothe each child in turn. Follow the rules of the Shuffle for the first three nights on pages 140 to 142. Make sure that by the third night, you are using your voice to soothe instead of relying too much on touch.

Both parents must be on the same page—one is not picking up the baby more often than the other, for instance. If one child is more of a problem sleeper than the other, have the parent who has an easier time with consistency sit next to that child. If the sleep crutch is nursing to sleep, let the non-nursing parent do the first few nights.

FREQUENTLY ASKED QUESTIONS
FROM PARENTS OF MULTIPLES

Q: **I have twins, and one is a better sleeper than the other and gets woken by the other twin. How should I sleep coach them?**

A: In those cases where one baby truly does disrupt the other's sleep, I do make exceptions and separate them at night during sleep coaching. It's usually a good idea to leave the poorer sleeper where he is and move the sounder sleeper to another room, using a portable crib if necessary. Good sleepers tend to be more flexible and can more easily adjust to a temporary new sleeping place, even if it's a little noisier or brighter than the babies' bedroom. Once the poorer sleeper is sleeping through the night fairly consistently (or waking for a single feeding if that's age appropriate and you're satisfied), you can return him to the shared room.

Q: **I have triplets. How can we do the Shuffle and sit next to their cribs when there are only two parents available? And sometimes only one of us is home at bedtime?**

A: If you have triplets or quads, you can still do this, but be gentle on yourself by not expecting too much at first. You are outnumbered, after all. You may need to have one parent sit between two babies or two parents tag teaming with three babies, and so on. If there is just one parent, gently move back and forth to stroke and soothe each child in turn. Follow the rules of the Shuffle for the first three nights on pages 140 to 142. Make sure that by the third night, you are using your voice to soothe instead of relying too much on touch.

SLEEP CRUTCHES AND SOLUTIONS

Babies who have trouble getting to sleep and staying asleep often have *negative associations,* or *sleep crutches.* These aren't actually bad behaviors; they only become negative when they block sleep independence. For instance, children should be hugged and snuggled. But if they are hugged and snuggled until they fall asleep and each time they wake up at night, they will never learn how to fall asleep on their own or get themselves back to sleep at night.

Similar negative associations involve being held or rocked to sleep, serenading or swinging a baby, or nursing or feeding a baby even when he is seeking food for comfort, not hunger. Our job as parents is to create positive sleep associations, letting our babies learn to fall asleep on their own. That's what's required by their growing bodies and miraculously expanding minds.

CRUTCH: NIGHTTIME FEEDING

Example: My ten-month-old nurses to sleep at bedtime and nap time and is still waking to nurse four or five times during the night! What can I do?

Even a smart, thoughtful mom who knows that her daughter is feeding enough during the day may still have a fear of letting her child go hungry—especially when that child is waking in the middle of the night. Check with your pediatrician to make sure your little one doesn't have a health issue requiring nighttime feeding, but the overwhelming odds are that a baby this age is still getting up in search of breast or bottle because that's the only way she knows how to go to sleep and get back to sleep. Don't be hard on yourself if your child has developed this habit. It's very common—because it works!—but it's time for your baby to learn another way to fall asleep.

Eliminating Nighttime Feeding

Families I've worked with have tried all the techniques outlined below for eliminating nighttime feedings; make the choice that best matches your child's temperament and what you can follow through with consistently. I suggest starting with the most gradual one, Method A, but if you feel confident that B or C makes more sense for you and your baby, go ahead. Please read through this entire section; many of the tips can be applied to any of the strategies.

Whatever approach you take, it will be easier if you try to reset your baby's hunger clock so she takes in more calories by day and therefore isn't looking for more at night. I know some babies, even this young, who do a remarkable job of lightly snacking all day so they can feast all night. Start by reviewing her daytime feeding schedule and keeping a written log for a week. Go over it with her doctor to make sure she's getting the right mix of breast milk and/or formula and solids. Try to nurse or bottle-feed her in a quiet, dim place without television, phone, or other distractions so that she can focus on taking a full feeding. This advice holds true during growth spurts, too. She may need an occasional night feeding mid-spurt, but by enhancing her daytime feedings, you'll minimize the nighttime ones.

Once you and your pediatrician have agreed that your baby can go eleven hours at night without a feeding, choose one of the methods. Ideally, eliminating that nighttime meal should be completed within a week. Choose your target day—and stick to it.

Three Options for Nighttime Weaning
Method A: The Taper-Off Technique

If you're nursing, gradually cut down the amount of time your baby is at the breast. For example, if she usually feeds for twenty minutes, let her go for only fifteen. Cut back every night until she's ready to give it up, or until you're down to five minutes. At that point, it's time to stop altogether. Make sure you unlatch her when she finishes eating heartily, even if it's faster than the time you allotted; don't let her gently suckle and doze. Get her back to bed while she's drowsy but awake.

If you're bottle-feeding, you can decrease the amount of formula she gets by a few ounces every few nights. When you get to two ounces, it's time to stop. That's usually the best way to do it, but you could also gradually dilute the formula until it gets so watery she decides it's not worth waking up for.

If your baby is waking to eat several times a night but only nursing for a couple of minutes or taking a couple of ounces, this method won't work for you. Choose Method B or C.

Method B: The Four-Night Phase-Out

Whether you're breastfeeding or giving a bottle, feed your baby just once during the night for three nights; it's best to *set a time* for when you'll give her that single snack, so you can either:

* feed her the first time she wakes after a set time, such as midnight, or
* the first time she wakes as long as it's been at least four hours since she's last eaten, or
* offer her a dream feed, in which you pick her up and feed her right before you go to bed. Note: Not all babies will feed well at a dream feed and then will be up an hour later. If this is your baby, then stick with a set-time approach.

Only feed her once at night and not again until at least 6:00 a.m., when you can both start your day. When she wakes at other times, sit by her crib and offer physical and verbal reassurance—but do not feed her! On the fourth night, don't feed her at all. Remember, she has had three nights to get used to receiving fewer calories at night. Usually, parents will move their seats away from the crib on the fourth night of the Shuffle, but we're going to modify it for this night. So on the fourth night when she wakes up, sit next to her crib for one more night. Comfort her from your chair as you did at bedtime. Don't pick her up unless she's hysterical, and then hold her only briefly. If you breastfeed exclusively, putting the other parent on night duty might help your baby adjust to the no-night-feeding reality more quickly.

Important note: Keep this in mind if you've decided that you'll feed your baby the first time she wakes after midnight. If you find yourself sitting with her and doing the Shuffle from 11:00 p.m. until midnight while she fusses or cries, don't feed her a minute after the clock strikes 12:00. Wait until she goes back to sleep and then wakes up again—even if she only dozes for half an hour. You don't want to send the message that crying for an hour will yield a feeding.

Method C: Cold Turkey

If your baby is barely feeding at night, whether from breast or bottle, you may decide that it will be easier to stop all the feedings cold turkey. Go to her crib side when she wakes at night as outlined in the Shuffle. Just make sure you and your partner are on the same page in this decision. If Mom has been breastfeeding, consider having the non-nursing parent handle all middle-of-the-night wake-ups, since your child knows that the other parent won't be there to nurse her.

PARENTS WHO WANT TO REDUCE THE NUMBER OF FEEDINGS AT NIGHT WITHOUT ELIMINATING THEM ALTOGETHER, THIS ONE'S FOR YOU

Let's say you and your pediatrician think your baby still needs to eat at night, or you want to reduce nighttime feedings but aren't ready to cut them out altogether; follow the first step of Method B, but don't stop feeding her on night 4. Restrict meals to once a night. Feed your child quickly, and avoid other interactions that will encourage her to stay up. Coach her back to sleep for all other wakings.

Daytime weaning came easily for Christina and Sally, but at ten months, Christina was still having trouble cutting out her daughter's two last breast-feedings. At bedtime, Christina nursed Sally to sleep in a rocking chair, staying there until she was sleeping soundly enough to be gently transferred into the crib. At 4:00 a.m., Sally woke up, and Christina and Andy took her into their bed to be nursed again.

Contemplating doing anything that would upset Sally was very difficult for Christina. She had about zero tolerance for tears, and she interpreted every cry as a sign of hunger. "She was my little baby, and I couldn't let her cry," Christina recollected. "I nursed her too much; every little cry, I thought she was hungry. I never let the poor child cry. I didn't realize that crying was part of her way of communicating."

Sleep Lady Tip

If the baby wakes before her set-time feeding and stays awake and fussy, don't feed her as soon as the clock strikes her set time. If you do that, you risk training her to cry and cry. Instead, get her back to sleep for at least a little while before you feed her. For example, if she wakes up at 11:00 and fusses until midnight, don't pick her up and feed her at the stroke of 12:00. Get her to sleep, even if it's just for thirty minutes, until she wakes up again. So if she wakes up at 11:00, fusses until 12:00, finally falls asleep at 12:10, and wakes up at 12:45, you can feed her. She learned to get to sleep without that food. While she's fussing, try not to pick her up, but if she gets hysterical, hold her briefly. Some babies adjust in three or four days; others take a little longer. Your consistency will help her adapt more quickly.

Christina was apprehensive about the Sleep Lady Shuffle and the prospect of tears but had become convinced that she owed it to herself and to Sally to help her daughter learn to sleep. She and Andy considered which parent should sit in the chair, and Christina decided that as hard as it would be for her to listen to Sally's tears up close, it would be absolutely unbearable for her to listen to them from farther away. "I knew if I was watching her, I would know she was okay," she said.

Sally was a classic example of an easily ritualized baby who just swapped one sleep crutch for another. She gave up her nighttime nursing—but within two nights was demanding bedtime patting instead. It was very hard for Christina to keep the touching intermittent, to let Sally go to sleep without Mom's hand resting on her through the crib. Christina also had to resist—and she didn't at first—putting Sally down over and over again when she stood up. Sally would keep doing it, because she knew Mom would rub and pat her as she got her to lie back down, and Mom would keep doing it because Sally would cry if Mom stopped.

Sally cried a fair amount the first three nights, even with her mom being much too involved. The first night was a tough forty-five minutes, the second was thirty, the third twenty. (This is why it helps to keep a log, because twenty minutes seems really rotten until you look at your log and see that night 3 was less than half the tears of night 1.) On night 4, it was time for Christina to move the chair to the door—and things began to fall into place. It took the rest of the week, but the awakenings grew shorter and less frequent. Within a week, Sally was sleeping through the night. Her mom said, "She became an awesome nighttime sleeper."

CRUTCH: WALKING, HOLDING, BOUNCING, AND ROCKING TO SLEEP

Example: My daughter sleeps poorly during the day and more poorly at night. When she was smaller, I nursed her a lot so she would get some sleep, but now at nine months old, nursing doesn't seems to be as reliable a solution. So I started to rock her to sleep after I nursed her, and it worked. But now I need to rock her for longer and longer periods of time! She is an extremely alert baby who hates missing out on any of the action; she even learned to jerk herself awake when she starts falling asleep while I am rocking her. I feel out of options!

When nursing no longer does the trick, or when we cut out nighttime nursing because we know it interferes with sleep, some of us end up walking or rocking our babies to sleep instead. A few minutes of walking or rocking at bedtime is fine, but if he demands prolonged rocking or a five-mile hike, or if he needs to be walked and rocked repeatedly during the night, it's time to stop.

How to Eliminate Walking, Holding, Bouncing, and Rocking to Sleep

As with so many sleep problems, the easiest time for you to institute changes is at bedtime, when you are more awake and more likely to be consistent. Begin by doing all the walking or rocking in the bedroom, not around the house, to create a positive association between the room and sleep.

Every few days, you can scale back the amount of time you walk or rock. Stop walking when you've reached the *magic moment*, when he's very fatigued but still awake, and put him down in his crib. We want him to be aware that he is going into the crib, while having him exhausted enough that he won't want to fight sleep. We don't want to somehow secretly slide him in or trick him, because when he has a partial awakening, he'll get mad if he thinks he went to bed in your arms but now he finds himself stuck in the crib. Or instead of scaling back, you can stop the rocking and read him a book and walk him as you slowly make your way to turn off his light. Blow kisses to the moon, give him a kiss and a hug, and put him into the crib.

Sit by the crib and soothe him. If he gets hysterical, pick him up briefly and put him down as soon as he's calm. If he calms down in two seconds once you've picked him up, you'll know he didn't need to be picked up as badly as you'd thought he did. Resume your Shuffle position and be consistent.

Warning: While the Sleep Lady Shuffle encourages parents to pick up to calm their crying and distraught child, it can be futile for children with the crutch of being walked, held, bounced, and rocked to sleep. Some babies with this crutch genuinely cry hard and then, when picked up to calm, can fall asleep in their parents' arms in under two minutes! If this happens during sleep coaching, you can inadvertently train your baby to cry hard until you pick him up. When parents are trying to eliminate this crutch, I always tell them to use "pick up to calm" as conservatively as possible. If you inadvertently train him to cry hard to be picked up and he falls immediately asleep, you won't be able to use the soothing technique of "pick up to calm" anymore, and you will have to endure what could be a lot of crying.

If you want to go slower than either of these two options, see "Switching Associations" on page 144 to learn how to replace one crutch for another until your baby sleeps through the night.

CRUTCH: THE PACIFIER REPLUG

Example: My almost-twelve-month-old is pulling up in his crib and throwing his pacifier out multiple times a night. He loves his pacifier but this is exhausting. What can I do?

You don't have to take away the pacifier at this age. It's your choice. The pacifier itself is not a crutch; the crutch is the baby's dependence on someone else to replug it when it falls out. You can't necessarily keep the pacifier from falling out, but there are ways to address the baby replugging it by himself.

Most babies have developed the pincer grasp—the ability to pick things up using their index fingers and thumbs—by eight or nine months. Many frustrated parents have reported that even after their child develops the pincer grasp and can replug the binkie during the day, he still cries out in the middle of the night for a replug—and that's a sleep crutch. So I help parents teach their already skilled baby how to do it herself during the night.

How to Teach Your Baby How to Replug Her Pacifier

Since she has likely developed the pincer grasp, she can learn how to replug her pacifier for sleep. To make it easier, leave several in her crib so one is always within easy reach.

Start by putting the pacifier in her hand, not her mouth, at bedtime and when she wakes at night. For a few nights, you might have to guide her hand to her mouth, but at this age, they learn pretty quickly. Some children want one pacifier in each hand. Then move to guiding her to one of the several pacifiers you've placed in her crib. Help her roll to her side to find one if need be. Do this for another few consecutive nights.

After about five or six days of guided practice in the crib, you are ready for the next step. At the next bedtime and during any subsequent wakings and demands for a replug, point to a pacifier for her to retrieve it. If she is having trouble finding her pacifier in the dark—even with a dim night-light—consider glow-in-the-dark pacifiers. (Yes, there is such a thing. There are several reliable brands.)

Throwing the Pacifier

As babies in this age group learn to pull up and begin to cruise along furniture, they may go through the pacifier-as-missile stage. They love to hurl it out of the crib and make you go after it.

It is somewhat like a game of fetch your baby is playing with you. He'll throw the pacifier (or lovey) out of the crib and then scream for you to come get it. What's a parent to do?

Note that this often happens when you are in a Shuffle chair position that is no longer seated crib-side. Let's say you are sitting in the hall, in view, and he throws the pacifier to the floor. Do not retrieve it. Instead, tell him, "Lie down, and I will come give you your binky." Keep repeating this until he lies down. Once he is down, go into the room and get his pacifier.

Now tell him, "No throwing binky." You can even talk for the binky and say, "Don't throw me out. I want to snuggle and sleep with you!" Make the binky seem sad that he was thrown out. You may have one of those toddlers who likes to try to test the limits, and even after you return the lovey to him, he throws it again. Repeat the above, instructing, "Lie down, and I will get the binky for the last time." (Some parents want to give their child one more chance, and others don't; it's up to you.)

When you return, tell him that if he throws it again, you will not give it back to him. If he were to throw it again (I have had a few who do), you must stand your ground and not return it despite the wailing and pleading for his lovey. Continue to use your voice to verbally reassure him from your Shuffle position. Once he is completely asleep or when you check on him one last time before you turn in, return his lovey without waking him (of course).

If You Decide to Wean from the Pacifier

You might be ready for this option if you don't have the stamina to keep replugging pacifiers so many times at night and if, despite the fact that your baby has learned to replug her pacifier, she's still waking up in search of it repeatedly. Pick a night (or a few nights) when you are ready to cope with some unpleasantness. On the day you start, it would help if your baby had an especially nice and calming bedtime routine after a great day of naps any way you can get them. Be especially careful about getting her to bed drowsy but awake.

Don't give her the pacifier. Stroke or soothe her. Use techniques similar to those I earlier advised for parents breaking nighttime feeding or walking habits while doing the Shuffle. Every time she wakes up at night, do the Shuffle without giving her the pacifier. I understand that if she cries and protests incessantly, it's rough on you. But please stick it out. Consistency really, really matters here—and it will have its reward. Because if you give her the pacifier to get some sleep, you will risk conditioning her to cry for an hour to receive the pacifier—over and over again, indefinitely. We definitely don't want to do that. Once you start, follow through. Consistency counts. Prepare for a rough few nights. Unfortunately, there is no gradual method for weaning from the pacifier. It's either in the mouth or it's not.

> ### Sleep Lady Tip
>
> Some parents take the pacifier away at night but leave it at nap time, when it is harder for babies to settle themselves. This may not sound logical but it really works! You will know it's time to wean the pacifier at nap time if you are going in to reset tle him multiple times at each nap time.

CRUTCH: REACTIVE CO-SLEEPING

Most of the families I speak to are either co-sleeping out of desperation or they really want to continue to co-sleep but find it's not working well for their family. Families who are co-sleeping out of desperation are practicing what I call *reactive co-sleeping*. These "we didn't plan it this way" co-sleepers are reactively co-sleeping when they end up with their baby in the bed part or all of the night. I am not against co-sleeping if that is your choice (and you do it safely). But with these families, it's not a choice or philosophical commitment; it's the only way they can get their toddler to sleep at bedtime or back to sleep in the middle of the night. If you are reactively co-sleeping—in the category of "we didn't plan it this way"—that means it has become a crutch (for both you and your baby). In Chapter 12, I address how to end reactive co-sleeping as well as how to improve safe co-sleeping if co-sleeping is your preference.

TEMPERAMENT CHECK

By now, your baby's temperament is starting to become crystal clear. You've identified some of her cues and are beginning to know her habits, behaviors, and responses. Perhaps you've noticed that your baby likes to sleep with her head in the corner of the crib or thinks 11:00 p.m. is time to throw a party. Perhaps your baby is "fussy" or has a mind of her own.

In Phase 1, I specifically addressed the temperament of what I call the *highly alert child*. In my experience, this is the temperament that leads most of my clients, probably around 80 percent, to seek out my help and the help of my Gentle Sleep Coaches. If you have come to realize you have been blessed with an active, stubborn, engaged child, you might be running the risk of being more sleep deprived or frustrated—even depressed—than if you were sleep training a child who was less spirited.

I expand on the sleep needs of the highly alert child in Phase 1 on page 43 as well as in the previous chapter, "Six to Eight Months." Sleep training isn't impossible once you recognize that your highly alert child has her own set of rules about how and when she gets some sleep. Like a river, it's better for everyone to go with the flow than to try to swim against it.

EARLY RISING

So many parents reach out to me because they started sleep coaching their child and their babies are now sleeping a much longer stretch but waking at 4:00 or 5:00 a.m. and seemingly not wanting to go back to sleep. Or perhaps your baby was sleeping through until 6:00 or 7:00 a.m. until daylight saving time, and now, months later, she is still waking at 5:00 a.m. Early rising is such a huge and common sleep struggle.

Early rising is not the same as having early risers, whom I refer to as *early birds,* so as not to confuse the two. Early birds wake up earlier than many parents would like, 6:00 or 6:30 a.m., but they do so refreshed and happy. Their temperament skews more toward simply being a morning person. And in this case, you don't have to look far and wide to find that at least one parent is a morning person, too. Interestingly, research suggests there is a genetic link.

Then there are those early risers who are not happy to be up before the crack of dawn. They are tired, unrefreshed, the opposite of bright-eyed and bushy-tailed. But there they are—grouchy, awake, and not going back to sleep. This is when early rising is a problem, because the sleep tank isn't filled efficiently. And by now, we know that not getting enough nighttime sleep will affect nap quality and quantity, and nap time affects nighttime sleep—and the cycle continues.

WHAT CAUSES EARLY RISING?

While this is a very common problem, often the solution isn't one that is instant, as so many parents wish. Like any new skill, learning how to stay asleep takes time. Early rising is essentially your child having a difficult time putting himself *back to sleep* after a long stretch of sleep at night or not getting quite enough sleep to make it to his nap without being overtired. This skill is more difficult to learn than putting himself to sleep at bedtime.

For instance, I know if I get up at 5:00 or 5:30 a.m. and I'm awake a little too long, my brain starts to tick-tick-tick-tick with all the things I have to do, and I will have a hard time going back to sleep. My body has gotten just enough sleep to make it hard to go back to sleep—but not enough to leave me feeling rested and restored.

Here are four factors that can cause early rising. Sometimes only one causes the early rising; for other kids, it could be all four. Note that you should first always rule out illness or undiagnosed medical conditions that can cause and contribute to sleep problems, such as obstructive sleep apnea, which we discuss more in Chapter 14. Then, consider the following reasons:

1. Too drowsy at bedtime
2. Too long of a wakeful window between the afternoon nap and bedtime
3. Insufficient naps
4. Too late of a bedtime

Too Drowsy at Bedtime

The paramount lesson of helping your baby to learn to fall asleep on his own is putting him to bed drowsy but awake. You want him to be tired and ready for sleep but not falling asleep as soon as his head hits the mattress. Putting yourself to sleep is a form of self-soothing, and for him to learn that skill, he needs to be awake enough at bedtime. Once he masters it at bedtime, he can eventually apply it to night wakings as well as early risings, which are the toughest to go back to sleep from.

Overestimating the Wakeful Window

This may seem counterintuitive, but an overtired child generally takes longer to get to sleep and will wake more often during the night, causing early rising. Review your baby's nap schedule to make sure you are not exceeding his wakeful window, and be sure there are no more than four hours between the end of his afternoon nap and his bedtime. At this age, this window will be shorter if he is not napping long enough (three to three and a half hours).

Insufficient Naps

We will discuss this a bit in the napping section, but it begs to be repeated. Short napping or not enough napping can cause increased night wakings and early rising. Quality nap time actually helps encourage quality nighttime sleep. If your child tends to take very short naps or finishes her naps early in the day, you are probably dealing with early rising. Review your child's sample schedule and the nap-coaching section and decide when you are going to start nap coaching.

Too Late of a Bedtime

Many parents are shocked when I tell them that their child's natural bedtime is likely *between 7:00 and 8:00 p.m.* And in this age group, more likely 7:00–7:30 p.m. If your baby's bedtime is well beyond this window, sleep in the night could be disrupted and can lead to early rising. If your schedule is wildly different from the sample schedule and your child is rising early, consider adjusting bedtime earlier. Do not keep your child up too late, hoping that he will wake less often during the night and sleep later in the morning. This rarely (if ever) works. Overtired children sleep less, not more.

WHAT TO DO? RETURN TO THE SLEEP LADY SHUFFLE

While you are making adjustments based on the tips above and your child wakes before 6:00 a.m., treat it like the other night wakings and do the Shuffle. The catch is that you must use your consistent response until 6:00 a.m. If he doesn't go back to sleep, use what I like to call *dramatic wake-up*! Leave the room for a full minute (literally, a full minute—watch the clock!). After sixty seconds, return to the room bright and cheerful with a "Good morning!" while you open the curtains and let the light flood in. This signals to your child that you are getting him up because it is morning—and not because he is waking up too early!

Keep using the Shuffle in the early morning until the habit resolves. If you allow it to persist, you could be introducing a new sleep crutch that will need to be broken eventually. Keep in mind that early rising happens during the sleep-coaching process and can often take two to three weeks to fully resolve as you are working on improving naps. The two hardest or last pieces of sleep coaching to fall into place are early rising and the afternoon nap. So don't give up!

> ### Sleep Lady Tip
>
> Keep in mind that early rising happens during the sleep-coaching process and can often take two to three weeks to fully resolve as you are working on improving naps. The two hardest or last pieces of sleep coaching to fall into place are early rising and the afternoon nap. So don't give up!

MUCH ADO ABOUT NAPPING

Naps are an essential part of both the baby and toddler sleep requirements. Naps allow little bodies to recharge and process the activities that have happened so far in their day. For some children, naps are a challenge, a daily struggle, and often frustrating for parents. Remember that babies from nine to twelve months need two naps a day, about one and a half to two hours apiece. Usually, a baby in this age range no longer needs the short third nap in late afternoon; however, if the earlier naps are skimpy and the child is not yet sleeping through the night, the short third nap is required during the coaching process. You can tackle naps at the same time you start the Sleep Lady Shuffle at night.

Once you are ready, begin with the Shuffle at night—and then tackle the first nap the next morning, then the afternoon nap (or naps). Then go on to the second night of the Shuffle. Make sure you're timing your child's naps correctly, based on his age (as indicated in this chapter). Also, be aware of his sleep cues and windows of wakefulness.

Nap coaching is hard for a plethora of reasons. The best defense is a good offense, so here are two major rules of nap coaching and preemptive strategies that will address head-on any nap-time snafus that may arise (and they will!). You probably noticed I don't usually talk about "rules"; I prefer to give you a range of choices that fit your own parenting style. But after many years of working with parents of balky nappers, I have learned that these rules really help!

#1: Focus on putting your child down for a nap *in her crib, twice a day.* If you are going to nap and night coach at the same time, then begin nap coaching the morning after the first night, with the morning nap. Go through an abbreviated version of your bedtime routine of reading a book or singing a song, and work on getting her down drowsy but awake.

Don't feel obligated to feed her before her nap; however, if nursing or bottle feeding is your preferred transition activity, be careful not to let her fall asleep while eating. Remember, she has to be put into her crib awake enough that she is aware she is being put down. Draw the shades, turn on your sound machine, and watch your little one begin to demonstrate her sleepy cues of eye rubbing and yawning. Place your chair in the same place as you did the night before and follow the same steps of the Shuffle along with the same soothing techniques. Move your chair every three days, even if she didn't nap well on day 3.

#2: Spend an entire hour trying to get your child to sleep at nap time. Stay in your chair, exercising your Shuffle techniques for one whole hour. There are three possible outcomes:

1. Your baby doesn't go to sleep for the entire hour.
2. Your baby only takes a forty-five-minute nap.
3. Your baby sleeps for *less than* forty-five minutes, which is less than a sleep cycle. I call these abbreviated naps *disaster naps.*

WHAT TO DO IF YOUR BABY DOESN'T
SLEEP FOR THE ENTIRE HOUR

At the end of your Shuffling hour, leave the room, count to ten, and go back into the room to do your dramatic wake-up routine (open the blinds, sing, "Nap time is over, baby!") and take your child out of bed. Since he hasn't had a morning nap, he won't be able to last (or wait) until the afternoon for his next nap. Watch his cues; if he starts yawning, dozing while you feed him, and so on—even if it's just forty-five minutes after you got him out of his crib—go ahead and try for a nap again, doing the Shuffle.

WHAT TO DO IF YOUR BABY ONLY
SLEEPS FOR FORTY-FIVE MINUTES

This is the bare minimum for a nap. If he wakes up happy and seemingly refreshed from a forty-five-minute morning nap, that's okay, but be aware that he might be ready for his afternoon siesta sooner rather than later (after two hours awake rather than three). Watch for drowsy cues so you don't miss his sleep window. I find that when babies wake up happy after a forty-five-minute morning nap, they often don't wake up happy and refreshed after a forty-five-minute afternoon nap. If your child naps for just forty-five minutes in the afternoon, use the Shuffle techniques to get him back to sleep. Try for at least thirty more minutes if you can.

WHAT TO DO IF YOUR BABY NAPS FOR
LESS THAN FORTY-FIVE MINUTES

This is a *disaster nap*. When a child sleeps for less than forty-five minutes, he doesn't go through a complete sleep cycle and awakens at a partial arousal; it's enough to take the edge off his exhaustion but not enough to be restorative and to make it to the next nap or bedtime without being overtired. So here's the tough message: I want you to go to him and do the Shuffle for an hour—what I call the *longest hour*.

Here's an example: You put your child in his crib at 9:00 a.m. He conks out at 9:30, but only sleeps until 10:00. You go in and work on getting him back to sleep—which he does, thankfully, by 10:30, after just half an hour. But he only sleeps for twenty minutes. Chances are the negative voice in you is going to say, *I can't believe the Sleep Lady told me to do that! He cried more than he slept. What's the point of that?* But think about it: Your baby did it! He put himself back to sleep after a partial arousal from a nap—one of the hardest things to do. Going forward, he'll begin to get back to sleep more quickly and will snooze longer if you stick with it.

NAP-COACHING TIPS

It's easier to get a baby to take the morning nap than the afternoon nap. Don't miss that opportunity.

Afternoon nap training is tougher. Don't get discouraged; it's normal.

Keep a sleep log during nap training.

If it's 2:00 or 3:00 p.m. and your baby has not napped well enough, you may need to resort to your backup plan, such as a nap in the stroller or car, to avoid an exhausted baby and bedtime disaster.

You will be tied to the house during nap coaching. If you feel like all you are doing all day is trying to get your baby to nap, then you are doing it right! The payoff: you'll have more freedom (and a happier, rested baby) once you have a predictable napping schedule.

If you have a nanny, babysitter, or childcare setting that can do the nap training, thank your lucky stars. If your caregiver is reluctant to do the training, see if you can win her over with a simple explanation of the sleep science. If not, explain that your child needs a full sleep tank, and if that means the sitter has to use a sleep crutch like rocking to get the child to nap or to resume a brief or interrupted nap, that's okay.

DEVISE YOUR NAP-TIME BACKUP PLAN

After you have tried the nap in the crib twice during the day, you will likely need to use a backup nap plan to help fill the daytime sleep tank so your baby doesn't face bedtime even more exhausted, making it harder for him to go to sleep and stay asleep. If you check your sleep log around 2:00 or 3:00 p.m. and realize your child hasn't had close to three hours of day sleep, you will pull out all the stops to make sure you get that sleep tank filled. A backup nap plan can be to get her to nap in the car, stroller, swing, or carrier, but try to make it different from a habit (crutch) you've been trying to break. For instance, if you've been working on ending co-sleeping at night, don't put him in your bed for your backup plan. Try a car ride or walk in the stroller instead. If nothing else works, you may have to nap coach for a third time in the crib.

Ideally, the backup nap will last at least forty-five minutes, and your child will be awake by 4:30 or 5:00 p.m. so that he's ready to sleep at his regular bedtime.

MY THREE BEST PIECES OF NAP-COACHING ADVICE

* No naps before 8:00 a.m.—even if your child has been up since 5:00! It will throw off the entire day and ingrain in him the habit of getting up too early. I realize this is a tricky dance and your child may get overtired, but it's worth it in the long run.
* Your baby's morning nap should be no longer than one and a half hours. Wake him if need be. I know this goes against the rule of "Never wake a sleeping baby," but I only want you to do it for the morning nap to help regulate your baby's sleeping times.
* Follow the same chair positions for naps as you do at night.

If you have an older child who can't be left alone while you sit in your baby's room, you can do timed checks (see Chapter 6 in Phase 1)—looking in on your baby at regular intervals. Base the timing on your little one's temperament, and be consistent. If you have no idea where to start, then try checking on him every seven minutes, slowly increasing the time. When you go to his crib, be reassuring but quick. You'll defeat the purpose if you pat him until he's asleep during your crib-side check.

DO I HAVE TO NAP COACH AT THE SAME TIME AS NIGHT COACH?

Don't feel guilty if you can't follow all my advice right now. Give yourself (or your babysitter) permission to let the nap coaching slide, and just do what you have to do to get your child some daytime sleep, preferably at predictable times. As nighttime sleep improves, the daytime sleep *might* fall into place on its own. If not, take a deep breath and tackle naps again in another month or two. Keep reminding yourself that good daytime sleep promotes better night-time sleep; it helps you get through it.

If you decide not to address naps and only work on nighttime sleep, then do what you can to help her sleep throughout the day, even calling upon sleep crutches. But know that it will eventually stop working. Either she will wake up the minute you put her down or shortly thereafter, or you will find yourself having to hold her longer and longer to get her to sleep, only to have her nap briefly. Those will be some of your signs to say, "Okay, now it's time to start nap coaching." If you've worked on those other pieces at night and your current nap crutches still work, you can continue to hold off on nap coaching. But if your nap crutches no longer work, you will have to start nap coaching and night coaching simultaneously.

HOW TO NAP COACH MULTIPLES

Although I normally keep twins together at nighttime, I often recommend separating them for naps. Daytime sleep is much more challenging for most babies, and it's even harder if there's a playmate to distract or be distracted by in the next crib. Some parents keep multiples apart for naps for days or weeks, others throughout childhood. Do whichever feels best to you and seems to work for your children.

Nap coaching more than one child can be difficult. If you are lucky and one naps well, you can put him down and nap coach the other in another room (just checking as necessary on the good sleeper). More often, both will need some coaching, so separate them and do timed checks: when you calm one, leave him, then go to the other and calm him, then after ten minutes or so, go back and check on the first baby, and in another ten minutes, check on the second, and so forth. If you are struggling with both or all multiples really not napping well, then you might as well nap train them together in the same room. Instead of timed checks, sit between their cribs and follow the Shuffle along with advice on soothing and chair position in the section "Shuffling with Multiples," on page 145 for the onset of the nap.

FREQUENTLY ASKED QUESTIONS FROM PARENTS OF MULTIPLES

Q: **I have started nap coaching my twins in the same room, but one twin is having short naps and is always waking the other twin. Baby B has always tended to nap longer than Baby A, and I feel like Baby A is disrupting Baby B's naps! What do I do?**

A: This is not uncommon, and often I recommend separating multiples for naps, especially if one multiple is a better napper but gets woken up by the other one. Sometimes I recommend separating them temporarily, but in other cases it's indefinite and only for naps, not nighttime. If you are coaching both, use timed checks.

If one multiple goes to sleep quicker and easier, you can put her down for naps first and then Shuffle Baby B in a separate room. Consider using a pack-and-play in another room for naps.

Use the third, backup nap to even out the scales and have both twins ready for bed between 7:00 and 7:30 p.m. This nap can be in a swing or stroller. If Baby A had two decent naps totaling around two and a half to three hours, then wake Baby A at the forty-five-minute mark, or by 5:00 p.m. Baby B might have had two forty-five-minute naps and therefore may need to go down for this third backup nap earlier or be allowed to sleep until 5:30 p.m. Baby B can still go to bed at the same time as Baby A—remember, Baby B is nap deprived.

Q: **My twins are ten months old, and Baby A is sleeping through the night and Baby B is not. Do they both need a third nap?**

A: Most babies who are sleeping through the night and napping approximately three hours a day will drop their third, bonus nap by nine months. Since Baby B is not sleeping through the night yet and likely not napping well, too, he will definitely need a third nap despite being over nine months old. Baby A will only need a third nap if he isn't napping well. If that's the case, then make sure it's on the shorter side—thirty to forty-five minutes, and awake by 5:00 p.m. Your end goal is to have both babies well fed and ready for bed between 7:00 and 7:30 p.m., regardless of how different their naps were during the day.

Q: **Baby A wants to start her day at 7:00 a.m., and Baby B wants to sleep until 10:00 a.m. (probably because she was up six times last night)—should I let her sleep in?**

A: No, do not let her sleep in. Wake Baby B within thirty minutes of Baby A. This will help regulate her wake-up and, more importantly, keep them on a similar schedule, which will make life oh-so-much easier!

Chapter 9

THIRTEEN TO EIGHTEEN MONTHS

SLEEP GOALS

* *an average of eleven and a quarter hours of uninterrupted night-time sleep*
* *two and a quarter to two and a half hours of daytime sleep spread over two naps, with readiness to transition to one afternoon nap by eighteen months*

At this age, toddlers need an average of eleven and a quarter hours of uninterrupted sleep at night and two and a quarter to two and a half hours during the day. Children at the younger end of this age bracket take two naps, in the morning and afternoon, but by eighteen months, most consolidate to one afternoon nap.

Toddlers are prone to behavioral sleep problems. Their increased mobility (including walking), a peak in separation anxiety around the first birthday, and emotional attachment to such objects as bottles and pacifiers can all complicate bedtime and contribute to nighttime awakenings.

At around fifteen to eighteen months, toddlers transition from two naps to one. That's a tricky stage because there is usually a point when one nap is not enough and two naps are too many. The result is an over-tired child who doesn't sleep well at night. This chapter will give you techniques to help speed up and smooth out that transition, but you will probably still face a bit of crankiness for about three weeks as her body adapts.

As if that weren't enough, temper tantrums often emerge at this age, and toddlers start testing their parents. Bedtime is a common battle-ground for toddlers flexing emerging willpower muscles. A soothing bed-time routine is extremely important for children this age, and adhering consistently to routines and setting clear boundaries is essential. Children are comforted by routines, particularly at this age and on. It is how they can tell what is going to happen next. Toddlers and infants don't know what will happen next without prompts. We know how to go about our days by having schedules and consistent repeatable routines, and the same is true for toddlers. I'm by no means a schedule hound, but I find time and time again that routines help children anticipate, and when they can do that, they feel in control and therefore secure and comforted.

FIRST THINGS FIRST: CREATE A SCHEDULE

We build toddlers' schedules around how much sleep they need, so de-termining how much sleep your toddler requires is the priority. I opened this chapter with the average nap and nighttime sleep goals for this age group—an average of what the American Academy of Pediatrics and the National Sleep Foundation recommend. (I have found over the years of working with families that those goals have worked very well for parents, but you can learn more about the two organizations' recommendations on their websites.) Sleep averages are a range, and you have to find where in that range your child fits. A chart alone can't tell you that—but watching your child's cues can. The best place to start when setting your schedule is the average amount of sleep and going from there.

By now, you probably are well acquainted with your toddler's sleep cues and temperament, and that information is useful when formulating a daily schedule.

Sample Schedule

(Shift earlier if your child wakes between 6:00 and 7:00 a.m.)

7:00–7:30 a.m.	**Wake-up and Breakfast.**
9:00–9:30 a.m.	**One-Hour Morning Nap.** If she's still taking a morning nap. She'll probably want a snack right before or after the nap.
11:30 a.m.–12:30 p.m.	**Lunch.** Depends on morning-nap timing.
12:30–1:30 p.m.	**Afternoon Nap.** About an hour and a half if it's a second nap; about two to two and a half hours if it's the only nap of the day. Snack after nap.
5:00–5:30 p.m.	**Dinner.**
6:00–6:30 p.m.	**Bedtime Prep.** Start bath and bedtime preparations.
7:00–8:00 p.m.	**In Bed.** Drowsy but awake. Bedtime should be at 7:30 or 8:00, and by *bedtime,* I mean in the crib, not in the bathtub or on your lap reading stories. Toddlers this age can fight sleep much more vehemently than younger babies.

Children need regular nap times, regular bedtimes, and three recognizable mealtimes. Their bodies need the routine to regulate day and night hormone cycles and to keep them in sync with their internal clocks. Their little hearts and minds need certainty and predictability to feel secure. But I also believe in some flexibility.

The sample schedule is a good starting point, but you can adjust it. For instance, if your child is an early riser, move the morning nap earlier.

You may also have to play with the schedule a bit to accommodate the needs of your other children. Sleep times are averages. Some kids sleep more, some sleep less, but the variations are a lot less than many parents think. If your child is napping and sleeping poorly, chances are you are underestimating how much sleep she needs.

Even when you do achieve a workable schedule, natural variations inevitably occur. Some days she will eat or sleep a little more, and some days she will eat or sleep a little less. Growth spurts, runny noses, new teeth, or just a bad mood—toddlers have their off days just like we do—can all create minor variations in her daily routine. But don't let the schedule get totally out of whack. As you learn to read her sleep cues and she becomes better rested, you will be able to tinker with the schedule more easily. Watch her daytime behavior. If she's easy and content, she's probably on a pretty good schedule. If she's fussy and demanding, she may need longer naps, an earlier bedtime, a later wake-up time—or all of the above.

If you have to skip a nap because of a doctor's appointment or some other essential interruption, most toddlers fare better missing the morning nap than the afternoon one. You can temporarily move the afternoon nap up a bit to compensate for a missed morning one.

Barring unusual dietary or health concerns, thirteen- to eighteen-month-olds should have three recognizable mealtimes a day. Most snack twice a day, after the morning nap and upon awakening from the afternoon nap. Check with your pediatrician, but healthy children in this age group on a normal growth curve can almost always go eleven to twelve hours at night without food. If your child is still waking to eat frequently, you have to adjust her body clock and change her sleep habits. I'll give you some tips on how to eliminate nighttime feeding on page 201. Let's explore your ideal routine a bit more.

Wake-up. A good wake-up time is anywhere from 6:00 to 7:30. Remember that one of the basic rules of sleep hygiene is to wake up and go to bed at about the same time every day (about a twelve-hour time frame). If your baby wakes up before 6:00, the following "Early Birds" section will help you teach him to sleep later.

Some toddlers sleep past 7:30. If it works for you and your family—and by *works*, I mean that she is getting good naps and at least eleven to eleven and a half hours of uninterrupted sleep at night—that's fine; leave it alone. When she gets closer to starting preschool, make sure you leave plenty of time for her to gradually adjust to an earlier wake-up. But an 8:30–9:00 a.m. wake-up throws off many toddlers. They nap too late or inconsistently, and they go to bed too late and don't sleep well at night. You can either just start waking her at 7:30—gently at first—or you can adjust more gradually. Get her up about fifteen to thirty minutes earlier each day until her wake-up is 7:30.

Morning rituals, the counterpoints of your evening ones, are still a good idea to reinforce her understanding of wake-up time versus sleep time. Throw open the blinds, switch on the lights, sing some cheery good-morning songs, and start your day. It's your choice whether you feed her immediately or have some playtime; however, if you choose to feed, don't do so in the dark, or you risk her falling back to sleep. The parent who comes home the latest from work can make mornings his or her special game time.

Morning Nap. While she's still on a two-nap-a-day schedule, her morning nap should begin around 9:00–9:30. If she's sleeping well at night, the morning nap should be two to three hours after she woke up. Watch the sleep windows to determine exactly what time is right for her. Remember to provide that wind-down time to get ready for sleep, maybe a book or two or an abbreviated version of her bedtime routine.

She will probably sleep about an hour, maybe an hour and a half. I discourage longer morning naps because the afternoon nap is usually the more important one, the one that she will hold on to for another two or three years. If she sleeps two or three hours in the morning, consider waking her after ninety minutes or else she is going to have a tough time going down for her afternoon nap. And if ninety minutes seems too long and she is still not wanting an afternoon nap, wake her up after forty-five minutes. After the morning nap is a nice time to visit the playground, go for a walk, or do some shopping. She will be refreshed and less likely to doze off in the car or stroller and throw off her afternoon nap schedule.

Lunch and the Afternoon Nap. A lot of parents don't realize that toddlers get hungry more quickly than we do. Lunch is often at 11:30, almost always by noon or 12:30. You've usually got some playtime after lunch and before the afternoon nap. Usually, you will aim for two to three hours between the end of the morning nap and the start of the afternoon one. Again, watch her sleep signals to get her down at the right time.

The afternoon nap usually lasts about one and a half hours. Once she consolidates to one nap, aim to get her down sometime between 12:30 and 1:30, and she'll probably sleep two to two and a half hours. A pretty typical afternoon nap runs from about 1:00 to 3:30, but it can vary thirty minutes in either direction. When she gets up, it's time for another snack and some playtime before dinner.

Dinner. An early dinnertime, 5:00–5:30, is usually wise, even if that means she doesn't eat with her parents. She can always have fruit or a bit of dessert with you while you eat dinner. The early schedule helps both her eating and her sleeping. I find that children have eating windows, too, and if you feed them too late, they don't

Sleep Lady Tip

Remember when we talked about emotional availability? (See Chapter 3, "Getting to Know Your Child.") That focused connection with your child is always important—but it's absolutely essential that we be patient and fully present at bedtime. Try as best as possible to leave your workday behind. Forget about your to-do list for a moment. Put aside that email or phone call that upset you. Better yet, at bedtime, put aside your phone! Leave it in another room while you focus on your child. It will still be there once he's asleep. Having so many screens and devices distracting us is probably the biggest change I've seen since I started developing the Sleep Lady system. I know it's not easy to ignore your phone, but the benefits—to both you and your child—are huge.

eat very well. The last thing you want is a poor dinner eater who then wakes up demanding a midnight snack. (You'll get enough of that in adolescence!)

Bedtime Prep. Bedtime prep is not your child's actual bedtime. Bedtime is when she is in her crib, drowsy but awake, and you are in your chair position during the Shuffle. Toddlers need a lot of transition time to prepare for sleep, in terms of both brain hormones and emotional readiness to separate from their parents until morning. Bedtime routines must be structured and predictable, and they absolutely cannot be rushed. Leave enough time—maybe it will be half an hour for your child, maybe an hour (including bath time)—and make it a fun and loving time, a time she eagerly anticipates. Keep the bedtime routine in her bedroom, not all over the house, so she incorporates the message that it is time to slow down and get ready to sleep. It's okay to start downstairs with some pre-bedtime evening rituals, but as soon as the bath is done, stay in the bedroom. Get any unpleasant aspect of bedtime over at the beginning so you can spend the rest of it calming down in enjoyable ways.

If your toddler is healthy and growing well, she won't need a feeding prior to bedtime, but some toddlers still like to nurse briefly or have a cup of water before bed. If she's taking a bottle at bedtime, switch to a cup and think about water instead of milk. You can do this gradually if you like, moving from an eight-ounce bottle to a four-ounce bottle and then to a cup. Some people use milk or formula and dilute it for a few nights before switching to water. If you walk or rock her before sleep, keep it brief and in her bedroom. If she still listens to music at bedtime, start phasing it out before she actually gets into her crib. Put her down drowsy but still awake.

BABIES ARE NATURAL BOOKWORMS

As you turn the pages of *Are You My Mother?* for the umpteenth time, you wonder how your baby cannot be tired of this book yet. Research shows, however, that picture books—even those ones that both you and your baby have memorized—are not just a great way to develop the brain. They do wonders for bonding and soothing, especially at bedtime.

While your baby is not actually "reading" the book, she is learning the important elements of reading—things like practicing page turning and distinguishing words. As your baby grows, you will notice she imitates your finger pointing and voice inflections as you read characters' dialogue.

Reading books can be a great way to cue bedtime. Some parents choose to play an audiobook, turn on cartoons, or read an illustrated bedtime story—but some recent research showed that of these options, the old-fashioned book is best for developing baby's brain. Try to avoid the e-book versions of classic childhood books, especially at bedtime and nap time, since the glow of the electronic device can disrupt sleep cycles and circadian rhythms, your child's natural "body clock." And swiping a tablet is not as gratifying for a child as turning a page and feeling the achievement of finishing a book, as you close the cover, saying, "The end."

By reading picture books, you are helping your child's neural connections and her ability to eventually learn to read all by herself. In fact, thirteen to eighteen months is the ideal age to incorporate more books into your baby's life. They are experiencing a slow but steady growth in vocabulary and can point to pictures and recognize faces and characters. You can watch them enjoy it.

This kind of engagement, especially when it is with a family member or caregiver, also fosters a closeness and interaction beneficial to promoting nighttime security, bedtime cues, and a healthy sleepy-time routine. Parents love this bedtime story time, too. You may keep reading together for years to come.

(For more on the detrimental effects of the blue light or "glow" emitted from pads, phones, tablets, even some light bulbs, please turn to page 30 in Phase 1.)

Bedtime. Aim to have her asleep—asleep, not getting ready for bed—between 7:00 and 8:00. Watch her cues and trust your own intuition. You might move bedtime a little later, to 8:00, after she has begun sleeping consistently through the night and at nap time and has caught up on all her missed sleep. Remember, she still needs, on average, eleven hours and fifteen minutes of sleep at night.

Now that your baby is standing and probably walking, be prepared for some crib gymnastics. Many babies stand in their cribs; you put them down, and they bounce right back up. For a one-year-old, this is literally stand-up comedy. But no matter how hilarious she thinks it is, try not to join in the merriment or she'll play jack-in-the-box all night. Pat the mattress, put her down once, when you think she will stay down (i.e., the magic moment), and then pat her. Experiment and use your intuition. If she gets up again, keep patting the mattress as a signal to her, but don't keep laying her down. This works better if you're sitting rather than standing over the crib. She'll get down when she's ready, and she'll be ready faster if you don't help her turn it into a game.

Note: On many occasions, parents who work in careers with atypical hours ask whether it is possible to keep their toddlers up later and start their days later. My answer is always "I can't make any promises that it will work, but we can certainly try!" A few conditions apply, however. The first is that everyone in the family has to be able to sleep later, which means the child isn't preparing to go to day care or preschool early in the morning. The second condition is the family has to be committed to filling the daytime sleep tank and shifting the entire schedule later, including naps, meals, and so on.

Because of circadian rhythms, which are pretty sturdy by this age, there is no guarantee this will work. Use your intuition and watch your child's sleep cues and behaviors to determine whether moving back to a more traditional schedule is best for your child's sleep needs and overall development. For example, if your child is now going to bed at 9:00 p.m. but continues to wake at 7:00 a.m., you should shift back to an earlier bedtime so your child can get the sleep she needs at nighttime.

HOW TO COMMUNICATE YOUR
SCHEDULE TO CAREGIVERS

Whether you have a stay-at-home nanny, a day care center, a once-in-a-while sitter, or a grandparent taking care of your toddler during the day, communicating and maintaining your new schedule can be tricky, but not futile. Even when playing by the rules of other providers and facilities, all does not have to be lost. Here are some strategies to help you all get on the same page when you become committed to sleep coaching:

1. Make a copy of your daily schedule—like the one in this chapter—and give it to your caregivers, letting them know you have begun sleep coaching and that for just a few weeks, you are asking them to be mindful of the schedule when they can.

2. Each morning when you leave your child, let the caregiver know what time your child woke up that morning, as well as how many times during the night she was up, and therefore what time she will most likely be ready for her first morning nap.

3. Ask the childcare providers if they can work toward a total of two and a quarter to two and a half hours of nap time no matter how they get the child to sleep. We cannot expect or presume they will be comfortable or allowed to adhere to the Shuffle or reduce the use of sleep crutches, but you can certainly ask. Sometimes that is the best we can do. Just remember that your child getting sleep throughout the day, no matter how it is accomplished, whether by rocking or another sleep crutch, will still help you with nighttime sleep coaching, as your child will not be overtired and will have two and a quarter to two and a half hours of daytime sleep in her sleep tank.

4. Some childcare providers just won't nap train (day care centers often have their own schedules and methods). If that is the case, you can still sleep coach by adhering to your morning and evening routines, focusing on getting the child to sleep through the night. Then, on weekends, nap coach diligently. Don't worry about how that might feel inconsistent. It will take longer, but it can still work. For instructions on nap coaching your thirteen- to eighteen-month-old and how to handle transitioning to one nap, see the section "Much Ado About Napping" on page 213.

TAKE NOTE OF DEVELOPMENTAL CHANGES

Walking and running and throwing fits, oh my! Just when you think you have your daily schedule and coaching plan, here come the developmental changes to throw a wrench in them. Developmental changes are those milestone moments that are super exciting to witness and indicate our child is thriving. How fast children grow and develop is a wonder to watch, but beware these milestones, as they can also introduce some new challenges, particularly when sleep coaching. Many times, clients come to me saying they were doing just fine with their coaching until suddenly their toddler seemed to go off the rails. We discussed sleep regressions in Phase 1, and often a developmental milestone will cause a regression in your baby's sleep progress. Maybe your toddler was a terrific sleeper and then suddenly refuses to go down. Or he would comply with his bedtime routine a few months ago but now has become quite opinionated! Once you learn to recognize the culprit, you will be able to set yourself and your baby right back on track. What follows are the most common developmental changes you can expect in the thirteen- to eighteen-month age range and strategies to help with sleep regressions they might cause, so you all may continue the journey to better sleep.

SEPARATION ANXIETY

Separation anxiety hits a peak right around the first birthday and can go all the way to eighteen months or beyond, depending on your child's temperament. Saying "Night-night" to parents can be tough. That nice, long transition to bedtime, good focused time with one or both parents, helps ease the fears. Although most one-year-olds can't say much, they understand an awful lot, so give plenty of verbal assurances that you are nearby.

Even after some parents complete the Shuffle successfully, they like to stay in the room as their toddler falls asleep to help with the separation. That's okay as long as you don't fall back into all your pre-Shuffle habits and she doesn't wake up at night needing you to go sit there again and again. If you choose not to stay in the room, it may help if you reassure the toddler that you'll be nearby—and then keep your word. Instead of going downstairs to clean the kitchen, which can seem very far away from the crib, stay in a nearby room so she feels your closeness as she nods off.

Use Loveys

Loveys, usually a special stuffed animal or security blanket, are very useful as children cope with separation anxiety. Many families have told me their babies resisted all attempts to have them bond with a special toy the first year but quickly attached to an object around age one. They may choose one of their own at this age, maybe from among that batch of first-birthday presents. They may also abandon the lovey they favored in infancy and choose a new one.

To encourage the bond, incorporate the lovey in bedtime and nap-time rituals. For instance, if you play peekaboo before bed, the lovey should play peekaboo, too. If you stroll around the room saying good night to favorite objects, the lovey should say good night, too. Tuck the lovey in the crib with her at bedtime and nap time. At some point, your baby might mimic bedtime activities for the lovey, giving her lamb or teddy bear a good-night kiss and tucking it in.

Even if the lovey bond hasn't stuck before, I strongly recommend making another effort now. Toddlers often get emotionally attached to the breast or their bottle, sippy cup, or pacifier, and they may wake up often at night wanting a bottle or cup, not because they are really hungry or thirsty but because it helps them feel secure. Easing the attachment to the breast, bottle, and so on goes hand in hand with strengthening the attachment to the lovey—you'll have trouble fostering the lovey bond if you don't reduce the previous attachment simultaneously.

Some parents worry if a toddler starts lugging the lovey around with him all the time. That may be a minor inconvenience, because you have to remember to take the lovey with you, but I don't regard it as a problem. Pacifiers are a little different, and I don't recommend having toddlers walk around with them all day. If a toddler is attached to a pacifier, it may well be this is his lovey. Overusing it at this age may interfere with communication and speech development. Consider getting rid of the pacifier, or restricting it to bedtime and naps, long car rides, or doctor's appointments. If you want to learn how to wean off the pacifier altogether, turn to the discussion on page 318 in Chapter 11, "Two and a Half to Five Years."

THROWING THE LOVEY (OR PACIFIER)

Some toddlers like to throw their loveys out of their cribs, mostly at bedtime or nap time. It is somewhat like a game of fetch your toddler is playing with you. He'll throw it out of the crib and then scream for you to come get it. What's a parent to do when a toddler continues to throw his lovey—or pacifier, which, if he still uses it, has probably become his lovey—out of the crib?

Note that this often happens when you are in a Shuffle chair position that is no longer seated crib-side. Let's say you are sitting in the hall, in view, and he throws the lovey to the floor. Do not retrieve it. Instead, tell him, "Lie down, and I will come give you your lovey/binky/whatever." Keep repeating this until he lies down. Once he is down, go into the room and get his lovey.

Now tell him, "No throwing lovey." You can even talk for the lovey and say, "Don't throw me out. I want to snuggle and sleep with you!" Make the lovey seem sad that he was thrown out. You may have a toddlers who likes to test the limits, and even after you return the lovey to him, he throws it again. Repeat above, instructing, "Lie down, and I will get the lovey for the last time." (Some parents want to give their toddler one more chance, and others don't; it's up to you.)

When you return, tell him that if he throws it again, you will not give it back to him. If he were to throw it again (I have had a few who do), you must stand your ground and not return it despite the wailing and pleading for his lovey. Continue to use your voice to verbally reassure him from your Shuffle position. Once he is completely asleep or when you check on him one last time before you turn in, return his lovey without waking him (of course).

TEETHING

Teething can interfere with sleep, but far less than many parents anticipate or believe. You have likely already encountered some cut teeth by this age, and it may seem like little white spots are appearing in your child's mouth all the time! Usually, children who sleep well will experience minor disruptions when they begin to teethe (except for the molars, which come in between ages one and two and can cause more pain). But children who are overtired or who don't know how to put themselves to sleep may have more trouble when teething. It's like she is saying, *I'm already tired, I'm not sure how to go to sleep, and now I have this pain in my mouth. That's going to put me over the edge, so I'm going to stay up and yell.*

To sort out how much of the sleep disruption stems from those new little teeth, compare day with night behavior. If she's her usual self all day but extra cranky or difficult at night, it is probably not the teeth. If a usually cheerful child is miserable around the clock, the trouble may well be a particularly painful tooth. The pain usually subsides as soon as the tooth comes through the gum. Ask your pediatrician about using infant acetaminophen or a similar painkiller. Occasionally, I've worked with children who have a slew of symptoms—diaper rash, low-grade fever, diarrhea, disturbed sleep, excessive drooling, poor appetite, and crankiness—but they are a minority, and the problems usually pass as soon as the tooth pops out.

If teething problems crop up while you are in the middle of the Shuffle, progress may slow down for a few days while the tooth comes through, but stick with it. You might want to be a little more soothing, do a little more holding or patting, but don't regress to all the patterns and crutches you are trying to change. If you are just about to embark on the Sleep Lady Shuffle and you suspect a tooth is about to erupt, consider delaying any changes for a day or two.

HEAD BANGING

Sometimes toddlers go to great lengths to tell you—when they can't verbalize—how they are feeling. And sometimes, they choose behaviors that look like self-harm and usually alarm parents (for good reason!). At this age, head banging is a big factor, with parents seeking help because the crib has become somewhat of a mosh pit. I spoke with occupational therapist Lindsey Biel about the complex nature of head banging and what to do about it. Here is what she advises:

One of the most disturbing things parents may see is when their children bang their heads—against the mattress, against the crib bars, against the walls, and against Mom or Dad's body. The first thing to do is check for an ear infection, vision problems, dental issues, and teething. [See the previous chapter for more on teething.] Some kids will head bang to distract themselves from headaches, and this behavior could, in rare cases, be the only noticeable sign of a seizure. If head banging is persistent, talk to your pediatrician, who may refer you to a pediatric neurologist. You certainly want to pad crib bars or any other hard surface to avoid a serious injury and pull your child's crib or bed away from the wall and place it on a thick rug. Use padded vertical crib liners that zip around each crib slat. If head banging is intense, your pediatrician may suggest an OT evaluation. Your OT may suggest that you have your child wear a helmet to prevent injury.

For some kids, head banging can be a form of intense sensory-seeking that can be horrendous to watch. [See Chapter 15 for information about sleep and sensory processing disorder.] A few quick things to try:

* Regularly massage her scalp and face with your hands or a vibrating massager.
* Let her sit on your lap, facing you, and grind her face into yours. Try pressing your chin against her forehead and moving your jaw back and forth as you hum.

* Let him push items with his forehead—for example, a pillow-filled box or a dust mop—across the floor.

At the same time, be a bit cautious about whether your child is engaging in this behavior to get your attention. Do you come running after a few head bumps? You may be reinforcing this behavior.

TANTRUMS

The dictionary's definition of a tantrum is "an uncontrolled outburst of anger and frustration, typically in a young child." For parents, it's a downright mortifying event, no matter which way you look at it. Toddlers understand more than they can say, which can be frustrating for them, especially if they want to negotiate with you (or outright protest). For instance, at this age, your toddler might know what you mean when you tell him no, but now he wants to have a conversation about it—but can't! Or you might be starting to make some changes like weaning from the pacifier or only giving a bottle once a day. When they make big changes (and these are huge in the world of toddlerdom), parents have to expect tantrums.

Parents scramble for advice and strategies on how to control tantrums. In my opinion, far too many child experts instruct parents to use time-outs as a response. I am not one of them. In fact, I believe placing a toddler who can't fully express himself in a corner or on a chair will inadvertently shame him for having what feels like big emotions for him that he doesn't know how to handle. It's not just time-outs that I avoid recommending but any kind of response that doesn't help a child learn the skill of self-regulation—like walking away from the child, which sends a message of dismissal, or avoiding eye contact when they are upset, which defies the act of compassion necessary for our child to bond and attach to us securely. We want children to know it's okay to have big feelings and to eventually learn to understand their emotions and over the years learn how to process them and manage them. It's one of our many tasks as parents to help teach and model to them. The same is true for learning the skill of putting oneself to sleep independently.

This all connects to the bottle weaning, pacifier weaning, and weaning from nursing and sleep coaching in general. It is all about how we teach toddlers to self-regulate with reassurance and don't leave them alone to figure it out. This is why it's important for parents to address daytime behavior in addition to bedtime behavior. If your toddler throws a tantrum for a bottle during the day and you give him a bottle, and then during a night tantrum you don't, that's confusing to a toddler. You must lay the groundwork during the day. Remember that toddlers experience our consistency and boundaries as comforting, and that helps them to feel safe and know what to expect.

I have found that the technique, which has origins in the positive parenting field, called *hug-hold* works the best for not only subsiding tantrums but to help toddlers process their emotions, name/identify them when they are a bit older, and calm themselves down on a physiological level. It also does wonders for parents' blood pressure! By their nature, the steps of hug-hold are calming, so it is an appropriate sleep-time strategy when your toddler throws a tantrum at bedtime.

Hug-Hold

Wait for a short lull in the tantrum so you can pick your toddler up, facing out.

1. Go to a quiet spot where the tantrum did not start. In my house, I took my girls to the stairway and sat them on my lap on the step.
2. Hold her on your lap facing out, put your arms around her arms so her arms are immobile at her sides.
3. Use a passive hold. The gentle pressure actually acts as comforting input for many toddlers.
4. Hold her and rock (remember your toddler's face is not facing yours). Rock her forward and backward slowly while you breathe

in through your nose and out through your mouth and whisper, "Shh, shh." No words, just soothing sounds. The breathing alone will calm *you* down, centering you and giving you more patience to continue the process.

5. Notice she starts to mimic you by breathing more steadily. You might now hear her breath rattle a bit as she catches her breath and begins to calm.

6. Once she is calm, redirect or distract her. We don't want to dwell; just move on. Release her and say something like "Let's go find your blocks," or "I wonder where bunny went."

7. As children get older, you can use this approach, expand on it, and have a conversation about it once they are calm. "I understand you were angry when Mommy said no cookie before dinner. We have a rule, 'No cookies before dinner,' and you threw your cup. What other ways can you show you are mad? Maybe you can go yell in a pillow or stamp your feet." You are acknowledging her feelings, helping name them, and offering options for what she could do with those feelings.

Note: Hug-hold along with a constructive discussion for older children acknowledges her feelings, calms her down, and gives her tools, *but she is still not getting the cookie.* It is the same thing at bedtime: we are calming, giving tools to sleep, *but you are not putting her to sleep.*

CHANGES IN EATING

Toddlerhood means milk isn't at the heart of our children's diets anymore. That's a huge change, as by the first birthday, they get most of their nutrition and their calories from solid foods. The American Academy of Pediatrics now recommends they take two to three glasses of milk (eighteen to twenty-four ounces)—the advice varies a bit, so consult your doctor, especially if you want to discuss nutritious alternatives to cow's milk. If your toddler eats a lot of dairy products like yogurt, she's getting her calcium and vitamin D and doesn't need to drink as many glasses of milk.

Remember, she's not an infant anymore, so feeding her before bedtime or offering the dream feed will not prolong her sleep. To the contrary, it might just fuel her habit of associating drinking with sleep and her wanting to drink all night. It may also invite her to wake up and let you know loudly that she has a soaking-wet diaper. Introduce a cup now if you haven't already, even if you plan to continue nursing. Offer the sippy cup—of water, milk of your choice, formula, or whatever your doctor recommends—at each meal.

Transitioning to a Cup

How long you breastfeed is a personal decision; however, at this age, the cup is recommended to be introduced at meals and to generally practice with. What this section aims to do is stop the breast or bottle from being needed by a toddler to fall asleep. The important point is to teach our toddlers how to go to sleep without sucking to sleep.

For bottle-feeders, it is recommended that by twelve months toddlers are weaned from a bottle and are drinking out of a cup. This isn't just a milestone, it's a lifestyle shift for everyone in the family, so it's no wonder toddlers throw so many tantrums! Weaning from the breast and/or bottle and introducing a cup (more on that in a bit) will change your bedtime routine and your child's eating and drinking habits, and it could disrupt sleep coaching, especially if your toddler has been feeding to sleep.

 Sleep Lady Tip

To transition from bottle to cup, start with the first morning bottle. Fill it with only three or four ounces, and then move quickly to breakfast. After a few days, offer a sippy cup of milk. Then start reducing the amount of milk in the bottles that you offer before (or after) lunch and dinner. Give him a cup with his meal instead. You may find that if you give him the bottle after his meal, he won't really want it much anymore, because he won't be hungry.

If you eliminate it completely, and many parents do around the first birthday, I recommend going from breastfeeding to a cup, not to a bottle. Weaning should be an easy, natural transition. It seldom disrupts sleep, but sleep that is already disrupted can make weaning harder for an overtired, unhappy baby. Weaning is more difficult if your toddler has not learned how to fall asleep without a breast or bottle in her mouth.

Many mothers continue nursing the first thing in the morning and once at bedtime well beyond the first birthday. That's only a problem when the baby can't go to sleep, or back to sleep, without being breastfed. (The same applies to bedtime bottle-feeding.) In that case, you are facing a sleep crutch issue, not a weaning issue, and I'll talk more about how to change those patterns later in the "Sleep Crutches and Solutions" section on page 201.

A CUP-UH-LA PIECES OF ADVICE
FOR WEANING FROM THE BOTTLE

* **Introduce a cup.** Ideally, you'll have been giving your baby sips from a cup by six to nine months old. If not, start giving him different kinds of cups until you find one he likes. Some kids take to sippy cups right away; others prefer flip-up straws. Others don't care what kind of cup it is as long as it's blue, or green, or has puppies or princesses on it.
* **Eliminate the bottle, starting with lunch.** Lunch is the meal at which the bottle is probably least important to him. Instead, serve his milk in his now-favorite cup.
* **Take away the dinner bottle.** Once he's used to having a cup at lunch, after around four to seven days, swap out the bottle for a cup at dinner.
* **Next, tackle the morning bottle.** Instead of handing your toddler a bottle as soon as he gets up, go right to the table for breakfast.
* **Finally, let the bedtime bottle go.** If your child has had a good dinner, which may not be as much food as you might think—he doesn't need a bottle before bedtime to sleep through the night. If he doesn't need the bottle to put himself to sleep, then you may be able to skip the bottle at this point, since he's gotten used to doing without it during the day.

THE SLEEP LADY SHUFFLE

So you have created a daily schedule and taken into consideration any developmental changes that may be occurring as you prepare to sleep coach, and now it's time to Shuffle! You've seen the step-by-step Sleep Lady Shuffle guide at the end of Phase 1. Here is where we put it to work for your thirteen- to eighteen-month-old. As you know by now, the Sleep Lady Shuffle is a gentle behavioral modification technique that lets you be a comforting presence as your child learns to put herself to sleep and back to sleep in her crib. The Shuffle is used to nap coach as well, but for the purpose of this section, I will first guide you through sleep coaching at night. I would be remiss if I didn't tell you that there is no such thing as a no-cry sleep-coaching system, so expect some tears. Remind yourself that you will always be there to assure her that she is not alone, she is safe, and she is loved and supported as she slowly learns this new skill.

Before beginning the Shuffle, please turn to Chapter 5: Prepping for Sleep-Coaching Success, where I lay the groundwork for sleep coaching. It is best to begin sleep coaching at bedtime, after a great day of naps, getting in naps any way you can. You will have better success at nighttime if your baby's daytime sleep tank is filled. You should follow the Shuffle schedule, moving on to the next position even if your child has had a bad night or two, fussing or waking more frequently. *Don't be surprised if there's a little regression or protest the first night of each new chair position.* If your child gets sick during the Shuffle, you might want to pause and freeze or maintain your position until she's feeling a little better. You might even have to move a little bit closer during an illness to offer more comfort, but then resume your sleep shaping when she recovers.

TIPS FOR THE FIRST THREE SHUFFLE NIGHTS

1. *Don't get into a power struggle about laying your toddler down—you won't win!* If he is sitting or standing in the crib, pat the mattress and encourage him to lie down. Stay calm and say things like

"Sh-sh," "Night-night," and "It's okay, lie down." Sit down in your chair to encourage him to lie down and be closer to your level.

2. *You can stroke, pat, rub*, sh-sh, *or sing to your child intermittently through the rails of the crib.* But don't do it constantly until he falls asleep, or it will become his new sleep crutch. Stop when he is starting to fall asleep. (Some toddlers don't like to be touched as they fall asleep; follow your instincts and his cues.) If you notice every time you stop patting your child that he starts crying, you are patting too much. Try to touch less and less during the first three nights, knowing that on night 4, you will be moving farther away.

3. *The parent controls the touch.* Don't let the toddler fall asleep grasping your finger or hand, for example, because he will wake up when you move, and it will start all over again. Pat or stroke a different part of his body or the top of his hand.

4. *If the toddler becomes hysterical, pick him up to calm him.* Stay in his room; don't walk around the house or sit down in the rocker. Don't let him fall asleep in your arms. Ideally, calm him while you are standing with him in your arms. When he's calm, kiss him, put him back in the crib, and sit near him in the chair. Make soothing sounds and pat or stroke him. If you pick him up and he's immediately calm, then you've been had. Instead of you training him to sleep, he trained you to pick him up! Wait a little longer next time. Trust your instincts and your knowledge of your child. You will know within a night or two whether picking him up helps or gets him more upset.

5. *Stay by his crib until he is sound asleep at bedtime and during all night awakenings the first three days of the Shuffle.* If you rush out of the room the second he closes his eyes, he will wake up and be upset, and you'll have to start all over.

6. *Return to your Shuffle position, and follow these rules each time the toddler wakes during the first three nights* (as long as you and your

pediatrician have decided to end night feeding). Go to the crib, give him a kiss, encourage him to lie down if necessary, and sit in the chair. Do this at each awakening until 6:00 a.m.

NIGHTS 1–3: NEXT TO THE CRIB

Once bath, stories, and songs are over, put the toddler in the crib calm and awake, and *sit in a chair next to the crib.* If she cries or fusses, you can stroke or pat her intermittently, but don't do it constantly or you'll just create a new negative association. You can touch more on the first night. You can sing during the get-ready-for-bed stage, but once it's time for her to sleep, stick to calming *sh-sh* or *night-night* sounds. You might want to try closing your eyes. That makes it easier not to talk to her too much, and it also conveys a sleepy-time message. Stay there until she falls asleep. If she gets up, remember not to keep putting her back down.

Make sure that you, the parent, control the touch. Instead of having her hold your hand or finger, you should pat her. Make sure that you do not caress her too steadily; do it on and off. Count to yourself if it helps—count to ten touching, then count to sixty not touching, then touch for another ten counts. You don't want to swap one sleep crutch,

> ### Sleep Lady Tip
>
> When you soothe your child by going to her crib to pat or rub her back, it is important that you control the touch. Instead of having her hold your hand or finger, you should pat her. Make sure you don't caress her too steadily, or else she might cry when you stop. Do it on and off. Count to yourself if it helps—count to ten touching, then count to sixty not touching, then touch for another ten counts. You don't want to swap one negative association like rocking for another—like your constant touch for the sound of your voice.

like rocking, for another—like your constant touch or the sound of your voice. You know you're touching too much if when you stop touching, she starts crying.

On night 1, if necessary or if you are not quite comfortable, you can do more touching. But don't touch steadily; do it on and off, and know that you will need to taper off or start patting more intermittently beginning on night 2. You will know that you are touching too much if you stop patting and your toddler cries. Similarly, during your first three nights next to the crib, try to be mindful of how much touch you are offering, because on night 4, you will be positioned farther away from your toddler and won't be touching as much. You will defeat moving away from the crib if you go crib-side each time to, for instance, pat him to sleep. (The no-snuggles or no-picking-up-the-toddler rules, by the way, do not apply to a child who is sick, frightened, or startled.)

Unlike many other sleep-coaching methods, with the Shuffle, you can pick up your toddler to calm him down when he gets extremely upset. Try not to do this either immediately after putting him in the crib at bedtime or as the first thing during the night when he wakes. Try patting him, shushing him, or handing him his lovey or pacifier, for example, and sitting in the chair. Tell him that it's okay, and stay in the chair until he falls asleep. *Do this for each wakening.*

Many parents I work with find solace when I remind them that their toddler isn't crying because she is hurt or abandoned. You are there with her in the same room, providing care and support and reassurance, teaching her a new skill and how to be independent. The toddler is simply learning something new (and so are you!), and doing things for the first time can feel like hard work.

NIGHTS 4–6: HALFWAY TO THE DOOR

Move the chair *about halfway to the door.* If the room is small, move the chair to the doorway as in night 7. Continue the soothing sounds, but stay in the chair as much as you can. Get up to pat or stroke him a little if necessary, or make the same soothing sounds with your voice as you have used the past three nights. Again, try not to pick him up unless he's hysterical, and if you do pick him up, follow the technique I described for the first three nights. Stay in the chair until he falls asleep. If you allow yourself to move to the crib side and pat him almost to sleep, you will create a crutch and undo any progress you've made.

Many parents during these nights create new sleep crutches without knowing it. They will move the chair farther away from the crib, and instead of picking up their crying child (an old crutch), they will sing him to sleep (a new crutch). As you move farther away on the following nights, the child will not be able to hear the song, and then you will have a crying toddler on your hands. Another trap is parents getting up and patting their child too much to soothe him. Naomi, a mother of a fifteen-month-old, found that if she just patted her toddler for thirty seconds during the Shuffle, he would fall right to sleep. It was that easy. But when Naomi worked late one night, her husband said the toddler was still awake—and grouchy to boot. Naomi went in to pat him, and thirty seconds later, her toddler was asleep. This mother had created a new sleep crutch without knowing it.

NIGHTS 7–9: CHAIR AT THE DOORWAY, INSIDE THE ROOM

Continue the same soothing techniques from your chair, remembering to intervene as little as possible. If he cries a little bit, keep calmly reassuring him. He'll know that you are there, and he will fall asleep.

NIGHTS 10–12: INTO THE HALLWAY, IN VIEW

Move into the hall with the door open enough so that he can still see you. You can keep making those *sh-sh* sounds, not constantly but enough to let him know that Mom or Dad is close by and responsive. Stay until he falls asleep.

NIGHTS 13 AND ON

Next, you are going to stay *in the hallway or in a very nearby room, where the child cannot see you but can hear you.* You can make some reassuring *sh-sh* sounds, not constantly but enough to let her know that Mom or Dad is close by and responsive. If she cries, try checking on her from her bedroom door—without going all the way into the room. Be calm and reassuring. Make some comforting sounds, conveying that you are not far away and that you know she can put herself to sleep.

A significant number of toddlers start falling asleep and staying asleep by now. But many parents have one more step to take: giving him the opportunity to fall asleep without their visual presence. Leaving him to fall asleep without a parent in his room may seem like a huge leap for you, but it's not as big for him anymore. All that chair moving has given him nearly two weeks of preparation. He has given up some negative associations, is starting to master a new skill, and has learned that you are always nearby.

Sleep Lady Tip

Children get ritualized easily. Make the changes every three days—or less. Dragging it out makes it harder, not easier, for your toddler. Give it more than three days, and he'll expect you to stay exactly where you are— and get mad or upset when you try to double that distance.

Occasionally, a toddler will cry or fuss a little for a few nights, but don't rush in prematurely. Let him calm down and nod off. If you check on him from the doorway, try to be fairly unobtrusive, and don't check too frequently. You want to reassure him you are nearby and have faith he can do this. Remind yourself of how far you and your toddler have come!

IF YOUR TODDLER IS STILL WAKING AT NIGHT

If these techniques don't eliminate those final night awakenings, you might be putting your child to bed when he's too drowsy. It's easier for a toddler to put himself to sleep at bedtime than in the middle of the night—particularly if he was 90 percent asleep before his head hit the pillow. Try putting him down when he's a bit more alert, even if it means backing up and doing a few more days of the Shuffle. You may find that an earlier bedtime also helps him conquer the night awakenings. Try moving bedtime a half hour earlier. If you are still nursing at bedtime, try doing that feeding a little earlier in the evening to further weaken the link between suckling and sleeping. Sometimes it helps to keep a light on while you nurse to help him break that suckle-sleep association.

JOB CHECKS

Some parents have to take one more step and move farther away, doing what I call a *job check,* telling the child where they will be, what they will be doing, and promising to be back very soon: "Mommy is going to get her pajamas. I'll be back in five minutes," or "Daddy is going to brush his teeth, and then I'm going to come back and blow you another kiss." These checks work best with older toddlers who have more developed language skills.

Some families stay in this position for a while; the toddler still needs those ten or fifteen minutes of reassurance. Others get to the point where they can put the child to bed, say good night, and leave. Sometimes they need to come back for one last "curtain call" before she goes to sleep, but the goal is to reduce the number of checks. Use your instincts about what will work best for your child. You might have to let her regress a little once in a while. For instance, if you are leaving her to fall asleep on her own, and she does it successfully, she may still have a spell now and then when she needs a little more reassurance and you have to stick closer by her for a few nights. I don't mean going back to the start of the Shuffle, but you might have to hang out in the hallway one or two nights or revert to making checks briefly before you can leave her on her own again.

NOT READY FOR THE SHUFFLE? YOU CAN TRY SWITCHING ASSOCIATIONS UNTIL YOU ARE

I believe *you* have to be ready to sleep coach, and often it feels like a huge leap. And if you can't take that leap, take some preparatory smaller steps before you sleep coach 100 percent.

For instance, if your child depends on you to put her to sleep by rocking, feeding, or lying down with her and you are not ready to put your toddler down drowsy but awake at bedtime, you can switch the crutch, or what I call *switching negative sleep associations*. If you nurse her to sleep, stop one night and instead have the other parent rock her to sleep. Yes, you are creating a new sleep crutch—from nursing to sleep to rocking to sleep—but because the behavior of the other parent rocking her is so new, the toddler is not as attached to it. It may be easier to stop rocking to sleep when you are ready to start sleep coaching.

Another small step you can take now is to work on gently fading out your child's current sleep crutch. For example, if you always hold your child until she's completely asleep, try holding her until she's almost asleep. Then put her in her crib and pat her all the way to sleep. You can also try patting her back to sleep during the night.

SHUFFLING WITH MULTIPLES

Your multiple toddlers shared a womb, and it's usually a good idea to have them share a room. Some families even put them in the same crib for a few months, until they start rolling over. Yes, you have probably heard them grunt, whimper, and make all sorts of strange toddler noises and marveled about how they didn't seem to disturb each other. Even when they wake each other, they almost always learn to sleep through each other's sounds, and you want to encourage them to do so. Be careful about responding too quickly if one makes a noise. Parents often rush in as soon as they hear a peep, fearing that one will wake up the other one. You may be reinforcing the troubled sleeper while you protect the one who is asleep. The sleeping twin may be oblivious, or she may stir but then get herself right back to sleep, or one parent might have successfully reassured her back to sleep, exactly as you want her to do. Parents of triplets or quadruplets can adapt these techniques for their children, although most don't separate them for naps simply because they don't have enough room! A parent can sit in the middle of the bedroom between the children to soothe them. The children learn quickly to sleep through their siblings' crying and fussing.

Just like with singletons, start the Sleep Lady Shuffle at bedtime after a day when your toddlers' daytime sleep averages have been met—which means getting naps in any way you can. Whether you need to rely on all your sleep crutches at the same time or take two car rides a day, getting the daytime sleep tanks filled—even if it means taking drastic measures—is a must before beginning the Shuffle at night. If possible, move the cribs closer so they are at least three feet apart, and have one parent sit in a chair between the cribs. If two people are available, this will be easier to do. Each parent can sit by a crib/multiple.

After your soothing bedtime routine, place your toddlers in their cribs drowsy but awake and sit in your chair position as described in the Sleep Lady Shuffle, beginning on page 191. If one parent is doing the Shuffle, sit in a chair between the cribs and go back and forth. If two parents or other caregivers are available, it will be easier and each adult can sit by a child. Stroke and soothe each child in turn. Follow the rules of the Shuffle for the first three nights; you are using your voice to soothe instead of relying too much on touch.

Both parents must be on the same page—one is not picking up the child more often than the other, for instance. If one child is more of a problem sleeper than the other, have the parent who has an easier time with consistency sit next to that child. If the sleep crutch is nursing to sleep, let the non-nursing parent do the first few nights.

FREQUENTLY ASKED QUESTIONS
FROM PARENTS OF MULTIPLES

Q: **I have twins, and one is a better sleeper than the other and gets woken by the other twin. How should I sleep coach them?**

A: In those cases where one child truly disrupts the other's sleep, I do make exceptions and separate them at night during sleep coaching. It's usually a good idea to leave the poorer sleeper where he is and move the sounder sleeper to another room, using a portable crib if necessary. Good sleepers tend to be more flexible and can more easily adjust to a temporary new sleeping place, even if it's a little noisier or brighter than the toddlers' bedroom. Once the poorer sleeper is sleeping through the night fairly consistently (or waking for a single feeding if that's age appropriate and you're satisfied), you can return him to the shared room.

Q: **I have triplets. How can we do the Shuffle and sit next to their cribs when there are only two parents available? And sometimes only one of us is home at bedtime?**

A: If you have triplets or quads, you can still do this, but be gentle on yourself by not expecting too much at first. You are outnumbered, after all. You may need to have one parent sit between two toddlers or two parents tag teaming with three toddlers, and so on. If there is just one parent, gently move back and forth to stroke and soothe each child in turn. Follow the rules of the Shuffle for the first three nights on pages 191–194. Make sure that by the third night, you are using your voice to soothe instead of relying too much on touch.

SLEEP CRUTCHES AND SOLUTIONS

Toddlers who have trouble getting to sleep and staying asleep often have *negative associations,* or *sleep crutches,* as discussed in Chapter 1. These aren't actually bad behaviors; they only become negative when they block sleep independence. For instance, children should be hugged and snuggled. But if they are hugged and snuggled until they fall asleep and each time they wake up at night, they will never learn how to fall asleep on their own or get themselves back to sleep at night. Our job as parents is to create positive sleep associations, letting our babies learn to fall asleep on their own. That's what's required by their growing bodies and miraculously expanding minds.

Here are some of the most common crutches that can disrupt sleep coaching for this age group.

CRUTCH: NIGHTTIME FEEDING

Example: My fifteen-month-old still wakes up to feed two to three times a night, even when I feed her right before bedtime! What can I do?

Eliminating Nighttime Feeding

If your child is using a bottle rather than a sippy cup, make the switch now, particularly if your toddler needs a bottle to go to sleep, which is a sleep crutch. Night weaning and perhaps complete weaning from a bottle to a cup will have to be built into your sleep-coaching plan. If you want to keep the bottle during the day, wean him off his nighttime bottles. Or if you are worried he isn't getting enough to drink, as long as he is not leaking through his diapers, give him a bottle at bedtime, then brush teeth to avoid cavities, read a book, and put him in his crib drowsy but awake. Reducing the number of ounces will also be helpful.

Check with your pediatrician; if there are any growth concerns and the doctor recommends sticking to the bottle for a while, you can still address the sleep associations. Give the bottle earlier in the bedtime routine, and then use the Shuffle to teach your toddler how to go to sleep without having to have a bottle to get drowsy or fall completely asleep. You want to move away from him associating sleep with feeding. If your child becomes fussy during the day and asks for a bottle or your breast, look at the clock and your sleep log. Is he really hungry, or does he want the bottle for comfort? Can you comfort or distract him in some other way? This also helps your toddler learn other ways to self-regulate. Maybe he's overtired and needs a few quiet hugs from you or a few minutes on your lap with a book. Maybe he's tired and it's time for his nap. Perhaps he is signaling that he needs to go to bed a little earlier than usual. We want him to learn there are other ways to feel calm and happy in addition to the bottle or breast.

When you are ready to wean him from the bedtime bottle or breast-feeding, reduce the amount every two or three days, from eight ounces, down to six ounces, to four, to two. Then offer him a sippy cup of water instead. Sometimes a toddler protests when he hits that four-ounce mark because it is no longer enough fluid for him to suck himself to sleep. Find other ways to comfort him and know that it means the very next night you have to go straight to a sippy cup of water at bedtime and no more bottles during the night or at bedtime. Be careful if he starts to want the water at each waking, and avoid the temptation to give it to him. You will be refilling the cup multiple times a night, and your responsiveness might teach him to keep waking.

If you are concerned your toddler is genuinely thirsty at night, you can offer one small sippy cup of water at the beginning of the night. When he wakes, point to the cup and say, "There is your water cup." No refills, however. Many times, the toddler won't want the cup, especially if it's not enough water to provide enough sucking time to go back to sleep. Talk to your pediatrician if you believe your child is overly thirsty throughout the day and night.

If all else fails, don't worry, you still have options!

Three Options for Nighttime Weaning
Method A: The Taper-Off Technique

If you're nursing, gradually cut down the amount of time your toddler is at the breast. For example, if she usually feeds for twenty minutes, let her go for only fifteen. Cut back every night until she's ready to give it up, or until you're down to five minutes. At that point, it's time to stop altogether. Make sure you unlatch her when she finishes eating heartily, even if it's faster than the amount of time you've allotted; don't let her gently suckle and doze. Get her back to bed while she's drowsy but awake.

If you're bottle-feeding, you can decrease the amount of formula she gets by a few ounces every few nights. When you get to two ounces, it's time to stop. That's usually the best way to do it, but you could also gradually dilute the formula until it gets so watery she decides it's not worth waking up for.

If your toddler is waking to eat several times a night but only nursing for a couple of minutes or taking a couple of ounces, this method won't work for you. Choose Method B or C.

Method B: The Four-Night Phase-Out

Whether you're breastfeeding or giving a bottle, feed your toddler just once during the night for three nights; it's best to set a time for when you'll give her that single snack. Decide on a time, such as first waking after midnight. If you are not sure what time to choose, think about when she tends to eat the most during her night feedings or a time that is harder to get her back to sleep—like 3:00 a.m. versus 11:00 p.m.

Only feed her once at night, and not again until at least 6:00 a.m., when you can both start your day. When she wakes at other times, sit by her crib and offer physical and verbal reassurance. On the fourth night, don't feed her at all. Remember, she has had three nights to get used to receiving fewer calories at night. Usually, parents will move their seats away from the crib on the fourth night of the Shuffle, but we're going to modify it for this night weaning. So on the fourth night when she wakes up, sit next to her crib for an additional night. Comfort her from your chair as you did at bedtime. Don't pick her up unless she's hysterical, and then pick her up to calm her. If you breastfeed exclusively, putting the other parent on night duty might help your toddler adjust to the no-night-feeding reality more quickly.

Sleep Lady Tip

In the event you decide to feed your toddler at a set time of midnight, and she wakes before her set-time feeding and stays awake fussing until the set time, do not feed her. For example, if she wakes up at 11:00 and fusses until midnight, don't pick her up and feed her just because the clock strikes 12:00. That will just teach her to fuss or cry for an hour until you feed her, and that's not the best way to minimize tears. So get her back to sleep, even if it's only for thirty minutes, until she wakes up again. So if she wakes up at 11:00, fusses until 12:00, finally falls asleep at 12:10, and wakes up at 12:45, go in and feed her. She learned to get to sleep without food. If she is consistently waking at an hour before her set time and you think you picked the wrong time, move the set time one hour earlier the next night.

Important note: Keep this in mind if you've decided that you'll feed your toddler the first time she wakes after midnight. If you find yourself sitting with her and doing the Shuffle from 11:00 p.m. until midnight while she fusses or cries, don't feed her a minute after the clock strikes 12:00. Wait until she goes back to sleep and then wakes up again—even if she only dozes for half an hour. You don't want to send the message that crying for an hour will yield a feeding.

Method C: Cold Turkey

If your baby is barely feeding at night, whether from breast or bottle, you may decide that it will be easier to stop all the feedings cold turkey. You can stop offering your baby a breast or a bottle when she wakes at night. Go to her crib side as outlined in the Shuffle. Just make sure you and your partner are on the same page in this decision. If Mom has been breastfeeding, consider having the non-nursing parent handle all middle-of-the-night wake-ups, since your child knows the other parent won't be there to nurse her.

WHEN IT'S TIME TO WEAN

Weaning from the breast should be an easy, natural transition and is not a requirement for successful sleep coaching. Weaning seldom disrupts sleep, but sleep that is already disrupted can make weaning harder if the toddler is already overtired and unhappy. Weaning is also more difficult if she has not learned how to fall asleep without a breast or bottle in her mouth. There's no "right" way to wean, but the most common advice is to drop one daytime feeding one week, drop a second one the second week, and so on (some moms go slower, which is fine—do what works for you). Many mothers continue nursing the first thing in the morning and once at bedtime well beyond the first birthday. That's only a problem when the toddler can't go to sleep, or back to sleep, without being breastfed. (The same applies to bedtime bottle-feeding.) In that case, you are facing a sleep crutch issue, not a weaning issue.

Many moms report that the easiest feeding to drop is a midday one It's easier on their bodies and on their babies. Start by giving your toddler a cup of milk with whatever meal corresponds most closely to the nursing time. After a couple of days or a week, or whatever feels right to you, do the same for another feeding.

The final two breastfeedings are usually the wake-up one and the bedtime one. Some families keep those two feedings for quite a while; it's your choice. When you decide to give up the morning feeding, have the non-nursing parent, if possible, get the toddler up in the morning and offer milk in a cup with breakfast. The nursing parent shouldn't join the breakfast scene until the toddler is fed.

When you are ready to stop the last pre-bedtime feeding, reduce the amount or time every two or three days, from eight ounces, down to six ounces, to four, to two. Then offer her a sippy cup of water instead during books.

Make sure you allow a little extra time for her routine so she has plenty if she needs some extra soothing. If your toddler has been breastfeeding at bedtime, it might help to have the other parent do the last step of the bedtime routine for a couple of nights. Remember that you don't want her drinking milk at bedtime indefinitely, as it's bad for her teeth.

CRUTCH: WALKING AND ROCKING TO SLEEP

Example: Xavier weighs eighteen pounds, and I can't rock him any longer! I tried putting him into his crib, but he grabs on to me and tries to crawl up me like a tree. I feel like I am losing the struggle. What happens when he keeps growing and my back goes out?

If you are walking or rocking your child to sleep and having to walk or rock him back to sleep over and over again all night long, walking or rocking has become a sleep crutch, and it's time to sleep coach.

How to Eliminate Walking, Holding, Bouncing, and Rocking to Sleep

Make sure you have a comforting bedtime routine. You can incorporate a wee bit of walking or rocking in it—like a few minutes in the rocking chair while you read a book, or a brief stroll around the room with the light on while saying good night to favorite toys. Then put him down, drowsy but awake. Sit by his bed and pat him, stroke him, whisper soothing words, but leave him in his crib. Follow the rules of the Shuffle and coach him to sleep. Whichever parent is likely to be more consistent and not rock him should be the one to do the crib-side duty the first few nights. Each time he wakes at night, go to him quickly and sit by his bed and pat him, stroke him, and whisper soothing words, but don't pick him up and walk or rock him to sleep.

Scaling back the amount of time you walk or rock every few days doesn't work as well at this age. He'll figure out rather quickly that you are going to secretly slide him into his crib once he is asleep. The safest bet is to read him a book and do a little rocking as you slowly make your way to turn off his light. Blow kisses to the moon, give him a kiss and a hug, and put him into the crib.

Sit by the crib and soothe him. If he gets really hysterical, pick him up briefly and put him down as soon as he's calm. If he calms down in two seconds once you've picked him up, you'll know he didn't need to be picked up as badly as you'd thought he did. Resume your Shuffle position and be consistent.

Warning: While the Sleep Lady Shuffle encourages parents to pick up to calm their crying and distraught child, it can be futile for children with the crutch of being walked, held, bounced, and rocked to sleep. Some toddlers with this crutch genuinely cry hard and then, when picked up to calm, can fall asleep in their parents' arms in under two minutes! If this happens during sleep coaching, you can inadvertently train your baby to cry hard until you pick him up. When parents are trying to eliminate this crutch, I always tell them to use "pick up to calm" as conservatively as possible. If you inadvertently train him to cry hard to be picked up and he falls immediately asleep, you won't be able to use the soothing technique of "pick up to calm" anymore, and you will have to endure what could be a lot of crying.

CRUTCH: THE PACIFIER REPLUG

Most pediatricians recommend weaning your child off the pacifier by eighteen months to two years, but if your child is waking up a lot at night seeking her paci, you might want to tackle it now. Be prepared for a few nights of unpleasantness. Start at bedtime after a great nap day, and put her in her bed after a soothing bedtime routine without her pacifier. Sit by her crib and offer physical and verbal reassurance. Comfort her and encourage the bond to a lovey. As you take the pacifier away, say something like "It's not paci time, but Teddy Bear is here and wants to hug you." I know this won't be a quick cure, but you are trying to distract her from the pacifier and provide a security substitute. It's worth a try. Do the same at all night wakenings. Follow the soothing rules of the Shuffle for the first three nights.

If you don't want to take away the pacifier yet, you should still be able to teach your toddler to find it herself so you don't have to keep chasing it for her all night long. Leave a few pacifiers scattered around the crib so she can find at least one of them in the middle of the night while she's still half asleep. You can find glow-in-the-dark options, too. I do encourage restricting pacifier use to sleeping, though, because research suggests 24-7 use can interfere with other aspects of development, including speech, or in the very least, communication. Some families with children this age get rid of the pacifier at night but use it for naps, long car rides, or trips to the doctor.

If your child is experiencing night wakings because she wakes and wants you to replug her pacifier, I have dedicated an entire section on how to nip the crutch of the pacifier replug in the bud in Chapter 7, "Six to Eight Months." Further, at this age, toddlers go through the pacifier-as-missile stage. They love to hurl it out of the crib and make you go after it.

It is somewhat like a game of fetch your toddler is playing with you. He'll throw the pacifier (or lovey) out of the crib and then scream for you to come get it. What's a parent to do?

Note that this often happens when you are in a Shuffle chair position that is no longer seated crib-side. Let's say you are sitting in the hall, in view, and he throws the pacifier or lovey to the floor. Do not retrieve it. Instead, tell him, "Lie down, and I will come give you your binky." Keep repeating this until he lies down. Once he is down, go into the room and get his pacifier.

Now tell him, "No throwing binky." You can even talk for the binky and say, "Don't throw me out. I want to snuggle and sleep with you!" Make the binky seem sad that he was thrown out. You may have a toddler who likes to test the limits, and even after you return the lovey to him, he throws it again. Repeat the above, instructing, "Lie down, and I will get the binky for the last time." (Some parents want to give their toddler one more chance, and others don't; it's up to you.)

When you return, tell him that if he throws it again, you will not give it back to him. If he were to throw it again (I have had a few who do), you must stand your ground and not return it despite the wailing and pleading for his lovey. Continue to use your voice to verbally reassure him from your Shuffle position. Once he is completely asleep or when you check on him one last time before you turn in, return his lovey without waking him (of course).

CRUTCH: REACTIVE CO-SLEEPING

Most of the families I speak to are either co-sleeping out of desperation or really want to continue to co-sleep but find it's not working well for them. Families that are co-sleeping out of desperation are practicing what I call *reactive co-sleeping*. These "we didn't plan it this way" co-sleepers are reactively co-sleeping when they end up with the toddler in the bed part or all of the night. I am not against co-sleeping if that is your choice (and you do it safely). But with these families, it's not a choice or philosophical commitment—it's the only way they can get their baby to sleep at bedtime or back to sleep in the middle of the night. If you are reactively co-sleeping—in the category of "we didn't plan it this way," that means it has become a crutch (for both you and your baby). In Chapter 12, I address how to end reactive co-sleeping as well as how to improve safe co-sleeping if co-sleeping is your preference.

TEMPERAMENT CHECK

By now, your toddler's temperament is crystal clear. You know her cues and her habits, behaviors, and responses. Perhaps you've noticed that your toddler likes to throw her pacifier out of the crib or thinks 11:00 p.m. is time to throw a party. Perhaps your toddler is "fussy" or has a mind of her own.

In Phase 1, I specifically addressed the temperament of what I call the *highly alert child*. In my experience, this is the temperament that leads most of my clients to seek out my help and the help of my Gentle Sleep Coaches. In fact, about 80 percent of my clients are parents of highly alert children. If you have come to realize you have been blessed with an active, stubborn, engaged child, you might be running the risk of being more sleep deprived or frustrated—even depressed—than if you were sleep training a child who was less spirited.

I expand on the sleep needs of the highly alert child in Phase 1 on page 43. Sleep training isn't impossible once you recognize that your highly alert child has her own set of rules about how and when she gets some sleep. Like a river, it's better for everyone to go with the flow than to try to swim against it.

EARLY RISING

So many parents reach out to me because they started sleep coaching and their toddlers are now sleeping a much longer stretch but waking at 4:00 or 5:00 a.m. and seemingly not wanting to go back to sleep. Or perhaps your toddler was sleeping through until 6:00 or 7:00 a.m. until daylight saving time, and now, months later, she is still waking at 5:00 a.m. Early rising is such a huge and common sleep struggle.

Early rising is not the same as having early risers, whom I refer to as *early birds,* so as not to confuse the two. Early birds wake up earlier than many parents would like, 6:00 or 6:30 a.m., but they do so refreshed and happy. Their temperament skews more toward simply being a morning person. And in this case, you don't have to look far and wide to find that at least one parent is a morning person, too. Interestingly, research suggests there is a genetic link.

Then there are the early risers who are not happy to be up before the crack of dawn. They are tired, unrefreshed, the opposite of bright-eyed and bushy-tailed. But there they are—grouchy, awake, and not going back to sleep. This is when early rising is a problem, because the sleep tank isn't filled efficiently. And by now, we know that not getting enough nighttime sleep will affect nap quality and quantity, and nap time affects nighttime sleep—and there ensues the cycle.

WHAT CAUSES EARLY RISING?

While this is a very common problem, often the solution isn't one that is instant, as so many parents wish. Like any new skill, learning how to stay asleep takes time. Early rising is essentially your child having a difficult time putting himself *back to sleep* after a long stretch of sleep at night, or not getting quite enough sleep to make it to his nap without being over-tired. This skill is more difficult than putting himself to sleep at bedtime.

For instance, I know if I get up at 5:00 or 5:30 a.m. and I'm awake a little too long, my brain starts to tick-tick-tick-tick with all the things I have to do, and I will have a hard time going back to sleep. My body has gotten just enough sleep to make it hard to go back to sleep but not enough to leave me feeling rested and restored.

Here are four factors that can cause early rising. Sometimes only one causes the early rising; for other kids, it could be all four. Note, you should first always rule out illness or undiagnosed medical conditions that can cause and contribute to sleep problems, such as obstructive sleep apnea, which we discuss more in Chapter 14, and then consider the following reasons:

1. Too drowsy at bedtime
2. Too long of a wakeful window between the afternoon nap and bedtime
3. Insufficient naps
4. Too late of a bedtime

Too Drowsy at Bedtime

The paramount lesson of helping your toddler learn to fall asleep on his own is putting him to bed drowsy but awake. You want him to be tired and ready for sleep but not falling asleep as soon as his head hits the mattress. Putting yourself to sleep is a form of self-soothing, and for him to learn that skill, he needs to be awake enough at bedtime. Once he masters it

Sleep Lady Tip

When transitioning to one afternoon nap, some parents get stuck with the nap being from 11:00 a.m. to 1:00 p.m. and then a very long stretch until bedtime. If your toddler was sleeping through the night before this nap transition, she will likely start to wake during the night and wake too early in the morning due to this too-long wakeful window between afternoon nap and bedtime. You will need to focus on pushing that nap later, until after noon.

at bedtime, he can eventually apply it to night wakings as well as early risings, which are the toughest to go back to sleep from.

Overestimating the Wakeful Window

This may seem counterintuitive, but an overtired child generally takes longer to get to sleep and will wake more often during the night, causing early rising. Review your toddler's nap schedule to make sure you are not exceeding his wakeful window, and be sure there are no more than four hours between the end of his afternoon nap and his bedtime. More about napping in the section "Much Ado About Napping" on page 213.

Insufficient Naps

We discuss this in the napping section, but it begs to be repeated. Short napping or not enough napping can cause increased night wakings and early rising. Quality nap time actually helps encourage quality nighttime sleep. If your child tends to take very short naps or finishes her naps early in the day, you are probably dealing with early rising. Review your child's sample schedule and the nap-coaching section and decide when you are going to start nap coaching.

Too Late of a Bedtime

Many parents are shocked when I tell them that their child's natural bedtime is likely *between 7:00 and 8:00 p.m.* And in this age group, more likely 7:00–7:30 p.m. If your toddler's bedtime is well beyond this window, sleep in the night could be disrupted and lead to early rising, not to mention night terrors! For more on night terrors, turn to Chapter 13. If your schedule is wildly different from the sample schedules and your child is rising early, consider adjusting bedtime earlier. Do not keep your child up too late, hoping that he will wake less often during the night and sleep later in the morning. This rarely (if ever) works. Overtired children sleep less, not more.

WHAT TO DO? RETURN TO THE SLEEP LADY SHUFFLE

While you are making adjustments based on the tips above and your child wakes before 6:00 a.m., treat it like the other night wakings and do the Shuffle. The catch is that you must use your consistent response until 6:00 a.m. If he doesn't go back to sleep, use what I like to call *dramatic wake-up*! Leave the room for a full minute (literally, a full minute—watch the clock!). After sixty seconds, return to the room bright and cheerful with a "Good morning!" while you open the curtains and let the light flood in. This signals to your child that you are getting him up because it is morning and not because he is waking up too early!

Keep using the Shuffle in the early morning until the habit resolves. If you allow it to persist, you could be introducing a new sleep crutch that will need to be broken eventually.

> ## Sleep Lady Tip
>
> Keep in mind that early rising happens during the sleep-coaching process and can often take two to three weeks to fully resolve as you are working on improving naps. The two hardest or last pieces of sleep coaching to fall into place are early rising and the afternoon nap. So don't give up!

MUCH ADO ABOUT NAPPING

It's hard to imagine how many changes—developmentally, emotionally, and lifestyle-wise—your child and your family have made. You've begun weaning and giving milk to your toddler in a cup, and now it's time to look at how she naps and whether she is ready to move from two naps a day to one. However, if this is your first go-round with sleep coaching or using the Sleep Lady Shuffle, we should first discuss nap coaching in general so you can give your toddler the foundation she needs.

When your child is taking two naps, the morning one should be about an hour (minimum forty-five minutes, maximum ninety minutes). The afternoon one should be about an hour and a half. A little variation is okay, but don't let her sleep so long in the morning that she can't go down in the afternoon. When she consolidates, the afternoon nap (which may be at midday for a while during the transition) is about two and a half hours up through eighteen months. Nap needs will slowly shrink to about ninety minutes by age three.

Ideally, you want to start nighttime sleep coaching before nap coaching. So do the Sleep Lady Shuffle one night, and start nap coaching the next day. Make sure you're timing your child's naps correctly, based on his age (as indicated in this chapter). Also, be aware of his sleep cues and windows of wakefulness.

Nap coaching is hard for a plethora of reasons. The best defense is a good offense, so here are two major rules of nap coaching and preemptive strategies that will address head-on any nap-time snafus that may arise (and they will!). You probably noticed I don't usually talk about "rules"; I prefer to give you a range of choices that fit your own parenting style. But after many years of working with parents of balky nappers, I have learned that these rules really help!

#1: Focus on putting your child down for a nap *in her crib, twice a day if she is still on two naps.* If you are going to nap and night coach at the same time, then begin nap coaching the day after the first night with the morning nap if on two naps and the afternoon nap if on one nap. Go through an abbreviated version of your bedtime routine of reading a book or singing a song. Place your chair in the same place as you did the night before and follow the same steps of the Shuffle along with the same soothing techniques. Move your chair every three days, even if she didn't nap well on day 3.

#2: Spend an entire hour trying to get your child to sleep at nap time. Stay in your chair, exercising your Shuffle techniques for one whole hour. There are three outcomes that can happen:

1 Your toddler doesn't go to sleep for the entire hour.
2. Your toddler only takes a forty-five-minute nap.
3. Your toddler sleeps for *less than* forty-five minutes, which is less than a sleep cycle. I call these abbreviated naps *disaster naps*.

WHAT TO DO IF YOUR TODDLER DOESN'T
SLEEP FOR THE ENTIRE HOUR

At the end of your Shuffling hour, leave the room, count to ten, and go back into the room to do your dramatic wake-up routine (open the blinds, sing, "Nap time is over!") and take your child out of bed. Since he hasn't had a morning nap, he won't be able to last (or wait) until the afternoon for his next nap. Watch his cues; if he starts yawning, dozing while you feed him, and so on—even if it's just forty-five minutes after you got him out of his crib—go ahead and try for a nap again, doing the Shuffle.

WHAT TO DO IF YOUR TODDLER ONLY SLEEPS
FOR FORTY-FIVE MINUTES IN THE MORNING

This is the bare minimum for a nap. If he wakes up happy and seemingly refreshed—which may happen at this age—that's okay, but be aware that he might be ready for his afternoon siesta closer to noon. If your child wakes up after forty-five minutes from his afternoon nap, use the Shuffle techniques to get him back to sleep (try for at least thirty minutes if you can).

WHAT TO DO IF YOUR TODDLER NAPS FOR
LESS THAN FORTY-FIVE MINUTES

This is a *disaster nap*. When a child sleeps for less than forty-five minutes, he doesn't go through a complete sleep cycle and awakens at a partial arousal; it's enough to take the edge off his exhaustion but not enough to be restorative and to make it to the next nap or bedtime without being overtired. So here's the tough message: I want you to go to him and do the Shuffle for an hour—what I call the *longest hour*.

Here's an example: You put your child in his crib at 12:30 p.m., he conks out at 1:00, but only sleeps until 1:30. You go in and work on getting him back to sleep—which he does, thankfully, by 2:00, after just half an hour. But he only sleeps for twenty minutes. Chances are the negative voice in you is going to say, *I can't believe the Sleep Lady told me to do that! He cried more than he slept. What's the point of that?* But think about it: Your toddler did it! He put himself back to sleep after a partial arousal from a nap—one of the hardest things to do. Going forward, he'll begin to get back to sleep more quickly and will snooze longer if you stick with it.

NAP-COACHING TIPS

It's easier to get a toddler to take the morning nap than the afternoon nap. Don't miss that opportunity.

Afternoon nap training is tougher. Don't get discouraged; it's normal.

Keep a sleep log during nap training.

If it's 2:00 or 3:00 p.m. and your toddler has not napped well enough, you may need to resort to your backup plan, such as a nap in the stroller or car, to avoid an exhausted baby and bedtime disaster.

You will be tied to the house during nap coaching. If you feel like all you are doing all day is trying to get your baby to nap, then you are doing it right! The payoff: you'll have more freedom (and a happier, rested baby) once you have a predictable napping schedule.

If you have a nanny, babysitter, or other childcare provider who can do the nap training, thank your lucky stars. If your caregiver is reluctant to do the training, see if you can win her over with a simple explanation of the sleep science. If not, explain that your child needs a full sleep tank, and if that means the sitter has to use a sleep crutch like rocking to get the child to nap or to resume a brief or interrupted nap, that's okay.

DEVISE YOUR NAP-TIME BACKUP PLAN

After you have tried the nap in the crib twice during the day, you will likely need to use a backup nap plan to help fill the daytime sleep tank so your toddler doesn't face bedtime even more exhausted, making it harder for him to go to sleep and stay asleep. If you check your sleep log around 2:00 or 3:00 p.m. and realize your child hasn't had close to two and a half hours of day sleep, you will pull out all the stops to make sure you get that sleep tank filled. A backup nap plan can be to get him to nap in the car, stroller, swing, or carrier, but try to make it different from a habit (crutch) you've been trying to break. For instance, if you've been working on ending co-sleeping at night, don't put him in your bed for your backup plan. Try a car ride or walk in the stroller instead. If nothing else works, you may have to nap coach for a third time in the crib. And if that doesn't work, move bedtime even earlier.

Ideally, the backup nap will last at least forty-five minutes, and your child will be awake by 4.30 so that he's ready to sleep at his regular bedtime.

MY THREE BEST PIECES OF NAP-COACHING ADVICE

* No naps before 9:00 a.m. at this age—even if your child has been up since 5:00! It will throw off the entire day and ingrain in him the habit of getting up too early. I realize this is a tricky dance and your child may get overtired, but it's worth it in the long run.
* Your baby's morning nap should be no longer than one and a half hours. Wake him if need be. I only want you to do it for the morning nap to preserve the afternoon nap.
* Consider shortening the morning nap to forty-five minutes if you notice that your toddler is pushing his afternoon nap later and later after a longer morning nap.

If you have an older or younger child who can't be left alone while you sit in your toddler's room, you can do timed checks (page 70 in Phase 1)—looking in on him at regular intervals. Base the timing on your little one's temperament, and be consistent. If you have no idea where to start, then try checking on him every seven minutes, slowly increasing the time. When you go to his crib, be reassuring but quick. You'll defeat the purpose if you pat him until he's asleep during your crib-side check.

DO I HAVE TO NAP COACH AT THE SAME TIME AS NIGHT COACH?

Don't feel guilty if you can't follow all my advice right now. Give yourself (or your babysitter) permission to let the nap coaching slide, and just do what you have to do to get your child some daytime sleep, preferably at predictable times. As nighttime sleep improves, the daytime sleep *might* fall into place on its own. If not, take a deep breath and try nap coaching again in another month or two. Keep reminding yourself that good daytime sleep promotes better nighttime sleep; it helps you get through it.

If you decide not to address naps and only work on nighttime sleep, then do what works to help her sleep throughout the day, even calling upon sleep crutches. But know that it will eventually stop working. Either she will wake up the minute you put her down or shortly thereafter, or you will find yourself having to hold her longer and longer to get her to sleep, only to have her nap briefly. Those will be some of your signs to say, "Okay, now it's time to start nap coaching." But if you've worked on those other pieces at night, and your current nap crutches still work, you don't have to start nap coaching. If, however, none of your nap crutches work, you will have to night and nap coach at the same time.

IS MY CHILD READY FOR ONE NAP A DAY?

The significant sleep event at this age is switching from two naps a day— morning and afternoon—to a single afternoon nap right after lunch.

Consolidating naps is a definite physical and psychological transition, and almost all children undergo the "one nap is too little, two naps are too many" phase. Many parents get very nervous about this transition, and even in the best-case scenario, you will probably have a little bit of crankiness and disruption for one, two, or sometimes even three weeks. Here are signs your child may be ready to consolidate to one nap a day:

> ## Sleep Lady Tip
>
> To preserve that afternoon nap, which is the one she's going to keep through most or all the preschool years (and occasionally longer), shorten the morning one. When she's ready to drop the morning nap, probably within a few months, you'll phase the morning one out and keep that afternoon snooze.

* She's about fifteen months to eighteen months old (later is not uncommon; earlier is rare).
* She's sleeping through the night consistently—ten to eleven hours of uninterrupted sleep. If she's not, work on improving nighttime sleep before you tackle the nap change.
* She's taking longer and longer—and longer—to fall asleep for the morning nap, or sleeping for such a long time in the morning that she won't take her afternoon nap or at least not until 4:00 p.m. (meaning you will have a very testy and overtired child by bedtime).

As you evaluate her daytime sleep schedule, remember that you are looking for a pattern, not just a one-day departure from the normal routine. Don't mistake one or two abbreviated morning naps or skipped afternoon naps for the sign that she's ready for the change; that might happen now and then as she gets older. But when her pattern becomes pretty consistent (perhaps seven to ten days in a row), the time is probably right to help her start the transition. If you aren't sure, keep a log of her napping and waking times for a week or two.

Sleep Lady Tip

If your child is not yet sleeping through the night, work on that before you tackle the change from two naps to one. When she's slept through the night consistently for a few weeks, then you can begin altering the nap schedule if you see that she is ready.

If your child is ready, your goal is to have your child's nap begin at around 12:30 or 1:00. The nap should last for two and a quarter to two and a half hours, although it will grow shorter during the next two or three years. The trick is to know when your child is ready to shift to a single afternoon nap and to make sure she doesn't get so overtired during the transition that she crosses the line between mildly cranky and totally sleep deprived. Be extra solicitous of her nighttime sleep while you are making this transition. If she's too overtired, her nighttime sleep may get disrupted, or she may wake up earlier, which in turn will make her tireder and crankier in the daytime, which then will make it harder for her to make it to her afternoon nap. As you know, that's a recipe for sleep disaster. So as you adapt to new daytime patterns, *get her to bed earlier than usual, around 7:00.* Allow plenty of time to follow her familiar and soothing bedtime routine. Most children make the transition in about ten days, but it could take up to three weeks for her to fully adjust. Don't be alarmed if she has a bit of trouble napping or wakes up occasionally during the night during the transition. It's normal and temporary.

CHANGES AND CHALLENGES: DROPPING THE MORNING NAP

Once you see the above signs that your toddler is ready to drop her morning nap for at least twelve to fourteen days straight, you can start the process of dropping her morning nap. It should take only seven to ten days. Here's how:

1. Gradually push her morning nap later—until around 11:00 a.m. for two days, then 11:30 for a couple of days, then noon, and so on. Don't let the nap get stuck in late morning. Some kids can adapt more quickly to a noon nap time, and others need to go slower. Watch your child. Your goal is for the afternoon nap to eventually start between 12:30 and 1:00 and last at least two and a quarter to two and a half hours.

2. If your toddler sleeps for only an hour and wakes up tired, then try to soothe and resettle her back to sleep. If all else fails, do dramatic wake-up and use one of your emergency techniques, such as putting her in the car or stroller to top off her sleep tank.

3. Do not let her sleep past 4:00 or 4:30 p.m, so as not to disrupt her bedtime.

4. Try to get your child to bed earlier than usual for two weeks or so during the transition—like 7:00 p.m.—to cushion her from being overtired.

5. Be open to an occasional two-nap day. If during the transition your child seems too tired, it's okay to let her nap twice—just limit the morning snooze to forty-five minutes.

Choose a sensible time, just as you did when you started sleep coaching. Don't try to change her whole routine, for instance, the day before you leave for a vacation or when you are under a particularly intense deadline pressure at work.

Proceed gradually, making small changes each day for about seven to ten days. Don't go cold tur-

Sleep Lady Tip

Toddlers who aren't sleeping through the night still need two naps—at least temporarily—and then after successfully completing the Shuffle and they are sleeping through the night, you can transition them to one nap.

key and just scrap that morning nap. Instead, *push the morning nap a bit later.* Delay it until around 11:00 a.m. for two or three days, then 11:30 for a few days, then noon, and so on. Don't let it get stuck at 11:00; make it to noon at the earliest. If your toddler is sleeping through the night and when transitioning her to one nap you got stuck with her napping from 11:00 a.m. to 1:00 p.m., she may start to wake during the night and have early risings due to the long wakeful window from 1:00 p.m. to bedtime. *You want her on that early-afternoon schedule within seven to ten days*, although it may take another week or so for her body's wake-and-sleep rhythms to fully adjust.

If she sleeps for only one hour and wakes up tired, which is common during the transition, try to coach her back to sleep. Try doing the Shuffle for at least thirty minutes before giving up and doing dramatic wake-up. If she only napped from, let's say, 1:00 to 2:00 p.m. and you weren't able to coach her back to sleep, then you will need to use your emergency backup nap plan, such as putting her in the car or stroller, to get her some more sleep. Remember not to let her sleep past 4:00 or 4:30 p.m. Even if she naps later than usual, don't delay her bedtime. Keep it on the early side.

If you've been working on the one nap for a few days and you see that she is a bit off, that she is too tired, *give her a two-nap day to catch up*. I know I keep telling you to be consistent, but in this particular situation, your priority is to see that she's rested, to keep her from crossing into that exhausted-but-wired state. Keep the morning nap short, about forty-five minutes, so you can still put her down after lunch for the second nap. The next day, get back on the one-nap consolidation path.

Try to avoid consolidating naps when *you* think she's ready; wait for *her* to give you the signal. Doing this prematurely won't work. Remember, watch your child, not the calendar. *Also, avoid consolidating the nap times in the wrong direction—getting rid of the afternoon one and keeping the morning one!* Parents may let a twelve-month-old take a two- or three-hour nap in the morning. The child will then refuse to sleep in the afternoon, but there's no way on earth she will make it from the end of that morning nap all the way until bedtime without melting down.

NAP COACHING AND DAY CARE PROVIDERS

If your toddler still needs two naps but goes to a day care where twelve-month-olds are automatically transitioned to one nap, ask if your toddler can go back to the "baby room" for a short morning nap and then return to the toddler room when he wakes. He can then have his afternoon nap with this toddler group. Another option is to request he not be moved to the toddler room and that he remain in the baby room until he is transitioned to one nap. Share with your day care center the signs and average age of transitioning to one nap. If they refuse because of a policy, then you may need to pick up your toddler early for a few weeks while you are night coaching and get him to take a second nap in the car on the way home so he is not running on vapors at bedtime. Plan on an "in crib at 7:00 p.m." goal during this time. At home on the weekends, let him have two naps a day to catch up on his sleep.

HOW TO NAP COACH MULTIPLES

Although I normally keep twins together at nighttime, I often recommend separating them for naps. Daytime sleep is much more challenging for most babies, and it's even harder if there's a playmate to distract or be distracted by in the next crib. Some parents keep multiples apart for naps for days or weeks, others throughout childhood. Do whichever feels best to you and seems to work for your children.

Nap coaching more than one child can be difficult. If you are lucky and one naps well, you can put him down and nap coach the other in another room (just checking as necessary on the good sleeper). More often, both will need some coaching, so separate them and do timed checks: when you calm one, leave him, then go to the other and calm him, then after ten minutes or so, go back and check on the first toddler, and in another ten minutes, check on the second, and so forth. If you are struggling and both or all multiples are really not napping well, then you might as well nap train them together in the same room. Instead of timed checks, sit between their cribs and follow the Shuffle, along with advice on soothing and chair position in the section "Shuffling with Multiples," on page 198, for the onset of the nap.

TRANSITIONING TO ONE NAP WITH MULTIPLES

Just as your twins may walk at different times or crawl at different times, they may very well transition to one nap at different times—especially if Toddler A, for instance, has started sleeping through the night before Toddler B. This means that you will have two different schedules, with Toddler B napping in the morning while Toddler A is not. You may want to keep Toddler B's morning nap to forty-five minutes to keep the afternoon naps somewhat close to each other in terms of timing. Toddler A may also nap longer in the afternoon, and you may need to wake her up within thirty minutes of Toddler B, or by 4:00–4:30 p.m.

You may need a third backup nap during nap coaching if your toddlers are solidly on one afternoon nap but it's not long enough to make it to bedtime without being overtired. Your end goal is to have both toddlers well fed and ready for bed between 7:00 and 7:30 p.m. regardless of how different their naps were during the day.

FREQUENTLY ASKED QUESTIONS FROM PARENTS OF MULTIPLES

Q: **My twins were born early, and one of them has sensory processing disorder (SPD) for which we are seeing an OT. Because that twin has such difficulty napping and sleeping in general, and then add in all our treatment appointments, where do we begin with sleep coaching?**

A: Sensory processing sensitivities can definitely affect sleep. Please turn to Chapter 15 for more information on sensory processing and sleep. Not only can your twin have more difficulty going to sleep and staying asleep, but his treatment schedule may be challenging. Talk with your treatment providers about the importance of naps and see if they can schedule their appointments with your twin around his naps. Try to catch up on naps with your twins on busy treatment days any way you can, to work toward the goal of the same bedtime.

It's possible that your twin with SPD needs to be sleep coached while the other twin does not. If need be, consider sep arating them temporarily at night while you sleep coach the one twin—and for naps, too, if only the one doesn't nap well. Move the good sleeper out of the room and return him at night when his sibling is sleeping through the night. They may need to remain separate for naps for some time.

Sometimes sleep coaching and especially nap coaching can take longer with children who have sensory sensitivities. Make sure you talk to your OT about the sleep difficulties and ask for any helpful presleep exercises you can do.

Q: **I have started nap coaching my twins in the same room, but one twin is having short naps and is always waking the other twin. Toddler B has always tended to nap longer than Toddler A, and I feel like Toddler A is disrupting Toddler B's naps! What do I do?**

A: This is not uncommon, and often I recommend separating multiples for naps. Especially if one multiple is a better napper but gets woken up by the other one. Sometimes I recommend separating them temporarily, but in other cases it's indefinite and only for naps, not nighttime. If you coach both, use timed checks.

If one multiple goes to sleep quicker and easier, you can put her down for naps first and then Shuffle Toddler B in a separate room. Consider using a pack-and-play in another room for naps.

Use the third, backup nap to even out the scales and have both twins ready for bed between 7:00 and 7:30 p.m. This nap can be in a stroller. If Toddler A had two decent naps totaling around two and a half to three hours, then wake Toddler A at the forty-five-minute mark, or by 5:00 p.m. Toddler B might have had two forty-five-minute naps and therefore may need to go down for this third nap earlier or be allowed to sleep until 5:30 p.m. Toddler B can still go to bed at the same time as Toddler A—remember, Toddler B is nap deprived.

Q: **Toddler A wants to start her day at 7:00 a.m., and Toddler B wants to sleep until 10:00 a.m. (probably because she was up six times last night)—should I let her sleep in?**

A: No, do not let her sleep in. Wake Toddler B within thirty minutes of Toddler A. This will help regulate her wake-up and, more importantly, keep them on a similar schedule, which will make life oh-so-much easier!

Chapter 10

ONE AND A HALF TO TWO
AND A HALF YEARS

SLEEP GOALS

* *eighteen-month-olds average eleven and a quarter hours of nighttime sleep and two and a quarter hours during one midday or afternoon nap*
* *at age two, average sleep requirements drop to eleven hours at night and two hours during the day*
* *age two to three, expect sleep to drop to ten and a half hours at night and one and a half during the day*

This chapter is written with crib sleepers in mind, but I recognize that some parents transition their child to a bed at a young age, and some of you may have already made the switch before learning that it may not be ideal. If that is the case, you can find lots of advice on doing the Shuffle with children in beds, as well as tools for the challenges that come along with sleep coaching children in beds, in the next chapter, "Two and a Half to Five Years." If your preference is co-sleeping, please turn to Chapter 12 for techniques on doing the Sleep Lady Shuffle while co-sleeping with your one-and-a-half- to two-and-a-half-year-old.

One of the hardest aspects of sleep coaching for one-and-a-half- to two-and-a-half-year-olds is that parents are a little skeptical that they can change deeply ingrained habits, and they are often so exhausted after two years of sleep deprivation that the required nighttime consistency of the Sleep Lady Shuffle feels insurmountable. I've met parents who have literally fallen asleep on the floor in the middle of the night as they've tried to carry out these changes. But as you will see, children can and do learn the skill of putting themselves to sleep.

FIRST THINGS FIRST: SET A SCHEDULE

Children need regular nap times, regular bedtimes, and reasonably regular mealtimes. Their bodies need the routine to regulate day and night hormone cycles, and their little hearts and minds need the predictability to feel secure. But I also believe in some flexibility. The following sleep times are averages, but the variations are a lot less than many parents think, and your child may well need a lot more sleep than he's getting. The American Academy of Pediatrics and the National Sleep Foundation recently updated their recommended sleep averages for all age groups. You can visit their websites to learn more, but for now, I am offering a sample schedule based on what has worked for many parents of one-and-a-half- to two-and-a-half-year-olds with great success.

Even when you do develop a workable schedule, you will experience some natural variations. Some days your baby will nap or snack a little more, and some days she will nap or snack a little less. As you learn to read her sleep cues and recognize her sleep windows, you'll be able to adjust the schedule more easily. Watch her daytime behavior. If she's easy and content, she's probably on a pretty good schedule. If she's fussy and demanding, she may need longer naps, an earlier bedtime, a later wake-up time, or all of the above.

Sample Schedule

(Shift earlier if your child wakes between 6:00 and 7:00 a.m.)

7:00 7:30 a.m.	**Wake-up and Breakfast.**
12:00–12:30 p.m.	**Lunch.**
12:30–1:00 p.m.	**Afternoon Nap.** Snack upon waking.
5:00–5:30 p.m.	**Dinner.**
6:00–6:30 p.m.	**Bedtime Prep.** Start bath and bedtime routine.
7:00–8:00 p.m.	**In Bed.** (Sometimes 8:30, depending on age and nap schedule.)

Let's explore your ideal routine a bit more.

Wake-up. Give her a *dramatic wake-up*. Throw open the blinds, switch on the lights, sing cheery good-morning songs, and start the day. Create morning rituals, just like you have evening ones, to reinforce her understanding of wake-up time versus sleep time. Any time between 6:00 and 7:30 is normal for this age group. If she sleeps much later than 7:30, start waking her up earlier to get her on a more age-appropriate schedule. Usually, sleeping later just pushes the rest of her schedule out of whack, particularly if she attends preschool. With younger children, I change wake-up time in ten-minute intervals over several days. At this age, do it faster, because they adapt well. Either just wake her up at 7:30 and put up with a little crankiness for a day or two, or make the adjustment by about half an hour a day.

Morning Nap. By eighteen months, most children have consolidated to one nap, usually afternoon or midday. If yours hasn't yet done so, don't worry; it's uncommon but not abnormal. Read the "Changes and Challenges: Dropping the Morning Nap" section in Chapter 9, "Thirteen to Eighteen Months," to make that rough spot a little less bumpy.

Lunch and Afternoon Nap. Lunch is usually around noon, give or take a half hour. Afternoon naps for this age group usually start around 12:30 or 1:00, maybe 1:30. They'll cut back from two hours and fifteen

> ## Sleep Lady Tip
>
> As toddlers turn into preschoolers, they may be able to skip an occasional nap without falling apart. Don't be fooled into thinking that she's outgrown naps completely. Most kids need about an hour or an hour and a half until age three and a half to four.

minutes at eighteen months, to two hours at age two, and to about an hour and a half by age three.

A little variation is normal. Don't worry as long as the rest of her schedule is fine; tweak the napping schedule a bit if it's causing other sleep problems. For instance, if your eighteen-month-old naps for three hours but is cheerful and sleeping well, leave it alone. But if she's taking those long naps and then doesn't want to go to bed on time, gradually shorten the nap or move it a little earlier in the day (as long as it is after noon). Aim for about a four-hour gap between the end of the nap and bedtime for an eighteen-month-old; it will get closer to five hours as you near age three.

Dinner. Fight the temptation to keep young children up late so the whole family can eat together. Feed them around 5:00 or 6:00, even if that means eating without the rest of the family. The early schedule better matches their natural rhythm for eating and sleeping. If an early dinner means less family time, find ways to compensate, such as building in a little more parental playtime in the morning or having playtime after an early dinner.

Bedtime Prep. A soothing bedtime routine is a must, so allow plenty of time to prepare her for bed, physically and emotionally. By that, I mean leave time not just for bathing, tooth brushing, and PJs but also for calming down and getting ready to separate from you for the night. First, let's talk a bit about bedtime mechanics, the whens and wheres, including a few minor differences between being in a crib and a bed. Then we'll see how to create that calm, soothing transition to dreamland.

The bedtime routine should be in the bedroom, not all over the house, so she knows it's time to slow down and prepare for sleep. You still need to get her down drowsy but awake. As I mentioned, she no longer needs a feeding prior to bedtime, but some toddlers still like to nurse briefly or have a cup of water before bed. Just don't nurse her all the way to sleep or let her use her sippy cup as a sleep crutch. If you walk or rock your toddler, keep it brief and keep it in her room. Keep any bedtime music very soft. Use it to cue her that it's time to sleep, but then turn it off. You don't want the lullaby to be a sleep crutch so that she can't get to sleep or back to sleep without it. Ditto for toys with music and lights; phase them out before she falls asleep. At this age, toddlers often like a moment or two of deep-pressure hugging before you put them into bed. Try the "hot dog or sandwich exercise" created by Carol Kranowitz, which she describes in her book *The Out-of-Sync Child,* or visit my blog (https://sleeplady.com /blog/), where I also outline how to do this. You might want to introduce yoga as part of your routine. You can find terrific information and poses in Chapter 17.

The routine should literally be a routine. Young children are very ritual oriented. In fact, your child may well demand that you keep to the exact same routine each and every night. This may include singing the same song, playing the same game, or reading the same book over and over again. They get to the point where they notice if you try to skip a page or shorten a sentence!

Each of my kids had her own rituals at this age. Carleigh liked to kiss a flying cow she had hanging in her room. Later, we made up a "two things" game, where we talked about two things about her day. She liked to hear stories about my childhood or about when she was a baby. Gretchen and I had our own silly little game. She liked me to kiss my pinkie and make it buzz like a baby bee. The bee would then kiss her nose. I always told both girls that I would check on them again before I went to bed—a promise I made and carried out well into their school years.

Telling children what to expect, particularly as they get older and more verbal, helps fill their cravings for predictability while underscoring the rules. "Now I am going to tuck you in and give you a big hug, and then you are going to go to sleep and have wonderful dreams." If they start stalling and negotiating, you might want to "blame the clock" instead of getting into a power struggle. For instance, if they want to

Sleep Lady Tip

Remember when we talked about emotional availability? (See Chapter 3, "Getting to Know Your Child.") That focused connection with your child is always important—but it's absolutely essential that we be patient and fully present at bedtime. Try as best as possible to leave your workday behind. Forget about your to-do list for a moment. Put aside that email or phone call that upset you. Better yet, at bedtime, put aside your phone! Leave it in another room while you focus on your child. It will still be there once he's asleep. Having so many screens and devices distracting us is probably the biggest change I've seen since I started developing the Sleep Lady system. I know it's not easy to ignore your phone, but the benefits—to both you and your child—are huge.

read three more books, point to the clock and say, "It's ten minutes before eight, when we have to turn out the light. Let's see how many books we can read in ten minutes."

You may also try to make her feel invested in her bedtime, which becomes even more important in the next two or three years. For instance, Jake and his long-eared bunny liked to watch the fish tank in his room, and Evelyn permitted Jake to decide whether the fish should have their little light on or not. Joanne always gave her son Ilan a two- or three-minute reminder before story time was over, and then she let him put out the bedside lamp by himself (at least, he thought his little hand was flicking that switch all by itself).

Talking about fun things that happened during the day or about pleasant things to anticipate the next day allays bedtime anxieties. You can even make a list of sweet things to dream about.

Bedtime, meaning asleep in bed, not thinking about going upstairs, should be between 7:00 and 8:00.

BEDTIME FINDER: DO THE MATH BACKWARD

Figuring out the exact time for your individual child is one part watching sleep cues and one part backward math. Start with her average wake-up time and count back the hours she needs. For instance, if your eighteen-month-old wakes up at 7:00 a.m. and needs eleven and a quarter hours of sleep, she should be *asleep by* 7:45 p.m. Start putting her down at around 7:00 or 7:15, depending on how long her bath and bedtime routine take. If your two-and-a-half-year-old wakes up at 7:00 a.m. and needs eleven hours of sleep at night, she needs to be asleep by 8:00 p.m., so you should probably be heading for bedtime prep around 7:15 or 7:30. These are averages. Your child may need a half hour more or a half hour less. Watch her for signs that she is getting tired, and make sure she's in bed drowsy but awake before she's overtired.

On many occasions, parents who work in careers with atypical hours ask whether it is possible to keep their toddlers up later and start their days later. My answer is always "I can't make any promises that it will work, but we can certainly try!" A few conditions apply, however. The first is that everyone in the family has to be able to sleep later, which means the child isn't preparing to go to day care or preschool early in the morning. The second condition is the family has to be committed to filling the daytime sleep tank and shifting the entire schedule later, including naps, meals, and so on.

Because of circadian rhythms, which are pretty sturdy by this age, there is no guarantee this will work. Use your intuition and watch your child's sleep cues and behaviors to determine whether moving back to a more traditional schedule is best for your child's sleep needs and overall development. For example, if your child is now going to bed at 9:00 p.m. but continues to wake at 7:00 a.m., you should shift back to an earlier bedtime so your child can get the sleep she needs at nighttime.

Sleep Lady Tip

Either parent should be able to put the child to bed, and it's okay if two parents have slightly different styles. But both parents should put the child to bed at the same time and should display a consistent response to such bedtime behavior as crying, throwing toys, and so forth. The united front sends a clearer, less confusing message that discourages such antics and lays the groundwork for all the co-parenting to come.

HOW TO COMMUNICATE YOUR
SCHEDULE TO CAREGIVERS

Whether you have a stay-at-home nanny, a day care center, a once-in-a-while sitter, or a grandparent taking care of your child during the day, communicating and maintaining your new schedule can be tricky, but not futile. Even when playing by the rules of other providers and facilities, all does not have to be lost. Here are some strategies to help you all get on the same page when you become committed to sleep coaching:

1. Make a copy of your daily schedule—like the one in this chapter—and give it to your caregivers, letting them know you have begun sleep coaching and that for just a few weeks, you are asking them to be mindful of the schedule when they can.

2. Each morning when you leave your child, let the caregiver know what time your child woke up that morning, as well as how many times during the night she was up, and therefore what time she will most likely be ready for her afternoon nap.

3. Ask the childcare providers if they can work toward a total of one and a half to two hours of nap time no matter how they get the child to sleep. We cannot expect or presume they will be comfortable or allowed to adhere to the Shuffle or reduce the use of sleep crutches, but you can certainly ask. Sometimes that is the best we can do. Just remember that your child getting sleep throughout the day, no matter how it is accomplished, whether by patting to sleep or another sleep crutch, will still help you with nighttime sleep coaching, as your child will not be overtired and will have the approximately two hours of daytime sleep in her sleep tank.

4. Some childcare providers just won't nap train (day care centers often have their own schedules and methods). If that is the case, you can still sleep coach by adhering to your morning and evening routines, focusing on getting the child to sleep through the night. Then, on weekends, nap coach diligently. Don't worry about how that might feel inconsistent. It will take longer, but it can still work. For instructions on nap coaching your one-and-a-half- to two-and-a-half-year-old, see the section "Much Ado About Napping" on page 266.

TAKE NOTE OF DEVELOPMENTAL CHANGES

Walking and talking and jumping out of cribs, oh my! Just when you think you have your daily schedule and coaching plan, here come the developmental changes to throw a wrench in them. Developmental changes are those milestone moments that are super exciting to witness and indicate your child is thriving. By now, your toddler's milestones go way beyond the physical ones you measured monthly at your pediatrician's back in the baby days. Your one-and-a-half- to two-and-a-half-year-old is learning to follow simple directions yet tests your rules and his limits, which can make bedtime more challenging.

Curious about their world, toddlers are extremely eager to explore, leading to more limit testing and boundary breaking. They climb, crawl, crash, and clamber, standing on furniture, trying to scramble out of the crib. Yet as they push their limits, they rely on their parents to keep setting boundaries, seeking safety, reassurance, and security. Their language skills are blossoming, but they understand more than they can say, leading to frustration and tantrums. Their favorite words seem to be *no, I do,* and *mine,* and they are particularly possessive about their toys and their parents. As their language skills improve, they just love to stall, bargain, and negotiate, particularly around bedtime.

They may go through periods when they have the "scaries" because of the dark, thunder, monsters, and the like. Nightmares and night terrors may start and may be a recurring problem for the next several years. Potty training can complicate bedtime behavior if you let it become a battle of wills rather than a cooperative venture. To prevent bedtime from becoming a battle, make sure that you have a very consistent, predictable, and soothing routine. Clear rules and parental consistency are essential, along with plenty of love, cuddles, and kisses.

SEPARATION ANXIETY

Separation anxiety may have peaked at the first birthday, but prepare for another big wave at about eighteen months and then spells of it throughout early childhood. A nice long, gentle, predictable transition to bedtime, quality time with one or both parents who are really focused on bedtime rituals—and not on the telephone, washing dishes, or paying bills—helps soothe those worries. Taking the tips above on how to bring emotional availability to bedtime can help your child separate from you more peacefully.

At some point, your child may begin to articulate that he wants you to stay with him at bedtime. It can be heartbreaking to hear him plead, "Mommy, sit," or "Daddy, stay." Be gentle but firm when the time does come to say good night. If your child isn't talking yet, she can probably still understand your verbal reassurances about how Mommy and Daddy love her and will be nearby.

Young enough to still experience some separation anxiety at night and old enough to suspect they may be missing excitement if they are asleep, children this age excel in stalling and delaying tactics at bedtime. I've heard some sleep doctors call these "curtain calls" because they aim to get the parent to come back to the bedside over and over again.

When a child repeatedly seeks to be tucked in, kissed, given a blankie, and so on after normal, reasonable limits have been reached, the parent should respond once. Define what you consider reasonable limits for your child, balancing his separation fears with his gift for manipulation! Maybe you want to say good night once and that's it; maybe you don't mind going in three or four times. But once you set those limits, make them clear to your child and remind him, "This is the last time."

The next time, if there is a next time, your response should be neutral but firm. Say, "Now it is time to go to sleep," or "I love you, sweetheart, but you know it's time to go to sleep now." It's important to remember consistently and follow through. Don't say anything like "Last time," if you are not absolutely committed to making it the last time.

Separation anxiety at bedtime is an opportunity to be emotionally available to your child, validating her fears, even helping her name them and process them, so she feels more secure in trusting that you are there when she needs you.

Use Loveys

Loveys, usually a special stuffed animal or blanket, are very important for those children who are gaining independence but still need that extra helping of security. Loveys help with separation, with fighting the scaries, and with breaking lingering emotional attachments to bottles, cups, or pacifiers.

> ★ **Sleep Lady Tip**
>
> Starting at about age two, tell her how sweet and cozy she looks when she sleeps. Children love to hear that; it also reassures them that you are watching out for them while they sleep.

Even children who have spurned loveys in the past may embrace one now. They may want a lovey from a favorite book or video. With their blossoming imaginations, they also like including loveys in games, including bedtime and nap-time rituals. For instance, if you look out the window and say good night to doggies or cars, have the lovey say good night to doggies and cars, too. Tuck the lovey in with her for bedtime and naps, and when she wakes up at night, remind her that she has her lovey to snuggle.

However, if your child's lovey is a pacifier, a bottle, a cup, or your breast, she may not accept a new lovey as easily. As you wean her from the bottle or start to weaken the association between nursing and sleep, she will be more receptive to a new security object, but it takes time.

Parents may worry if their child wants to carry the lovey everywhere. If the lovey is a pacifier, restrict it first to the house, then to sleep time. But if it's a toy or blanket, I don't regard carrying it as a problem before age two. Just have a few of them in case you lose one! When your child reaches two years of age, you might want to restrict the lovey to the house and car or maybe a special occasion, such as going to the doctor or an anxiety-provoking unfamiliar place or situation.

Jeffrey, at two and a half, could not get to sleep or back to sleep without his bottle or twirling his mother's hair, a fixation he had formed when he was only six months old. Jenn took Jeffrey to one of those workshops where you can make your own teddy bear; they have them at malls and crafts shops. Jenn helped Jeffrey make a "fireman bear" to match his fireman bed theme. His excitement made it easy to weave the fireman bear into the bedtime routine and ease out of the bottle drinking and hair twirling. "Making it himself really got him invested in it," Jenn said.

Later, Jeffrey adopted a long-eared bunny as a lovey, and yes, he twirled its ears to his heart's content. Jeffrey, whose own hair was too short to twirl, still wanted Mom's hair when he was sick or particularly tired, even after she got a short, tousled cut. "I don't know why he likes it so much; he is always telling me, 'I love your hair.'" But while it still may be a habit, it is no longer a constant need that disrupts his sleep.

NEW MOBILITY

Escaping the Crib

All too often, parents rush to get their child out of a crib and into a bed, as though it were a sign of achievement, maturity, or their guaranteed success as adults. One woman I worked with even reported an unspoken competition in her child's playgroup to see which toddler could move first to a bed. Children who switch too young to a bed may experience sleep disruption and difficult bedtimes with tears and tantrums. Safety is also a factor. I worry a lot about a twenty-month-old roaming around in his room at night, pulling out drawers, unplugging lamps, exercising all that wonderful but potentially hazardous curiosity.

Even if the child is trying to climb out of the crib, I almost always advise parents to keep him in as long as possible, definitely until two and a half and preferably until three. By then, a child has the verbal skills to understand the big-bed rules and the beginning of *some* impulse control to help him stay in his bed.

I like keeping toddlers in a crib as long as I can, but they sometimes have their own agendas. If your child starts climbing out, dissuade him by making the climb harder by lowering the mattress. If you have determined he has mastered jumping out of the crib every time, put pillows on the ground for safety in case he attempts Olympic-style hurdling. Remove large toys or stuffed animals from the crib that might serve as a launchpad.

If he does get out, put him right back in the crib with minimal interaction—except to say, "No climbing." Be firm, but don't yell at him. Try stationing yourself outside the bedroom door, out of his line of vision if possible, and peek in. When he starts to raise his leg again, say, "No climbing." Sound like you mean it, and keep putting him back in the crib if you have to.

If your child still seems determined to get out, particularly if he's under age two, try a *sleep sack*, which will make it more difficult to get that leg over the side and torpedo out. That may buy you a few months before you switch to the bed. Visit my website (https://sleeplady.com/products) for recommendations on sleep sacks that can help with this.

They may also miss that feeling of cozy containment in their crib. I know some families who regretted moving the child to the bed and managed to get him back to a crib, particularly if he was talking about his crib or trying to climb into a younger sibling's crib. It's not too late to transition back to a crib, particularly if your child was not jumping out of it. I have worked with families who thought their children "hated" their cribs and therefore assumed a bed would be better. But with this age group, it turns out usually to be less about the crib and more about not having good sleep associations. Now with tools in this book, you can hit the Reset button and retry the crib with the sleep manners and sleep hygiene reinforced in the Shuffle. It's not too late!

Some kids do hate cribs and start talking about big-boy or big-girl beds. If they can articulate it, that's a reasonably good sign that they have the verbal ability to understand big-bed rules. In the event you have already moved your child out of her crib and into a bed for safety reasons or otherwise, please turn to the next chapter, "Two and a Half to Five Years," to learn how to use the Sleep Lady Shuffle in a bed along with other troubleshooting advice for challenges that come along with children and beds (such as walking around the room or getting in and out of their bed while you do the Shuffle).

TANTRUMS

The dictionary's definition of a tantrum is "an uncontrolled outburst of anger and frustration, typically in a young child." For parents, it's a downright mortifying event, no matter which way you look at it. Toddlers understand more than they can say, which can be frustrating for them, especially if they want to negotiate with you (or outright protest).

Parents scramble for advice and strategies on how to control tantrums. In my opinion, far too many child experts instruct parents to use time-outs as a response. I am not one of them. In fact, I believe placing a toddler who can't fully express himself in a corner or on a chair will inadvertently shame him for having what feels like big emotions that he doesn't know how to handle. It's not just time-outs. I avoid recommending any kind of response that doesn't help a child learn the skill of self-regulation. I don't recommend walking away from the child, which sends a message of dismissal, or avoiding eye contact when he is upset, which undermines the compassion a child needs to bond and attach to us securely. We want children to know it's okay to have big feelings and to eventually learn to understand their emotions and over the years learn to process and manage them. It's one of our many tasks as parents to help teach and model to them. The same is true for learning the skill of putting oneself to sleep independently.

This all connects to the bottle weaning, pacifier weaning, and weaning from nursing and sleep coaching in general. It is all about teaching toddlers to self-regulate with reassurance and not leaving them alone to figure it out. This is why it's important for parents to address daytime behavior in addition to bedtime behavior. If your toddler throws a tantrum for a bottle during the day and you give him a bottle, and then during a night tantrum you withhold the bottle, that's confusing to a toddler. Remember that toddlers experience our consistency and boundaries as comforting, and that helps them to feel safe and know what to expect.

I have found that a technique called *hug-hold*, which has origins in the positive parenting field, works the best not only to soothe tantrums but to help toddlers process their emotions, name/identify them when they are a bit older, and calm themselves down on a physiological level. It also does wonders for parents' blood pressure! By their nature, the steps of hug-hold are calming, so it is an appropriate sleep-time strategy when your toddler throws down at bedtime. For step-by-step instructions for the hug-hold, see page 187 in the previous chapter.

CHANGES IN EATING AND SLEEPING

When our babies are little, we strive to get them to bed on a full tummy, hoping it will help them learn to sleep longer at night. That's no longer necessary. Those youngsters who are still breastfeeding may want to nurse briefly before sleep. That's fine, unless she must nurse to get herself to sleep at bedtime, nap time, or when she wakes up at night. (I'll talk more about how to gently modify night feeding when we address specific sleep crutches and solutions on page 255.)

In general, children this age should be able to go twelve, even fourteen hours from dinner until breakfast without a bedtime snack except perhaps a glass of water. Most pediatricians recommend limiting milk to sixteen ounces a day maximum (three or four four-ounce cups). The milk amount may be lower if your child eats cheese and yogurt. Kids who drink milk (or juice) all day tend not to be hungry at mealtimes and don't get enough solid foods, or enough of a variety of solid foods, to meet their expanded nutritional needs.

Barring any unusual dietary or health concerns, children eighteen to thirty months should have three anticipated mealtimes—breakfast, lunch, and dinner—plus snacks in the midmorning and following their nap in the afternoon. Some will want a third nibble, but keep it very light if it's close to a meal.

If you haven't already introduced a cup, do so now even if you are still nursing. Offer the sippy cup of water, milk, toddler formula, whatever your doctor recommends, at each meal. If he takes a bottle at night, switch to a cup, and if he takes milk at bedtime, switch to water. You don't want the milk bottle to become a sleep crutch, something he needs every time he tries to fall asleep. If you need more help with weaning from a bottle, see Chapter 9, "Thirteen to Eighteen Months."

EXPERIENCING THE SCARIES

Children at this age may get the scaries, conjuring up all sorts of gremlins and monsters at bedtime. The monsters might not be real, but your toddler's fears are very real to him. The scaries are an opportunity to flex your emotional availability muscle and model empathy and compassion as you sleep coach, so he never forgets you are near and he knows you are validating his emotions and concerns.

There are no hard-and-fast rules; trust your instincts and see what works. Try shining a flashlight into the closet or under the bed. Enlist that lovey to help you look. "See, your snuggly bear says there are no monsters under your bed, and now snuggly bear will get in bed with you and you'll both be safe and sound."

> Teddy was sleep coached at seven months and slept well for many months but began experiencing some bedtime fears just shy of his third birthday. Although Teddy used to like to sleep in total darkness, Ellen now found that a small night-light helped. "He'll ask me, 'Mom, are monsters real?' and I'll say, 'No, they are only in your imagination.' We have to go through this every single night." He also clung to the book It's OK! Tom's Afraid of the Dark! and she read it to him every night for many months.

For a list of other bedtime books that help with the scaries, visit my website (https://sleeplady.com/products/).

POTTY TRAINING

I don't see any problem doing sleep training and daytime potty training simultaneously, as long as the child is ready, able, and reasonably enthusiastic. Indeed, children often have a window between eighteen and thirty months (later is not abnormal, so don't worry) when they are quite interested in at least starting daytime potty training. Seize that moment or you might have to wait months for another chance. Talk to your doctor about whether your child shouldn't wear a diaper at night. Staying dry at night depends on whether your child's body is ready—whether his bladder is big enough yet, whether he has the hormones to quiet down the kidneys, and even genetics. I'm not going to review all the different theories and techniques of potty training. A good rule of thumb is to start potty training in the daytime and consider nighttime potty training when he wakes up in the morning with a dry diaper ten mornings in a row. This is an indication his bladder can hold it and you can stop using a diaper at night.

At nap time, give him a diaper or pull-up until he stays dry for at least a week. Leave nighttime for last. In fact, as far as I'm concerned, you can leave a diaper or pull-up on at night all the way up to age four or five. (I address bed-wetting for older children in Chapter 14, "Could Sleep Disturbances Be a Medical Condition?") Children often learn to stay dry at night on their own in time, and it is counterintuitive to expend all this energy teaching a child to sleep all night and then confuse him by waking him up to go to the bathroom! Many toddlers this age don't want to wear diapers at night or feel like they aren't "big kids" if they wear one, yet their bodies are not ready to stay dry all night long. As you potty train during the day, you can explain to your child, "Your bladder has to grow bigger to hold the pee-pee all night long." Reassure her that she isn't doing anything wrong, but her body will tell her when she is ready to stop wearing the diaper. You can even say, "When you are dry for ten nights in a row, then we can have big-girl underwear at night!"

If your child is already day and night potty trained, meaning he is staying dry at night, ask your child to sit on the potty before naps and before bed (but don't insist). If your child starts saying "I need to go potty" as a stalling tactic at bedtime, bring him to the bathroom. The trick to stopping this stalling tactic is to keep it boring, *really* uneventful, as the engagement with you is what the toddler is after. No talking, no games, no show-and-tell. At first, walk with your child to the bathroom; do not carry him there. The goal is for him to do everything as independently as he can, making it feel like a chore, not parent fun time. As much as possible, have him do the pants pulling, getting on to the potty, lifting the seat, washing and drying his hands, pulling his pants back up, and so on. Some parents graduate to not even entering the bathroom with the child, standing in the doorway with their back facing the hallway. You don't want to turn lights on, as that will disrupt the winding down you have achieved, so keep a night-light on in the bathroom at all times. Finally, if he still uses the potty as an excuse to prolong bedtime, try saying you'll wait in his room for him while he goes. Some parents put a portable potty in the bedroom to really make their point that the potty is not to be used to have a party.

THE SLEEP LADY SHUFFLE

As you know by now, the Sleep Lady Shuffle is a gentle behavioral modification technique that lets you be a comforting presence as your child learns to put himself to sleep and back to sleep in his crib. The Shuffle is used to nap coach as well, but for the purpose of this section, I will first guide you through sleep coaching at night. I would be remiss if I didn't tell you that there is no such thing as a no-cry sleep-coaching system, so expect some tears. Remind yourself that you will always be there to assure her that she is not alone, she is safe, and she is loved and supported as she slowly learns this new skill. I explain my Sleep Lady Shuffle here for toddlers who are still in cribs, but it's quite similar to the Shuffle for those in beds, and I outline the modifications in the next chapter, "Two and a Half to Five Years."

Before beginning the Shuffle, please turn to Chapter 5: Prepping for Sleep-Coaching Success, where I lay the groundwork for sleep coaching. It is best to begin sleep coaching at bedtime, after a day when she had a great nap, no matter how you got her to nap. You will have greater success at nighttime if your toddler's daytime sleep tank is filled.

You should follow the Shuffle schedule, moving on to the next position even if your child has had a bad night or two, fussing or waking more frequently. *Don't be surprised if there's a little regression or protest the first night of each new chair position.* If your child gets sick during the Shuffle, you might want to pause and maintain your position until he feels a little better. You might even have to move a little closer during an illness to offer more comfort, but then resume the Shuffle when he recovers.

TIPS FOR THE FIRST THREE SHUFFLE NIGHTS

1. *Don't get into a power struggle about laying your toddler down—you won't win!* If he is sitting or standing in the crib, pat the mattress and encourage him to lie down. Stay calm and say things like "Sh-sh," "Night-night," and "It's okay, lie down." Sit down in your chair to encourage him to lie down and be closer to your level.
2. *You can stroke, pat, rub,* sh-sh, *or sing to your child intermittently through the rails of the crib.* But don't do it constantly until he falls asleep, or it will become his new sleep crutch. Stop when he is starting to fall asleep. (Some toddlers don't like to be touched as they fall asleep; follow your instincts and his cues.) If you notice every time you stop patting your child that he starts crying, you are patting too much. Try to touch less and less during the first three nights, knowing that on night 4, you will be moving farther away.

3. *The parent controls the touch.* Don't let the toddler fall asleep grasping your finger or hand, for example, because he will wake up when you move, and it will start all over again. Pat or stroke a different part of his body or the top of his hand.

4. *If the toddler becomes hysterical, pick him up to calm him.* Stay in his room; don't walk around the house or sit down in the rocker. Don't let him fall asleep in your arms. When he's calm, kiss him, put him back in the crib, and sit near him in the chair. Make soothing sounds and pat or stroke him. If you pick him up and he's immediately calm, then you've been had. Instead of you training him to sleep, he trained you to pick him up! Wait a little longer next time. Trust your instincts and your knowledge of your child. You will know within a night or two whether picking him up helps or gets him more upset.

5. *Stay by his crib until he is sound asleep at bedtime and during all night awakenings the first three days of the Shuffle.* If you rush out of the room the second he closes his eyes, he will wake up and be upset, and you'll have to start all over.

6. *Return to your Shuffle position, and follow these rules each time the toddler wakes during the first three nights.* Go to the crib, give him a kiss, encourage him to lie down if necessary, and sit in the chair. Do this at each awakening until 6:00 a.m.

NIGHTS 1–3: NEXT TO THE CRIB

Once bath, stories, and songs are over, *sit in a chair next to the crib.* If he cries or fusses, you can stroke or pat him intermittently, but don't do it constantly or you'll just create a new sleep crutch or negative association. You can sing during the get-ready-for-bed stage, but once it's time for him to sleep, stick to calming *sh-sh* or *night-night* sounds. You might want to try closing your own eyes, which conveys a sleepy-time message and makes it harder for him to talk to you or try to engage you, particularly at this age when he is probably going to try very hard to get you to interact.

Stay there until he falls asleep. If he stands up, pat the mattress and tell him to lie down. Once he does get down, stroke or pat him intermittently if he finds it comforting. This works better if you are sitting, not standing, by the crib.

On night 1, if necessary or if you are not quite comfortable, you can do more touching. But don't touch steadily; do it on and off, and know that you are touching too much if you stop patting and your toddler cries. Similarly, during your first three nights next to the crib, try to be mindful of how much touch you are offering, because on night 4, you will be positioned farther away from your toddler and won't be touching as much. You

> ### Sleep Lady Tip
>
> When you soothe your child by going to her crib to pat or rub her back, it is important that you control the touch. Instead of having her hold your hand or finger, you should pat her. Make sure you don't caress her too steadily, or else she might cry when you stop. Do it on and off. Count to yourself if it helps— count to ten touching, then count to sixty not touching, then touch for another ten counts. You don't want to swap one negative association, like rocking, for another—like your constant touch or the sound of your voice.

will defeat moving away from the crib if you go crib-side each time to, for instance, pat him to sleep. (The no-snuggles or no-picking-up-the-toddler rules, by the way, do not apply to a child who is sick, frightened, or startled.)

Unlike many other sleep-coaching methods, with the Shuffle, you can pick up your toddler to calm him down when he gets extremely upset. Try not to do this either immediately after putting him in the crib at bedtime or as the first thing during the night when he wakes. Try patting him, or pointing to his lovey, for example, and sitting in the chair next to his crib. Tell him that it's okay and stay in the chair until he falls asleep.

Each time your *child calls for you in the middle of the night, resume the position you were in at bedtime that night as you calm him back to sleep.* We want a consistent response to all awakenings.

NIGHTS 4–6: HALFWAY TO THE DOOR

Explain, particularly to an older child who can understand better, that because he has done such a wonderful job of learning to go to sleep, you are now going to move your chair farther away but will still stay with him until he falls asleep. *Move the chair about halfway to the door.* (If the room is very small or the crib happens to be very close to the door, you should instead move to the center of the room *or sit by the door in his room.*) Continue the soothing sounds, but stay in the chair as much as you can. Get up to pat or stroke him a little as needed, or make some of those same soothing sounds you've been using. Make sure you don't go crib-side and end up patting him to sleep or holding his hand, as you will defeat the purpose of moving away and will teach your toddler to fuss until you go pat him to sleep or hold his hand to sleep. Try not to pick him up, but if he's really upset and you do need to pick him up, go ahead and do so, over the crib if possible. Hold him until he's calm, but keep it brief and don't let him fall asleep in your arms or on your lap. Sometimes a minute of deep-pressure holding will really help him calm down. Stay in the chair until he falls asleep.

> ### ★ Sleep Lady Tip
>
> Be careful that you don't create new sleep crutches. One mother, using the Shuffle to teach her son to sleep without being rocked on and off all night, introduced a new song about the night sky, which immediately assumed the same psychological importance for him as the rocking had! Within a few nights, she found herself singing it three times, then four times and then five, because the instant she stopped, he roused himself from semi-slumber and demanded, "Sky! Sky! Sky!" He also demanded the song each time he woke up at night.

Some children in this age group resist the changes that occur when starting the Shuffle. That usually doesn't happen during the first few nights; it's more likely to occur a little way down the road (like when you are no longer sitting by the crib), when they realize this isn't a passing whim of yours, that it's their new reality. He might start throwing his lovey out onto the floor. Then he'll want you to pick it up and put it back for him. Then he'll throw it out again. It's both a way of expressing frustration at you for making new sleep demands and a way of engaging you. Don't fall for it. Let everything stay on the floor. If he throws out his lovey or pacifier and then gets upset about it, tell him you will give it back as soon as he lies down. If the lovey or pacifier is being used as a game of fetch when it is time to go to sleep, see page 183 of Chapter 9, "Thirteen to Eighteen Months," for more advice on how to stop the madness.

NIGHTS 7–9: CHAIR AT THE DOORWAY, INSIDE THE ROOM

Again, explain he is doing a great job and tell him that you are going to move the chair again. Sit close to him and hug him for a minute before you make that move, but don't get so entwined that you have to struggle to get loose. Then move the *chair next to the doorway inside his room*. You should be dimly lit but still in his view. Continue the same soothing techniques, intervening as little as possible. He may cry a little bit, but gently reassure him and he will fall asleep.

NIGHTS 10–12: INTO THE HALLWAY, IN VIEW

You are now going to move out into the *hallway with the door open enough so that he can still see you*. Explain this move carefully before you make it, and praise him again for what a good sleeping boy he is becoming. You can keep making *sh-sh* sounds from the hallway—not constantly but enough to let him know that his parents are close by and responsive.

NIGHTS 13 AND ON

Next you are going to stay in *the hallway or in a very nearby room, where the child cannot see you but can hear you*. You can make some reassuring *sh-sh* sounds, not constantly but enough to let her know that you are close by and responsive. If she cries, try checking on her from her bedroom door—without going all the way into the room. Be calm and reassuring. Make some comforting sounds, conveying that you are not far away and that you know she can put herself to sleep.

A fair number of children start falling asleep and staying asleep by night 7 or 10—occasionally even sooner—but most parents have to take one more step and leave the child alone for five-minute intervals—doing what I call *job checks*. Tell him that you will keep checking on him until he is asleep. Leaving the child may seem like a radical change for you, but think about it: all that chair shuffling has given him nearly two weeks of preparation. He has given up some sleep crutches, and he has learned "Mommy is right down the hall even though I can't see her." Or "Daddy is sitting on the floor right near my room, and he loves me." Describe exactly where you will be sitting and explain that you will be close by even though he won't see you.

Don't go too far away. Stay on the same floor, maybe in a nearby room, maybe just read a magazine or a book for the first few nights. He may cry for a few minutes, but keep going back every five minutes to reassure him. You don't have to leave him more than five minutes, and unlike the cry-it-out approaches, you don't keep making the intervals longer. In fact, I strongly encourage you to keep a close eye on the clock so you don't exceed five minutes and upset him more.

IF YOUR TODDLER IS STILL WAKING AT NIGHT

If these techniques don't eliminate those final night awakenings, you might be putting your child to bed when he's too drowsy. It's easier for a toddler to put himself to sleep at bedtime than in the middle of the night—particularly if he was 90 percent asleep before his head hit the pillow. Try putting him down when he's a bit more alert, even if it means backing up and doing a few more days of the Shuffle. You may find that an earlier bedtime also helps him conquer the night awakenings. Try moving bedtime a half hour earlier. If you are still nursing at bedtime, try doing that feeding a little earlier in the evening to further weaken the link between suckling and sleeping.

JOB CHECKS

Because toddlers don't really understand what five minutes is but older toddlers can, you can explain time in terms of what I call *job checks*. "Mommy is going to change her clothes, and then I will be right back to check on you." Or "Daddy is going to brush his teeth, but I'll be right back." (If your child becomes more awake each time you come to check, you may want to consider longer intervals, or you may want to start with five minutes and slowly lengthen it.)

He may cry a bit the first few nights, but very rarely do children cry for more than a few minutes after going through the chair routine. If he does cry, check on him from the doorway. Be reassuring but calm. Keep in mind, he has gained confidence that you are nearby and responsive. He's ready to learn this skill.

Some parents decide this is as far as they want to go for now, and they stay in the hallway a few feet away from the child's room. That's fine as long as it's not taking an hour and the child doesn't need you in the doorway on and off all night long. Other parents gradually move away and phase out the checks. If you are using job checks, always return as promised.

Sleep Lady Tip

Children get ritualized easily, like that boy with the "Sky" song. Make the changes every three days—or less. Dragging it out makes it harder, not easier, for him. Give it more than three days and he'll expect you to stay exactly where you are—and get mad or upset when you try to double that distance.

NOT READY FOR THE SHUFFLE? YOU CAN TRY SWITCHING ASSOCIATIONS UNTIL YOU ARE

Some parents are more sensitive to tears and want to take sleep coaching in even slower steps if possible. *You* have to be ready to sleep coach, and often it feels like a huge leap. And if you can't take that leap, take some preparatory smaller steps before you sleep coach 100 percent.

For instance, if your child depends on you to put her to sleep by rocking, feeding, or lying down with her and you are not ready to put your toddler down drowsy but awake at bedtime, you can switch the crutch, or what I call *switching negative sleep associations*. If you nurse her to sleep, stop one night and instead have the other parent rock her to sleep. Yes, you are creating a new sleep crutch—from nursing to sleep to rocking to sleep—but because the behavior of the other parent rocking her is so new, the toddler is not as attached to it. It may be easier to stop rocking to sleep when you are ready to start sleep coaching.

Another small step you can take now is to work on gently fading out your child's current sleep crutch. For example, if you always hold your child until she's completely asleep, try holding her until she's almost asleep. Then put her in her crib and pat her all the way to sleep. You can also try patting her back to sleep during the night.

SHUFFLING WITH MULTIPLES

Your multiple babies shared a womb, and it's usually a good idea to have them share a room. Some families even put them in the same crib for a few months, until they start rolling over. Yes, they may grunt, whimper, and make all sorts of strange toddler noises, but they almost always learn to sleep through each other's sounds, and you want to encourage them to do so. Be careful about responding too quickly if one makes a noise. Parents often rush in as soon as they hear a peep, fearing that one will wake up the other one. You may be reinforcing the troubled sleeper while you protect the one who is asleep. The sleeping twin may be oblivious, or she may stir but then get herself right back to sleep. Parents of triplets or quadruplets can adapt these techniques for their children, although most don't separate them for naps simply because they don't have enough room! A parent can sit in the middle of the bedroom between the children to soothe them. The children learn quickly to sleep through their siblings' crying and fussing.

Just like with singletons, start the Sleep Lady Shuffle at bedtime after a day when your toddlers' daytime sleep averages have been met—which means getting naps in any way you can. Whether you need to rely on all your sleep crutches at the same time or take a daily car ride, getting the daytime sleep tank filled—even if it means taking drastic measures—is a must before beginning the Shuffle at night. If possible, move the cribs so they are at least three feet apart, and have one parent sit in a chair between them. If two people are available, this will be easier to do. Each parent can sit by a crib/multiple.

After your soothing bedtime routine, place your toddlers in their cribs drowsy but awake and sit in your Shuffle chair position. If one parent is doing the Shuffle, sit in a chair between the cribs and go back and forth. If two parents or other caregivers are available, it will be easier, and each adult can sit by a child. Stroke and soothe each child in turn. Follow the rules of the Shuffle for the first three nights on page 244. Make sure that by the third night, you are using your voice to soothe instead of relying too much on touch.

Both parents must be on the same page—one is not picking up more than the other, for instance. If one child is more of a problem sleeper than the other, have the parent who has an easier time with consistency sit next to that child. If the sleep crutch is nursing to sleep, let the nonnursing parent do the first few nights.

If you can't move the cribs and they must remain far apart and out of your arm's reach, each parent can sit by each crib for the first three nights. By night 4, you will be sitting in the middle of the room or by the door, depending on the room size. Only one parent needs to sit there. I have had both parents eager to sit in the second position—you certainly can if you want—but it's not necessary.

FREQUENTLY ASKED QUESTIONS
FROM PARENTS OF MULTIPLES

Q: I have twins, and one is a better sleeper than the other and gets woken by the other twin. How should I sleep coach them?

A: In those cases where one toddler truly disrupts the other's sleep, I do make exceptions and separate them at night during sleep coaching. It's usually a good idea to leave the poorer sleeper where he is and move the sounder sleeper to another room, using a portable crib if necessary. Good sleepers tend to be more flexible and can more easily adjust to a temporary new sleeping place, even if it's a little noisier or brighter than the toddlers' bedroom. Once the poorer sleeper is sleeping through the night fairly consistently, you can return the sounder sleeper to the shared room.

Q: I have triplets. How can we do the Shuffle and sit next to their cribs when there are only two parents available? And sometimes only one of us is home at bedtime?

A: If you have triplets or quads, you can still do this, but be gentle on yourself by not expecting too much at first. You are outnumbered, after all. You may need to have one parent sit between two toddlers or two parents tag teaming with three toddlers, and so on. If there is just one parent, sit in the middle of the room and gently move back and forth to stroke and soothe each child in turn. Follow the rules of the Shuffle for the first three nights on page 244. Make sure that by the third night, you are using your voice intermittently to soothe instead of relying too much on touch.

SLEEP CRUTCHES AND SOLUTIONS

Toddlers who have trouble getting to sleep and staying asleep often have *negative associations*, or *sleep crutches*, as discussed in "What's a Sleep Crutch?" on page 50. Here are some of the most common crutches that can disrupt sleep coaching at this age.

CRUTCH: NIGHTTIME FEEDING

Example: My two-year-old still wakes up and wants a bottle two to three times a night, even when I feed her right before bedtime! What can I do?

Eliminating Nighttime Feeding

Many kids do still have the nighttime milk habit, possibly because we as parents were so concerned about getting that last meal in them as infants that we haven't let go of it now that they are toddlers. In those cases, feeding and sleeping patterns may still be closely entwined. Let's talk first about nursing, and then about cups or bottles.

There's a subtle but important difference between nursing at bedtime and nursing to sleep. Some moms breastfeed until age two or older, and bedtime may be the nursing time they hold on to the longest. Avoid letting your child fall asleep at the breast. Either nurse until he's drowsy but still awake and then put him down or, better yet at this age, nurse him as part of the bedtime ritual but not as the last activity. In other words, nurse and then brush teeth, play a quiet game, read a book, or sing a song. Create a little space between nursing and sleep. Try keeping a light on while you nurse, so he is less likely to link breastfeeding with conking out.

With cups and bottles, you want to move from a bottle to a cup, from milk to water, from in bed to shortly before bed. How fast you make those changes depends on your temperament and your child's, but your end point is a cup of water before lights-out. (Or no drink at all, eventually.)

Some kids switch in a few days, if you explain it to them, with no problem. Others take it slower and may resist a little, but even a gradual transition should not take more than a week to ten days. The more they resist, the more emotionally attached they were to the cup or bottle.

If your child is using a bottle rather than a sippy cup, make the switch now, particularly if your child needs the bottle to go to sleep and back to sleep. Bottle weaning has to be built into your sleep-coaching plan. If you really want to keep the bottle, at least decide the child is not going to sleep with it. If you want to keep the bottle during the day, take him off at night. Or if you are worried he isn't getting enough to drink, as long as he is not leaking through his diapers, give him a bottle at bedtime, then brush teeth to avoid cavities, read a book, and then put him in his crib drowsy but awake. Reducing the number of ounces will be helpful. Some parents like to wean over the course of a few nights and offer some water after a bottle to swish the milk off.

Check with your pediatrician; if there are any growth concerns and the doctor recommends sticking to the bottle for a while, you can still address the sleep associations. Give the bottle when your child is awake—after a nap, for instance—instead of right before nap time or bedtime. The last thing you want is to keep him associating sleep with feeding; there has to be some separation between the two. Some parents create this separation by no longer feeding the toddler in his bedroom. This way, he decreases the link between drinking and bedtime.

If your child becomes fussy during the day and asks for a bottle or your breast, look at the clock and your sleep log. Is he really hungry, or does he want the bottle for comfort? Can you comfort or distract him in some other way? This also helps to teach the child to self-regulate. Maybe he's overtired and needs a few quiet hugs from you or a few minutes on your lap with a book. Maybe he's tired and it's time for his nap. Perhaps he is signaling that he needs to go to bed a little earlier than usual. We want him to learn there are other ways to feel calm and happy in addition to the bottle or breast.

If all else fails, don't worry, you still have options!

Three Options for Nighttime Weaning
Method A: The Taper-Off Technique

If you're nursing, gradually cut down the amount of time your toddler is at the breast. For example, if she usually feeds for twenty minutes, let her go for only fifteen. Cut back every night until she's ready to give it up, or until you're down to five minutes. At that point, it's time to stop altogether. Make sure you unlatch her when she finishes eating heartily, even if it's sooner than the time you've allotted. Don't let her gently suckle and doze. Get her back to bed while she's drowsy but awake.

If you're bottle-feeding, you can decrease the amount of formula she gets by a few ounces every few nights. When you get to two ounces, it's time to stop. That's usually the best way to do it, but you could also gradually dilute the milk until it gets so watery she decides it's not worth waking up for. I usually find reducing the total ounces in each bottle every few nights works best. Sometimes a toddler protests when he hits that four-ounce mark because it is no longer enough fluid for him to suck himself to sleep. The very next night of the Shuffle, don't offer any bottle and instead sleep coach him back to sleep.

If your toddler is waking to eat several times a night but only nursing for a couple of minutes or taking a couple of ounces, this method won't work for you. Choose Method B or C.

Method B: The Four-Night Phase-Out

Whether you're breastfeeding or giving a bottle, feed your toddler just once during the night for three nights; it's best to set a time for when you'll give her that single snack. Pick a time, such as the first time she wakes after a set time such as midnight.

Only feed her once at night, and not again until at least 6:00 a.m., when you can both start your day. When she wakes at other times, sit by her crib and offer physical and verbal reassurance. On the fourth night, don't feed her at all. Remember she has had three nights to get used to receiving fewer calories at night. Usually, parents will move their seats away from the crib on the fourth night of the Shuffle, but we're going to modify it for this night weaning. So on the fourth night when she wakes up, sit next to her crib for an additional night. Comfort her from your chair as you did at bedtime. Don't pick her up unless she's hysterical, and then pick her up to calm her. If you breastfeed, putting the other parent on night duty might help your toddler adjust to the no-night-feeding reality more quickly.

Important note: Keep this in mind if you've decided that you'll feed your toddler the first time she wakes after midnight. If you find yourself sitting with her and doing the Shuffle from 11:00 p.m. until midnight while she fusses or cries, don't feed her a minute after the clock strikes 12:00. Wait until she goes back to sleep and then wakes up again—even if she only dozes for half an hour. You don't want to send the message that crying for an hour will yield a feeding.

Method C: Cold Turkey

You can stop offering your toddler a breast or a bottle when she wakes at night. Go to her crib side as outlined in the Shuffle. Just make sure you and your partner are on the same page in this decision. If Mom has been breastfeeding, consider having the non-nursing parent handle all middle-of-the-night wake-ups.

If you are considering completely weaning your toddler off breast-feeding—during the day and night—please see page 205, "When It's Time to Wean."

CRUTCH: WALKING, HOLDING, BOUNCING, AND ROCKING TO SLEEP

Example: Julian is two years old and still needs to be rocked for forty-five minutes before he conks out. Both my husband and I are losing patience, and with my swelling pregnant belly, rocking is uncomfortable for me. I need to get him off this crutch soon before my next baby is born!

If you are still walking or rocking your child to sleep and having to walk or rock him back to sleep over and over again all night long, then it becomes a sleep crutch and it's time to start sleep coaching.

How to Eliminate Walking, Holding,
Bouncing, and Rocking to Sleep

Many of us rock our newborns to sleep, but after eighteen or twenty-four or thirty months, we want our toddlers to put themselves to sleep, especially if they will soon be transitioning to a bed, and reading time and other bedtime rituals might not be done in a rocker anymore.

Make sure you have a comforting bedtime routine. Begin by doing all the walking or rocking in the bedroom, not around the house, to create a positive association between the room and sleep.

You can scale back the amount of time you walk or rock every few days, but the safest bet is to read him a book and do a little rocking as you slowly make your way to turn off his light. Blow kisses to the moon, give him a kiss and a hug, and put him into the crib. Toddlers can catch on quickly, though, that you are scaling back, so the method might not work as well as it would with younger children.

Sit by the crib and soothe him. If he gets really hysterical, pick him up briefly, and put him down as soon as he's calm. If he calms down in two seconds once you've picked him up, you'll know he didn't need to be picked up as badly as you'd thought he did. Resume your Shuffle position and be consistent.

Warning: While the Sleep Lady Shuffle encourages parents to pick up to calm their crying and distraught child, it can be futile for children with the crutch of being walked, held, bounced, and rocked to sleep. Some toddlers with this crutch genuinely cry hard and then, when picked up to calm, can fall asleep in their parent's arms in under two minutes! If this happens during sleep coaching, you can inadvertently train your toddler to cry hard until you pick him up. When parents are trying to eliminate this crutch, I always tell them to use "pick up to calm" as conservatively as possible. If you inadvertently train him to cry hard to be picked up and he falls immediately asleep, you won't be able to use the soothing technique of "pick up to calm" anymore, and you will have to endure what could be a lot of crying.

CRUTCH: THE PACIFIER

Example: Our pediatric dentist urged us to get rid of the pacifier for our two-year-old. She loves her pacifier, and we are afraid she will throw a tantrum at bedtime and not go to sleep. Where do we begin?

How to Eliminate the Pacifier

Create designated times throughout the day for pacifier use. Slowly decrease the amount of time over a week until your child is only using it for sleep and stressful times, such as long car rides or trips to the doctor. This is when the art of distraction can really help. If your child is not cooperating and begins to whine and plead for the pacifier, try to distract him with another activity, such as getting out of the house, turning on music, playing hide-and-seek, and so on.

In the meantime, make sure you work on strengthening his bond with his lovey. "It's not paci time, but Teddy Bear is here and wants to hug you." That both distracts him from the pacifier and provides a security substitute. Better yet, try getting him a brand-new lovey as you take away the pacifier; the newness might further distract him. You could even try taking him shopping and letting him choose his own new bedtime pal.

If he's old enough, read some books about children who get rid of pacifiers, such as *Little Bunny's Pacifier Plan* or *The Last Noo-Noo* or *Bea Gives Up Her Pacifier / Ben Gives Up His Pacifier* or *Bye-Bye Binky*. Some pediatricians have advised parents to keep cutting the tip of the pacifier more and more until it's so mutilated the child no longer wants it. And I know one mom who had her son put it inside a Build-a-Bear, and he slept with the bear! Whatever you do, once you send it away or give it away or throw it away, don't go out and buy another one after an hour of whining.

When you are ready, you and your child should talk about how it's time to get rid of the binky—and reassure him that he's ready. Pick a target day to act, but give him a little while to get used to the idea, because it's an adjustment. That also gives you time to prepare alternative ways to soothe your child when there are bumps along the way.

Your child might agree to get rid of his pacifier at first and then suddenly have a change of heart at bedtime, which is understandable; after all, he may not have fully understood what he was agreeing to. Acknowledge that this is hard and that you are there to support him and suggest he might try snuggling the new stuffed animal he picked out in lieu of the pacifier. If you have already mailed off the pacifiers to the fairies or dropped them off at the hospital for the babies, you will need to follow through on no more pacifiers that night.

On your first night with no pacifier, make sure he had a good nap and has an early enough bedtime. Have a relaxing bedtime routine, and share how you will stay with him while he learns how to put himself to sleep without his pacifier. Talk about how his lovey or new lovey can help him. Be empathetic and calm him, soothe him, pat him, stroke him when he cries and whines. Expect a few rough nights and naps.

CRUTCH: REACTIVE CO-SLEEPING

Example: I need to nurse and rock my twenty-month-old to sleep and back to sleep all night long. She used to start her night in her crib but would wake so frequently that we gave up, and now we all go to bed together in our bed. She still wants to nurse several times during the night and sometimes lies on top of me. Most of the time, my husband ends up on the couch. I am exhausted and want her to sleep in her crib all night long. Where do I start?

Most of the families I speak to are either co-sleeping out of desperation—like this family—or they really want to continue to co-sleep but find it's not working well for their family. Families who are co-sleeping out of desperation are practicing what I call *reactive co-sleeping*. These "we didn't plan it this way" co-sleepers are reactively co-sleeping when they end up with their child in their bed part or all of the night. I am not against co-sleeping if that is your choice (and you do it safely). If you find that you are reactively co-sleeping—in the category of "we didn't plan it this way"—and want to make a change, go to Chapter 12, "Making Choices About Co-Sleeping, Bed Sharing, and Room Sharing," where I give you step-by-step guidance on ending reactive co-sleeping, as well as safety tips if co-sleeping is your preference.

TEMPERAMENT CHECK

In Phase 1, I specifically addressed the temperament of what I call the *highly alert child*. In my experience, this is the temperament that leads most of my clients, probably around 80 percent, to seek out my help and the help of my Gentle Sleep Coaches. If you have come to realize you have been blessed with an active, stubborn, engaged child, you might be running the risk of being more sleep deprived or frustrated—even depressed—than if you were sleep coaching a child who was less spirited.

I expand on the sleep needs of the highly alert child in Phase 1 on page 43. Sleep coaching isn't impossible once you recognize that your highly alert child has her own set of rules about how and when she gets some sleep. Like a river, it's better for everyone to go with the flow than to try to swim against it.

EARLY RISING

So many parents reach out to me because they started sleep coaching their child and she is now sleeping a much longer stretch but waking at 4:00 or 5:00 a.m. and seemingly not wanting to go back to sleep. Or perhaps your toddler was sleeping through until 6:00 or 7:00 a.m. until daylight saving time, and now, months later, she is still waking at 5:00 a.m. Early rising is a huge and common sleep struggle.

Early rising is not the same as having an early riser, whom I refer to as an *early bird*, so as not to confuse the two. Early birds wake up earlier than many parents would like, 6:00 or 6:30 a.m., but they do so refreshed and happy. Their temperament simply skews more toward being a morning person. And in this case, you don't have to look far and wide to find that at least one parent is a morning person, too. Interestingly, research suggests there is a genetic link.

Then there are the early risers who are not happy to be up before the crack of dawn. They are tired, unrefreshed, the opposite of bright-eyed and bushy-tailed, but there they are—grouchy, awake, and not going back to sleep. This is when early rising is a problem, because the sleep tank isn't filled efficiently. And by now, we know that not getting enough nighttime sleep will affect nap quality and quantity, and nap time affects nighttime sleep—and there ensues the cycle.

WHAT CAUSES EARLY RISING?

While this is a very common problem, often the solution isn't as instantaneous as many parents wish. Like anything to do with learning a new skill, learning how to stay asleep takes time. Early rising is essentially your child having a difficult time putting himself *back to sleep* after a long stretch of sleep at night or not getting quite enough sleep to make it to his nap without being overtired. This part of the skill is more difficult than putting himself to sleep at bedtime.

For instance, I know if I get up at 5:00 or 5:30 a.m. and I'm awake a little too long, my brain starts to tick-tick-tick-tick with all the things I have to do, and I will have a hard time going back to sleep. My body has gotten just enough sleep to make it hard to go back to sleep but not enough to leave me feeling rested and restored.

Here are four factors that can cause early rising. Sometimes only one causes the early rising; for other kids, it could be all four. Note: You should first always rule out illness or undiagnosed medical conditions that can cause and contribute to sleep problems, such as obstructive sleep apnea, which we discuss more in Chapter 14. Then consider the following reasons:

* Too drowsy at bedtime
* Insufficient naps
* Too long of a wakeful window between the afternoon nap and bedtime
* Too late of a bedtime

Too Drowsy at Bedtime

The paramount lesson of helping your toddler learn to fall asleep on his own is putting him to bed drowsy but awake. You want him to be tired and ready for sleep but not falling asleep as soon as his head hits the mattress. Putting yourself to sleep is a form of self-soothing, and for him to learn that skill, he needs to be awake enough at bedtime. Once he masters it at bedtime, he can eventually apply it to night wakings as well as the early risings, which are the toughest to go back to sleep from.

Insufficient Naps

We will discuss this in the napping section, but it begs to be repeated. Short napping or not enough napping can cause increased night wakings and early rising. Quality nap time actually helps encourage quality nighttime sleep. If your child tends to take a very short nap or finishes her naps too early in the day, this could be causing early rising. Review your child's sample schedule and the nap-coaching section and decide when you are going to start nap coaching.

Overestimating the Wakeful Window

This may seem counterintuitive, but an overtired child generally takes longer to get to sleep and will wake more often during the night, causing early rising. Review your toddler's nap schedule to make sure you are not exceeding his wakeful window, and be sure there are no more than four to five hours between the end of his afternoon nap and his bedtime. For a one-and-a-half-year-old, this window will be on the shorter side, like four hours, if he is not napping long enough. More about napping in the section "Much Ado About Napping" on page 266.

Too Late of a Bedtime

Many parents are shocked when I tell them that their child's natural bedtime is likely between 7:00 and 8:00 p.m. And if they are not napping or sleeping through the night, then more likely 7:00–7:30 p.m. If your toddler's bedtime is well beyond this window, sleep in the night could be disrupted and lead to early rising, not to mention night terrors! For more on night terrors, turn to Chapter 13. If your schedule is wildly different from the sample schedules and your child is rising early, consider adjusting bedtime earlier. Do not keep your child up too late, hoping that he will wake less often during the night and sleep later in the morning. This rarely (if ever) works. Overtired children sleep less, not more.

WHAT TO DO? RETURN TO THE SLEEP LADY SHUFFLE

While you are making adjustments based on the tips above and your child wakes before 6:00 a.m., treat it like the other night wakings and do the Shuffle. The catch is that you must use your consistent response until 6:00 a.m. If he doesn't go back to sleep, use what I like to call *dramatic wake-up*! Leave the room for a full minute (literally, a full minute—watch the clock!). After sixty seconds, return to the room bright and cheerful with a "Good morning!" while you open the curtains and let the light flood in. This signals to your child that you are getting him up because it is morning and not because he is waking up too early! Keep using the Shuffle in the early morning until the habit resolves.

USING A WAKE-UP CLOCK OR LIGHT

Some children closer to two years of age can benefit from using a wake-up clock to cue him to know when his day can begin. The wake-up light tells

Sleep Lady Tip

Early rising happens during sleep coaching and can often take two to three weeks to fully resolve as you are working on improving naps. The two hardest or last pieces of sleep coaching to fall into place are early rising and the afternoon nap. So don't give up!

the child to try to go back to sleep and when it's okay to get up and start his day. Set it for about 6:00 a.m., and once he sleeps pretty consistently until 6:00, you can gradually try setting it later. Each time your child wakes before 6:00 a.m., go into his room and point to the clock and say, "Your wake-up light is not on yet. It's still sleepy time," and resume your Shuffle position. When you do dramatic wake-up, point to the light and show your child that the wake-up light is now on, which means he can get up and start his day. It will take repetition and consistency on your part for your young child to understand this, but it can work! Visit my website (https://sleeplady.com/products/) for a list of wake-up clocks or lights that I recommend.

MUCH ADO ABOUT NAPPING

Children this age still need naps, even if they think they don't. Most children this age have consolidated to one nap a day or will do so shortly. (If your child hasn't, see "Is My Child Ready for One Nap a Day?" in the previous chapter, "Thirteen to Eighteen Months.") Usually, they nap from roughly 1:00 to 3:00 in the afternoon. As you no doubt know, napping can be difficult for children, just as it is difficult for many adults to sleep during daylight. They need plenty of time to change gears. You should have a whole routine, shorter but similar to bedtime. Quiet stories or songs in his room are good pre-nap activities.

Ideally, you want to start night coaching before nap coaching. So do the Sleep Lady Shuffle one night, and start the nap coaching the next day. Make sure you're timing your child's nap correctly, no earlier than noon at this age if he is on one nap. Also, be aware of his sleep cues and windows of wakefulness.

Nap coaching is hard for a plethora of reasons. The best defense is a good offense, so here are two major rules of nap coaching and preemptive strategies that will address head-on any nap-time snafus that may arise (and they will!). You probably noticed I don't usually talk about "rules"; I prefer to give you a range of choices that fit your own parenting style. But after many years of working with parents of balky nappers, I have learned that these rules really help!

#1: Focus on putting your child down for a nap *in her crib, once a day.* If you are going to nap and night coach at the same time, then begin nap coaching the day after the first night. Go through an abbreviated version of your bedtime routine of reading a book or singing a song. Cut the rocking or swinging time in half at the beginning if you want to go slowly, and work on getting her down drowsy but awake.

Don't feel obligated to feed her before her nap; however, if nursing or bottle-feeding is your preferred transition activity, be careful not to let her fall asleep while eating, especially if that is your toddler's sleep crutch. Remember she has to be put in her crib awake enough that she is aware she is being put down. Draw the shades, turn on your sound machine, and watch your little one begin to demonstrate her sleepy cues of eye rubbing and yawning. Place your chair in the same place as you did the night before and follow the same steps of the Shuffle along with the same soothing techniques. Move your chair every three days, even if she didn't nap well on day 3.

#2: Spend an entire hour trying to get your child to sleep at nap time. Stay in your chair, exercising your Shuffle techniques for one whole hour. There are three outcomes that can happen:

1. Your toddler doesn't go to sleep for the entire hour.
2. Your toddler only takes a forty-five-minute nap.
3. Your toddler sleeps for *less than* forty-five minutes, which is less than a sleep cycle. I call these abbreviated naps *disaster naps.*

WHAT TO DO IF YOUR TODDLER DOESN'T
SLEEP FOR THE ENTIRE HOUR

At the end of your Shuffling hour, leave the room, count to ten, and go back into the room to do your dramatic wake-up routine (open the blinds, sing, "Nap time is over!") and take your child out of bed. Since he hasn't had an afternoon nap, he won't be able to last (or wait) until bedtime. Watch his cues; if he starts yawning or acting tired—even if it's just forty-five minutes after you got him out of his crib—go ahead and try for a nap again, doing the Shuffle.

WHAT TO DO IF YOUR TODDLER ONLY
SLEEPS FOR FORTY-FIVE MINUTES

This is the bare minimum for a nap. I find that most toddlers who wake up after forty-five minutes don't wake up happy and refreshed, or if they initially do, they are tired and cranky thirty minutes later. If your child wakes up after forty-five minutes from his afternoon nap, use the Shuffle techniques to get him back to sleep (try for at least thirty minutes if you can). If he doesn't go back to sleep, plan for a backup nap (see below) and an earlier bedtime—or both!

WHAT TO DO IF YOUR TODDLER NAPS FOR
LESS THAN FORTY-FIVE MINUTES

This is a *disaster nap*. When a child sleeps for less than forty-five minutes, he doesn't go through a complete sleep cycle and awakens at a partial arousal; it's enough to take the edge off his exhaustion but not enough to be restorative and to make it to bedtime without being overtired. So here's the tough message: I want you to go to him and do the Shuffle for an hour—what I call "the longest hour."

Here's an example: You put your child in his crib at 1:00 p.m.; he conks out at 1:30, but only sleeps until 2:00. You go in and work on getting him back to sleep—which he does, thankfully, by 2:30, after just half an hour. But he only sleeps for twenty minutes. Chances are, the negative voice in you is going to say *I can't believe the Sleep Lady told me to do that! He cried more than he slept. What's the point of that?* But think about it: Your toddler did it! He put himself back to sleep after a partial arousal from a nap—one of the hardest things to do. Going forward, he'll begin to get back to sleep more quickly and will snooze for longer if you stick with it.

DEVISE YOUR NAP-TIME BACKUP PLAN

After you have tried the nap in the crib once (perhaps twice if he had a catnap) during the day, you will likely need to use a backup nap plan to help fill the daytime sleep tank so your toddler doesn't face bedtime even more exhausted, making it harder for him to go to sleep and stay asleep. If you check your sleep log around 2:00 or 3:00 p.m. and realize your child hasn't had enough day sleep, you will need to move to your backup nap plan. You want to make sure that he sleeps one way or another for a decent interval before the afternoon is over so that you're not set up for a bad night. A backup nap can take place in the car or stroller or, if need be, the nanny's or grandparents' arms, but try to make it different from a habit (crutch) you've been trying to break. For instance, if you've been working on ending co-sleeping at night, don't put him in your bed for your backup plan. Try a car ride or walk in the stroller instead.

Ideally, the backup nap will last at least forty-five minutes, and your child will be awake by 4:00 or 4:30 p.m. so that he's ready to sleep at his regular bedtime.

If you have an older or younger child who can't be left alone while you sit in your toddler's room, you

Sleep Lady Tip

No naps before noon—even if your child has been up since 5:00! It will throw off the entire day and ingrain in him the habit of getting up too early. I realize this is a tricky dance and your child may get overtired, but it's worth it in the long run.

can do timed checks (page 70 in Phase 1)—looking in on your toddler at regular intervals. Base the timing on your little one's temperament, and be consistent. If you have no idea where to start, then try checking on him every seven minutes, slowly increasing the time. When you go to his crib, be reassuring but quick. You'll defeat the purpose if you pat him until he's asleep during your crib-side check.

DO I HAVE TO NAP COACH AT THE SAME TIME AS NIGHT COACH?

Don't feel guilty if you can't follow all my advice right now. Give yourself (or your babysitter) permission to let the nap coaching slide, and just do what you have to do to get your child some daytime sleep, preferably at predictable times. As nighttime sleep improves, the daytime sleep *might* fall into place on its own. If not, take a deep breath and try nap training again in another month or two. Keep reminding yourself that good daytime sleep promotes better nighttime sleep; it helps you get through it.

If you decide not to address naps and only work on nighttime sleep, then do what works to help her get daytime sleep at appropriate times. But know that it will eventually stop working. Either she will wake up the minute you put her down or shortly thereafter, or you will find yourself having to hold her longer and longer to get her to sleep, only to have her nap briefly. Those will be some of your signs to say, "Okay, now it's time to start nap coaching." But if you've worked on those other pieces at night, nap coaching should be much more successful. Remember, night sleep develops first, and it's easier than daytime sleep, and she has shown you that she has started to learn the skill at night.

HOW TO NAP COACH MULTIPLES

Although I normally keep twins together at nighttime, I often recommend separating them for naps. Daytime sleep is much more challenging for most toddlers, and it's even harder if there's a playmate to distract or be distracted by in the next crib. Some parents keep multiples apart for naps for days or weeks, others throughout childhood. Do whichever feels best to you and seems to work for your children.

Nap coaching more than one child can be difficult. If you are lucky and one naps well, you can put him down and nap coach the other in another room (just checking as necessary on the good sleeper). More often, both will need some coaching, so separate them and do timed checks: when you calm one, leave him, then go to the other and calm him, then after ten minutes or so, go back and check on the first toddler, and in another ten minutes, check on the second and so forth. If you are struggling with both or all multiples are really not napping well, then you might as well nap train them together in the same room. Instead of timed checks, sit between their cribs and follow the Shuffle along with advice on soothing and chair positions in the section "Shuffling with Multiples" on page 252 for the onset of the nap.

Chapter 11

TWO AND A HALF TO FIVE YEARS

SLEEP GOALS

* between ages two and three, average sleep needs drop to about
  ten and a half hours a night, plus an hour-and-a-half afternoon
  nap
* four-year-olds need eleven and a half hours at night, and most no
  longer nap daily, but should be encouraged to try for the occasional afternoon nap
* encourage forty-five minutes of quiet time each afternoon
* five-year-olds sleep about eleven hours a night, and afternoon
  quiet time is still beneficial

Sleep coaching for this age group requires a mix of techniques. As preschoolers begin to cut back and eventually outgrow their naps, we
have to keep tinkering with their sleep and wake-up schedules and introduce afternoon quiet time unless we enjoy meltdowns before dinner.
They need structure and boundaries at bedtime, while of course still
keeping it loving and cozy.

Many clients who seek assistance in sleep coaching for this particular age group sleep coached their children at an earlier age but have experienced some regressions in the now-older child as they transitioned to preschool or a big-kid bed or for a variety of other reasons. Others have not sleep coached in the past and are now ready to help their child learn the skill of putting herself to sleep, set schedules that work for their family, and tackle sleep crutches and cumbersome bedtime rituals and habits. If you are new to sleep coaching, please keep in mind that solutions to ingrained problems that date back to infancy can take some time. You aren't going to undo four years of night awakenings or pacifier dependency in three days, so remember my advice about patience and consistency. Luckily, from about age three on, sometimes even a few months earlier, children understand on some level that they need sleep, that sleeping poorly is a problem, and that you are concerned about it. They can then become an ally in your attempt to change things and begin to own the solutions.

FIRST THINGS FIRST: CREATE A SCHEDULE

I opened this chapter with the average nap and nighttime sleep goals for this age group; however, you might be interested to learn what the American Academy of Pediatrics and the National Sleep Foundation recommend, which you can find on their websites. The sleep goals I suggest here are averages of what those two organizations suggest and have guided my clients sufficiently over the years. When you do your research, you'll find sleep averages are fairly broad in range. Use these averages as ballpark numbers as you figure out your own child's sleep needs. See where your child now falls—and where she needs to be. Watch your child's cues. Some children who fall on the lower end of the scale might do just fine, while others might not. When first devising your schedule, aim for the average amount of total sleep she needs, and go from there.

Scheduling isn't as elaborate or as difficult for these children as it is for younger ones, and the schedule may well be shaped largely by their preschool or childcare hours. Generally, you want your child to wake up between 6:00 and 7:30 a.m.; 6:00 is quite common and, unless by 7:00 they are already tired, it's perfectly acceptable if they are sleeping through the night. I'll address later how to help a child who is an early riser, largely sleeping through the night but persistently waking up before 6:00.

Usually, preschoolers need a midmorning snack and then have lunch around noon or 12:30. If they are still napping, a common time is about 1:00–3:00 in the afternoon. When they stop napping, usually at around age three and a half to four, they should still have some quiet time in the late afternoon.

As napping decreases, bedtime comes earlier. If your three-year-old has been going to bed at 8:30, when she eases out of the afternoon nap, she'll probably need to go to bed at around 7:30. By age five, you probably want her to sleep from about 8:00 p.m. to 7:00 a.m. Adjust it, of course, depending on your family schedule and her school start time, but aim for at least eleven hours of unfragmented overnight sleep.

BEDTIME ROUTINE

For this age group, the bedtime routine is typically the most challenging part of the day. Now that your child is older, you may want to modify her routine a little but make sure it remains soothing and predictable. Bedtime preparations should be in her room (or perhaps the early stage can be in a younger sibling's room), not all over the house. Include stories, songs, or games that soothe, not those that stimulate. Make sure the rules for how many stories, or how long you will read, are completely clear and nonnegotiable. Avoid wild, fast-moving games and scary stories.

Leave plenty of time, at least a half hour, for her to unwind and to get the attention from you she needs. If you rush it, she'll be more likely to run out of bed or stall or manipulate you into staying longer. If she starts bargaining for an even longer time with you, more stories or more songs, blame the clock. Tell her the clock says you have to stop reading at 8:00, so you have ten minutes. You can also use a wake-up clock or light that doesn't necessarily tell time but turns colors—green for *go* or red for *stop*—anything that signals to your child that time's up. If two parents take turns at bedtime, you don't have to follow an identical script, but you should have a similar routine, style, and response to bedtime power plays, fears, or game playing.

Sleep coaching and bedtime routines are great opportunities to emotionally connect and bond deeply with your child. This is especially true in this age group, when your little one is more aware of the world, is exposed to more people, and is more verbally responsive. The quiet time you spend together during the bedtime routine can be a time when you check in with your child without distractions about her emotions, questions, curiosities, confusion, dilemmas, and the like. In Phase 1, I explained in detail the importance of emotional availability (page 37), so please do flip back to it to learn more. Basically, it means that having a good quality of community and connection between parent and child pays off in sleep. We all struggle with this in today's hyperconnected world, but when you are reading a bedtime story, watch your child, not your phone! Your emotional availability helps your children feel safe and secure, which helps them separate from you at nighttime and go to sleep and stay asleep.

BEDTIME FINDER: DO THE MATH BACKWARD

Figuring out the exact bedtime for your individual child is one part watching sleep cues and one part backward math. Start with her average wake-up time and count back the hours she needs. For instance, if your three-year-old wakes up at 7:00 a.m. and needs ten and a half hours of sleep, she should be *asleep by* 8:30 p.m., so depending on your routine, you should probably be heading for bedtime prep around 7:30. These are averages. Your child may need a half hour more or a half hour less. Watch her for signs that she is getting tired, and make sure she's in bed before she's overtired.

Common sleep cues at this age include yawning, rubbing her eyes, sucking a thumb or pacifier, or just general fussiness. You may also see that your child's attention span is shorter or she is whining and throwing a tantrum more than usual. If she falls asleep on the floor, you probably missed the cue! Take note, however, that preschoolers are adept at hiding their sleep cues, so you must also pay attention to the clock. If you miss the sleep window and she gets that cortisol-fueled second wind, get her to bed a half hour or so earlier the next night. Avoid that vicious cycle where the less she sleeps, the less she sleeps. Similarly, if she dozes during her bedtime routine or falls asleep the very second you turn out the lights after story time, you are probably putting her to bed too late. Move bedtime earlier by fifteen to thirty minutes.

Kids at this age learn to pick up on the sleep-window concept. Occasionally, they'll just say, "Mommy, I'm ready for bed," or "Nye-nye," or just crawl into bed by themselves. But that's not too common, even with much older children—until they learn the skill of putting themselves to sleep and back to sleep independently.

Note: On many occasions, parents who work in careers with atypical hours ask whether it is possible to keep their preschooler up later and start their days later. My answer is always "I can't make any promises that it will work, but we can certainly try!" A few conditions apply, however. The first is

Sleep Lady Tip

Remember when we talked about emotional availability? (See Chapter 3, "Getting to Know Your Child.") That focused connection with your child is always important—but it's absolutely essential that we be patient and fully present at bedtime. Try as best as possible to leave your workday behind. Forget about your to-do list for a moment. Put aside that email or phone call that upset you. Better yet, at bedtime, put aside your phone! Leave it in another room while you focus on your child. It will still be there once he's asleep. Having so many screens and devices distracting us is probably the biggest change I've seen since I started developing the Sleep Lady system. I know it's not easy to ignore your phone, but the benefits—to both you and your child—are huge.

that everyone in the family is afforded the flexibility of sleeping later, which means the child isn't preparing to go to day care or preschool in the morning. The second condition is the family has to be committed to shifting the entire schedule later, including naps, meals, and so on. Everyone can sleep later; they can't sleep less.

Because of circadian rhythms, which are pretty sturdy by this age, there is no guarantee this schedule shift will work. Use your intuition and watch your child's sleep cues and behaviors to determine whether moving back to a more traditional, earlier schedule is best for your child's sleep needs and overall development, especially as he or she prepares to start school.

TAKE NOTE OF DEVELOPMENTAL MILESTONES

Walking and talking and heading toward preschool, oh my! Just when you think you have your daily schedule and coaching plan, here come the developmental changes to throw a wrench in them. Developmental changes are those milestone moments that are super exciting to witness and indicate our children are thriving. By now, your child's milestones go way beyond the physical ones you measured monthly at your pediatrician's back in the baby days. Your two-and-a-half- to five-year-old follows directions, has a vivid imagination, can tell you how she feels and what she wants, and tests your rules and their limits, which can make bedtime more challenging than ever! This section introduces some major developmental changes that occur for this age group and advice on how to not let them shatter your sleep coaching.

SEPARATION ANXIETY

Children this age often still experience lingering separation anxiety, which is why so many of them demand that you lie down with them at bedtime or they'll wander out of bed looking for you. A good, comforting bedtime routine is essential. Don't rush through it, but don't let him keep stalling, negotiating, and bending the rules. A promise to check on him again before you go to bed is very reassuring. And if you say you are going to check on him, make sure you really do.

You might also want to teach your child deep-relaxation techniques, the kind you do at the end of a good exercise class or before going into labor! Have her relax her toes, feet, ankles, shins, knees, and

> ### ★ Sleep Lady Tip
>
> Children love it if you tell them how snuggly and cozy and peaceful and beautiful they look when they sleep. I think they take it as a confirmation that you really are checking on them and watching over them while they are asleep, that you aren't that far away, that they are as safe and sound as you promise.

so forth, all the way up her body. If you don't want to do this yourself, you can play relaxing music, try a sleep meditation app, or check out the "Good Night Yoga Flow" section in Chapter 17. (See my list of suggestions at the back of the book, or try my sleepy music compilation, *The Sweetest Dreams*, which also has a relaxation exercise, available at https://sleeplady.com/products/).

Children also like applying their imaginations to a dream agenda. "Tonight, I'll dream about playing basketball." Or "Tonight, I will dream about building a sandcastle." Or "Tonight, I will dream about being a beautiful ballerina." It helps them feel more in control of what happens to them after they fall asleep, particularly if they are worried about having nightmares. My Dream Cards (also available at https://sleeplady.com/products/) might help children feel in control of their dreams. The cards guide children through a progressive relaxation exercise and have several images for dream ideas, such as a tree house, a beach scene, a field of flowers, and a rainbow. I based them on my experiences with creating dreams with my own daughters.

For children this age with separation anxiety, fear of monsters (a.k.a. the scaries), or a newly emerging anxiousness in general, the Excuse Me

Drill is an effective tool. See page 292 in this chapter for instructions on implementing this strategy.

See page 292 in this chapter

> ## Sleep Lady Tip
>
> Sometimes a child who is not normally afraid will have a few days of palpable anxiety and may have transferred that anxiety onto imaginary ghosts or monsters. Depending on her verbal skills, you may be able to tease out what's bothering her—a schedule change, a classmate being mean at preschool, an upcoming event that is worrying her.

Use a Lovey

Preschoolers and kindergartners are definitely not too old for a lovey at bedtime. I strongly encourage it. My own daughters had them for years. The lovey helps them cope with separation and nighttime fears. Some children are and always will be indifferent to loveys, but some kids will get attached now, even if they spurned one toy after another when they were younger.

Include the lovey in your nighttime games, stories, and rituals. Be creative, and give your child a role in choosing her lovey. Go shopping together, or make a lovey together on your own or at a workshop at a local craft store. Some children switch alliances, first bonding to this bedtime toy, then latching on to that one. That's fine; it's their way of satisfying their own evolving tastes and needs. One little boy outgrew his baby lovey and started lining up all his action-hero toys around his bed to keep him safe at night. No monster would dare cross Spider-Man, Superman, and a big green Hulk! If your child sleeps with the same lovey every night, make sure you tuck it in with her and say good night to them both. If she likes different loveys, let her make that night's selection pretty early in the routine or else it becomes another excuse for stalling at lights-out.

Many kids this age have some kind of self-soothing ritual that involves the parent. They may want to twirl Mom's hair (surprisingly common!) or hold Dad's hand. They might do something a little more eccentric, like poking fingers in Dad's belly button or holding a parent's earlobe. Try to transfer this habit to a lovey. One mother of a hair twirler went to a fabric store and made a lovey out of satin with a tassel the child could twirl. Others have found stuffed animals, blankets, and dolls with fringes or other twirlable features. She may not accept the substitute immediately, but ease her into it. Let her do her ritual, like the hair twirling, for a few minutes

> ### ★ Sleep Lady Tip
>
> Make the lovey a part of the search team. The lovey can help you check the room and then snuggle into the child's arms and say, "See, everything is safe and sound. There are no monsters, bears, ghosts"—whatever she fears.

while you are reading good-night stories, but then once lights are out, direct her to her new lovey by saying, "Lights are out, which means no more twirling Mommy's hair. You can twirl your stuffed horse's tail."

NEW MOBILITY

Switching to the Big Bed

I generally recommend that parents wait until their child is two and a half and preferably until three years of age to transition from a crib into a big-kid bed, and the American Academy of Pediatrics recommends that once the crib rail falls below a child's chest (while standing in the crib), it's time to transition. For most children, this coincides with my age recommendation, especially when the crib mattress is dropped to the lowest position available. Some parents believe transitioning to a bed will solve an already-existing sleep problem, but it rarely does; so before you make the move, check your motivations and expectations.

Why do I recommend waiting until your toddler is at least three? For starters, there's a maturity issue. Between two and a half and three years old, your child will have the verbal skills to understand the big-bed rules and the beginning of *some* impulse control to help him stay in his bed. In addition to maturity, safety is a huge factor. An eighteen-month-old roaming your house at night is scary. Even if you are a babyproofing expert, it's not worth the potential risk of your toddler finding a lamp, plug-in, or pull cord.

If your child is ready to make the transition, there are a few things you can do to help her through this change gently and with minimal resistance.

Have a Conversation

Talk to your child about the upcoming change. Explain why she will be getting a new bed and when. Get excited! Be sure to mention a new bed often so that your toddler has time to process the information. At three, she may have myriad questions for you, so be prepared.

Make It Special

This is a big deal and a big transition for your toddler. Make it special by having him help you pick out new sheets, blankets, even the bed itself if you'd like. This may also be a good opportunity to redecorate his room if you've been thinking about it. Have your child as involved as possible, as it will help him take ownership of this new responsibility and big-kid status.

When choosing a bed, be sure to pay attention to the distance from the mattress to the floor, and consider purchasing a bed rail or even a toddler bed to help with safety (especially if your child is petite).

Discuss the Big-Bed Rules and Stick to Them

Now that your child is moving into a bed, a crib will no longer confine him. This is a big step, and many children will test their boundaries (and your patience) until they've found the limits. Testing limits is completely normal, but when it involves bedtime, it can be both trying and exhausting. A few basic things to think about:

1. **Baby gates.** You may want to consider placing a gate on the bedroom door, at least in the beginning, as a coaching device and a safety measure. The gate delineates boundaries, helping a child

understand that he has to stay in his room. It also prevents him from wandering around and possibly getting hurt in a dark house in the middle of the night—or from turning the TV on in the living room!

2. **Bathroom trips.** Decide if your potty-trained child needs to ask for help or if she can visit the bathroom alone. You may want to consider placing a potty chair in her room if you are sure she will not spill it. Refer to page 243 for tips on handling repeated potty trip requests.

3. **The boomerang effect.** Explain the privileges, but also review the rules. Let him understand that you will still put him to bed, but then he's expected to stay there. Be consistent from the very start. If he gets out of bed, take him right back without any fuss. Praise him for staying in bed. Give him plenty of stickers or other little rewards that you've found motivate him. Let him call his grandparents or aunts or cousins to brag about the new bed.

4. **Early rising.** If your child is prone to early rising (and you haven't already), consider purchasing a wake-up clock or light that will tell her when it's okay to awaken, and make it part of her room makeover. Visit my website (https://sleeplady.com/products/) for wake-up clocks or lights I recommend.

USE A WAKE-UP CLOCK OR LIGHT

Children between two and six years of age (and even older) can benefit from you using a wake-up clock to cue them to know when their day can begin. The wake-up light tells a child to try to go back to sleep and when it's okay to get up and start his day. Set it for about 6:00 a.m., and once he sleeps pretty consistently until 6:00, you can gradually try setting it later. Each time your child wakes before 6:00 a.m., go into his room and point to the clock and say, "Your wake up light is not on yet. It's still sleepy time," and resume your Shuffle position. When you do dramatic wake-up, point to the light and show your child that the wake-up light is now on, which means he can get up and start his day. Repetition and consistency are essential for success. If you allow your child to get out of bed and start his day even fifteen or twenty minutes before the wake-up light comes on, he will not take the light seriously the next day. Visit my website (https://sleeplady.com/products/) for a list of wake-up clocks or lights that I recommend.

You may want to consider leaving the crib in your toddler's room, at least for a short period of time. Some children like to have a choice, and being able to choose a big-kid bed is empowering. On the other hand, some children will merely be distracted by having their crib in the room (and may even try to climb back in, which is usually an indicator that they aren't ready to make the switch). As a parent, it's up to you whether you remove the crib immediately or after a few weeks.

Note: If you are about to embark on my Sleep Lady Shuffle or other major nighttime changes like taking away a bottle or pacifier, consider whether it would be easier if you kept him in the crib a little longer. It keeps him in a safe and familiar environment while you are changing other aspects of his sleep, and it may be simpler if you don't have to worry about him getting up and out of bed while you are trying to teach him how to sleep in it. However, I have also found that many older children do better if you change everything at once. You give him the privilege of the new big-boy bed and incorporate the changed sleep expectations into the big-bed rules. There's no right or wrong decision here. Trust your instincts about which approach is a better match for your child's temperament.

Sleep Lady Tip

It might not be a good time to introduce a big bed at the same time as a new baby, as it can seem as though you are bringing in a "replacement" baby. Try to introduce the new bed either several months prior to the baby's arrival, or a few months after so that the events are separate in your child's mind.

WHEN YOUR CHILD DOESN'T WANT A BIG BED

If your child, even up to age four, still likes the crib, leave it alone. You can bring up the topic occasionally. You can look at beds and sheets, but there's no rush unless, of course, your child's weight exceeds the crib's limit. He'll move when he's ready, and he'll be ready soon enough. Some families use toddler beds as an interim step, but I don't see a need for it. If he really wants one, fine, but it's certainly not an essential investment. The one advantage is that they are usually too small for you to fit into alongside him, which children often demand when they move into a bed of their own. Some preschoolers go through a phase when they don't want to sleep in their bed; they want to sleep or nap on a little couch, a pad on the floor, a beanbag chair, whatever. It may happen right after the transition from the crib; it may happen later. You can use some kind of system of rewards and incentives to lure him into the bed, such as reading his favorite story together in the bed, giving him an extra back rub in bed, or something like that.

Probe whether something in the bed is frightening him. Remember, emotional availability and having conversations about his feelings or fears will reinforce his security. Maybe he's afraid of falling off, in which case, you can put extra pillows on the floor or get bed rails for the side. But I would ask myself if it's worth fussing over. If he's sleeping reasonably well in his room, I wouldn't worry about it, and he'll probably move into the bed himself pretty quickly.

CHANGES IN EATING AND SLEEPING

Children this age should have a regular meal routine: three meals a day plus healthy snacks in the midmorning and midafternoon—after their nap if they still take one. They do not need a bottle anymore. Sucking on one at night is not good for their sleep, their teeth, or their overall nutrition. If your child is still using a bottle, go back and review my information on bottle weaning your toddler in Chapter 9, "Thirteen to Eighteen Months."

At bedtime, she can have a cup of water, but no milk or juice in bed. I'd prefer you give her the water during story and song time, not after lights-out. If she makes you fill the water cup a zillion times at bedtime, set clear limits, and stick to them. You can leave a cup of water by her bedside overnight (I'd recommend a sippy cup or a sports bottle, not a baby bottle or an open cup until she gets used to groping for it in the dark). But again, explain at bedtime that this has to last her all night; you aren't going to keep coming back to give her more. Joanne, my cowriter, convinced her little boy to leave a few ounces in his nighttime water cup. Ilan gave it to a stuffed animal, his "backup lovey," who slept near his bed but not in it, to hold for him in case he needed it.

STALLING AND CURTAIN CALLS

One father I worked with called his eldest daughter "Captain Loophole"— and that pretty much summed it up. Children this age are brilliant procrastinators, and any separation anxiety or nighttime fears only hone their skills. They get out of bed—or call you in—over and over again, what I refer to as *curtain calls*. The best defense is a sensible bedtime, a good routine, and the ability to gently disengage when they start to pepper you with all sorts of questions and requests.

Children this age are brilliant procrastinators, and any separation anxiety or nighttime fears only hone their skills.

If your child wants you to tuck him in three hundred times, try to do it just once or twice. Tell him what you expect, when the "last time" will be. Then stick to it. You can come back to his doorway in a few minutes to quickly praise him for understanding and following the bedtime directions. Once you've given him that dollop of praise and reassurance, leave before he starts trying to engage you all over again. Skip this step if it makes matters worse. Use your judgment. Put up a gate if he insists on coming out of bed a zillion times; he'll get the message.

Sometimes children know exactly which maternal anxiety button to push. I know one little boy who got out of bed and told his mother his tummy hurt. She was naturally solicitous and fussed over him a bit as she got him back to bed. A half hour later, he wandered out again, this time declaring that his hair hurt!

> "She stalls, stalls, stalls," Marcy said of Ariella. "She's so smart; she says she needs certain things, and she chooses things that push my buttons. It all seems so rational to me—she asks for such normal things. I'll ask her if she really needs a glass of water, and she'll tell me she didn't get that toothpaste taste out of her mouth. She'll tell me she needs a new diaper, she has pee-pee and can't sleep, so I go back in and change her. She'll say she needs that fuzzy blanket; it's a lot warmer. I try to plan ahead. I try to think of what she'll need at bedtime and set her up for total success. But she always manages to think of one last thing."

If a child says he is hungry, it's very hard for a parent to say no and then guiltily wonder if he was truly hungry. If he's a picky eater or seems to have added epicurean demands to his stalling repertoire at bedtime, just firmly say, "No, you had dinner. We'll have breakfast when you wake up tomorrow." If it's a real aberration and you think he might genuinely be hungry, give him a quick, healthy snack but explain very carefully that you are doing this tonight but won't be doing it every night. The next night, consider a preemptive strike. Ask him if he needs a snack right before you start his bath and bedtime routine, and tell him he can have the snack now but not after bath and tooth brushing. Encourage enough eating during the day and have a sensible meal schedule.

The Bedtime Pass is a strategy that helps stop the curtain calls, minimizing your child's laundry list of nighttime demands or sudden "needs," like a drink of water, to go to the potty, or switching out which stuffed animal gets to sleep with her.

The Bedtime Pass
The Bedtime Pass is a get-out-of-bed-free card. There is a lot of research that shows it works! It's a great tool for kids age three and up who do

know how to put themselves to sleep but still stall by hopping out of bed and asking for a million different things. You can find examples online or create one yourself—maybe your child will even want to help. The pass is good for one special request, question, concern, hug, or drink after bedtime or lights are out.

Try to introduce this when you child is in a good mood, and say something like this: "I understand that sometimes you think you need something after you go to bed, and so I've come up with a great idea." You could certainly say it's the Sleep Lady's suggestion if you want to blame somebody else.

Be clear with your child about the rules from the start. Explain that you will give him a special card at bedtime that he can exchange for one, and only one, request after lights-out. The request has to be for something reasonable or at least acceptable—like answering a question or giving a hug. Emphasize that once he surrenders the pass, you're not coming back again into the room and he must be quiet and go to sleep. (Some children may need two passes to start, but explain from the outset that she'll get so good at it you will be able to scale it back to one. Make the transition after a few nights.) Praise your child in the morning for doing such a good job with her Bedtime Pass. If you're using a sticker chart, you can add one for this. To download a sample sticker chart and bedtime pass, visit https://sleeplady.com/charts.

If you think your child needs a little extra motivation to follow the new rules, you can tell her that if she doesn't use her pass, she can trade it in for a little treat in the morning, such as a sticker or an extra few minutes of a favorite activity. It shouldn't be a big-ticket item; it should be fifteen minutes more playground time or an extra bedtime story, that sort of thing. You might want to keep a little treat box in the kitchen—inside put slips of paper with things that she enjoys or you can do together, not things that you buy her. After a good night, let her pick a reward, but make sure you deliver on it quickly. Make sure you leave time to do this in the morning, amid the get-to-school-and-work rush. Delayed gratification won't work; you need to keep your own end of the bargain.

Here's what it should look like: When you tuck the child in, leave the pass within her reach and remind her of the rules. Say, "Good night," leave the room, but stay nearby. If the child calls out or gets out of bed, collect the pass, respond to the request quickly, return her to her bed, and say, "Good night"—gently but firmly. Keep the whole Bedtime Pass exchange short and sweet, remind the child that she's used her pass and that now it's time to be quiet and go to sleep.

If the child gets out of bed again, show her that you mean business. Simply walk her back to her bed with minimal interaction. If she calls out, respond with a quick little "Good night," or, if it feels right to you, don't respond at all. The point is that you need to engage as minimally as possible and absolutely under no circumstances cave in to those additional requests.

Tuck-ins

If your child asks you repeatedly to come to his bedside and tuck him in—and no sooner have you tucked him in and are returning to your chair than he has kicked his blankets down and is asking you to tuck him in again . . . then you must limit the number of tuck-ins. Explain to your child that Mommy or Daddy will only do one tuck-in after lights-out, and if he kicks his blankets down after that, he will need to pull the blankets up himself. Brace for protest and stand your ground.

Remember, for sleep coaching to work, you need to follow through on behavior modifications during daytime and nighttime. Don't expect that if you tuck a child in thirty times at nap time, he'll settle for one tuck-in at night.

Experiencing the Scaries

Almost all children at some point in this age bracket experience vague fears in the evening: monsters, ghosts, shadows, or just things they can't quite put a name on. The monsters might not be real, but your toddler's fears are very real. The scaries are an opportunity to flex your emotional availability muscle, to model empathy and compassion for your child as you ease him further along sleep coaching. The trick is learning how to validate his emotions and ease his concerns without allowing him to turn the scaries into an excuse to prolong bedtime or to get out of bed repeatedly during the night.

Spend a minute looking under the bed or in the closet, if that's what she needs you to do. You might hold hands and check together, unless that seems to intensify her fear.

"Wes has never mentioned being scared of monsters or ghosts, but he's afraid of the dark. We use night-lights in his room, the hallway, adjacent bedroom, and bathroom. He always takes a lovey and Blackie the bear to bed as security, which helps," Amanda said.

At three and a half, Sam began saying he was afraid of voices outside. Nora thought he might be using it as a ploy to delay bedtime, but she gave him the benefit of the doubt. "We reassure him that we've locked and double-checked all the doors and that we are downstairs to keep anyone out. And when we're at my parents' house, we do the same thing and also tell him that their dogs won't let anyone in."

Giving the child a physical prop to reassure himself can also help. Not a weapon, of course, but something he can see or hold or touch to know he will not be left at the mercy of the scaries. James, for instance, was a great sleeper, but he started experiencing bedtime anxieties when he was three and a half. He was a small child with a very soft voice, so Ellen gave him a bedside bell. He could ring it, knowing that Mom or Dad would hear it right away. They even rehearsed during the day so he could see how quickly Mom and Dad would respond.

Obviously, if your child is truly terrified, give her the extra comfort she needs. It's usually better to sit by her and stroke her and hug her rather than lie down and go to sleep with her. If she really needs a lot of physical reassurance, hold her in your lap for a moment or two and then put her back down and continue patting her. You can also do a lot of snuggling and cuddling with the lights on, before the final stage of bedtime. You may have to spend a few nights sitting in the doorway while she falls asleep, rather than leaving her completely alone.

If your child has a nightmare, return her to bed and offer extra reassurance. Help her turn her thoughts away from the nightmare and to more pleasant images—"rainbows and flowers," as my older daughter used to say. Rita, a mom you'll meet in a moment, used to circle four-year-old Isabel's bedroom, saying, "Bad dreams, go away!" Occasional nightmares are normal; just about all kids have them. Read Chapter 13, "Nightmares, Night Terrors, and Sleepwalking," for more tips on coping.

WHEN YOUR CHILD HAS ANXIETY

Children's anxieties begin to expand as they become more aware of the larger world around them, especially in the early school years. They may begin to worry about personal harm, being hurt or robbed. They worry about one of their parents or grandparents getting sick. They start to worry about school, their friends, or their pets. They can absorb far more than you may realize from even a brief glimpse of television news or a snippet of a radio report, and they can be quite worried about earthquakes, hurricanes, and the like, however distant. Many youngsters will also have explicit fears or perhaps a more vague unease about war or terrorism or gun violence.

Again, this is an opportunity to exercise being emotionally available to your child. Assuaging anxieties can sometimes be as simple as talking to your child and getting the fears out in the open, where they don't seem so terrifying. But the depth of childhood anxiety is often underestimated. Don't overreact—a little bit of fear and anxiety is normal at this age, and your child being afraid of a monster doesn't mean she will grow up to be neurotic. But if your child seems excessively fearful or phobic during the day, too, talk to your pediatrician and her teachers and consider whether she needs professional intervention.

Often, I advise parents to use what is called the Excuse Me Drill, a terrific strategy for children who are generally anxious or have separation anxiety at bedtime.

The Excuse Me Drill

This is a responsive, simple approach to anxiety, developed by Brett Kuhn, a professor of pediatrics and psychology at the University of Nebraska. It fits very well into the Sleep Lady method and philosophy. It's designed for children who are at least three years old who sleep in a bed, although it can work for an older preschooler who is still in a crib. As we'll see, the Excuse Me Drill starts with you leaving your child's room before bedtime literally for just a few seconds—not long enough for her to get scared and come running after you. The Excuse Me Drill uses positive reinforcement to help address your child's resistance to having you leave her room at bedtime. It's all positive reinforcement; you build on the good bedtime behavior and, for now, overlook any other behaviors you want to change. It's about teaching her, or reteaching her, how to let you go at night while knowing you are nearby and responsive. In some ways, it reminds me of playing peekaboo with a baby, when babies learn that even when they don't see you, you are still there.

Warning: It's not a quick fix. Parents need to plan on investing a couple of weeks or a month before things are really improved. Start your bedtime routine earlier to build in time for this. As you know by now, letting bedtime run later only makes things worse.

Here are some scenarios for how you can use the Excuse Me Drill:

* If you are planning to start sleep coaching with my Sleep Lady Shuffle, you might want to spend some time on the Excuse Me Drill first. Once you see some progress, you can incorporate it into the first days of the Shuffle (and you might need to extend those first three nights of the Shuffle—but not so long that the drill itself becomes a sleep crutch).
* Similarly, if you are ready to start the Shuffle, you can lengthen the bedtime routine to include this drill. And instead of three nights

for the first stage of the Shuffle, you might need a few more days before moving your chair to position two.

* If your child was a pretty solid sleeper but is now having trouble because of anxiety (either as a developmental stage or because of an event or experience that triggered it), the Excuse Me Drill might be all you need to do, and then he'll rediscover his sleep independence. You can always go through the Shuffle again to reinforce, although you may find his sleep stabilized after only a few nights.

Here's how it works: The Excuse Me Drill is done during your typical soothing bedtime routine, while you still have some lights on. You can start this approach during book reading or after tuck-in (before lights-out). For example, you can sit next to your child while you both look at books, and you can use physical touch to calm your child, such as stroking her hair, rubbing her back, or tickling her arm if the child finds that relaxing and not overstimulating.

Then, after a couple of minutes, when the child is really calm and relaxed, make an excuse to go out of the room—for a very short period of time. It doesn't matter what your excuse is. You could just say, "Oh, excuse me, I need to go and get a tissue. You stay in your bed. I'll be right back." Then leave the room for a couple of seconds and come right back, ideally before the child has had the chance to get out of the bed and follow you out of the room. You may not make it out of the room the first couple of times, but that's okay.

Often in sleep coaching, we warn the child that we will not come back if she calls out. That's the right approach for the curtain calls and stalling—but it's definitely not the right message for this drill. This anxious child needs to know you are coming back ASAP. You only give attention to the positive. If she comes out of the room after you, don't chastise her. Instead, gently and quietly take her back and perhaps say, "I got my tissue. Come on, let's go back to bed."

When you return, go right back to what you were doing. You sit back on the bed again and resume all the soothing physical touch and then—this is the important part—you describe the positive behavior that you are seeing. So you might say something like "Wow, look how nicely you were lying in your bed. Ooh, I love that your head is on the pillow."

That's it. Return to the intermittent patting and the stroking and whatever book or bedtime activity you were doing. Then after a few more minutes, make up another excuse. It could be "Oh, I need to go get a pair of socks. You stay in bed quietly, and I'll be right back."

So you leave for another short amount of time, and then return and repeat the process, including more praise, and you're doing this often. Kuhn refers to this as a fixed-schedule reinforcement. You may do this twenty times on night 1. You might not even be out of the room when the child falls asleep. That's okay. It's just a start. The parent keeps getting up, making little excuses to just leave the room for a second or two, and then returning. The goal, of course, long term, is to try to be outside the room when the child falls asleep. But don't worry if that doesn't happen immediately.

Each night, try to stretch the amount of time you stay out of the room. It's key that when you go back into the room, you describe and praise what you see. Sometimes children get out of bed and follow the parent. Don't focus on that at all. Just take the child by the hand, say, "Come on, let's go back to bed," and resume the reassuring touch. Obviously, if the child starts to do well, you can stay out for longer and longer periods of time. You also want to vary the amount of time that you're out of the room. It's very labor-intensive, but it can accomplish the result with virtually no crying under certain circumstances.

RESISTANCE TO BEDTIME OR NOT TIRED ENOUGH

Research tells us that bedtime resistance—and by that, I mean crying, calling out, coming out of the bedroom, all those curtain calls—reaches a peak occurrence at around four years of age. In fact, about 50 percent of all kids in this age group, at some point, are going to demonstrate some kind of resistance to going to bed and staying in bed. She might go to bed—but not fall asleep for a long time—partly because she's just not tired enough. So if your child is falling asleep at, say, 10:30 and you want to get her back to around an 8:30 sleep time, we use an approach called *bedtime fading.* Really, we're helping her overcome her bedtime resistance—while also doing a little adjustment to her internal clock. With younger children, as I've told you, you really don't want them to get overtired. That makes it harder, not easier, for them to fall asleep. Addressing sleep resistance at this age, however, we're looking for that balance. We do want them more tired, but not meltdown-inducing exhausted.

Bedtime fading works on the premise that if a child is resistant to going to bed and he's not really tired, he's not going to fall asleep easily. He's going to lie there and call for you—or get up and look for you. So if you delay the bedtime, you can reduce the resistance and get a rapid initiation of sleep. Some sleep medicine doctors and behaviorists recommend this as the first change to make in a sleep plan with older children. (And most parents prefer this gentle approach, with lots of positive reinforcement, to threats or even using medication like antihistamines or melatonin to get kids to sleep.)

Here's how it works. Start by logging your child's sleep patterns for one week, specifically looking at the gap between the time you put her to bed and when she actually falls asleep. You look for the average time she goes to sleep in a week, and that is where you start. You then back up the bedtime routine ten, fifteen, twenty minutes before that determined time. You are matching the child's bedtime with her natural sleep onset time. So if you want your child to eventually go to bed at 8:30 p.m., if that's the age-appropriate bedtime, but she isn't falling asleep until 10:30 p.m., choose 10:30 p.m. as that temporary bedtime or asleep time. Then do the typical calm, relaxing bedtime routine, using whatever coaching method you decide with her. Once the child is falling asleep easily at 10:30, start moving bedtime earlier in ten- to fifteen-minute increments every few days, until you get back to the age-appropriate bedtime. You can use bedtime fading in tandem with the Shuffle. Be careful not to move the bedtime too quickly or you will start to have problems again. Slower is always better. If the Shuffle is going well, you can start moving the bedtime earlier on night 4 or 5, but this is not a set rule.

While you fade bedtime, I don't recommend letting the child sleep more during the day, which parents are going to be tempted to do. The child can have his regular nap time, but don't allow him to extend those naps at all. Cut the sleep off after 4:00 p.m., and absolutely no napping in the car if it can be avoided.

POTTY TRAINING

I don't think there's any problem with working on changing sleep patterns at the same time you are potty training, as long as you don't turn potty training into a tug-of-war. Focus on daytime training, and leave a diaper on at nap time until he stays dry for at least a week. At night, I think it's fine to keep a diaper on until age four or five; children can develop overnight control on their own if you give them time. You want to see your preschooler waking up dry for at least ten days in a row before switching to underwear at night. Bladder size and genetics play a part in when a child can stay dry all night long. To learn more about staying dry at night, check out Dr. Howard Bennett's book *Waking Up Dry: A Guide to Help Children Overcome Bedwetting*. For more information on potty training while sleep coaching, see Chapter 10, "One and a Half to Two and a Half Years," and for bed-wetting in older children, see Chapter 14, "Could Sleep Disturbances Be a Medical Condition?"

SLEEP-COACHING PREP: PARTNERING WITH YOUR CHILD

Parents have an array of techniques available to them to help shape their toddlers' sleep habits and routines. By this age, children can get vested in improving their own sleep and can feel pride and self-worth when they achieve it. Positive reinforcement goes a long way.

At this age, children can get vested in improving their own sleep and can feel pride and self-worth when they achieve it. Positive reinforcement goes a long way.

THE FAMILY MEETING

Start with a family meeting, where both parents sit down with the child and talk about sleep in an age-appropriate manner. Choose a time when your child is happy and receptive. Sunday morning after pancakes is a lot better than 5:00 p.m. on a weekday when she skipped her nap and is starving for dinner.

Tell her that you consulted (or read a book by) the Sleep Lady and learned about how children can learn to put themselves to sleep without a mommy or a daddy lying down with them and sleep all through the night in their cozy bed. That way, you can blame me for any changes or rules she doesn't like. For instance, if your child begs you to lie down with her, you can say, "The Sleep Lady said we can't do that, but we can stay with you in your room."

Some children get furious with me. "The Sleep Lady can't come over to play with me!" "I don't like the Sleep Lady." They may pick up this book and throw it! Practice empathy, telling your child you understand this is hard for her, but you will be there the whole way through to help her, and you are confident she can do it. But when the children succeed, when they start feeling good about their new sleep skills, they often want to call me on the phone and tell me how proud they are of themselves! You can visit my website (https://sleeplady.com/certificate) and download a certificate—add their name and some stickers and give it to them.

Keep the discussion upbeat and positive. You don't want your child to feel she has a problem or that she's doing something wrong. To the contrary, you should portray it as your responsibility. "We should have helped you learn to put yourself to sleep without lying down with you when you were younger. But the Sleep Lady helped us understand that, and now we are going to stay with you as you learn."

Explain that children who go to bed without fussing and who sleep all night feel better in the morning and have more fun during the day. Encourage her to brainstorm about how she can participate, maybe by deciding what she can take into her bed to touch, hug, or twirl or what extra game she will get to play in the morning if she uses her good sleep manners at night. You want her to have a stake in success.

If you think it will help, you can give your child examples, preferably of an older friend or cousin she looks up to. Say something like "We are going to teach you how to put yourself to sleep and sleep all night long in your own bed, just like Cousin Johnny and Cousin Jenny and Grandma and Aunt Rachel." Be careful; you want to frame this in a positive way, not to make your child feel ashamed that she's not doing something you want or expect of her, or that other children are able to do.

At four, Isabel had trouble falling asleep and seldom slept through the night. She usually ended up in a sleeping bag on the floor next to her parents. Her little sister, Deirdre, in contrast, didn't mind just hanging out in her crib for a half hour or so until she fell asleep. Rita and Elliott put up with Isabel's problems until their third child, Rebecca, was born, and then it just got too hard to deal with three young children, two of whom were up half the time. Rita and Elliott convened a family meeting and learned that Isabel was already well aware of the problem. "I told her that Daddy and I found out we were supposed to have taught her how to fall asleep by herself, like Deirdre. We said we talked to the Sleep Lady, and she gave us some ideas. Isabel said she wanted to go to sleep like Deirdre. She was totally intrigued," Rita remembered. Isabel was more aware of the problem, and more ready to make changes, than her parents had realized.

Explain clearly what changes your family will make so the child knows what to expect. Warn her about an earlier or more structured bedtime or a new routine. "Daddy is not going to lie down with you anymore, but Daddy will sit next to you until you fall asleep." Or "If you come to our bed at night, we are going to tell you we love you and take you back into your bed, where you can snuggle with your teddy bear." Adapt the script to the appropriate sleep challenge, but you don't have to give a lot more detail. Introduce a sleep manners chart to clearly define your expectations.

Marcy said of her three-year-old daughter, "Ariella is a real creature of habit, so I always prep her about change. If I do something one night, she'll expect it the next night. She'll say, 'Why don't you have your hand on my leg? You had it there yesterday.' I prep her all day long, letting her know about change in advance. I'll say, 'Tonight, we're going to do this, but tomorrow it's going to be that.' If I don't tell her, she starts asking about tomorrow."

Sleep Lady Tip

You may be surprised at how sensitive children already are to sleep issues and how quickly they pick up the lingo. Many children are relieved when parents bring this up. They know that something is wrong, that their parents are frustrated and want them to sleep differently. They are happy to know you are going to help them fix it.

SLEEP MANNERS CHART

There is something very powerful about having a visual representation of the sleep goals and skills you are teaching your child. By creating and using a sleep manners chart, you and your child can keep track of his progress, tally up his own achievements, and see where he needs work. This fosters independence and accountability and keeps sleep coaching from feeling utterly divisive. Children in this age group want to feel in control and proud of themselves, and they want to know you are proud of them, too.

Howard Glasser, the psychotherapist who created the Nurtured Heart Approach, talks a lot about the power of acknowledging positive behavior. Glasser teaches that you praise the positive behavior you want to keep seeing and ignore the behaviors you don't want. The key is including both the acknowledgment and an added verbal response, such as "I see that you're lying in your bed," and then you add, "That shows me"—and then fill in the blank in a specific way. For instance, you might say, "That shows me that you're using control," or "That shows me you're following your sleep manners," or "That shows me you're being a great listener." This specificity is so much more effective than parents just saying, "You're doing a great job," which every child hears often enough that it begins to become ineffective.

A sleep manners chart is not a sticker chart (although stickers are part of it). I agree that your child, who may have never been sleep coached before, won't suddenly comply just for a silly sticker! But a sleep manners chart, customized by you for the skills you and your child are working on, is a way for your child to see and celebrate his progress. It's less about the sticker and more about your acknowledgment—the sticker, the words you say out loud to praise his sleep progress, all the positive reinforcement. And for the child, the chart makes his skills and achievement tangible. That clear visualization of success goes a long way with this tough crowd! Plus the chart will help you *and* your child keep focused on the behaviors you want to see more—that positive reinforcement. And without criticizing,

---

Sleep Lady Tip

I like to call it a sleep *manners* chart, instead of sleep *rules*. Rules imply judgment or even potential punishment. Manners connote expected daily behavior. It's a reminder that we want to incorporate manners in our lives all the time, not just when we are getting stickers.

you can gently guide him to work harder on any remaining sleep manners trouble spots.

Create a one-page chart for each week so he can see his track record and maybe get a little extra bonus at the end of each week. Ariella, for instance, got an assortment of stickers, but the special sparkly gold one was her reward at the end of a good week. To make a weekly chart, turn the paper horizontally, put the days of the week along the top, and add the manners across the left, or short, side. Visit my website (https://sleeplady .com/charts/) to download a sample sleep manners chart.

Choose three to four manners that best apply to your child. You can change them over time if you need to, but not so often that you confuse your child about goals. Phrase the manners in positive terms—*dos*, not *don'ts*. Here are a few examples:

* "Lie quietly in bed." (This means no shouting or yelling; talking or humming quietly to themselves or their stuffed animals is okay.)
* "Put yourself to sleep without Mommy or Daddy lying down with you."
* "Put yourself quietly back to sleep during the night without Mommy or Daddy lying down with you."
* "Stay in bed quietly until 6:00 a.m." (or whatever realistic time you choose) or "Stay in bed quietly until the wake-up light comes on."
* "Cooperate at nap or quiet time."

In the beginning, include one relatively easy bedtime rule so your child can always get some positive feedback. For instance, one category can be "Cooperate at bedtime" a.k.a. "Put on your pajamas without making Mommy have to chase you around the room!" This is a competence builder. It helps her feel she can live up to the new sleep expectations, that it's not too hard for her.

When your child becomes satisfied with that easy one, raise the bar. Tell her she is so very good at getting that sticker that she will now have to focus on a new manner. Get her invested in the new chart—give her a bunch of stickers as a "graduation" present for that item, if it helps, or let her go to the store with you and select the stickers she will earn for the next task.

Hillary positively beamed with pride when we reviewed her sleep manners in the morning after a great night, but after a good start in modifying her poor sleep habits, her progress stalled; she even regressed a bit. Her mom, Hope, changed the chart. She took off that easy "Brush your teeth and put on your pajamas" and replaced it with "Lie quietly in bed." Which of course meant no yelling or calling out or shenanigans at bedtime. Hillary was not pleased. She called out fifty-five times for Mom (Hope counted) that night. She finally asked for a book instead of Mom, and Hope gave it to her. She then fell asleep.

Give the chart some good, focused attention every night at bedtime, even if your child appears to be ignoring you. Remind her of her sleep manner that says, *Stay in bed quietly until your wake-up light comes on.* "That means when you wake up and it's quiet and your light is not on, you need to snuggle back into your bed." Using a wake-up light to cue her to know when her day can begin can be very helpful in the sleep-coaching process. Set it for about 6:00 a.m., and once she sleeps pretty consistently until 6:00, you can gradually try setting it later. You can talk about the sleep manners during the day, too, emphasizing her successes, gently reminding her of expectations but not dwelling on failures. But the nighttime review is essential.

In the morning, review all the manners—those your child accomplished (putting stickers or stars next to them) and those she needs to try again that night. Praise her for what she did well (and watch her beam with pride) and what she needs to practice and get better at. Try not to make her feel that she is bad if she failed; just tell her that she can try again that night and that you know she can do it. Remind her of some other achievement that she is proud of, sleep related or not. If she's done a really good sleep job, you can give her an extra sticker for her jacket or her hand so she can show it to her grandmother, her babysitter, her preschool teacher, or the cashier at the grocery store.

REWARDS

Some parents promise a reward, a gift, or a trip if the child earns a certain number of stickers. This isn't necessary—the stickers, the praise, the hugs, and the sense of accomplishment can be adequate rewards themselves. If you do want to give an extra reward, or if you've been using the sticker chart for some time and need a little extra pizzazz, go ahead and add a carrot, but start small and be realistic. If you promise a trip to Disney World, what are you going to do for a follow-up? With a small reward, you can withhold it if he regresses, but are you really going to cancel a trip to Disney World if he wakes up a few nights and climbs into your bed? You are probably better off just promising him a trip to the nearest zoo!

Occasionally, children, particularly when they are a little older, need sticks in addition to carrots—although I'm not big on punishment, so maybe we should talk about *twigs* instead of *sticks*. They may also need some privileges taken away to get them to change sleep behavior. It can be a little thing—like not letting her help you switch the kitchen light on in the morning if she woke you up before 6:00—or not so little—like taking away a favorite video, computer time, or morning TV if she still gets up in the middle of the night. I use this as a last resort, usually with older children, and I don't use it very often. And I never use the twig without the carrot. When I take away a privilege, I continue to offer a lot of praise and positive reinforcement for what the child is doing right.

Think of family outings and activities as rewards, instead of toys and games. Tell your child that if he earns his sleep chart, he can decide whether you are going out for pancakes Sunday morning or for pizza Saturday night. Treats can be free. Tell him Daddy will take him for an extra trip to the playground, or they can go sledding twice in one day.

(Don't promise sledding in July; you want the reinforcement of a reward to come quickly after the behavior.) You can say Mommy will read three extra stories one afternoon or watch a special video with him twice. You have enough plastic junk in the house already, and time with you is more valuable to your child than anything you can get at the store.

THE SLEEP LADY SHUFFLE

It is important to recognize that the success of the Sleep Lady Shuffle depends on parental consistency. Whatever soothing techniques or boundary-setting or behavioral consequences you uphold during the Shuffle, you must apply them throughout the day. Not just for naps, bedtime, and nighttime wakening—you need to be consistent, period. For instance, if your child wants a cookie before dinner and he throws a tantrum, and you give in so he'll stop his antics, you will not have success calming him and/or helping him learn the skill of putting himself to sleep at night without him expecting you to give in to his nighttime outcries. To drive the point further: if during a daytime tantrum you give your child the pacifier that you are trying to wean him from, and then during a night tantrum you don't, that's confusing to the child. His tantrums may just get fiercer. Remember that children experience our consistency and boundaries as comforting, helping them to feel safe and know what to expect.

Additionally, before you begin the Shuffle, you might want to rule out any medical conditions or sensory processing difficulties. For more information on both, please turn to Chapters 14 and 15, respectively.

My Sleep Lady Shuffle is still a useful tool for this age group, but I'll warn you that it isn't as easy doing the Shuffle with a three- or four-year-old in a bed as with a six-month-old in a crib. The Shuffle is gentle and gradual, but older children still get upset and fight the change. Don't get angry, but don't give up, either. Keep reminding him that he can learn to put himself to sleep in his wonderful big bed without Mommy lying down with him. You can use his sleep manners chart to show him his progress.

Throughout the Shuffle, we try to minimize tears, but I can't promise to eliminate them completely. Luckily, by the time our children are three or four, most of us aren't as worried about tears damaging them. We've inevitably had to listen to our share of tears by now, and we find it easier to cope with crying now that our children can also use words to communicate their wants and worries. To keep the tears in check, give plenty of reassurance, love, and praise. In addition to reviewing rules and expectations with him every night at bedtime, you should also pay your child some sleep compliments during the day. Don't dwell on his sleep failures, but keep praising his sleep achievements. (The directions that follow are for children in beds. If your child is still in a crib, follow the version of the Shuffle in the previous chapter, but do a little more explaining about each step, which helps an older child with better verbal skills buy into the Shuffle.) If you are co-sleeping, please turn to Chapter 12 for how to do the Shuffle when sharing a bed.

If your child wakes up in the middle of the night—and he will at first—pat or soothe him briefly in bed and then return to where you were sitting at bedtime that night until he falls asleep again. We want a consistent response to every wakening. I give tips later in this chapter on ways of dealing with specific bedtime and middle-of-the-night sleep crutches.

Keep moving your Shuffle position every three days, even if he had a bad night, woke up frequently, or protested a lot. Expect some regression or resistance each time you move a little farther from his bed, but stick to it. Particularly with this age group, it's essential not to backtrack or give mixed signals. If he gets sick during the Shuffle, give him extra hugs and kisses, and then maintain or freeze your Shuffle position or sit closer if needed. When he starts to feel better, continue with the Shuffle. Try not to drag it out too long.

As you go through the Sleep Lady Shuffle with children this age, remember, your biggest challenge will probably be that they will get out of bed and try to climb onto your lap or hug or hold on to you. To make the Shuffle more successful and less stressful, remember:

* Children do better when they know what to expect, so explain things carefully.
* Review sleep manners and expectations at *every* bedtime and in the morning and repeat the explanations as you move through the Shuffle.
* Children respond well to positive reinforcement, so give them plenty of praise and encouragement.
* Allow plenty of time for bedtime routine; this isn't the time to rush.
* If your child wakes up in the middle of the night, go to him, calm him quickly, and then resume the Shuffle position you had at bedtime that night.
* They will test you—particularly if you haven't been consistent with them in the past.

BIG-KID BED TIPS FOR THE FIRST THREE NIGHTS OF THE SLEEP LADY SHUFFLE

1. *Don't get into a power struggle.* Doing the Shuffle with a child who is in a bed, not a crib, can be a challenge. If she sits up in bed, ignore it; if she gets out, pat the mattress and encourage her to get back in. Do not chase her around and put her in bed. Patiently sit in your chair and encourage her to get back into her bed.
2. *You can reach over and stroke, pat, or rub your child intermittently in her bed.* But don't caress her constantly until she falls asleep, or it will become her new sleep crutch. Stop the stroking when she is starting to fall asleep. (Some children don't like to be touched as they fall asleep; follow their cues.)
3. *The parent controls the touch.* Don't let your child fall asleep holding your hand, for example, because she will wake up when you move, and it will start all over again. Pat or stroke a different part of her

body or the top of her hand. If she keeps putting her legs on yours, or persists in trying to touch you, scoot your chair away. You can still lean in to touch or reassure her.

4. *If she becomes hysterical, hug her in her bed to calm her, but don't lie down in her bed.* Don't let her fall asleep in your arms. Tantrums are not uncommon at this age, although the toughest nights are probably later in the Shuffle when you are sitting in the hallway but still in her view. If at any point during the Shuffle (or anytime) your child becomes hysterical, scared, or throws a tantrum, you can use the hug-hold technique discussed on page 187.

5. *Return to your Shuffle position and follow these rules each time she wakes at night.* When she wakes, go to her or return her to her bed, give her a kiss, encourage her to lie down if necessary, remind her that her wake-up light is not on, and sit in the chair. Do this at each awakening until 6:00 a.m.

NIGHTS 1–3: NEXT TO THE BED

Once you've completed bath, stories, and your review of his sleep manners chart and your expectations, turn off the lights and *sit in a chair or on the floor next to his bed.* Stroke or pat him intermittently if he fusses or cries, but don't do it constantly, or he will form a new negative association and will need you to pat him constantly to fall asleep. You can be a little more generous with touch the first night, when the whole system is new to him, but be careful about creating difficult new patterns, starting on the second night. Children this age will almost certainly try to engage you. Try closing your eyes, which not only conveys an unambiguously sleepy message but also makes it easier for you to resist getting drawn into a conversation or philosophical seminar about the nature of the universe. Stay there until he falls asleep.

Some children get quite upset even on this first night if you won't lie down with them. In desperation, some parents have put their heads down on the pillow next to their child. Try not to do it, and if you do, please restrict it to the first night, or you aren't going to make much progress. You will not be changing your child's ritual or teaching him to learn new skills if you are sharing a pillow! You can stroke or pat intermittently if he fusses or cries, but don't do it constantly, or he will form a new sleep crutch and he will need you to pat him to sleep. You, not the child, should be in charge of the touching. For instance, if he grabs your hand, gently remove it but then touch his hand sporadically. If he puts his leg or arm on your lap to keep you nearby, gently remove it and tell him, "Legs or arms have to stay on the bed," then scoot your chair a few inches away so that you have to lean in to touch him. Close your eyes and *sh-sh* him. *Stay there until he is asleep.*

Each time he wakes, go to him or return him to his bed, give him a kiss, encourage him to lie down if necessary, remind him that his wake-up light is not on, and sit in the chair. *Do this at each awakening until 6:00 a.m.*

Remember, in three more nights, you won't be sitting next to him and won't be able to touch him constantly. You want to be able to fade out of his sleep picture, not add to his fury each time you make a change.

NIGHTS 4–6: TO THE DOOR

Tell him how proud you are of him as you see him learning how to put himself to sleep. For instance, if you notice that he has started to talk quietly to his stuffed animal as he is lying in bed, you could point out to him that you noticed that he is finding ways to calm himself down and get ready for sleep. Focus on his strengths, and try to be specific in your praise. Explain the next move. Tell him that you are going to give him a big hug, and then *move your chair to the door inside his room.* Keep the door closed at this point—partly to keep him from running out of the room. Reassure him that you will be able to see each other. Promise him that you will still stay in the room until he falls asleep, but that once you turn out the lights, there's no more talking.

Once you are in the chair by the door, stay as quiet as possible, but an occasional soothing *sh-sh* is okay. If he gets so upset that he needs some help calming down, go to his bedside, reassure him, and give him a deep-pressure hug. Remind him that you aren't going to leave him, that you'll stay until he falls asleep. Don't let him fall asleep in your arms or lap, and don't lie down with him in his bed. Keep telling him what a good job he's doing and how proud you are of him. Return to your chair. *Stay there until he is asleep.*

Each time he wakes, go to him or return him to his bed, give him a kiss, encourage him to lie down if necessary, remind him that his wake-up light is not on, and sit in the chair. *Do this at each awakening until 6:00 a.m.*

NIGHTS 7–9: IN THE HALLWAY, IN VIEW

Continue the praise, positive reinforcement, and clear explanation of what he can expect and what you expect of him. Keep praising him on what he is learning. *Sit in the hallway in view.* (Obviously, keep the door open for this stage!) You can keep making those *sh–sh* sounds from the hallway, not constantly but with enough frequency to remind him you care. Some kids have the most trouble with this chair position, as you are no longer in their room, and they will keep coming to you in the hallway and asking you to come back in the room. Tell him if he gets back into his bed *on his own*, you will come in and tuck him in. If this happens repeatedly, you will have to put a limit on the number of tuck-ins. If it gets excessive, consider putting up a gate in the door. See advice below on how to present the gate.

Sit in the hallway, in view, until he is asleep. Each time he wakes, go to him or return him to his bed, give him a kiss, encourage him to lie down if necessary, remind him that his wake-up light is not on, and sit in the chair. *Do this at each awakening until 6:00 a.m.*

NIGHTS 10–12: IN THE HALLWAY, NOT IN VIEW

Go through the same routine—praise and positive reinforcement and an explanation of the next step. Now you will be *sitting in the hallway, but out of his view.* Leave his door open a crack or a few inches. Tell him you will be nearby, and use your voice intermittently to reassure him of your presence. If he comes out of bed, go through the same recommended options that you've used the last few nights. Some parents use a baby gate at bedtime. If you want to try that, put the gate up at bedtime so the child knows you are doing it. Blame it on the Sleep Lady. "The Sleep Lady said your body is so used to waking up and jumping right out of bed, it forgets all about your sleep manners. We are putting the gate up so when you wake up tonight and pop out of your bed and go to the gate, you will say, 'Oh yeah, I am supposed to stay in my bed quietly.' Once your body remembers its sleep manners and you stay in your bed all night long, we won't need the gate anymore." This gives him a say in when you no longer need to use the gate.

NIGHTS 13 AND ON

Next you are going to stay in the hallway or in a very nearby room, where your child cannot see you but can hear you. You can make some reassuring *sh-sh* sounds, not constantly but enough to let him know that Mom or Dad is close by and responsive. If he cries or calls out for you, try checking on him from his bedroom door—without going all the way into the room. Be calm and reassuring. Convey that you are not far away and that you know he can put himself to sleep.

JOB CHECKS

A fair number of children start falling asleep and staying asleep by the end of two weeks (it takes longer with older kids)—occasionally even sooner. Some parents have to take one more step and move farther away, doing what I call a *job check,* telling the child where they will be, what they will be doing, and promising to be back very soon: "Mommy is going to get her pajamas. I'll be back in five minutes," or "Daddy is going to brush his teeth, and then I'm going to come back and blow you another kiss." It is important that you come back to your child after your "job" is done so you follow through with your promise. Children don't really understand what "five minutes" means, so explaining where you will be and what you will be doing can help. Tell him that you will keep checking on him until he is asleep. When you check on him, just go as far as the doorway; don't go into the room, where it will be easier for him to reengage you or tug at you all over again.

Some parents decide to stop the Shuffle at the point when they are sitting in the hallway a few feet from the child's room. If that feels right to you, go ahead and try it, as long as it's not taking an hour and the child doesn't need you to come back to the doorway on and off all night long. Other families continue to make the five-minute checks for weeks or months, if that's what

> ### Sleep Lady Tip
>
> Children get ritualized easily. Make the changes every three days—or less. Dragging it out makes it harder, not easier, for him. Give it more than three days, and he'll expect you to stay exactly where you are — and get even more frustrated and angry when you try to double that distance.

makes everyone comfortable. That's okay as long as he's sleeping through the night and falling asleep reasonably quickly, not using those checks as an excuse to keep himself awake so he can keep seeing you. But most families do get to the point where they can do their bedtime routine, say good night, and leave.

Sometimes even children who have "graduated" from the Shuffle and sleep well regress a little. Routines get disrupted, illnesses occur, or they experience normal waves of fear or insecurity. Don't return to whatever prolonged and convoluted bedtime techniques you used before the Shuffle. Be particularly wary of relapsing into co-sleeping. Instead, sit quietly in the doorway for two or three nights, where he can see you. That allows you to be present and comforting, without abandoning all your progress. Then move on to the final steps of the Shuffle. It should go pretty smoothly.

SHUFFLING WITH MULTIPLES

Just like with singletons, start the Sleep Lady Shuffle at an age-appropriate bedtime after a day when your children's daytime sleep averages have been met. For the younger children in this age group, get their nap in any way you can. Whether you need to rely on all your sleep crutches at the same time or take a car ride every day, getting the daytime sleep tank filled—even if it means taking drastic measures—is a must before beginning the Shuffle at night. For older kids who no longer nap, choose a Shuffle start night when the children are as rested as you can get them. If possible, move the beds closer so they are at least three feet apart, and have one parent sit in a chair between the beds. If two people are available, this will be easier to do. Each parent can sit by a bed/multiple.

After your soothing bedtime routine, have your children get into their beds after reviewing their sleep manners. Sit in your Sleep Lady Shuffle chair position described in the previous section. (See page 304.) If there is just one parent, gently move back and forth to stroke and soothe each child in turn. Follow the rules of the Shuffle for the first three nights. Make sure that by the third night, you are using your voice to soothe instead of relying too much on touch.

If you can't move the beds and they must remain far apart and out of your arm's reach, each parent can sit by each bed for the first three nights. By night 4, you will be sitting by the door. Only one parent needs to sit there. I have had both parents eager to sit in the second position—you certainly can if you want—but it's not necessary.

FREQUENTLY ASKED QUESTIONS
FROM PARENTS OF MULTIPLES

Q: I have twins, and one is a better sleeper than the other and gets woken by the other twin. How should I sleep coach them?

A: In those cases where one child truly disrupts the other's sleep, I do make exceptions and separate them at night during sleep coaching. It's usually a good idea to leave the poorer sleeper where he is and move the sounder sleeper to another room, using a portable crib or making a makeshift bed on the floor in your room. Good sleepers tend to be more flexible and can more easily adjust to a temporary new sleeping place, particularly if it's a little noisier or brighter than the kids' bedroom. Once the poorer sleeper is sleeping through the night fairly consistently, you can return the good sleeper to the shared room.

Q: **I have triplets. How can we do the Shuffle and sit next to their beds when there are only two parents available? And sometimes only one of us is home at bedtime?**

A: You may have one parent sitting between two children or two parents tag teaming with three children, and so on. If there is just one parent, sit in the middle of the room or by the door, and gently move back and forth to stroke and soothe each child in turn. Follow the rules of the Shuffle on pages 306–308 for the first three nights. Make sure that by the third night, you are using your voice to soothe instead of relying too much on touch.

SLEEP CRUTCHES AND SOLUTIONS

We want our children to learn to self-regulate and self-soothe, but sometimes parents have been coming to the rescue since their children were babies to offer additional soothing and regulating techniques, such as rocking, feeding, holding, and so on. Now that your child is almost a preschooler, you might notice some of these techniques have morphed into other ones. Your bouncer now wants to be cuddled to sleep, your feeder now wants you to lie down with him, or maybe your rocker needs to twirl your hair to nod off. The issue is not the soothing itself; it is the development of an association a child might make *between* that technique and sleep. We call them *negative associations*, or *sleep crutches*, that babies and children need to get themselves to sleep or back to sleep. (See "What's a Sleep Crutch?" on page 50.)

This age group, more than others, experiences numerous sleep crutches, mostly ones that involve a ritual between the child and parent. In this section, we will learn how to weaken those associations to minimize night wakings and set you up for success with the Shuffle. Remember that overtired children wake up more at night, so keep working on napping. Most kids in this age group still need it.

CRUTCH: HAIR TWIRLING, SKIN-ON-SKIN CONTACT, HAND-HOLDING, CUDDLING

Example: My four-year-old son loves to twirl my hair until he falls asleep. I now have to remember to take my hair out of a ponytail before I kiss him good night or else he will hold on to it for dear life.

Helping Your Child Put the "Self" in the Self-Soothing Rituals (and Leave You Out of It)

Many kids this age have some kind of self-soothing ritual that involves the parent, whether it's twirling Mom's hair (surprisingly common!) or something a little more eccentric like poking fingers in Dad's belly button. Try to transfer this habit to a lovey. One mother of a hair twirler went to a fabric store and made a lovey out of satin with a tassel. Others have found stuffed animals, blankets, and dolls with fringes or other twirlable features. She may not accept the substitute immediately, but ease her into it. Let her do her little ritual like the hair twirling for a few minutes while you are reading good-night stories, but then slowly start to move away, letting her gradually hold the lovey instead. Tell her something like "Once lights are out, no more twirling Mommy's hair. You can twirl your stuffed horse's tail instead."

If her crutch is having you lie down with her, she may still want that at 3:00 a.m., even if she no longer needs that at 8:00 p.m. She may want to be snuggled or given yet another cup of water when she wakes up at night. Or maybe she's still sending you scurrying to find that pacifier under the bed. Dealing with the normal nighttime fears and worries of the preschool years, a child may just wake up to say, "Hi, Mom, just testing! Just checking to make sure you're where you're supposed to be!" We want to give our children enough comfort so they feel safe and can go back to sleep, but not so much reinforcement that they still have incentives to keep these awakenings—and the crutches that go with them.

I believe in responding when our children need us. Leaving them to scream in the dark does not promote good sleep for them or for us. Checking on them makes them feel better, and it makes us feel better. (You do need to make sure she's truly awake before you rush in to "rescue" her. If she's whimpering or crying out briefly during a partial awakening, don't charge in with parental sirens blaring when she's about to drift back into a deeper sleep on her own.) But we don't want to overdo it. Check on her, soothe her—but don't perpetuate the crutch, or she'll keep waking night after night.

When your child wakes up at night during the Shuffle, give her a brief, reassuring pat and return to the position you were in that night at bedtime. Sometimes after children have finished the Shuffle and are sleeping well, something may throw them off, and you may have a few night awakenings. If she gets up, quietly return her to her bed and sit in a chair or stand in the doorway. You might want to start in the chair, and then after a night or two, move to the door, similar to what you did during the Shuffle to fade yourself out of her middle-of-the-night picture.

Remember, do not engage her. Bore her. Do not take her into your bed. Do not get into her bed. Do not pick her up and walk around the house. Do not criticize or scold or talk about consequences or punishments at this particular time. In fact, do not talk at all except for a few soft phrases like "Night-night," or "I love you. Go to sleep." Hand her the lovey and give her a quick hug and a kiss, but don't do too much hugging, patting, and cuddling, or she'll keep waking up every night wanting her fix of snuggles. Leave as soon as you can without engendering hysterics.

CRUTCH: REACTIVE CO-SLEEPING

Example: At least twice a week, I wake up with my five-year-old's foot in my face, except I know I put him into his bed the night before. I am completely unaware when he enters my bed, so I'm not awake to stop it.

Eliminating Sneaky Co-Sleepers

If your child sneaks into your bed while you are sound asleep, you need to outsmart him. Hang a plastic kitchen utensil or a bell from your bedroom door and close the door enough so the child has to push it to enter. The bell or spoon will probably make enough noise to wake you up. Warn her that you are going to do this, and let her hear what it sounds like, so it doesn't terrify her in the middle of the night.

One mom said it didn't really bother her if her two-and-a-half-year-old sneaked into her bed—she didn't even notice, and everybody slept. She had second thoughts, however, after the night her daughter crawled into bed with some unsuspecting houseguests.

WHEN YOUR CHILD WON'T STAY IN HER BED

If during the Sleep Lady Shuffle your child is having difficulty staying in her bed when you are no longer sitting by her side and she is coming to you or trying to crawl into your lap despite your redirecting her to "get back in your bed" multiple times, here's what you can do:

1. Stand up and say calmly but firmly, "Get back in your bed." If she doesn't, say, "I'm going to count to three. Get back into your bed, or I am going to leave the room." We want to avoid you chasing her down, and you putting her in her bed; the goal is to get your child to do the behavior.
2. Count to three. If she is not back in her bed, leave the room, close the door, and count to ten in your head while she is crying. It is important that you follow through with your threat. If you tell her you are going to leave the room if she doesn't get back to bed, and you don't leave the room when she protests, all bets are off.
3. After you count to ten, open the door and from the door say, "Get back into bed, and Mommy (or Daddy) will come back in the room." Usually by

this point, children get back into their beds because they want you in the room.

Usually, children get tired and stay in bed, particularly if they become more confident that you are going to stay there until they fall asleep. Remind her that if she stays in bed and follows her sleep manners, you will stay there as long as she needs you to fall asleep and that you will check on her before you go to bed. Most children then stay in bed.

Some preschoolers (especially if they are particularly alert or determined) will test you to see if you are going to follow through on your threat, particularly if you have not been consistent about consequences in the past. If she does not get back in the bed, then repeat the counting to three and closing the door. Don't yell; be calm and firm but not exasperated or impatient. If closing the door gets your child overly upset and hysterical, try using a baby gate.

CRUTCH: NIGHTTIME FEEDING

Example: My three-year-old still wants her bottle of milk in bed with her.

Time to Say Bye-Bye to the Bottle—Without
Spending All Night Refilling Her Water Cup

If your child still takes a bottle, it's definitely time to get rid of it. Explain that she is a big girl now and doesn't need a bottle. She may well realize this herself by now. Offer her a cup of water during story time, and if she cries for her bottle, soothe, comfort, and distract her but don't give her the bottle. In fact, you should get the bottles out of the house or at least out of sight (or adapt some of the following strategies for getting rid of the pacifier). Focus on strengthening her attachment to a lovey as you remove the bottle, or let her choose a new lovey as an incentive. Alternatively, please review the advice on how to wean from a bottle in Chapter 9, "Thirteen to Eighteen Months."

If she is emotionally attached to the water cup and it has become a sleep crutch, help her learn to go back to sleep without it. Go to her when she calls for it in the middle of the night, but either just quietly point to the cup you left by her bed and encourage her to take a sip or two and go back to sleep or try to soothe her into going back to sleep without it. Don't refill the cup. It will probably take a few nights, and you'll probably have some tears, but you can sit with her, stroke her intermittently, *sh-sh* her, and comfort her like you would a younger child.

CRUTCH: ROCKING TO SLEEP

Example: Even though I can't rock him anymore, my five-year-old wants to sit on my lap in the dark. I've resorted to getting rid of the rocker we used all his life (which was really upsetting to me as well as him), but now he just sits on my lap while I'm in my Shuffle position on the floor.

If Your Child Still Wants to Be Rocked to Sleep, It's Time to Stop It

By this age, children aren't usually rocked like they were as infants, but some still like to be lulled to sleep on their parents' laps during or after story time. Use the Shuffle to try to break that habit, just as you would for a child who wants you to lie down with him. Rock or hold him during the bedtime routine while you read books with the light on, but don't rock him after lights-out. If he tries to climb out of bed and get in your lap, just put him back to bed and soothe him. If he wakes up at night wanting to be rocked or held, return to your Shuffle position. For tools on how to get your child to stop getting out of bed while you are doing the Shuffle, see pages 316–317.

CRUTCH: THE PACIFIER

Example: My child wants to take his pacifier with him everywhere and wants me to help him find it during the night. I am afraid it will ruin his teeth, but I don't know how to get rid of it.

Getting Rid of the Pacifier—or at
Least Restricting It to Sleep

If you still aren't ready to get rid of the pacifier, at this age, definitely restrict it to sleep. Hide it or at least keep it by the bed but out of reach during the day, except at nap time and bedtime. If your child wakes up one or more times during the night, summoning you to help her find her pacifier, put several in and around her bed, or leave a spare in a little basket or bowl where she can find it herself. If she demands that you get it for her, go to her and gently remind her where they are and reward her for learning to do it by herself. If she absolutely cannot find it herself, then as an interim step, you should retrieve it but hand it to her and make her put it into her mouth. Next, try pointing to the pacifier and have her grab it and put it in her mouth. Consider glow-in-the-dark pacifiers if even you are having trouble finding them! You can add this as a manner to her chart—"Find pacifier on your own during the night."

Now that your child has pretty good verbal skills, consider eliminating the pacifier completely. Talk to her about the decision; she's old enough to be part of it. I offered some ideas on how to do this in the previous chapter. (See page 260.) When you are ready, choose a time when she's relatively rested and relaxed—not right after she's been sick, when you've been traveling, or she's in her first week at preschool. Work on transferring some of her attachment from the pacifier to a lovey, and expand the lovey's role in bedtime rituals.

If you haven't already restricted the pacifier to bedtime and naps (not awake and playtime), do that first before you get rid of it completely. You'll get a little resistance, but distract her and praise her for not using it. When she adapts to not having it during the day, take it away at bedtime, but let her keep it for a while longer at naps. Pick a big day when she will no longer have the pacifier. Give her a few days to get used to the idea. She may agree to it—but then get very upset when the big day arrives. Get the pacifiers out of the house; she can't demand them quite as much, and you can't give in if they just aren't there anymore. If you yield when she cries, she will learn that you don't really mean it, and the next time you try to wean her from the pacifier, she will cry and fuss even more.

Start the Shuffle the same night you decide to dispose of the pacifier. Brace yourself for a few rough naps and bedtimes. She will probably cry. Give her that lovey and offer extra reassurance. Cuddle a little longer on the first night and follow the rules for the first three nights of the Shuffle (outlined on pages 306–308) before the lights go out, or sit by her bed until she falls asleep. Don't do this for more than a week, or you will create a new sleep crutch. If you've been sitting by her bed for several days, you might want to do a truncated version of the Sleep Lady Shuffle again to get out of her room. If it's the second (or third!) time you've done it, move through it quickly: just one or two nights in each position, or go straight from her bed to the doorway. Use your instincts and your knowledge of your child's temperament, but try to do it on the speedy side. Offer plenty of praise, and keep encouraging attachment to a lovey.

CRUTCH: THUMB SUCKING

Example: I feel a little embarrassed that my four-year-old sucks his thumb in his pre-K class.

Address the Thumb Sucking—and Be Very Patient

If your child is still sucking his thumb, I don't think he'll outgrow the habit on his own. Age four or five is a good time to address it because your child now has the language skills to communicate with you about what can be a process taking several months.

My daughter Carleigh was a determined thumb sucker, and I decided to address the habit when she was five, already in kindergarten. She had sucked her thumb since she was six months old and had the callus to prove it! She had a lovey, a small pillow she'd used since she was a baby, but instead of being a substitute for the thumb, it was a companion. When she snuggled against that pillow, the thumb went right into the mouth.

I enlisted her dentist's support in encouraging her to stop sucking her thumb because she was going to get big-girl teeth soon, and we wanted them to grow in straight and strong and beautiful. Use whatever words and images will reach your child and get her invested. Her father and I empathized a lot and told her we knew it was very hard and we were very proud that she was going to try. We also enlisted other people, including her grandmother, to share their memories of how they stopped sucking their thumbs as children and how proud they felt.

Praise and encouragement will, however, get you only so far. Bribery will get you the rest of the way. We asked Carleigh what she wanted as a prize or reward. Her first choice was pierced ears, but I managed to dodge that for a few more years. I let her talk me into her second choice: adopting the class hamster at the end of kindergarten. I wasn't thrilled, but at least it wasn't a class snake. We found a picture of a hamster that we pinned on her bulletin board so she could see it from her bed for the rest of the school year. I also talked to her about the hamster a lot, and of course, she had the hamster in class as an additional reminder all day. We found an unexpectedly large selection of hamster books at our local library, and I think we read them all.

We started by giving up daytime thumb sucking. Children are often not even aware that they are sucking, so she agreed to let me point it out to her by gently removing her hand. I noticed patterns: Carleigh was much more likely to rely on her thumb when she was frustrated, upset, overstimulated, or overtired. Once we had cut down on daytime sucking, we got rid of the thumb sucking at nap time—she still needed an occasional nap at five and a half. (I usually recommend getting rid of thumb sucking at bedtime before napping, but I reversed that with Carleigh because at that age her naps were sporadic, while bedtime was daily.) When she napped, and later when she slept, we put bandage tape not just on her thumb but on all her fingertips. Carleigh, a partner in this process, suggested that herself because she thought she would suck other fingers if we taped just the thumb.

As I'd expected, the first night in the thumb-free zone was the hardest. Carleigh was generally an excellent sleeper, but I recognized that falling asleep without the familiar association of thumb and lovey pillow was a struggle that night. She snuggled with her special pillow, looked at books, and talked to me about what she wanted to dream about. I told her I would check on her a lot that night, which I did. I reassured her that she could do this, that she would love having a hamster. It was hard for me as her mother to watch her that night, but she eventually did fall asleep.

We kept the tape for several weeks and slowly reduced the number of fingers being taped. Carleigh told me which fingers she would be most likely to suck at night. We then went tapeless but still didn't bring the hamster home until she was no longer sucking any fingers when we checked on her at night. Her callus disappeared, the nail changed shape, and she even said her thumb no longer tasted as good! (Someone once told me a sucked thumb does taste different from an unsucked thumb; it has something to do with the oils in the skin. But I confess I don't recall seeing any scientific confirmation of this phenomenon.) We finally celebrated Carleigh's accomplishments and brought home the hamster. (That hamster, alas, died, as did two of his successors.)

Although this plan worked for Carleigh, it took several months. We might have been able to do it faster, but I think it would have meant more tears, more trauma, and probably a higher risk of failure. Be patient and be creative. Involve your child and respect her insights; she may know well what will help. I can't imagine doing this with a younger child or one who lacks good language skills.

EARLY RISING

So many parents reach out to me because they started sleep coaching their child and she is sleeping a much longer stretch but waking at 4:00 or 5:00 a.m. and seemingly not wanting to go back to sleep. Or perhaps your child was sleeping through until 6:00 or 7:00 a.m. until daylight saving time, and now, months later, she is still waking at 5:00 a.m. Early rising is such a huge and common sleep struggle.

Early rising is not the same as having an early riser, whom I refer to as an *early bird*, so as not to confuse the two. Early birds wake up earlier

than many parents would like, 6:00 or 6.30 a.m., but they do so refreshed and happy. Their temperament skews more toward simply being
a morning person. And in this case,
you don't have to look far and wide
to find that at least one parent is a
morning person, too. Interestingly,
research suggests there is a genetic
link.

> ## Sleep Lady Tip
>
> Early rising happens during the
> sleep-coaching process and can
> often take two to three weeks
> to fully resolve as you are work-
> ing on improving naps. The two
> hardest or last pieces of sleep
> coaching to fall into place are
> early rising and the afternoon
> nap. So don't give up! It is a hard
> pattern to change, and it usually
> takes three or four weeks of
> very consistent coaching, or lon-
> ger if she's had early wake-ups
> for more than six months.

Then there are the early risers
who are not happy to be up before
the crack of dawn. They are tired,
unrefreshed, the opposite of bright-
eyed and bushy-tailed, but there
they are—grouchy, awake, and not
going back to sleep. This is when
early rising is a problem, because the
sleep tank isn't filled efficiently. And
by now, we know that not getting
enough nighttime sleep will affect
nap quality and quantity, and nap
time affects nighttime sleep—and there ensues the cycle.

WHAT CAUSES EARLY RISING?

While this is a very common problem, often the solution isn't one that is
instant, as so many parents wish, especially now that they can get up and
try to begin their day whether you like it or not! Like anything to do with
learning a new skill, learning how to stay asleep takes time. Early rising is
essentially your child having a difficult time putting himself *back to sleep*
after a long stretch of sleep at night or not getting quite enough sleep to
make it to his nap without being overtired. This part of the skill is more
difficult than putting himself to sleep at bedtime.

For instance, I know if I get up at 5:00 or 5:30 a.m. and I'm awake
a little too long, my brain starts to tick-tick-tick-tick with all the things

I have to do, and I will have a hard time going back to sleep. My body has gotten just enough sleep to make it hard to go back to sleep but not enough to leave me feeling rested and restored.

Here are four factors that can cause early rising. Sometimes only one factor is needed to cause early rising; for other kids, it could be all four. Note: you should first always rule out illness or undiagnosed medical conditions that can cause and contribute to sleep problems, such as obstructive sleep apnea, which we discuss more in Chapter 14, and then consider the following reasons:

1. Too drowsy at bedtime
2. Insufficient naps
3. Too long of a wakeful window between the afternoon nap and bedtime
4. Too late of a bedtime

Too Drowsy at Bedtime

The paramount lesson of helping your preschooler learn to fall asleep on his own is putting him to bed drowsy but awake. You want him to be tired and ready for sleep but not falling asleep as soon as his head hits the mattress. Putting yourself to sleep is a form of self-soothing, and for him to learn that skill, he needs to be awake enough at bedtime. Once he masters it at bedtime, he can eventually apply it to night wakings as well as the early risings, which are the toughest to go back to sleep from.

Insufficient Naps

We will discuss this in the napping section, but it begs to be repeated. For children under three and a half years old, short napping or not enough napping can cause increased night wakings and early rising. Quality nap time actually helps encourage quality nighttime sleep. If your child tends to take a very short nap or finishes her naps too early in the day, this could be causing early rising. Review your child's sample schedule and the nap-coaching section and decide when you are going to start nap coaching.

Overestimating the Wakeful Window

This may seem counterintuitive, but an overtired child generally takes longer to get to sleep and will wake more often during the night, causing early rising. Review your child's nap schedule to make sure you are not exceeding his wakeful window, and be sure there are no more than five hours between the end of his afternoon nap and his bedtime. More about napping in the section "Much Ado About Napping" on page 326. If your child is over three and a half years old and no longer napping, make sure his bedtime is early enough and that you have ruled out underlying medical conditions.

Too Late of a Bedtime

Many parents are shocked when I tell them that their child's natural bedtime is likely between 7:30 and 8:30 p.m. And if they are not napping or sleeping through the night, then more likely 7:30–8:00 p.m. If your child's bedtime is well beyond this window, sleep in the night could be disrupted, which can lead to early rising, not to mention night terrors! For more on night terrors, turn to Chapter 13. If your schedule is wildly different from the sample schedules and your child is rising early, consider adjusting bedtime earlier. Do not keep your child up too late, hoping that he will wake less often during the night and sleep later in the morning. This rarely (if ever) works. Overtired children sleep less, not more.

WHAT TO DO? RETURN TO THE SLEEP LADY SHUFFLE

While you are making adjustments based on the tips above and your child wakes before 6:00 a.m., treat it like the other night wakings and do the Shuffle. The catch is that you must use your consistent response *until* 6:00 a.m.

If she gets up at, say, 5:00 or 5:15 and comes looking for you or calling you, get her back to bed with minimal conversation. Remind her that it isn't morning time yet, that her wake-up light hasn't come on yet. Decide whether you will stay in her room until 6:00 or whether you will leave and check on her every ten or fifteen minutes. Base your decision partly on which approach is more likely to get her back to sleep—or even get her to stay in her bed. You don't want her chasing you every thirty seconds if you leave, and you may need to gate her door. Nor do you want her to keep talking and chatting and trying to engage you if you stay in her room.

You can try both approaches for a day or two to get an idea of which will work, but don't keep switching back and forth. Choose a system and stick to it for a while. You may find a two-stage approach works best. Stay in her room in your Shuffle position in the morning for a while, maybe a week or so, to communicate that she has to stay in bed. Then leave the room to give her more space to fall asleep again on her own.

Ideally, she should get back to sleep until 6:00 or later, and you can snooze in a chair, lie on her floor, or get back to your own bed. If she does go back to sleep, wake her up at 7:30 a.m. If she doesn't get back to sleep, wait until 6:00. Then go back into her room (if you are already in the room, leave for a minute or two but explain you'll be right back) with your dramatic wake-up and morning routine. Convey the message that she is starting her day because it's 6:00 a.m. and her wake-up light has come on—not because she cried, fussed, and screamed.

Some children naturally start sleeping later as they get a little older and outgrow napping. If that happens, it will happen on its own; you can't force it. You should not take away or shorten naps in the hopes of persuading her to sleep later (unless her naps are much longer than typical for her age). That usually backfires, and you just end up with an even more overtired child who will still wake up early and be even grouchier.

Even when they stop napping, quiet time in the late afternoon or before dinner is a must for four-year-olds and a wise idea for five-year-olds.

MUCH ADO ABOUT NAPPING

Sleep needs shift year to year for this age group. As their naps shrink and disappear, they need to sleep a little longer at night. You'll have to adjust bedtime, unless they naturally begin to sleep a little later in the morning. Even when they stop napping, quiet time in the late afternoon or before dinner is a must for four-year-olds and a wise idea for five-year-olds.

With the two-and-a-half- or three-year-old, you still need to be vigilant about daily naps. He can skip an occasional one, but put him to bed earlier that night. Naps also remain essential for older children who aren't sleeping through the night or who are obviously tired during the day. You will have to nap coach. For how to nap coach your child, see the section "Much Ado About Napping" on page 266; the advice applies to this age group, too. That information includes tips for nap coaching multiples.

At around age four, you may find that your child no longer needs a daily nap but still needs a "nap day" every three or four days. Carleigh napped daily until age five and slept every other day after school for the first few months of kindergarten, which was only a half day at the time. That's longer than most children, but I could tell by her behavior that she still needed that extra sleep in the afternoon. My second daughter, Gretchen, in what was probably a more typical pattern, stopped napping at home when she was about three and a half but still napped at preschool.

If your child is getting about eleven hours of unfragmented sleep at night and seems well rested during the day, it may be time to go from naps to quiet time. You might want to cut out naps every other day rather than eliminate them completely, or you may find that he naps great on the days he's with his sitter or at preschool but won't nap on days he's with you (or vice versa). Children who were good nappers but who now take a very long time to fall asleep in the afternoon may also be ready to phase out the nap and start quiet time.

When Kerry was three years old, Laurel abandoned her struggle to make him nap on the days he was home with her, but he still napped beautifully on the days he had a sitter. A few months later, Laurel noticed that he was much more difficult at bedtime on nap days. "I'd put him to bed, and he'd be up and out of bed six times. It more than made up for the nap," she said. "Everybody would be angry—I felt so bad for him." Although I usually urge families to continue the nap until around three and a half or four, in this case, Mom's instincts were right. When they cut out the nap, bedtime became simple and pleasant. "We can shut off the light and say good night, and he goes to sleep," Laurel said.

Quiet time is exactly what it sounds like—about forty-five minutes of structured, solitary play, preferably at about the same time every afternoon. It's a time for children to rest their bodies and, to a lesser extent, their minds. It helps pave the way for a peaceful dinner hour and easy bedtime. Good activities include looking at books; watching an age-appropriate, calm children's video (leave fast-paced, action-packed shows for another time); coloring; or playing in their room with dolls, trains, trucks, or the like. The activity should not need a lot of adult interaction or supervision, so make sure the child is in a safe place. Please remember to not have your child on an electronic device during quiet time, as the glow emitted from the device has an arousing effect on the brain. (See "Say No to the Glow" in Phase 1.)

Quiet-time activities: lacing cards, LEGO, Colorforms, Wikki Stix, Imaginetics (which are like the modern version of Colorforms), matching games, *I Spy* books, dot-to-dot books, coloring books, and puzzles.

Phase 3

SLEEP MAINTENANCE AND TROUBLESHOOTING THROUGH AGES AND STAGES

Chapter 12

MAKING CHOICES ABOUT CO-SLEEPING, BED SHARING, AND ROOM SHARING

The topic of co-sleeping is a hotly debated one, especially with the American Academy of Pediatrics taking an official stance against bed sharing at any age. Making matters worse is the confusion over terms that apply to families who want to remain close to their children at night and sleep in a family setting. It becomes even blurrier because the AAP takes a firm stance against bed sharing, but *recommends* room sharing with a child from birth to at least six months and ideally one year. First, let's try to define the terms.

The AAP opposes sharing a bed with a child. When the pediatrician group says it supports co-sleeping, it is referring to *room sharing*. This is what it sounds like: parents bring home a newborn and place him in a bassinet in their own room or a co-sleeper that attaches to the side of their own bed for easy access and safety. Having the baby in a crib right next to you, in a bassinet that you can reach over and touch, or a co-sleeper attached to the bed—Arm's Reach (www.armsreach.com)

is one brand—may well be the best of both worlds. It's easy to feed the baby at night without everybody having to get up and walk around. You have the peace of mind of having her literally at your fingertips. But you don't have to worry about the safety challenges of bed sharing. For moms who have had C-sections and have difficulty getting up and moving around for the first few weeks, it may be particularly helpful.

When parents talk about making the decision to co-sleep with their children, many are considering room sharing; however, the divisive line that causes passionate debate and criticism typically centers around co-sleeping, as in *bed sharing*—or, as it is popularly known, *the family bed*.

This chapter is not about choosing which camp you fall into, and it isn't aimed at talking you into or out of either lifestyle choice. But here is the ironic reality. Even for families who have decided not to co-sleep or room share or bed share, a whopping 60 percent of them wind up doing so in the first year of their child's life out of mere sleepless desperation. These "we didn't plan it this way" folks are reactively co-sleeping—responding to awakenings by bringing the child into their bed, sleeping in their child's room, or some other combination of room sharing.

So with that reality alone, I want to make sure that families who end up sharing a bed, whether they planned to or not, are able to do so safely. And if you are in a situation, planned or unplanned, that isn't working for your family—if it's all *co* and no *sleep*—I want to give you tools to change it. That is what this chapter aims to do.

REACTIVE CO-SLEEPING

Adele and Geoff read every book and tried every technique with Alex before they came to me. By then, he was fifteen months and very confused about what he was supposed to do to get to sleep. "Everything worked a little bit, but nothing worked completely," Adele said. They had Ferberized him earlier, and while it helped him fall asleep, it didn't keep him asleep. Eventually, they tried letting him cry it out for those middle-of-the-night awakenings, too, but it was intolerable; he cried and cried, three or four hours at a stretch. "I couldn't take it. It was 2:00 a.m., he was in there crying, showing no sign of stopping, and just crying himself more awake. That panicked me. So I went back to nursing him to sleep. That would work; it would only take five minutes. But I'd have to do it three or four times a night."

Later, she weaned him at night, but it was a slow process, taking about six weeks, partly because he got sick several times around then and Adele would nurse him again while he wasn't feeling well. By age one, the nighttime weaning was over, but he was still waking up all night, and Adele wasn't about to put up with all those tears anymore. Desperate, she started taking him into her bed. "He'd go back and forth, shuttling between the crib and the bed. It was horrible, and I felt like a complete failure because I had been so anti–baby-in-bed."

I encourage you as parents to make a decision about the shared bed before the baby is born, reserving the option to change your minds without any guilt if your decision turns out not to be the best one for *you*. It's important to understand that co-sleeping is not magic. Although some proponents of the family bed would disagree, I have worked with numerous couples whose babies did not necessarily sleep deeper or longer because they were in bed with their parents. In fact, some parents found that their child slept longer and woke less frequently when they stopped co-sleeping and moved her into her own crib. Perhaps this is temperament or sensitivity to sound, movement, texture, or smell, or all of the above. What is important is that we figure out what works for your child and family.

I can't tell you how strongly I feel about finding a solution that feels right for you, even if it wasn't what you'd planned, hoped, or expected. If you are constantly exhausted, you can't be the mother or father you want to be, and you aren't going to be as adept at reading your baby's cues and responding to her needs. And you have a higher risk of ending up depressed, which isn't good for you or your child.

CO-SLEEPING CATEGORIES AND GOALS

I divide *co-sleeping* into three categories: the committed co-sleepers, the short-term co-sleepers, and the "we didn't plan it this way" co-sleepers.

The *committed co-sleepers* are couples (also a lot of single moms) who choose the family bed as a philosophy and lifestyle. Many are influenced by the *attachment parenting* philosophy popularized by William and Martha Sears. These parents consciously decide to have the baby (or, later, all the children) sleep with them until he expresses a desire for his own bed, even if that takes several years. I hear from these families when they no longer want to go to sleep at 7:00 p.m. or find that their children won't stay in bed unless they lie down with them and go to sleep at the same time and stay there for the night. Or their child beyond nine months still wants to nurse several times a night and the parents are frazzled. They want to continue to co-sleep—without having everyone be an exhausted wreck.

A subsection of committed co-sleepers who seek out my help are those I call the "caught-off-guard co-sleepers." These parents have successfully bed shared for years with their first child or children, only to be surprised that their latest addition is either not interested in sleeping with her family or is such a frenetic, wiggly sleeper that parents aren't getting the rest they need. Additionally, temperament and sensory sensitivities can be a factor. This can be disappointing for families and a reminder that we have to remember that each child is unique and we may have to parent them differently from their siblings.

The *short-term co-sleepers* and room sharers want the baby with them the first few months, but know their child will move to her own room at around six months. Bed sharing for the first six months is the riskiest time to bed share (see Appendix C, "Safe Sleeping Recommendations for Babies"). They like the bonding, and they like the convenience of having the newborn right there when they are nursing frequently. As new parents are often anxious parents, they may also feel less worried if the baby is by their side. These parents may do well by choosing room sharing (having the bassinet in their room or an attachable co-sleeping bed) as an alternative because it satisfies the need for closeness and convenience, while minimizing the safety risks. I recommend that if you choose to co-sleep in the same bed short term with your newborn (fully aware of the safety requirements), plan to transition to the crib, bassinet, or co-sleeper at about three months and then room share until your baby is six months to a year. But even during the three months in which you are co-sleeping in the same bed, you should have the baby nap in his crib, bassinet, or co-sleeper consistently. Having him sleep on his own at nap time will make the eventual switch to nighttime sleep in the crib much smoother, preparing him to fall asleep on his own—whether he learns that skill all by himself or you do the Sleep Lady Shuffle.

The "we didn't plan it this way" co-sleepers, or *reactive co-sleepers*, are the parents who end up with the baby in the bed part or all of the night, not by choice or philosophical commitment but because it's the only way they can get their baby to sleep at bedtime or back to sleep in the middle of the night. Some started out as short-term co-sleepers but never figured out how to stop it. Others put the baby in the crib at bedtime but take her into their bed out of desperation when she wakes up for the third or fourth time at night. And there are those who are ambivalent and either can't decide where they want the baby to sleep or are conflicted, with one parent advocating the family bed and the other favoring the crib. Disagreement usually results in a mishmash of crib sleeping and co-sleeping, which can make even a very young baby confused about where and how she is supposed to fall asleep. Even the most enthusiastic proponents of bed sharing don't promote reactive co-sleeping.

Some experts, including Elizabeth Pantley, author of *The No-Cry Sleep Solution*, recommend placing the baby between the mother and the wall or rail, not between the two parents. She believes that fathers, grandparents, older siblings, and babysitters don't have the same "instinctual awareness of a baby's location" and won't respond as well to the baby's needs and positioning. Pantley also says that mothers who are very deep sleepers, who won't wake up at the baby's subtle cues, might want to refrain from co-sleeping.

WHAT'S RIGHT FOR YOU

When you are deciding whether long-term co-sleeping is right for you, an array of practical and emotional issues bear consideration. Think about your own childhood, your nighttime fears, your feelings of closeness to or isolation from your parents. Mothers working outside the home need to consider whether they want the extra closeness at night because they feel guilty or are afraid they are hurting the baby by being away during the day. I don't mean to imply that all parents who co-sleep do so out of guilt, but understanding your motives can often clarify your decision. Ask yourself, too, whether nighttime physical proximity is really the key to a secure bond or attachment with your child. As a mother and as a family therapist, I am not convinced that it's a requirement; most of our bonding, our attachment, and our interaction take place during the day. How we touch, care for, play with, listen to, respond to, and laugh with our children when we are awake seems more essential to the formation of our relationships than where and how we choose to sleep.

You also need to think carefully about how having a child in bed with you all the time will affect your marriage. Think, too, about how you will deal with a growing family. Will you have two or three children who are in bed with you? If you are a single parent, consider the implications of integrating a new partner into your life when your child is sharing your pillow.

Keep in mind that co-sleeping is a long-term commitment, a practice that you will need to continue until the child *chooses* to transition to her own bed. Sometimes that takes a year or two, sometimes seven or eight. Reid and Julia, for instance, co-slept with their first two children, and it was easy, pleasant, and emotionally gratifying. Both children quickly transitioned to their own beds. Then along came Todd, their third child, who was a very disruptive co-sleeper and didn't want to move until I helped them ease him into his own room at fourteen months. Also take more mundane matters into account. How light a sleeper are you? Will a wriggling baby keep you up at night? Will you worry more if he's with you or if he's away from you? Will you miss being able to read in bed with the light on or watch television late at night?

If you change your mind during the first three to six months, the transition isn't much of a problem. After that, it gets harder, but it's not impossible. I've worked with many families who have practiced co-sleeping for two years and then decided they needed to change their sleeping arrangements. I will give you advice on how to transition a two-year-old into her own bed as smoothly and gently as possible, but I must emphasize that I don't recommend letting a child sleep in your bed for two years and then abruptly sending her down the hall to her "own" bed. After all, she thinks your bed *is* her bed. And I definitely don't encourage abruptly ending co-sleeping with one child to make room for a new baby in your bed. (I'll have some suggestions later in this chapter for coping with that situation.)

SAFETY CONCERNS AND PRECAUTIONS

As you consider the pros and cons of the family bed, you should be aware of some safety issues. Some studies have found a higher risk of sudden infant death syndrome (SIDS) and other sleep-related infant deaths, such as accidental suffocation and strangulation, for babies that bed share. As I noted, the American Academy of Pediatrics has formally recommended against bed sharing for the first year. In 2016, the AAP stated that evidence shows sleeping in the parents' room on a separate, safe surface lowers the chance of SIDS by as much as 50 percent. It also helps prevent suffocation, strangulation, or entrapment that can happen when babies are sleeping in bed with adults.

First Candle, an organization devoted to reducing the rates of sleep-related infant deaths, notes an increase in the rate of accidental suffocation by 115 percent over the past decade, with many of these cases directly attributable to bed sharing.

Further, First Candle reminds parents that beds that are perfectly safe and comfortable for adults or older children can be very hazardous

Sleep Lady Tip

Do not sleep with your baby if you are very overweight or if you have been drinking alcohol or using drugs or medications. I've included a full list of child safety rules—for all babies, not just co-sleeping ones—at the back of the book. Please read it.

for babies. Adult beds are not made with infant safety in mind. "Especially dangerous are pillow top and memory foam mattresses that can conform around a baby's mouth and nose and obstruct their breathing," writes First Candle in the appendix of this book. "Soft bedding and other items in the adult bed increase the risk of SIDS and suffocation, especially for young babies. A baby or small child can also fall from the bed or get trapped between the mattress and the structure of the bed (the headboard, footboard, side rails, and frame), between the bed and the wall or nearby furniture, or even between railings in the headboard or footboard. Fatalities have been documented."

The remaining sections of this chapter will provide information for the following:

* Improving the family bed you already share and plan to keep
* Ending co-sleeping and/or room sharing
* Sleep coaching and room sharing

HOW TO IMPROVE SLEEP IN THE FAMILY BED

Those of you who are co-sleeping happily and healthily may still benefit from steps I outline here that can improve the quality of everyone's sleep. You can help your baby develop good sleep patterns and at least a degree of sleep independence even in a family-bed setting.

As I mentioned, I very strongly recommend having the baby nap in his bassinet or crib and restricting the co-sleeping to nighttime. (An occasional exception of a parent-child nap will not create a problem.) Not only does this promote better sleep habits for the child, it also gives the parent a lot more freedom. If your child knows how to fall asleep on his own, you won't have to lie down with him for every nap or go to bed at 7:00 every night.

Some couples who co-sleep but also want to foster a degree of sleep independence in their baby and a little early-evening freedom for themselves put the baby down in her crib at bedtime. Then they move her into the family bed when they get ready for sleep themselves, or the first time she wakes up at night.

Remember that sleep is a learned skill, regardless of whether your child is in your bed or her crib. Helping her develop the ability to fall asleep without being nursed, held, or rocked each and every time is an important foundation.

Decide where you want your baby or child to start at night:

Option 1: She starts in her crib or her bed and then can join the family bed at your bedtime or her first waking after you go to bed.

Option 2: She will start in your bed, and everyone goes to bed at the same time.

Option 3: Make a safe sleeping area (e.g., a mattress on the ground with ideally a bare room and put baby to bed there and parents join later).

I prefer #1 for safety reasons; #2 doesn't mean that bedtime is 10:00 p.m., either; and with #3, you have to feel really comfortable leaving your baby or child alone, knowing he may roll off the bed and/or get up and crawl or walk around the room.

If you decide to have your baby or child start the night in his own crib or bed, then you can follow the age-appropriate chapter and do the Shuffle at bedtime. Address his sleep crutch by using the steps described in those chapters. Bring your baby or child into your safe bed the first time he wakes after you go to bed, or get him out of his bed and bring him to your bed when you go to sleep.

SAFE CO-SLEEPING TIPS

If you decide to co-sleep, talk to your doctor about the most recent safety recommendations, and do everything you can to reduce the hazards. Some experts recommend placing a firm, smooth mattress or futon on the floor away from all walls. Use well-fitted sheets that can't be easily pulled off. Don't use any pillows or blankets in the early months, and make sure the baby can't get stuck in a mattress pad. Never use waterbeds or any other soft and flexible surfaces. Make sure there are no crevices or soft spots where the baby can get caught or smothered.

If your mattress is not on the floor, use well-designed guardrails that cannot entrap a baby. If your bed is next to the wall or other furniture, make sure there is no place the baby can get stuck or smothered. Or move your bed away from the walls.

ELIMINATING NIGHTTIME FEEDINGS WHILE CO-SLEEPING

If you want to wean your baby from all night feedings or reduce them to one while you co-sleep, then you can: nurse or feed when you bring your child to bed or their first waking after you go to bed and then coach back to sleep for all other wakings. You can keep this one feeding as long as you want, or if you want to completely night wean, do this for three nights and then stop.

After you feed her, unlatch her while she's still awake, and pull your shirt down. Then place her facing away from you, and put a lovey in her arms. You might also want to create a little space between you and the baby as she falls asleep after nursing. Comfort her to sleep, but don't let her have your breast again to go to sleep. Pat, shush, and snuggle to sleep. If you are keeping an additional feeding, then build that into your plan and coach for all the other wakings. If you feel this is becoming too confusing for you and your child (which is a possibility), Mom can sleep in another room for a few nights and return for the feedings. The other parent would co-sleep with the child and coach through the wakings. If she wakes up wanting the breast again sooner than that, use one of your other comforting techniques to help her get back to sleep. If that proves too hard, Mom might sleep in another room between nursings for a few nights, letting the non-nursing parent comfort and share the bed with the baby.

If your baby is eating much more at night than during the day, keep track of her nursing patterns and then try to shift them. Consult the age-appropriate chapter in this book for techniques on cutting back on nighttime nursing, even if you don't want to eliminate it completely, and adapt those strategies to the family bed. For instance, if your child were not co-sleeping, you would nurse her before putting her to bed and keep some separation between the two activities.

Some parents want to continue to co-sleep and wean a child from all night feedings (with the green light from their pediatrician). You can follow the *three-night taper-off method* as outlined in the "Eliminating Nighttime Feeding" sections in the age-appropriate chapters. Some parents will decide on doing the three-night method or cold-turkey method so that Dad or the other parent will co-sleep with the baby or child—snuggling, patting, and spooning to sleep while Mom sleeps in another room for three or four nights, creating that separation from the sleep-nurse association. Dad will be focused on night awakenings and coaching. Then, when Mom returns to the bed after night 4, she should wear a bra and fitted shirt to avoid struggles over the breast.

Some parents who want to night wean decide to move from the family bed to co-sleeping in the child's room for a few nights because they feel the new environment might help lessen the association between nursing and sleeping and give opportunities for new associations. Base your decision on what you can follow through with consistently. If you start with trying to wean in the family bed and are finding it too difficult, then switch to the option of co-sleeping in her room, with the goal being to have her in her own crib in her own room, completely weaned. There are two ways to do that:

1. **Three-night taper-off method,** ideally with the non-nursing parent co-sleeping with the child. The nursing parent will come in at the set time for feeding. Then, on the fourth night, there will be no feedings, and the nursing parent will coach the child back to sleep. On the fifth night, the parents will put the child in the crib

and begin the Shuffle (both parents can be involved), or you can delay Mom's involvement for a few more days if nursing was the primary sleep crutch. Expect some regression when Mom joins the sleep-coaching process.

2. **Cold turkey** is an option if the baby or child was barely nursing before. Then Dad or the non-nursing parent co-sleeps for two or three nights in the child's room, and then on the third or fourth night puts the baby in the crib and starts the Shuffle.

MOVE OUT OF THE FAMILY BED

Many of the couples who consult me started out committed to co-sleeping and later found it didn't quite work out for them. I also encounter a lot of "we didn't plan it this way" couples seeking help in finally breaking the pattern. These families end up missing their privacy, or they are just not getting very much sleep. Babies can be very noisy, squiggly sleepers, thrashing around or burrowing down to the foot of the bed, where you then worry about them being smothered in bedding. Some babies may not learn to sleep very well in bed with their parents, nursing frequently because the opportunity is always present or because they are too stimulated to sleep much of the night simply by being so close to their parents. It can be a bit of a jolt for a couple who opted to co-sleep because they believed their baby truly needed their constant presence, only to find that this particular child sleeps better without them.

Although I told you my preference is that you make an informed decision about co-sleeping early on and stick to it, if you find it isn't working, do not hesitate to make a change. Don't feel guilty, and don't let anyone else make you feel guilty or incompetent. You can and will have a strong and healthy attachment with your child even if you don't co-sleep. Typically done in three stages, the switch is made pretty quickly for babies who are six months and older, and I'll guide you through that. For older children in beds, expect the adjustment to take at least three weeks, and then give it another two or three months until you can be confident the change has really taken root.

When you do move a child out of your bed, you must be consistent. You can't take her into your bed sometimes, not even when it's almost morning, or you are going to confuse her. This can be emotionally difficult for a parent who still enjoys aspects of sleeping with her child. If you miss that little baby head curled against your neck, find another way to satisfy that yearning with some extra cuddling throughout the day.

After a baby has been in your bed for months or years, I suggest making changes in several stages over several weeks (though not every family goes through every step): daytime acclimation to her room, daytime napping, sleeping with the child in her room, and the Sleep Lady Shuffle to teach sleep independence. I'll explain each stage in more detail below.

If your child is old enough, try to prepare her by talking through the imminent change. Even a one year-old may comprehend more than you realize, and certainly from eighteen months or so, they can

Sleep Lady Tip

The one time I do not recommend ending co-sleeping with your child is with the birth of a new baby. It's not ideal to move one child out of your bed to make room for the next, particularly since fears, rivalries, and feelings of displacement are so common even without making dramatic changes. I know a few kids age three and older who have graciously gotten up and out of Mom and Dad's bed to accommodate the new baby, but that is really asking an awful lot of them. Either complete the transition a good three to six months before the new baby comes, or keep the older child in your bed for a few more months. You can put the newborn in a bassinet or co-sleeper sidecar nearby. Then simultaneously transition both children to their own room or rooms. Some couples divvy up the co-sleeping tasks, with the nursing mom in one room with the newborn and the other parent in another room with the older child. They usually do that for a few months, until the newborn is sleeping through the night, and then end co-sleeping with both kids.

understand a good deal. Letting them know what is coming—and making it sound enticing and exciting—often helps the transition.

STAGE 1: DAYTIME AND PLAYTIME

Start by getting your baby used to his room awake and in daylight. In fact, he shouldn't just be used to it, he should like it. Play with him there, change him there, and hug him and kiss him there. If he needs some incentives to venture into the unfamiliar room, put some fun new toys or books in his room. (You can skip this stage if your child is already playing in his room or napping there.)

STAGE 2: ADDRESS NAPPING

If she's not already napping in her bedroom, you can start there by co-sleeping in her room for naps in a safe makeshift bed or a mattress put temporarily in her room where her crib is. Or if you are transitioning an older child to a bed, rather than a crib, in her room, you can co-sleep for naps there. Spend a week or two getting her accustomed to napping in her own room before you make the nighttime transition. Go ahead and nap in her room with her for two or three days if your intuition tells you she needs that extra assistance. Then if she has trouble falling asleep in her room, sit with her for the next few days but try to be a fairly neutral presence. Calm and soothe her a bit, but don't let her constantly engage you, or all the interaction will be an excuse for her not to sleep. After a few days, you can try the Sleep Lady Shuffle to help her learn to nap on her own.

It is up to you whether you want to address the napping first or napping and nighttime sleep simultaneously—it doesn't matter if you are sitting in exactly the same position day and night at this point. Instead of the Shuffle, you have the option of trying to settle her in for a nap with her lovey and then leaving the room, checking on her every four or five minutes if she's crying. If that feels too abrupt to you, remember that either approach is fine and that you should choose the one that feels best for you and suits your child. Read the chapter relevant for your child's age for details on the Shuffle and nap training.

STAGE 3: CO-SLEEP IN HIS ROOM AND STARI THE SLEEP LADY SHUFFLE

When you are ready for night coaching in his room, you should start the Sleep Lady Shuffle, my method of gradually teaching the baby or child to put himself to sleep without you. On the day you start, make sure the child gets a great day of naps any way you can get them.

With most babies, you start the Shuffle by sitting right next to the crib or bed. With co-sleeping, you can spend a few nights co-sleeping in his room with him to create a bridge between the family bed and independent sleep. Then you are ready for the heart of the Shuffle. Begin by sitting next to your child's crib or bed for three nights to soothe him. If the thought of leaving your child once he is asleep feels too abrupt, you can sleep in the room in a makeshift bed for two to three nights so you can attend to him quickly when he wakes. *But stay only two or three nights.* Any longer, and he will become accustomed to having you there, and it will be harder for him when you try to leave. If he is in a bed and not a crib and he gets out and tries to join you during the night, simply put him back immediately without a word. If he does this repeatedly or if you wake up at night and find he has joined you in your bed, remove the makeshift bed the next morning and stop sleeping in his room. Continue with the Shuffle from a chair.

Every three nights, move your Shuffle position a little farther away so that he can gradually fall asleep more independently. Move across the room, then to the doorway, then out the door, into the hall. Within about two weeks, you will be able to leave him alone while still checking on him and reassuring him frequently. The fine points of the system vary a little bit by age, so please review my directions in the age-relevant chapter.

If your child has been going to bed in her crib but ending up with you in the middle of the night, you can't ease out of this habit gradually. You have to set new sleep associations. With older children, discuss their sleep manners and "jobs" in exercising those manners, which are discussed in Chapter 11, "Two and a Half to Five Years." Enforce them and positively reinforce them consistently. As always, if your child is upset, you can pick up to calm, but do so briefly. Additionally, you can stroke, soothe, whisper, murmur, and pat your child when she gets up and expects to come to your bed, but don't give in, not if you really want to end co-sleeping. That means you have to keep her in her crib or bed every time—at 2:00, 3:00, 4:00, and 5:00 a.m. If you reassure her but make her stay in her crib at 2:00, 3:00, and 4:00, but take her into your bed at 5:00, you have confused her and possibly trained her to cry longer and harder next time. Babies can't tell time. She can't understand why you take her into your bed at some times and not others.

SLEEP COACHING AND ROOM SHARING

Example: We have a one-bedroom apartment and initially co-slept with our baby in the early months, but she is nine months old now and still waking a lot at night to nurse back to sleep, and we are exhausted. We want her to sleep in her own crib. We don't have another bedroom, so her crib will need to stay in our room. Can we still sleep coach?

The short answer is absolutely! And I get this question both from parents who have no choice but to share a room and from parents who want to keep the family environment without sharing a bed. Here's how to sleep coach while room-sharing:

Decide if you want to begin the Shuffle with her crib next to your bed, and every three days, move the crib farther away from your bedside (this only works in a big room). Or you can move her crib as far from your bed as possible and start the Shuffle there at bedtime. In both scenarios, you'll start the Shuffle sitting right near the crib at bedtime—and make sure you start after a great day of naps. When you begin the Shuffle, review the "Tips for the First Three Shuffle Nights." Put her down drowsy but awake at bedtime in her crib in your room, and sit next to her crib at bedtime and when she wakes during the night. Don't pat or stroke her constantly. Give her enough contact to feel loved and secure, but not so much contact that it becomes a sleep crutch—that she needs you to be there stroking her all the time at bedtime and during the night.

After night 3 or 4 (depending on your night-weaning plan), follow the usual Shuffle chair positions at bedtime only. When your child wakes during the night, do an initial crib-side check to make sure all is okay and to reassure your baby, and then return to your bed and verbally reassure from there. Like the "traditional" Shuffle, you can go crib-side to reassure, but be careful not to do this too much and inadvertently create a new crutch. Please refer to age-appropriate chapters for tips on calming your child during the Shuffle.

Some parents create a barrier or wall for privacy and to foster an idea of independent sleeping between the crib and the bed, such as an accordion room separator, or they thumbtack a sheet to the ceiling (make sure your child can't grab it and pull it down). Mobile toddlers and children who see their parents might be more tempted to want to go to them, so creating privacy could instill an out-of-sight, out-of-mind idea and better assist in sleep coaching and keeping your child from becoming a human boomerang—in and out of bed (theirs and yours) all night long.

After she gets accustomed to sleeping in her crib, keep your bed strictly off-limits for at least three months, or else you'll start the whole cycle all over again, which is not fair to her. Snuggle—but not in your bed. Find a comfy chair or couch somewhere, and don't let her fall asleep in your arms.

FOUR FAMILIES' JOURNEYS

CANDICE (ELEVEN MONTHS)

At eleven months, Candice had a severe aversion to her room. She had been co-sleeping with her mom, Patty, while her dad, Don, afraid of squishing her, had been sleeping in another room. When Candice was six months old, her parents had made an attempt at reclaiming their bed and tried to Ferberize her. It was a disaster. Candice cried and cried, and the more she cried, the more awake she became. The experience traumatized her so badly she would not even go into her room anymore, not even to play, not even accompanied by parents. She went back into their bed—and Don went back into the guest room. Five more months passed, and her parents finally decided something had to give.

The first step was to reacquaint Candice with her room. Patty put a lot of enticing new toys there, and the two of them played there together each day. This went on for two weeks. We actually altered the usual order. Instead of working on naps, which were difficult for Candice, we addressed bedtime. Patty co-slept with Candice in her room for a few days. Then Patty put Candice in her crib and started the Sleep Lady Shuffle, while she slept on an air mattress on the floor. When Candice protested or awoke in the middle of the night wanting Mom, Patty was near her and could respond to her quickly by reaching through the crib slats to pat and reassure her daughter and pick up when necessary. Patty noticed that Candice was beginning to develop her own techniques for soothing herself to sleep—twirling her hair, playing with her crib, and using her pacifiers not only to suck on but to play with.

Finally, it was time for the big move after four or five days of sleeping in the room at night—removing the mattress from Candice's room. Mom sat in the chair by the door at bedtime and during the night and continued to Shuffle out. There were some tears, but Candice never got so hysterical that she couldn't calm herself down, nor did the tears ever get so intense that Patty and Don couldn't tolerate them.

Then, just when Patty and Don thought they were done and Candice was sleeping through the night, she got sick. They handled it well. Instead of taking her back into their bed and ending up back at square one, Patty would sit in a chair in Candice's room until the baby was very calm and drowsy, but not completely asleep. When she recovered, they checked on her from the doorway for a few nights. Candice quickly became an excellent sleeper. Soon Patty and Don could even leave her with a sitter and go out for dinner. "It's a totally different world for us," her mother said. "Now she loves to sleep in her crib."

TODD (FOURTEEN MONTHS)

Julia and Reid were committed to attachment parenting and had enjoyed co-sleeping with their first two children, now both in school. Then came Todd. He was fourteen months old when his family consulted me. All was not well.

Todd had a number of health problems, including allergies and one prolonged and severe ear infection that led to surgery to insert tubes. Although those conditions aggravated Todd's disjointed sleep, they didn't fully explain it. And once his ears were better and his allergies addressed, he still didn't sleep any longer or better. He nursed much more frequently than his sisters had, slept more poorly, and had a less malleable temperament. "Todd wasn't an easily detached baby. We even had to leave a co-op preschool because he didn't separate well," his mom said.

Getting so little sleep with him in their bed, they first tried to move him to a crib at eight months. It didn't work. Instead of Todd napping in the crib, Julia ended up taking thirty-minute walks around the house with the stroller. "It gets pretty boring making endless loops on those hardwood floors," Julia said.

Bedtime was a struggle. They had to rock and nurse him to sleep, and he didn't stay asleep unless he was in their bed, nursing and snuggling. "We had to add all these layers of shenanigans on top of all the rituals," Reid recalled. At the same time, they were dealing with two other young children with their own bedtime needs and demands. So they put Todd back in their bed and tried to make the best of it.

Julia and Reid knew that Todd was capable of sleeping all night and in a crib if he wanted to. He had proved that when Julia had surgery for kidney stones and pumped so Todd could have breast milk in a bottle. Todd didn't like bottles, so he just slept all night, albeit not very happily. "That worked until those breasts were back in his world, and that's what he wanted," she ruefully recalled.

When I saw them, we talked a lot about their parenting styles, what changes they would be able to make, what changes just weren't realistic given their personalities, values, and lifestyles. "I am not a schedule person—you give me hours to follow, and I come unhinged," Julia said. She identified which tasks *she could accomplish and which she had to turn over to Reid. She agreed to work on limiting feedings to six times a day and to try comforting techniques other than nursing, not an easy task with an agile and determined fourteen-month-old who, whenever he got distressed, would try to climb up his mom, lift up her shirt, and wriggle himself underneath. They also switched the dinner hour from 6:00 to 5:00 so they'd have plenty of time to eat as a family and to start Todd's bedtime routine at 6:30 and have him asleep by 7:30. Before, he had gone to bed at 9:00 or 9:30, too late for a one-year-old.*

At night, as we began the Sleep Lady Shuffle, we wanted to create a distinct separation between nursing and sleep. Julia nursed downstairs in the sunroom at about 6:30. (Most families I work with nurse in the child's bedroom, being careful not to nurse the child into a deep sleep. In Todd's case, we thought additional separation was warranted.)

Julia knew that she wouldn't be able to cope with the initial phase of sleep training, so Reid took charge. Todd went down more easily than they had expected the first night in his own room, with his dad sitting by his side. But he woke up at 11:00 p.m. and again at midnight. The second time was the worst. He screamed furiously for an hour and twenty minutes. Reid sat next to him, calm and consistent. "I knew it was okay to touch him but not to hold his hand. I knew to pat him on the back and then stop, or to pat the mattress gently. It was almost more difficult for me than for him, because you want to reach out— you want to take care of your kid. But I knew I couldn't start out holding his hand because I would be moving farther away in a few nights, and I wasn't going to be able to hold his hand when I was five feet away," Reid said.

Julia sat outside the bedroom and tried to empathize through the door until she finally realized that she needed to stop listening, ignore the baby monitor, and try to get some sleep for herself.

The second night, Todd got mad. Reid, who is pretty laid-back, remembered thinking, Oh, my God, I've got a demon child in the crib! *Todd threw things out of the crib and tried to crawl out. They put a sleep sack on him so he couldn't get a leghold.*

"I just kept repeating the same reassuring words. I just kept repeating them like I was teaching a dog a trick. 'Todd, you can do this, go night-night. You can

do this, go night-night.' By three days, I just shortened it to 'Night-night, night-night,'" Reid remembered.

The third day, Reid saw an improvement. It still wasn't easy, but looking at his log, Reid could see that Todd had cried for twenty-two minutes. "That felt like a lot—until I looked back and saw he had cried one hour and twenty minutes the first night. It was bumpy and not a lot of fun, but it was getting better." Reid and Julia were still having doubts and second-guessing themselves at this point, but decided to stick with it and gave each other moral support.

By the time Reid reached the point where he had to leave the room, he was feeling much more optimistic. "I realized the next step didn't have to be a big step. I was confident he could do it." Reid came back and checked on Todd every five minutes or so. The nights Julia took bedtime duty, she made less frequent checks because Todd would get furious if he saw her but didn't get to nurse himself to sleep. "It was tough for a few nights," she recalled. "But we knew he was pulling it together."

Julia says she is a little more open to modifications and alternatives based on her children's temperaments, less afraid that she will hurt her children or weaken her bond with them if she doesn't do everything by the attachment-theory book. Partly because they were still a little ambivalent about the co-sleeping and partly because the family experienced a lot of changes and adjustments in the next few months—Reid lost his job when the high-tech bubble burst, and the family spent several months traveling around, trying to decide where to relocate—they were not always completely consistent. Sometimes Todd didn't cry at all at bedtime, and sometimes he'd cry for four or five minutes, but never longer than that and never as ferociously as he had those first two nights. Among Todd's first full phrases was "Mommy, lie down, bed." And sometimes one parent did give in and lie down with him, particularly while they were traveling or going through one transition or another. "We've had some recidivism," said Reid. "And then it takes a few days to get back. The lesson to be learned is the more you get into a routine and stick to a routine, the easier it is for the kids to know what to expect."

Months later, Todd was generally restricting his bedtime screaming to hotel stays with his sisters. His father confided, "He only does that because he thinks it's a riot."

KERRY (TWO AND A HALF YEARS OLD)

Laurel and Richard were classic "we didn't plan it this way" co-sleepers. Kerry slept in a crib—except when he didn't. When he fussed and wanted his mom, Laurel slept with him in the family room or guest room. He was quite young when he moved into a toddler bed, where she couldn't fit alongside him, but when he got out of bed, as toddlers often do, they often ended up asleep together on the floor.

Philosophically, she didn't object to sleeping with him, only neither of them slept very much. "If I had to sleep with him—well, okay. But sleeping with him wasn't even resolving the issue. He was extremely restless. He would be perpendicular in the bed, kicking me in the head, rolling around a lot. I was so worried about him rolling off, he was moving so much, I couldn't sleep," said Laurel, a therapist who knew about behavioral modification with older children but found it was "a lot different when you are dealing with your own emotional stuff and your own child."

Before starting the Sleep Lady Shuffle, we tweaked his bedtime routine to change, but not shorten, his snuggle time. They did the bath, tooth brushing, and so forth, and then Laurel and Kerry snuggled up to read books on a little couch in his room. To earn his last story, his special reading of Toy Story, *he had to get into bed. "That was the incentive; we could entice him into bed," Laurel said. They also used a sleep manners chart for good bedtime behavior.*

After reading to Kerry, Laurel turned off the light and began the Shuffle, sitting by his side on the floor. The first night, she kept her hand on him because she knew he was going to need that contact. By the second night, she was careful to make the hand touching more sporadic lest it become another sleep crutch. She patted his hand, without lying down with him, each time he woke those first nights.

Since Kerry was on the floor and was used to having Laurel there as well, she never used a chair. She sat on the floor, but she moved through the Shuffle, to the end of the bed, the doorway, then out in the hall.

Kerry had progressed nicely, in less than two weeks. Initially, he was still getting up at night to look for Mom. She would take him back to his room silently. Resisting the impulse to lie down and sleep with him—and it can be a strong impulse when you are tired and want to get both you and your baby back to sleep quickly—she would assume whatever position she had been in at bedtime that night and sit there until he drifted back to sleep. The night awakenings tapered off. There were some bumps, because he'd regress each time he got sick or traveled, but the overall progress was good.

TWO CHILDREN (DYLAN, FIVE YEARS; LEILA, FIFTEEN MONTHS)

While earning her master's degree in education and working with at-risk pre-schoolers, Shauna had studied cross-cultural child-rearing and become convinced that co-sleeping was the right and natural path. When she and Nick had children, they were drawn to attachment parenting. Shauna nursed Dylan on demand, breastfeeding until he was almost two and a half. She carried him in a sling and co-slept, including lying down with him at nap time. Although they had been trying to transition him to a bed, it was not very successful, and he usually stayed with them. That's where he was at age four, when Shauna went into labor with his little sister, Leila.

Shauna didn't initially bring Leila full-time into an already-crowded bed. Instead, she placed her in an adjacent co-sleeper for six months, and then brought her into the family bed. In the meantime, they worked on shifting Dylan into his own bed. They managed to get him out of their bed, but one of the parents often ended up sleeping in his bed! Or they'd get him to sleep and he'd crawl back in their bed, or someone, somewhere, would end up sleeping on the floor to be near someone else.

Exhausted by this routine, Shauna set goals. She wanted Dylan sleeping all night in his own bed. She wanted Leila to stop nighttime nursing and be in her crib at fifteen months. With my help, she and Nick tackled both children's sleep issues simultaneously, with Nick concentrating on Dylan and Shauna on Leila, who was still being breastfed at bedtime and during the day.

They called a family meeting for Dylan, who was now five, and explained their expectations. They made him a star chart with five sleep manners. He also had both moral support and a little peer pressure in his preschool, where another little girl had worked with me. She became his sleep buddy as they compared their star tallies.

They began the Sleep Lady Shuffle. "He cried at the beginning. He'd say, 'I want Mommy.' Then he would be really proud of himself for quieting down and falling asleep," Shauna said. If he came to them at night, one of them would quietly walk him back to his own room and resume their chair position and remind him that his wake-up light was not on yet and he had to stay in his bed quietly. "If he was having a bad dream or he was scared, we would help him think of happy things," she said.

After five years of co-sleeping and emotional ambivalence about ending it, they were not always consistent. They knew it was unwise to lie down with Dylan, but they relapsed, sometimes because their hearts tugged their heads toward their little boy's pillow, sometimes because they were just too tired to do anything else. They had become a sort of hybrid of backsliding committed co-sleepers and "we didn't plan it this way" co-sleepers.

When Nick traveled overseas, Shauna, by then pregnant with a third child, allowed Dylan to have a "sleepover" in Mom's bed. "He was getting up and walking in, and I just let him—I couldn't deal with both his and Leila's sleep issues while I was pregnant and Nick was away. It was just too much for me to handle." She knew there would be sleep consequences but decided to face them, believing she would be able to cope better when Nick was back home and she could get more rest.

Meanwhile, Leila was making progress, partly because Shauna was determined to improve Leila's sleep before the next baby came. Nighttime weaning took only two nights. Shauna still nursed her before bed, but during the night she would offer her a cup of water; Leila wasn't all that interested in it, so Shauna stopped. Then she would pat Leila and hold her until she fell asleep without anything in her mouth. At the same time, she introduced a lovey to distract Leila from touching Shauna's hair as she fell asleep.

Leila had sometimes spent at least part of the night in a crib, but it was in her parents' room. Now they moved the crib to her own room. Shauna and Leila slept on the floor together for one night, but Leila kept trying to sleep on top of Shauna's chest. Although Shauna's own style and preference were to be very slow and gradual, something told her not to sleep on the floor too long, that Leila would start expecting to sleep this way. The next night, she nursed Leila until she was drowsy but still awake and then put her into her crib and began the Shuffle.

Leila accepted the changes reasonably well during the first few nights when Shauna was sitting by her side, but once Mom moved that chair away, Leila stood up in her crib and let everyone know she was mad. Shauna at first tried to be a calming, soothing presence, but by the end of a week realized that Leila did better if her mom just left the room. She cried for three minutes—tear-sensitive Shauna clocked it—and then put herself to sleep and pretty much stayed asleep. She woke up too early, 5:00 a.m., so for the first few mornings, Shauna lay on a mattress on the floor, and her presence helped Leila get back to sleep. Later, Shauna would go in and pat and reassure Leila if she woke up too early and then leave the room as Leila drifted back to sleep.

Leila's sleep for the next six months or so was good but not perfect, partly because the family went away for a month that summer shortly after the Shuffle. Leila potty trained early, which had its advantages, but she would yell, "Potty, potty, potty!" wanting to get out of the crib at night. She slept through the night for a while but then began waking up again in the early morning, between 4:00 and 6:00. She also tried to climb out of her crib before age two, but Shauna stopped it. "I wasn't ready for her to get out of the crib. I had just gotten her in it!" Like many toddlers, she also went through those spells of separation trouble at bedtime, and Shauna experimented with how to ease those fears. She found that at times Leila sought her presence but not her touch. She sat in a chair in Leila's room at night and knew that soon she would have to start leaving the room, despite Leila's protests, or else face sitting there for the next few years. Pregnant with her third child, that was not in Shauna's game plan.

Shauna and Nick still believed in co-sleeping but decided to limit it even further with their third child. The plan was to co-sleep for four months, and then get the baby into a crib. With each child, they also paid more attention to how often he ate, and whether he was really seeking the breast or expressing some other infant needs and desires. "I still believe in nursing on demand—but

I have to be more aware and recognize what he's demanding, whether he's hungry. I have to be aware when I'm nursing him to sleep," Shauna said.

She's also seen her own attitudes evolve and keep evolving with each child. She attributes much of Dylan's warm and affectionate personality to his attachment-parenting infancy and still can't bear to hear him cry. "If he needs us, we go in." With Leila, it's different. Shauna can tolerate more tears, and she doesn't feel the need to be as physically close as much of the time. "With each child, I have more knowledge and experience. I'm still Sears and Sears oriented, I like the attachment-parenting philosophy, but I'm also fascinated by the science of sleep. It's what my heart wants versus what my brain knows I should do about sleep. What feels natural is not the most sleep promoting; what feels natural often gets in the way."

Napping with your baby is a great idea sometimes, particularly during those tiring newborn months, but you won't want to be locked into napping with him all the time for several years. It can also create a big child-care napping problem if you go back to work or want to get out of the house now and then. It gets really complicated if you have two children napping at different times or one who needs you to lie down with her and a slightly older one who isn't napping at all anymore and needs your supervision and attention. If she's in a crib, you also have a little more freedom to move around your home. You don't have to stay in the room every minute to make sure she doesn't get smothered by your bedclothes or, when she gets a little older, roll out of bed.

Chapter 13

NIGHTMARES, NIGHT TERRORS, AND SLEEPWALKING

Nightmares, night terrors, and sleepwalking are distinct phenomena—and none of them is a sign of serious emotional disturbance or disorder.

Nightmares are part of normal development, peaking between ages two and three. Children at this age have wondrously rich imaginations and some difficulty distinguishing reality from fantasy. Nightmares occur during REM sleep, and the child wakes up feeling anxious or afraid, but he recognizes his parents and seeks comfort.

Night terrors are less common, occurring in about 5 percent of children, more boys than girls, and can last into the school years. They occur in non-REM sleep, when we do not dream, so the child will not remember the terror. (See Chapter 4, if you want to review REM and non-REM sleep.) Night terrors can be disturbing for parents to watch, but they are not a sign of serious emotional disturbance or disorder. You may not be able to eliminate them completely, but you can take steps to minimize them. Usually children outgrow them, and they seldom last past early adolescence.

Like night terrors, *sleepwalking* is a partial-arousal parasomnia disorder that happens during non-REM sleep, when a child is coming out of a deep-sleep cycle. Unlike nightmares, children do not remember night terrors the next day. Safety is generally the biggest concern with sleepwalking, as the child can wander around, open doors, and climb stairs.

NIGHTMARES

Nightmares occur toward the end of a sleep period. The child can recall the dream or at least know she had a bad one, and it may take her a while to get scary thoughts out of her head and fall asleep again. Nightmares are, of course, common after difficult events or when children are experiencing change or stress or are reliving a trauma. They can also occur when a child is overtired, either because she still hasn't learned to sleep well enough or she's been thrown off her routine for a few days by illness, travel, or a change in the family's schedule. But sometimes they occur for no particular reason, just like we as adults may have a bad dream when nothing particularly unusual or unpleasant is going on in our lives.

You can't prevent all nightmares—they are part of childhood, just as they are an occasional part of adulthood. But you can try to minimize them and make them less frequent. Avoid scary videos, books, games, and stories prior to bed. Don't play scary games, not even during the day if your child is fearful, unless you can turn them into empowering games where your child transforms the scary monsters into giggly monsters or something like that.

When a child does have a bad dream, respond very quickly and assure her that she is safe. Hug her and hold her if she needs it, even if you are in the middle of a sleep-shaping program or a step in the Sleep Lady Shuffle that asks you to minimize your nighttime physical engagement. Stay in her room until she falls asleep again. It's tempting to lie down in her bed with her, but try to avoid it, or to keep it brief, particularly if you are trying to break a co-sleeping pattern or if you have been co-sleeping until recently.

The same rich imagination that contributes to the nightmares may also help combat them. For instance, many three- and four-year-olds have imaginary friends, and you can help the child enlist those friends to ward off bad dreams or monsters. Draw on the lovey, too; remind her that the lovey is by her side all night and will make her feel safe and sound. Children also like applying their imaginations to a dream agenda. "Tonight, I'll dream about playing basketball." Or "Tonight, I will dream about building a sandcastle." Or "Tonight, I will dream about being a beautiful ballerina." It helps them feel more in control of what happens to them after they fall asleep, particularly if they are worried about nightmares. My Dream Cards (available on my website, https://sleeplady.com /products) might help children feel in control of their dreams. Based on my experiences in "creating" dreams with my own daughters, the cards guide children through a progressive relaxation exercise and have images for dream ideas, such as a tree house, a beach scene, a field of flowers, and a rainbow.

By age five, many children understand the difference between dreams and reality. Despite that cognitive leap, they still need TLC and reassurance, just as we adults still want an extra hug when we have a bad dream.

Sometimes kids become fearful of their own rooms because of the nightmares or just start stalling more at bedtime or running out of bed more at night. Spend more time playing with her in her own room during daylight so that she feels safer and more comfortable there. At night, allow a little extra time for the bedtime rituals and relaxation. Include bedtime stories about children conquering their fears.

Review her sleep chart to remind her of good sleep manners, and then reward her liberally for following them. If she wakes with a nightmare and comes to your room, take her back to her own bed and stay near her until she feels better.

Sometimes parents sleep in a child's bedroom after bad dreams, but be careful about doing this too long or too often. It can become a negative association, or a sleep crutch, and she will need you to be there all the time. (You may decide lying down with her is worth it if you feel you will be able to retrain her out of that habit fairly quickly, when the fear of nightmares subsides.)

At bedtime, if she's apprehensive about bad dreams, tell her you will be nearby, and be very specific. "Mommy will be in her room reading," or "Daddy will be right down the hall hanging up his suits." Promise to check on her frequently and then live up to that promise. Not only will those checks make her feel safer, but they will also help keep her in her own room instead of scrambling out every five minutes in search of you. Leave the door open a little if that makes her feel better, and keep a night-light on or even a little more hall light than usual. Discuss bad dreams if your child brings them up, but don't "lead the witness." In other words, you shouldn't be the one to remind her about last night's scary dream, and if she runs into your bedroom at night, your first words should not be "Did you have a nightmare?" Be sympathetic—don't yell at her for getting out of bed when she may be frightened, but don't plant the idea of bad dreams if it isn't already there.

A few other suggestions follow. Not every idea will help with every child, but experiment to see which works for you or which leads you and your child to your own helpful variants:

1. Allow a pet to sleep in the child's room.
2. Try letting your children share a room as long as they both have good sleep manners and won't keep each other up.
3. Use some kind of "monster-away spray," or if it seems too confusing to be chasing away monsters at the same time you are trying to teach your child that monsters don't exist, use a "bad-thought spray."
4. Let your child create his own bad-dream defenses. One slightly older girl I worked with, about eight, made a shield with pictures and images that she felt protected her, which she kept by her bed. Another one put up a dream catcher. Several kids I know have arranged their stuffed animals or action figures around their beds in a way that makes them feel protected. I heard about one insightful

preschool teacher who had families make a "monster box"—with a lid to capture monsters and keep them confined.

5. Include in your bedtime preparations some kind of prayer for safety if that fits your beliefs, or create a more secular anti nightmare ritual or mantra. Your child might imagine a guardian angel watching over him, or recite a prayer with you that surrounds him with love, light, and protection.

6. Help your child act out throwing away his bad thoughts in a concrete way that can make him feel they are really gone. Throw them out the window (you don't really have to open the window) or dump them in the trash or flush them down the toilet (just make sure he knows that they are flushed far away so he doesn't get afraid of the toilet in the morning!). One mom I know made a "worry tree" with her kindergartner. She made the trunk and branches out of brown construction paper and formed leaves out of green Post-it notes. Each night, the child plucked a leaf off the tree and ripped it up, eliminating a worry.

7. If your child has adequate verbal skills, teach him progressive relaxation techniques, tightening and releasing muscles starting at the toes, then the feet, and all the way up to the top of the head. If you don't want to do this yourself, you can play a relaxation CD (see my suggestions at the back of the book, or try my album, *The Sweetest Dreams,* available on https://sleeplady.com/products). You can also try creative visualization, helping your child imagine playing on the beach with his cousins or walking in the park as the leaves change color—any image that will make him feel happy and calm. Children sometimes like to pretend they are a character in a favorite (non-scary) book or like making up stories where they are a prince or princess or magic fairy in a beautiful garden. (I have some resources on my website at https://sleeplady.com/products.)

8. It is also wise to avoid high-dose vitamins close to bedtime, and if your child takes any medication, talk to your pediatrician about whether it might interfere with sleep and whether you can find an alternative or at least change the dosing times.

NIGHT TERRORS

Night terrors are not bad dreams or nightmares. They are still distressing to witness, although the first time your child experiences one, you may not immediately recognize it as a terror.

> ### Sleep Lady Tip
>
> Children may pick up more than we realize about frightening events, whether it be a distant hurricane, a fire down the block, or the unsettling news of our world. Through snippets of television news or adult conversation, they may get just enough information to be frightened and not enough to truly comprehend how abstract or distant a threat is to them or their loved ones. Keep your antenna up for what they may be hearing or seeing that may cause fear and anxiety. It's often wise to avoid television or radio news when young children are present.

A child experiencing a terror may scream, shout, sweat, have a racing heart, appear anxious, and seem inconsolable. His eyes may be wide open and he will look awake, but this is a partial-arousal disorder and he is actually still asleep and probably won't recognize you. He may even push you away or flail at you, even while he is calling out for you. The terror usually lasts five to fifteen minutes and then subsides. It is often more upsetting for the parent to endure than for the child to experience, since the child usually won't remember it—and the parent will.

Night terrors occur during non-REM sleep (when children are coming out of deep sleep) and usually within two hours of falling asleep. The single biggest risk factor is probably not getting enough sleep. Usually, night terrors stop once a child gets more sleep. For a reminder of the sleep averages for your child's age, see the age-appropriate chapter. Sleep apnea can also be a factor, so discuss that possibility with your doctor. Stress that disturbs sleep, such as a major change in the child's sleep schedule or a new place to sleep, can also be a factor. A child who has an erratic sleep schedule is also at higher risk. Terrors may also occur during developmental milestones, or when a child is sick or running a fever.

> "My child didn't have too many bad dreams, and I don't think he had any full-fledged monstery nightmares that I was aware of," one mother told me. "Then, one night when he was sick and had a slight fever, just before his third birthday, I heard this earsplitting, terrorized screech at about 10:30 or 11:00. He was screaming, 'Mommy, Mommy!' and when I ran to him and told him I was there, he kept alternating between screaming for me and hitting me, like he didn't recognize me and I was scaring him. I picked him up and held him, which I later realized I probably shouldn't have done, and he kept screaming for me, and I kept telling him I was there, and he seemed to go back and forth between recognition and terror.
>
> "Then, all of a sudden, it was over. The tension went out of his body, and he went right back into a peaceful sleep, looking perfectly calm and content. I was so shaken that I slept in his room the rest of the night, but he was fine and never said a word about it in the morning. He didn't have any problems again, including the next time he had a cold and tummy ache, but then, a few months later, it happened again when he was running a fever. It still took me a few minutes to realize what was going on, but at least I was a little better prepared. It still felt horrible to watch, and I felt helpless, but at least I knew it was only the fever and that he would be okay in just a few minutes."

Children are more likely to experience night terrors if either parent had night terrors as a child or if a parent had a partial-arousal sleep disorder like sleepwalking. If your child gets up and walks around while having a terror, which can happen occasionally even with children who do not otherwise sleepwalk, make sure she is safe. Think about placing a gate at the top of any nearby stairs.

During a terror, monitor the child to make sure he is physically safe and not thrashing around in a dangerous way during the episode. But don't interfere, as this could intensify it. Try not to touch your child or

Sleep Lady Tip

Although this may not be a psychological problem or an illness, you might want to discuss frequent ongoing terrors with your pediatrician to make sure there is no underlying trauma, illness, or apnea that must be addressed. Check to see if any medications he is taking, including any over-the-counter drugs, could be interfering with his sleep and contributing to the terrors.

pick him up, since this can actually prolong the terror. Go to him, stay in his room, and calmly reassure him. Don't talk to him about the terror in the morning. Since sleep deprivation plays a major role in night terrors, put him to bed earlier, even if only by thirty minutes. Be extra vigilant about keeping him on a consistent sleep schedule.

If night terrors seem to be regular events, not an occasional side effect of a fever or temporary schedule disruption, keep a sleep log to monitor the timing and frequency. If they are occurring two to three times a week at set times (e.g., two hours after going to sleep), try waking him fifteen minutes before the typical onset of the terror. Don't get him completely wide awake, rouse him just enough for him to mumble, move, or roll over. Then let him fall asleep again and see if you can disrupt the sleep cycle that leads to the terrors. Do this every night for seven to ten days. If the terrors return, do the waking again, but this time do it for two full weeks to see if you can extinguish the problem.

SLEEPWALKING

Like night terrors, sleepwalking is a partial-arousal disorder that occurs during non-REM sleep, when the child is not dreaming. Episodes usually occur within two hours of falling asleep, and the child doesn't remember sleepwalking later. A sleepwalking child looks awake but usually appears confused and may be clumsy and do strange things. He may not want comfort from a parent, although he probably won't scream and act afraid as he would if he were having a terror. Sleepwalking, as with terrors, often runs in families.

You may be surprised to find that sleepwalking is actually quite common, although chronic or frequent sleepwalking is relatively rare. In *Pediatric Sleep Problems: A Clinician's Guide to Behavioral Interventions,* Lisa Meltzer and Valerie Crabtree write that "confusional arousals and sleepwalking occur in approximately 17% to 40% of children and typically begin around the age of 2 years."

The most important concern is, of course, safety. You don't want a sleepwalking child to fall down the stairs, climb anywhere he shouldn't be, stumble into the basement, or go outside. You should put gates on the stairs and lock doors. If you hear him walking around, don't wake him, but try to gently guide him back to bed. If you are afraid you won't hear him, think about installing an alarm, or even some kind of makeshift system, like a bell that will ring if he opens his bedroom door. Sleep deprivation is a risk factor for sleepwalking, so make sure he gets plenty of sleep and is on a consistent schedule. With sleepwalking, I do recommend you contact your pediatrician. Depending on the frequency of the episodes and his risk of injury, she may want to prescribe a short-term sleep medication.

It's important to know that in most cases, it's possible to identify a medical cause for the partial arousal that leads to the confused awakening, sleepwalking, or night-terror event. One-third of the time, the arousal is related to obstructive sleep apnea. One-third of the time, it is due to a combination of the other medical conditions, such as restless legs syndrome, asthma, allergies, acid reflux, and chronic pain. The remaining third of the time, the non-REM parasomnias have no identifiable source for the arousal. These occur normally throughout childhood and will eventually go away on their own. But it's worth talking to the doctor and doing a medical sleep evaluation. If the cause is identified and fixed, the confused arousals, sleepwalking, and night-terror events will resolve.

Chapter 14

COULD SLEEP DISTURBANCES
BE A MEDICAL CONDITION?

Coughs, colds, ear infections, and tummy aches, those routine child-hood illnesses, can temporarily disturb sleep, and Chapter 16, "Routine Busters," will help you through those rough spots. Here I will talk about some of the complexer and more persistent medical problems. As I'm not a medical doctor, I called on my own family pediatrician, Dr. Faith Hackett, as well as Dr. Anthony Loizides, pediatric gastroenterologist at the Children's Hospital at Montefiore, to review this chapter. If you have consistently applied a behavioral modification program—whether it's my Sleep Lady approach or one of the crying-it-out alternatives—and your child is still not sleeping well, please consult your doctor to determine whether her sleep problems have medical roots and to refer you to a specialist if necessary.

When you do talk to your pediatrician, including at routine check-ups, make sure you mention your child's sleep patterns, even if the doctor doesn't bring it up herself. Provide her with enough information to evaluate the problem. Keep a sleep log, or at least jot down some notes, and be prepared to explain the behavioral approach you have adopted. If your child throws up regularly and you wonder if it may be a symptom of reflux, try to keep track of how often and when. For example, telling your doctor that your baby throws up five to seven times a day, ten minutes after eating, is more helpful than telling the doctor that the baby throws up "a lot." Similarly, if you think your child may have allergies, note the circumstances of the reactions. If you suspect apnea, make a five-minute recording of the snoring, snorts, or those other loud and strange nighttime noises so the doctor can hear for herself.

REFLUX AND COLIC

Spitting up is a normal part of infancy. It may create a laundry problem, but it's not a health problem. Doctors call it *GER*, or *gastroesophageal reflux*, and you can learn how to manage it until it resolves.

> ### Sleep Lady Tip
>
> Even children with medical components to sleep difficulties can benefit from behavioral modification techniques. For instance, your child might have health concerns that require night feedings past the age when most other infants are learning to sleep longer intervals. But you can still work on teaching good sleep habits at bedtime and nap time, even if you can't grapple with those night awakenings yet.

Regurgitation—what a lot of parents just call *reflux*, is common, reported in 40–65 percent of healthy infants. It becomes much less common, affecting just about 1 percent by the first birthday. Gastroesophageal reflux disease (GERD) is less common—in about one in three hundred infants. It can be caused by a host of factors, often related to a temporary relaxation of the valve between the esophagus and the stomach. Basically, that means stomach contents—breast milk, food, formula, and stomach acid—can go back up into the esophagus, the mouth, sometimes even the nose. In mild cases, it's akin to baby heartburn. In some cases, it's more severe. Luckily, GERD can usually be managed, and your doctor can suggest many techniques, possibly including medication. In most babies, the prevalence of regurgitation or GER in infants peaks at four months of age, with 50–85 percent of infants reported to have regurgitation at least once a day.

Babies with reflux can develop sleep problems that can persist even after symptoms are controlled. More than a third of the children I work with have, or have had, GER past the age of three to four months. (If they get over it very early, you should be able to follow the sleep-shaping ideas in the age-by-age section of this book without having to worry too much about longer-term sleep disruption.) My own second child, Gretchen, had the more severe form, GERD, and her first few weeks were not easy. But with our doctor's help, we were able to manage her condition with medication and have a happy, healthy baby who slept well.

Parents often confuse reflux with colic, but they are not the same. GER is a structural, though not permanent, problem with the digestive system. *Colic* is a term that basically involves recurrent and prolonged periods of infant crying, fussing, or irritability that occur without obvious cause and cannot be prevented or resolved by caregivers. Up to one in four babies under age three months experiences these crying jags, but to fulfill the criteria for colic, the infant must be less than five months of age when the symptoms start and stop, and there should be no other concerns, such as failure to gain weight. When colic occurs, it doesn't mean you are a bad or incompetent parent, or that your baby is in pain, or that he will be a fussy or unhappy child. Some people believe that colic can be explained by sensory processing that differs from that of infants who do not have colic and that your attempt to calm the baby will only add to the problem. For more on sleep and sensory processing, see Chapter 15. Dr. Richard Ferber, for instance, says that if the colicky baby doesn't respond to our soothing, then soothing isn't what he is seeking. He recommends that you let the colicky baby cry for fifteen to thirty minutes and see if he can calm himself down. My own preference is for you to review the soothing techniques, such as swaddling and swinging, that I outline in Phase 1. *Remember, don't get in the habit of nursing him every time he cries.* Since the crying might make it harder to read his sleep-window cues, keep an eye on the clock so you know how long he's been awake. Try taking him into a quiet, dimly lit room where he may start showing signs of tiring.

HOW TO RECOGNIZE GER

Reflux symptoms can emerge in very young infants. They can include:

* Frequent vomiting—sometimes and quite unpleasantly through the nose. (Some babies have *silent reflux*, meaning they have the pain and surges of acid without spitting up.)
* Slow weight gain (fortunately, not all babies with reflux fail to thrive).
* Reluctance to eat or signs of pain when eating, such as stiffening up, arching his back, or pushing away from the breast or bottle.
* Wanting to eat, but just a little at a time.
* Discomfort/irritability.

Don't panic if your child displays a few of these signs once in a while. You are looking for a pattern, not a single episode. But if you do suspect a problem, particularly if you are worried about GERD—call your pediatrician.

WHEN TO WORRY ABOUT GERD

* Failure to thrive
* Severe feeding refusal
* Dystonic neck posturing (muscles contract involuntarily)
* Vomiting blood
* Trouble swallowing or pain when swallowing

* Wheezing
* Stridor
* Cough
* Hoarseness
* Apnea spells
* Asthma
* Recurrent pneumonia associated with aspiration

It's important to get an accurate diagnosis. You might think the baby has reflux when he actually has another reason to make him uncomfortable. In severe or stubborn cases, your pediatrician may suggest you consult a pediatric gastroenterologist.

MANAGING REFLUX

Sometimes we can control reflux with a few simple positioning and feeding tricks, which I'll address in a moment. But sometimes we face slightly more complicated choices, and the solutions you choose will be a blend of your values and parenting style and your doctor's advice. For instance, if you are completely committed to breast milk and don't want formula, you may opt for medication and modify your own diet by reducing or eliminating dairy. Conversely, if you don't want to put your infant on medication, you might prefer to cut back on breast milk and try to find a formula that has been optimized for GERD instead of or in addition to nursing. (Some doctors recommend that you thicken your own formula, adding one teaspoon of dry cereal to two ounces of formula, but ask your pediatrician before you try this on your own, particularly with young infants.) Sometimes you won't have a choice. Your baby will clearly need medication, and your doctor will explain why.

The following suggestions are widely accepted by pediatricians, but check with your own doctor anyway. Not every pediatrician agrees with every element on this list, and your doctor may feel that some aspect of GER management is inappropriate, unwise, or even unsafe for your unique child. Keep in mind, too, that some of these tools will tame the spitting up but will not necessarily stop all the surges of pain.

Gravity is your baby's friend. Keep your baby upright, but not slumped over, for twenty to thirty minutes after all daytime and bedtime feedings to help digestion. You can seat her in an infant chair or hold her in your arms—*but don't get into the habit of holding her until she falls asleep in your arms.* Time the feeding early enough so that you can feed her, hold or sit her down for a half hour, and then put her to sleep drowsy but awake.

* Offer frequent, small meals.
* Burp your baby several times during the feeding, not just once after feeding.
* Consider different formulas under the direction of your pediatrician. If you are using a thickened formula for reflux, you might find that your baby does better with one brand over another or that he still throws up the powdered version but does better with a thicker (and alas usually costlier) premixed canned variety. Some babies do better with a hypoallergenic formula, particularly if they have an allergy to cow's milk protein. These allergic babies may experience regurgitation and vomiting indistinguishable from that associated with GER or GERD, so work with your doctor to rule that out. I'll talk more about allergies in a moment.
* Elevate his crib or bassinet under the head. You can buy a simple, inexpensive wedge at a baby store that goes under the mattress cover or the fitted bottom sheet (and is also helpful when he has a cold). One family I worked with, following their doctor's advice, rolled up a baby blanket in a U shape to make a nest in the elevated crib so the baby wouldn't roll down to the bottom of the crib. For safety's sake, they stuck the U-shaped blanket under the fitted sheet, and placed the baby with his feet at the bottom curve of the U. The sides of the U shouldn't reach past his chest. Some families use a Tucker Sling, which keeps the baby elevated, or an Amby bed, which is like a baby hammock. Both are available online. Of

course, review the safety precautions. For other products that may help, visit: https://sleeplady.com/products.

* Dress him in outfits that are loose at the waist, and avoid tight elastic waistbands on diapers.

* Consider having him sleep on his left side, once he is old enough to do so safely. Left lateral positioning results in reduction in the total number of reflux episodes as per several studies. Talk to your physician and familiarize yourself with safety precautions to avoid SIDS.

* Encourage him to sleep on his tummy, once he learns to roll over in both directions and the SIDS risk lessens (usually around six months; check with your doctor). Citing a few small studies showing that even younger infants with reflux do better on their tummies, some websites urge this sleeping position for reflux. The Joint Recommendations of the North American Society for Pediatric Gastroenterology, Hepatology, and Nutrition and the European Society for Paediatric Gastroenterology, Hepatology, and Nutrition are not to use positional therapy (i.e., head elevation, lateral and prone positioning) to treat symptoms of GERD in sleeping infants.

* It also helps to have a sense of humor and a mommy or daddy wardrobe that does not require dry cleaning! Carry around a lot of spare clothes in your car, stroller, or diaper bag—for your baby and for you!

HOW TO HELP BABIES WITH REFLUX SLEEP

As parents, our natural instinct is to soothe a baby who hurts. That's exactly what we should do. But we need to pay attention to how we soothe a reflux baby. While a baby without tummy problems is learning to rock himself to sleep, a reflux baby dealing with repetitive vomiting may miss out on the chance to learn how to self-soothe and fall asleep on his own! As we comfort our babies, we may inadvertently reinforce poor sleep habits. Then, even after the reflux (or colic) has passed or been controlled, our

Sleep Lady Tip

Babies tend to like bouncy chairs even if they don't have reflux, and not just after eating. Bouncy seats hold babies at an angle that "folds" them less than a car seat. You don't need all the bells, whistles, and elaborate sound and light effects; a simple seat is fine.

babies still don't sleep well. They must then learn, or relearn, how to put themselves to sleep without being walked, rocked, fed, put in the swing or car seat, or ridden around the block—you know the drill.

I will give you two related sets of suggestions—one on how to deal with sleep while you and your child are still handling the worst of the reflux, and a second one on how to get him on a better sleep path once the medical part is under control or he has outgrown it. In both cases, he'll do better if you tackle bedtime first, then naps. Before the nap piece falls into place, do whatever you need to do to get him some sleep during the day, even if it means breaking my usual rules of not using the car to get him to sleep. If you are feeding him at night for medical reasons, don't worry about changing that right away, although the night awakenings might diminish on their own as other aspects of his sleep improve. Work with the information here as well as the age-relevant chapter earlier in this book.

As with a colicky baby, reading reflux babies' sleep cues can be difficult. I suspect this is because they don't learn to differentiate their cries because pain, vomiting, hunger, and tiredness all sort of blur together for them. We then have more trouble figuring out what they're crying about and may not respond as consistently to whatever they're trying to tell us. So you have to be more diligent about watching the clock, not just your baby. Keep track of when he ate. As he gets older, you'll want to stretch out the time between feedings as long as you can without provoking more vomiting, particularly overnight. Also pay attention to how long he has been awake. Make sure he naps on time. The last thing he needs is an overlay of exhaustion on top of his symptoms of GERD. Taking him into a quiet, dimly lit room for a while before nap or bed often helps. He may show his sleepy signals more clearly in such a setting. Also, the quiet environment may cue him that it's time for bed.

As I mentioned, your doctor will probably recommend that you hold or seat your baby upright for about twenty to thirty minutes after he eats. Don't hold him until he falls asleep. You don't want him to develop an association between sleeping and being in your arms, or you'll have to hold him to sleep all the time, including overnight, for months to come. Don't worry if he falls asleep in your arms occasionally. Just don't teach him that your arms are his bed. Allow enough time between feeding and bedtime for another activity. Feed him, hold him upright, and then read him a book, give him a bath, and let him get some tummy time on a play mat. When it's time for him to sleep, put him down drowsy but awake. Try to arrange his daytime schedule so that you are feeding him when he wakes up in the morning and when he gets up from naps, instead of before he takes naps, to avoid that holding-sleeping association. That gives him time to digest before he lies down, a position that increases the reflux.

Some babies with reflux fare better if they eat small, frequent meals. That might mean you will have to feed him overnight to an older age than you would a baby without reflux. But the night feedings can also add to his discomfort, so talk to your doctor about when you can stop them. At some point, the nighttime nursing (or bottle-feeding) ceases to be a physical requirement and starts being a sleep-disrupting habit. When that happens, you need to stop those nighttime feedings. Please don't let this go on too long—address it before his first birthday. If not, you may well have a child who wakes you up, demanding a drink every few hours, well into his second or third year.

Babies who feed at night also tend to get emotionally attached to the cup or bottle, as though it were a pacifier or a teddy bear. Some babies give up the night feeding much more easily than you might guess, in a night or two. Some resist longer. In each age-specific chapter, I give detailed advice on nighttime weaning. For older babies who did not have reflux but still have a nighttime eating pattern, I usually recommend a pretty quick end—maybe not quite cold turkey, but something close. However, with children who had reflux, you might want a gentler and more gradual approach. I give many suggestions about night weaning in the age-specific chapters (with the most details in Chapter 7, "Six to Eight Months").

In my own sleep practice, I have found that post-reflux babies often remain very sensitive to their environments. They react more to such stimuli as bright lights, crowds, food, and textures. You then need to be sensitive to their sensitivities! (I talk a little more about sensory processing issues and give some resources in the section on attention-deficit disorder and attention-deficit/hyperactivity disorder later in the next chapter.) Continue to be very careful about his schedule. Watch the clock, and keep using that quiet, dimly lit room to help him calm down.

Tracy and Drew's son, Lucas, had been diagnosed with reflux shortly after his birth. His pediatrician prescribed Zantac. It took a while to get the dosing and timing right for Lucas, but by four months, the medication and reflux management techniques had brought the problem under control. But they didn't do anything for his sleep. If anything, his sleep was getting worse. While other babies had been learning rudimentary self-soothing techniques, Lucas had his mind on his hurting tummy. Now he was getting up every three or four hours—more on a bad night. Naps were also problematic, and sometimes he woke well before dawn.

Tracy started paying a lot more attention to his schedule and the timing of his meals. She shortened his feedings, sometimes letting him nurse only two or three minutes. "I shaved minutes off nursing to convince myself it was about soothing, not feeding. He was doing it for fun!" she said. "I knew he really didn't need to eat that often. And it wasn't the reflux cry anymore—it was the unhappy cry." At four months, the pediatrician said they should try to get Lucas to sleep, without food, for about seven hours a night. Seven hours seemed beyond comprehension to the sleep-deprived couple. They called me.

Tracy still breastfed Lucas before he went to bed, at about 7:00 p.m. But for the next feeding, at about 10:00 or 11:00, the parents decided to give him a bottle of formula or expressed breast milk. They also gave him his medicine then. Then they would not feed him again until at least 6:00 or 6:30 a.m. if he slept that late. They would stay with him and comfort him if he cried and protested, but they did not feed him or lie down with him. (I gave them the option of picking him up briefly if they needed to calm him down, although they chose to soothe him without lifting him out of the crib, a decision that might have made their first few nights a little tearier than they had to be.)

"The first night, he cried for a long time. Then he collapsed. We soothed him, but we didn't pick him up. It took about two weeks before he wouldn't cry at all, but other nights, he didn't cry as long," Tracy said. By the end of the two weeks, he was getting up once for ten minutes or less in the middle of the night, but they wouldn't feed him, and he woke up less and less. At about six months, they took the next step and gave up that dream feed. "It was pretty easy," she said. "He woke up and fussed, and we went in and said, 'Sorry, buddy!'" So then he went to bed at 7:00 at night and slept all the way through until 7:00 in the morning.

Although those first two weeks of transition were unpleasant, Tracy and Drew's wholehearted belief that Lucas needed to learn to sleep better made it a lot easier for them to be consistent. And with Tracy having to go back to her job at five months, they knew they needed to deal with his sleep problems now. "We couldn't have done it if we had to leave him alone crying. Being in the room made it easier. But we really believed he would be better off if he could sleep. He had to learn how to do it."

Tracy was also motivated by the confessions of her girlfriends that some of their kids were still waking multiple times at night at ages two and three. She was also clear-sighted enough about herself to know that she needed more sleep to be the mother she wanted to be. "I was so tired, I couldn't function, and I wasn't enjoying him as much as I wanted to," she said.

Those first few nights, she let Drew give Lucas a bottle and deal with his protests. That was partly to avoid getting Lucas even more upset by letting him see his mother but not letting him nurse. But it was also because, by then, Tracy really needed a break. She went downstairs, put in some earplugs, and slept for three nights. "I felt I'd been reborn."

ALLERGIES

Milk sensitivities, eczema, and environmental allergies can all hamper a baby's ability to learn how to sleep, and they can disrupt sleep at any time from infancy through childhood.

FOOD AND MILK ALLERGIES

If you are nursing and suspect your child is allergic or intolerant to milk, you can try eliminating all dairy products (check labels, as dairy ingredients can be hidden) from your diet. Cow's milk is the most common allergy in infants. A trial elimination diet, with the strict elimination of cow's milk protein from the mother's diet for two to three weeks, should result in the disappearance of symptoms in the child. Keep in mind that it may take up to seventy-two hours to clear breast milk antigens ingested by the lactating woman. Make sure you get alternative sources of calcium for your sake and your baby's. Some mothers mistakenly expect to see a difference in a few days, so they don't stick to it. Milk sensitivities can contribute to mild reflux and may also cause nasal congestion that can contribute to apnea.

Talk to your pediatrician about giving your baby a milk test. You might also, with your doctor's guidance, try hypoallergenic formula if you think your baby may have a cow's milk protein allergy. Think about eliminating or cutting out caffeine and alcohol if you are nursing. Because peanut and other nut allergies are now more common and can be dangerous, some pediatricians advise nursing mothers to eliminate peanuts, peanut butter, or other nuts from their diets. Also, if either parent had childhood food allergies, tell your pediatrician. She may want you to delay introduction of certain solid foods—like wheat, eggs, citrus, shellfish, berries, chocolate, or corn—or modify the timetable. For instance, she might want you to introduce one food a week, instead of trying a new one every few days, so you can more easily monitor reactions.

ECZEMA AND DERMATITIS

Numerous allergies can cause hives, rashes, and itchy skin—and it's hard to sleep if you itch like crazy. According to *Guide to Your Child's Sleep: Birth Through Adolescence,* from the American Academy of Pediatrics, allergic children can have trouble sleeping even at those times when they are symptom-free. Some research suggests that children with skin allergies may be at higher risk for developing asthma. There are a lot of treatments—some over the counter, some by prescription—for eczema and related conditions, so you and your pediatrician should be able to get this problem under control with relative ease.

STUFFY NOSES, COUGHING, AND
OTHER ALLERGY SYMPTOMS

Allergies can disturb sleep as well, and for a myriad of reasons, which can include coughing from postnasal drip and heavy breathing from nasal congestion. Medications used to treat allergies (and asthma) can sometimes have side effects that disturb sleep as well—keeping a child super wide awake or causing irritability. Antihistamines can dry secretions so well sometimes that it makes them hard to cough up and out; this can also make it difficult to get comfortable enough to sleep. Depending on your child's age and the severity of symptoms, your doctor may recommend a saline spray, decongestant, bedroom humidifier, or allergy medicine. (A lot of over-the-counter cold and allergy medicines are no longer recommended for children under age six, so be careful and talk to your physician.)

Your child might have seasonal allergies or a sensitivity to dust, pollutants, mold, or a household pet. Seasonal allergies can also inflame adenoids and tonsils, which in turn can cause sleep disturbances or sleep apnea. (More on apnea below.)

Because children with allergies or asthma may have such disrupted sleep, they may then struggle to stay awake during the day and may perform poorly in school. Sometimes they are judged to be hyperactive or to have behavioral problems when in fact all that fidgeting is just their attempt to stay awake. Good diagnosis and treatment lead to better sleep—and to a better-behaved, higher-functioning daytime child.

ASTHMA

For advice on asthma, apnea, and related sleep disorders, I turned to Dr. Lewis J. Kass, a Yale-trained certified pediatric pulmonologist and sleep medicine specialist. Asthma can be associated with sleep apnea, but asthma all by itself can disturb sleep. A child with poorly controlled asthma can have nighttime coughing and wheezing that wake him up repeatedly. Labored breathing makes it difficult to fall asleep and stay asleep. And many medications used to treat asthma can disturb sleep. Bronchodilators can make the heart race and make a child feel jittery—and sometimes kids are instructed to take them every four hours through the night. Oral steroids can likewise result in difficulty falling asleep.

But it's not just severe or poorly controlled asthma that can be a sleep impediment, Kass tells us. What's much subtler and more difficult to pick up is how very, very mild asthma can still disturb sleep—even asthma that is so mild that it doesn't result in any coughing or wheezing and doesn't disrupt the routine during the daytime. "When asthma is this mild, there may not be much fanfare, but oftentimes it might be just enough to increase one's sleeping respiratory rate from a normal sixteen breaths per minute to an elevated twenty breaths per minute," Dr. Kass explains. "Just that four-breath-per-minute increase (which is actually 25 percent) can be enough to change the quality of sleep from deep and restorative to light and easily disturbed."

Sleeping this way for weeks and months or even years shows how sleep deprivation can mount slowly but surely. Yet, on the surface, it would be hard to figure out why. Luckily, once asthma is identified and treated, sleep can improve dramatically and quickly.

OBSTRUCTIVE SLEEP APNEA

Some children have disturbed nighttime sleep because they are having trouble breathing. Said simply, if it's hard to breathe, it's hard to sleep. Think back to the last cold you had. How easy was it to get comfortable enough to fall asleep quickly and deeply and then stay asleep the whole night? Now imagine that your nostrils and nasal passages and airways are much, much smaller. For some toddlers and young children, obstructive sleep apnea (OSA) is why they have difficulty falling asleep and staying asleep.

"At one point, we used to believe that snoring was the most important symptom," Dr. Kass says, "but we've learned in recent years that not all children with OSA snore. One symptom, however, that is nearly universal in children with OSA is restless sleeping; and by *restless*, we're talking about really, really restless!"

Some parents tell Dr. Kass how their children "circle the clock" in their bed. Kids and toddlers will flip and flop and kick and toss and turn, and often all that restlessness makes them sweat profusely in their sleep. "Parents can be very descriptive about that observation as well, describing the room as smelling like a gym locker room or feeling so much wetness from perspiration that they wondered if the child had actually wet the bed," Dr. Kass said.

Snoring is something that you should certainly discuss with your pediatrician—or even record it so your doctor can hear what the child sounds like. Not all snoring is a problem—but it should *always* be looked into, Dr. Kass stressed. "At the very least, the presence of snoring in a baby, toddler, or child should prompt the asking of a series of questions designed to figure out if there is more to the snoring than meets the *ear*. I've found that parents can be very vivid in their descriptions of their child's snoring. 'He sounds like an old man!' 'I can hear her from two floors down with the doors closed and through earplugs!' 'He snores worse than I do!'"

If you co-sleep and your toddler or preschooler wakes up frequently, you might want to also think about apnea. This isn't true if she is nursing on demand and still wakes up to nurse frequently, but it is a possible indicator for a child who may wake up, sit up and reposition herself, and then go back to sleep.

I worked with a two-year-old who slept with his parents and would sit up, cry out, and plop back down in the middle of the night. He didn't need them to do anything else for him to get back to sleep. We worked on bedtime and nap time, and we did a lot of sleep coaching to reduce night awakenings. But we didn't eliminate them completely. He didn't snore, but he was a mouth breather, and he had milk allergies. His doctor finally ordered an x-ray of his adenoids, and sure enough, they were quite enlarged—often a factor in apnea. He had them removed and started sleeping all night almost immediately.

According to Dr. Kass, other symptoms of pediatric obstructive sleep apnea can include:

* Audible breathing
* Mouth breathing
* Unusual sleeping positions
* Nighttime awakenings
* Bed-wetting
* Early morning awakenings
* Difficulty waking up in the morning
* Tardy arrivals at school because of sleepiness
* Daytime sleepiness
* Poor focus in class
* Poor behavior in school or at home
* Hyperactivity or impulsivity

* Diagnosis of attention-deficit/hyperactivity disorder (ADHD) or attention deficit disorder (ADD)
* Poor school grades
* Daytime irritability
* Daytime napping (after five years of age)
* Difficulty falling asleep at night

Of course, we see these behaviors and symptoms in children a lot—and it doesn't mean they have a physical disorder. My whole Sleep Lady method centers on behaviors—and modifications—that address these sleep problems in healthy kids. The point is to pay attention—and talk to your doctor. Together, you can figure out which problems are medical (apnea, chronically inflamed tonsils, recurrent ear infections, and the like) and which are behavioral sleep-learning challenges you can resolve on your own, with my Sleep Lady method or another approach. But if you find yourself saying, "My child is always sick!" Dr. Kass stressed, take action. If it is apnea or a related disorder, your child can and should be treated not just for the sake of his sleep but for his overall healthy development and well-being.

HOW TO HELP A CHILD WITH APNEA SLEEP BETTER

If your child has even mild sleep apnea, behavioral modification will get you only so far. You can teach him to get himself to bed at night and at nap time, but you will have a very hard time stopping the night awakenings since it is a physical condition that is getting him up. So you need a double-pronged approach. Get him evaluated by a pediatrician and by an ear, nose, and throat specialist if necessary. You may need to take him to a special clinic for an overnight sleep study. Few clinics deal with pediatric behavioral sleep problems, but many do evaluations for apnea or other breathing disorders. Your doctor can refer you, or check the Sleep Education website (http://sleepeducation.org/find-a-facility), developed by the American Academy of Sleep Medicine, to find an accredited sleep center near you. Sometimes treatment, which can include surgery or allergy medication, solves all the sleep problems. In many cases, however, you will still have some behavioral problems to address. Follow the advice in this book for your child's age. You should find that improvement comes quickly.

BED-WETTING

Most children are daytime potty trained sometime between ages two and three, some earlier, some later. Girls are usually, but not always, earlier than boys. Listen to your child's signals regarding potty training—if he isn't ready, it won't go smoothly. I don't see any problem in working on daytime potty training, with a receptive and enthusiastic child, at the same time that you are doing Sleep Lady coaching. But I would not make a big push about using the potty at night in the midst of sleep coaching. Think of how confusing it would be for him to go through this behavioral modification program to learn to go to bed and stay in bed—and then be told he'd better get up and pee!

It often takes until age four or five for a child's bladder to grow big enough to contain the night's urine production or for his sleepy brain to learn how to respond when his bladder shouts, "Full!" Do get in the habit of having him go to the bathroom before bed, but just keep him in a diaper at night until he wakes dry for seven to ten days in a row. Then you can get rid of the diapers.

After age five, bed-wetting still affects about one in ten children. It's twice as common in boys as girls. The reasons for bed-wetting are not well understood, but there is often a family history. Many doctors now regard it as a *parasomnia,* a sleep disorder found in deep sleepers. Sometimes bed-wetting—particularly if the child was trained at night but then started wetting the bed again—can be a sign of sleep apnea, so discuss that possibility with your doctor.

In *Waking Up Dry: A Guide to Help Children Overcome Bedwetting* (2015), Dr. Howard Bennett says the main factors in bed-wetting include:

* Family history—75 percent of bed-wetters have at least one parent or a first-degree relative who wet the bed as a child
* Small bladder, which limits nighttime urine storage
* Deep sleep so that the child does not respond to the bladder's signals
* Constipation, which can create pushing on the bladder and confusing signals
* Minor illness and fatigue

Some families report success when they wake up the child an hour or two after he goes to bed, or right before the parents go to bed, to use the bathroom. But it isn't a surefire solution.

RESTLESS LEGS SYNDROME

Restless legs syndrome (RLS) is a very common but underappreciated cause of disturbed nighttime sleep in our children. Studies have placed the incidence of RLS occurring as high as 10 percent among children in the United States. Technically, that means that more children in the United States suffer from RLS than suffer from asthma! The definition of RLS is "an unpleasant sensation in the legs, during periods of quiet time, relieved by movement." According to Dr. Kass, "unpleasant" can take a variety of interpretations, from frank pain, to growing pains, to feeling creepy crawlies running up and down the legs, the sensation of water or electricity flowing through the legs, tingling, or numbness.

"The worst description I ever heard was from an older teenager who described the sensation as spiders crawling on the inside of her legs and that the spider legs were sharp knives," says Dr. Kass. "While it is described as occurring in the legs, in truth, it can occur in any muscle group. Variant presentations of restless legs have presented as restless arms, restless belly (nausea and vomiting), restless head (headaches), and even restless vocal cords (vocal cord dysfunction)."

Kids with RLS can experience symptoms even when not in bed. Any required stillness—during long car rides, plane rides, during movies, or while sitting at a desk in school—can feel intolerable to children with RLS. Relief is felt by moving; therefore, it feels better to move than not to move. This means that the most common symptom could be a child appearing in constant motion.

Dr. Kass says parents will often notice:

* My child "bicycles his legs" in bed while trying to fall asleep.
* She kicks all night long.
* He's constantly fidgeting.
* He's always changing positions.
* She can't sit still.
* He's always bouncing his legs.
* He gets detention because he gets out of his seat without permission.
* They tied her legs to the desk with an elastic band!
* I need to massage his legs before he can sleep.
* She burrows her legs under us like she needs to feel the pressure.
* He sleeps better with a weighted blanket.

Dr. Kass further explains, "Restless legs syndrome runs strongly in families and can occur in all age groups. As a matter of fact, it's not at all uncommon to consider RLS in babies and toddlers for whom a story exists of where the baby is in constant motion, is constantly kicking the legs, can't sleep through the night, or can't even sleep for more than twenty or thirty minutes straight; and all of this occurs without any breathing difficulty or symptoms of acid reflux. What's left is restless legs!"

Restless legs syndrome is frequently driven by low stores of iron in the body. RLS can improve simply with a doctor prescribing the proper amount of iron if the level of ferritin—a protein involved in how the body stores and uses iron—is found to be low.

Chapter 15

SLEEP COACHING FOR SENSORY PROCESSING DISORDER, SPECTRUM DISORDERS, ADD, AND ADHD

In the ten years since the second edition of this book was published, there's been a lot more awareness and discussion of attention-deficit disorder, attention-deficit/hyperactivity disorder, autism spectrum disorders, and other diagnoses. One issue that's particularly come to the forefront—both among clinicians and parents—is sensory processing disorders—which can definitely affect sleep. Books, research, and outreach about sensory processing have exploded in the past decade, and we now know so much more about how children with these difficulties sleep and how a tailored response during sleep coaching can meet their specific challenges.

Sensory processing disorder (SPD) is a condition in which the brain has trouble receiving and responding to information that comes in through the senses. The STAR Institute for Sensory Processing Disorder (www.spdstar.org) describes it this way: "For those with Sensory Processing Disorder, sensory information goes into the brain but does not get organized into appropriate responses. Those with SPD perceive and/or respond to sensory information differently from most other people. Unlike people who have impaired sight or hearing, those with Sensory Processing Disorder do detect the sensory information; however, the sensory information gets 'mixed up' in their brain and therefore the responses are inappropriate in the context in which they find themselves."

For assistance on these topics, I asked Lindsey Biel, MA, OTR/L, a pediatric occupational therapist who specializes in sensory processing issues, developmental delays, autism spectrum disorders, and other challenges in young adults. She is also the coauthor of *Raising a Sensory Smart Child: The Definitive Handbook for Helping Your Child with Sensory Processing Issues,* which is one of the best resources for parents. (Visit her websites, www.sensorysmarts.com and www.sensoryprocessing challenges.com, which contain many other excellent resources.)

For further information, I also recommend Carol Stock Kranowitz's *The Out-of-Sync Child,* Angie Voss's *Understanding Your Baby's Sensory Signals,* and Lucy Miller's *Sensational Kids.*

• •

Sensory Challenges / Sensory Processing Disorder / SPD, by Lindsey Biel

Children first learn through their senses. They see people and things; hear a variety of sounds; feel different touches, textures, and temperatures; taste and smell a range of flavors and aromas. They get vestibular input from their inner ears, telling them about movement and gravity; proprioceptive input from their joints, muscles, and connective tissue, giving them body awareness; and interoceptive information from internal organs, signaling their bodies' physiological state. Sensory processing is how children transform all those messages into a meaningful picture of the world and their place in it.

This complex neurological process develops automatically and perfectly for most children. However, because of unusual nervous system wiring, some children—as well as teenagers and adults—experience our rich sensory world differently. They do not take and use sensory input in the expected way, so they do not always get the accurate, reliable information that helps people feel safe and secure. Sensory challenges range from the preferences, intolerances, and quirks many young children have to more distressing and sometimes painful sensory experiences. There is a big difference between a child who is annoyed by clothing tags and one who throws hours-long tantrums because his "socks hurt." For kids with significant sensory issues, their brains and bodies just can't handle the constant barrage of sensory information that doesn't bother others.

Sensory processing challenges are estimated to affect 10–15 percent of children. Most at risk are children born prematurely, especially the youngest and smallest; children adopted from overseas; children exposed to alcohol, drugs, and heavy metals; and children with autism, attention deficits, and other developmental disorders as well as those who are intellectually quite gifted. Recent studies show that children who otherwise seem to be developing typically can also have significant sensory processing problems.[*]

When sensory processing challenges disrupt daily life at home, at school, or in community settings like the supermarket, developmental pediatricians, child psychologists, and neurologists may diagnose a child with sensory processing disorder, also known as SPD.

The gold standard of treatment for sensory processing challenges is occupational therapy with a specialist who has obtained advanced training. Meanwhile, there is a lot that parents can do to help their child with sensory challenges!

---

[*] Y. Chang, M. Gratiot, J. Owen, et al., "White Matter Microstructure Associated with Auditory and Tactile Processing in Children with and Without Sensory Processing Disorder," *Frontiers in Neuroanatomy* 9, January 26, 2016, doi:10.3389/fnana.2015.00169.

COMMON SIGNS OF SENSORY
PROCESSING CHALLENGES

* Out-of-proportion reactions such as:
    * Oversensitivity to certain loud or unexpected sounds, such as the vacuum cleaner or automatic hand dryer; or distress when a lot of people are talking
    * Annoyance with clothing tags, seams, fabrics, and too-tight or too-loose fit
    * Distress in visually busy environments, certain patterns and colors, and bright lights, especially fluorescent lighting
* Very limited food repertoire with strong objections to certain food tastes, smells, textures, and temperature
* May seek out or avoid physical contact and movement, including hugs and kisses, rocking, swinging, jumping, and rough-and-tumble play
* May tend to become uncomfortable or easily overstimulated in group settings
* May have low muscle tone or seem somewhat weak, clumsy, or accident prone
* May have decreased attention and focus, with delays in fine-motor, gross-motor, and other developmental skills

With a nervous system that is not functioning optimally, it can be difficult for a child with sensory challenges to establish regular eating and toileting routines and, unfortunately, to develop healthy sleep habits.

Many kids with sensory difficulties become hypervigilant about avoiding unpleasant or noxious input, putting them in a stressed-out, high-arousal state that makes it hard to drift off to sleep. They complain about any kind of noise in the house, whether it's the television, radiator, or air conditioner; a sibling snoring nearby; or parents talking quietly in another part of the house. They may object to how their pajamas feel, the texture and weight of their blanket, or complain that the room is too hot or cold. Tastes and smells bother them—their PJs or bed linens, their toothpaste, lingering kitchen aromas, or a sibling's body odor. They may be afraid of the dark but unable to sleep if the light is on. They may seek out movement when it's time to go to bed, bouncing and jumping around, and rock themselves in bed even as they get older. It's no wonder your sensitive child struggles to get a good night's sleep!

LINDSEY BIEL'S TEN SENSORY-SMART STRATEGIES THAT CAN HELP

1. *Bedtime routines.* Work *with* your child's nervous system rather than *against* it. While you do need to keep a regular, predictable bedtime routine, your sensitive child may need to start much earlier—perhaps up to two hours—before you want him to be asleep. You may need to engage your child in physical activity before bed to recalibrate his nervous system. It may seem counterintuitive, but jumping on a mini-trampoline with a safety bar, climbing a few flights of stairs, or another form of intense exercise may be exactly what your child needs to get the ya-yas out, stimulate production of the body's happy chemicals, and enable him to start to wind down for the night.

2. *Rethink bath time.* For some kids, taking a bath or shower before bed can actually rev them up, especially if they dislike the feeling of water on their faces. If evening baths do seem to soothe your child, try adding Epsom salts, which contain magnesium, which helps calm nerves and relax muscles, but only if you are sure your child won't drink the bathwater.

3. *Reading or meditation.* Many kids love to be read to before bed, often requesting the same book over and over because they love the

predictability. If books don't seem to help, try a bedtime meditation designed to help children slow down their breathing and quiet their minds. There are many guided meditations for kids on the Internet as well as apps you can use. A great, simple method is called *Take 5 Breathing*, which you can learn about at Childhood 101 (childhood101.com).

4. *Consider light.* Some children insist on a night-light, while others are disturbed by it. Follow their lead, but avoid fluorescents and daylight LED bulbs. Consider using blackout shades, especially if you are in an urban area. If you're not sure, try the blackout shades that attach with suction cups, which you can find online. It's best to avoid screen time before bed, but if you and your child absolutely must (or you suspect he is sneaking it), use built-in nighttime settings to shift to a more yellow-based light since the blue light normally emitted interferes with melatonin production.

5. *Noise.* Some kids do well with a fan to block out noise. You can also play music over speakers; use a white-noise or nature-sound machine or CD, the SleepPhones Sheep, which contains an MP3 player; or try the Cloud b Sleep Sheep, which plays eight prerecorded sounds. The iLs Dreampad connects to an app playing vibration-generating, ambient music only the user can hear. It's recommended for twelve months and older, but infants can use the iLs Dreampad with supervision for less than thirty minutes.

6. *Smell.* If your child complains about smells, do your best to eliminate offending items, and try using therapeutic-grade essential oils. It may take some trial and error to find an oil that your child enjoys that masks any perceived unpleasant odors and calms rather than stimulates her. Sweet orange oil, lavender, and rose are often favorites and work especially well through a diffuser. Very pure vanilla essential oil is especially worth trying if your child is a preemie or wakes up frequently. A neonatal intensive care unit study found that pleasant odors, particularly vanilla, led to improved breathing

during sleep for premature infants and reduced awakenings due to sleep apnea.[*]

7. *Temperature.* Many people sleep best in a cool room, but of course you don't want your child to get a chill. If your child runs warm during sleep, try a Bouffi Breathable 3-D mesh (for newborns to two-year-olds) or a cooling pillow, gel cooling pad, or bamboo pillow for your older child. Other kids need greater warmth to fall asleep. Try layering flannel and fleece. If you must use an electric blanket, it's best to supervise and turn it off once the bed warms up.

8. *PJs and linens* Avoid scented laundry products and fabric softeners that leave a chemical residue. Experiment with snug PJs versus loose PJs or wearing nothing. It can also help to use sensory-friendly seamless underwear from SmartKnitKIDS or switching from briefs to boxers or going commando. You may need to experiment with different kinds of sheets; cotton, knit, flannel, and percale all provide different sensory experiences. Kids who crave deep pressure may enjoy sleeping under a Lycra compression sheet.

9. *Blanket weight.* Some kids like lightweight blankets while others sleep best under a heavy blanket or two or three. Weighted blankets, available online and now in some stores, can be almost miraculously relaxing for some people, helping them fall asleep and stay asleep. But be aware of these safety factors: the blanket should be no more than 10 percent of body weight plus a pound or two. It's essential to keep the blanket appropriate to your child's weight, size, and respiratory status; he must be able to independently remove the blanket by *peeling it aside.* Weighted blankets are generally *not* recommended for use for children under age three since the enclosed pellets are a choking hazard and little ones cannot remove the blanket by themselves. Consult with your pediatrician

---

[*] L. Marlier, C. Gaugler, and J. Messer, "Olfactory Stimulation Prevents Apnea in Premature Newborns," *Pediatrics* 115, no. 1 (2005): 83–88.

if your child has any breathing, cardiac, or circulatory problems, epilepsy, extreme low muscle tone, fragile skin, or other medical issue.

10. *Self-regulating tools,* such as stuffed toys, loveys, and pacifiers can really help children with sensory issues. Weighted toys can give additional deep pressure input that your child may like. Many kids find vibration calming, so try placing a vibrating toy under the mattress or attaching it to the bed frame or crib bars. A vibrating mattress may also give the sensory input your sleeper needs.

ADD AND ADHD

The conditions ADD and ADHD are not usually diagnosed in very young children, but they sometimes do become an issue in preschool years. Children with other behavioral or attention problems, including sensory processing issues, may be mislabeled as ADD/ADHD, particularly in these early years.

Whatever the cause, hyperactive children often have trouble falling asleep. These children, even more than others, need a lot of consistency and a steady parental hand. Set bedtime rules, and make sure your child understands that they are rules, not suggestions! Give your child an extra-long wind-down period before bed—maybe forty-five minutes will do the trick.

Try to get tension-producing activities out of the way in the afternoon or early evening, leaving plenty of time for the child to switch into a calmer gear before bed. Stimulating games (including computer games and DVDs) should also be over and done with well before bedtime—and keep them out of his bedroom. Bedtime activities should be quiet, gentle, borderline boring. ADD/ADHD kids, even more than other children, may stall, engage, delay, provoke—they do whatever it takes to keep themselves up and you at their side before bed. Be patient but firm.

If your child takes medication for ADD/ADHD, it may make it harder for him to fall asleep. Work closely with your doctor on timing and dosage. You want to time the medication so it helps the child during the day but wears off early enough that it does not interfere with sleep. If you think medications are keeping your child up or making him have trouble falling asleep, talk to your doctor about alternatives. There are several medications on the market now for ADD/ADHD, and if one is creating sleep difficulties, it might be worth trying another.

AUTISM

Autism, also referred to as *autism spectrum disorder (ASD)*, is currently estimated to affect one in fifty-nine children in the United States per the Centers for Disease Control and Prevention, with autistic traits typically appearing between ages two and three.

Autism is indeed a spectrum, as some people have relatively mild challenges while others face profound difficulties. Some are nonspeaking, while others are quite chatty. Some have strong special interests and talents, while others are generalists. Some have superior intellectual ability, while others do not process information well. This is why it's essential to remember that once you've met one person with autism, you've met just one person with autism. Each person is unique.

What kids with ASD *do* have in common is varying degrees of difficulty with:

Social communication and interaction, such as poor back-and-forth conversations, reduced sharing of interests and feelings, reduced interest in peers, and problems adjusting behavior to different social contexts

Restricted, repetitive patterns of behavior, interests, or activities, such as lining up objects, echolalia (repetitive vocalizations), insistence on sameness, rigidity in thinking, and inflexible adherence to routines

Hyper- or hyposensitivity to sensory input or unusual interest in sensory aspects of the environment, as exemplified by strong responses to certain sounds and textures, excessively smelling or touching objects, and fascination with lights and moving objects

Many children with ASD also have medical issues, such as seizures or gastrointestinal issues, and mental health issues, such as anxiety, depression, obsessive-compulsive disorder, and attention-deficit disorder.

Sleep problems are common in kids with special needs and affect up to 80 percent of kids with ASD,[*] due to neurobiological and genetic factors including dysregulation of melatonin production, which interferes with sleep-wake cycles.[**] A recent study[***] shows that children ages two to five diagnosed with autism are twice as likely to have sleep difficulties than typically developing peers or those with developmental delays unrelated to autism. Children with ASD were found to be much more likely to resist going to bed, have sleep-related anxiety, have trouble falling asleep, and experience night terrors. Exhaustion, of course, makes raising a child with special needs such as autism all the more difficult.

• •

Lindsey Biel is coauthor of the award-winning *Raising a Sensory Smart Child: The Definitive Handbook for Helping Your Child with Sensory Processing Issues*, with a foreword by Temple Grandin. She is also the author of *Sensory Processing Challenges: Effective Clinical Work with Kids & Teens* and cocreator of the *Sensory Processing Master Class* DVD program.

---

[*] F. Cortesi, F. Giannotti, A. Ivanenko, and K. Johnson, "Sleep in Children with Autistic Spectrum Disorder," *Sleep Medicine* 11, no. 7 (2010): 659–664.

[**] O. Veatch, S. Goldman, K. Adkins, and B. Malow, "Melatonin in Children with Autism Spectrum Disorders: How Does the Evidence Fit Together?," *Journal of Nature and Science* 1, no. 7 (2015): e125.

[***] A. Reynolds, G. Soke, S. Sabourin, et al., "Sleep Problems in 2- to 5-Year-Olds with Autism Spectrum Disorder and Other Developmental Delays," *Pediatrics* 143, no. 3 (2019), https://doi.org/10.1542/peds.2018-049.

Chapter 16

ROUTINE BUSTERS

Dealing with Travel, Illness, and Life's Other Disruptions

No matter how hard you try to keep your child on a predictable and comforting routine, disruptions are inevitable. Some routine busters, such as a vacation or a weekend visit to the grandparents, are planned and welcome. Others—like illnesses—strike without warning and can turn a child's sleep upside down.

In this chapter, I explore ways to get through such common disruptions as travel, illness, teething, the birth of a sibling, and moving to a new home. I also offer some advice in the event of big life changes, like Mom returning to work or a divorce. I offer guidelines but not rigid rules. Some children are more adaptable than others and get back into their normal routines without missing a beat. Parents also react differently. Some families strive to keep the schedule in place at all costs. Others consciously decide that the circumstances warrant breaking the sleep rules temporarily, knowing they may have to pay a price later.

During the fall when Ilan turned three, Joanne's normal three-day workweek became a grueling marathon of fifteen-hour workdays—sometimes even longer—five or six days a week. Ilan didn't see her before bedtime and woke up frequently wanting to see her at night. She was exhausted, he was miserable, and she decided to co-sleep temporarily. After the work crisis ended, she took several days off and spent a lot of time with him and explained he was going to sleep alone in his fire truck bed again. She cuddled him a lot right before bedtime and sat in the hallway while he fell asleep. He began sleeping through the night again within a week.

As a rule, if you have deviated, it's a good idea to return to your normal routine as soon as possible. Most kids adapt quickly, particularly if they have already developed fairly good sleep skills. Sometimes you'll have to do another round of sleep coaching (often accompanied by some intense crying or, as I like to call it, *the intermittent-reinforcement shriek*), but it usually goes faster than the initial go-round because you are reminding them of a learned skill, not introducing it from scratch. At the end of this chapter, I give some help on how to do a refresher version of training, and, as always, you can comfort your child as you ease him back into his routine.

I like reminding children of sleep rules even while we're bending them. "You are sleeping in the same room as Mommy and Daddy while we are at the lake, but as soon as we get home, you and Teddy Bear will be back in your princess bed and Mommy and Daddy will be in our bed, but we'll come check on you every night." Or "I'm going to pick you up and hold you until you fall back asleep to make you feel better, but as soon as your tummy ache goes away, you won't need Mommy to do this. You are going to sleep great again, and I'll give you so many stars and stickers because I will be so proud." Even very young toddlers understand some of this, and older ones get it quite well. It helps

Sleep Lady Tip

If your child has only recently started sleeping through the night or going to bed without a great deal of fussing, try to postpone any discretionary travel for at least three weeks.

to make the rule breaking less confusing to them and makes the intermittent reinforcement less powerful. By understanding your expectations, they may have an easier time readapting to their old routine once the disruption has passed.

TRAVEL

The better a child sleeps at home, the better the odds are that he will sleep well when you travel. Even if he does get off kilter while you are away, if he's a good sleeper, he'll probably return to good patterns when he gets home. Conversely, if your child has only recently started sleeping through the night or going to bed without a great deal of fussing, try to postpone any discretionary travel for at least three weeks.

When you travel, your child will probably backslide a little bit, but try not to throw out all your gains, and try not to rely on whatever sleep crutch you've just eliminated. For instance, if you stopped nursing during the night, don't start again. Go ahead and do a lot more soothing and comforting on the road than you would at home, but find some way of soothing that won't lead you back to where you started, that won't let you get caught in the intermittent-reinforcement trap. You don't want him thinking, *You got me up to nurse when we were in that strange place; maybe you will still get me up to nurse now that we are home!* You can't blame him for trying.

Always bring along the lovey and pack a night-light, and since there's no such thing as traveling light with a small child anyway, go ahead and take along favorite books and toys. Many families bring crib sheets or blankets, too. (Some hotels don't provide much in the way of bedding with a crib or portable crib, so check in advance or pack linens just in case.) You want the child to have items that feel and smell comforting and familiar. If you are one of those parents who always keeps a small bag stocked with first-aid supplies, travel-size medications, and baby toiletries, stick the spare night-light and bulb in there as well so you don't have to worry about forgetting them. If you are staying at a relative's home or a rental condo, you may want to take your baby monitor with you, too, so you don't feel like you have to stay by his side in a dark room from 7:00 p.m. on!

> "We visit my parents, just about an hour away, pretty frequently. I used to bring the whole sheet set—including the bumper and the mobile! But I don't do all that anymore," said Jayne, who worked with me when Cynthia was four months old. "She sleeps in a crib there, and although she usually doesn't sleep well the first night, she's okay the second night. I try to be consistent with her routine there. I don't skip naps, and I put her down at her usual bedtime. She's fine as soon as she gets home."

One obvious drawback to staying in a hotel or motel is that young children go to bed early, and you may not want to sit in the dark all night. (Some couples take turns reading in the lobby or even in the hall. A balcony can be a good alternative, weather permitting. If you have older children, one of you might want to put the baby to bed in the hotel room while the other keeps the big kids occupied—ice cream, mini-golf, or something like that—but then try to have them tiptoe into the hotel room and get into bed as quietly as possible.)

Think about how to position the child's crib or bed so that you may be able to turn on a small lamp later without having it shine in his eyes, or maybe take one of those little travel book lights along. Some all-suite hotels oriented toward long-term business travelers have good deals for families on weekends and holidays. Even in a suite, you may have to turn off all or most of the lights for a few minutes when you put the baby to bed, but then you have some adult space to talk or read or watch a movie with the volume on low (and the kitchenettes are great when traveling with children). One creative mom I know packed an extra sheet and thumbtacks with her every time she stayed in a hotel with her child. She could make a curtained "wall" between the crib and the bed à la *It Happened One Night* so the child wouldn't think she was going to get to sleep in Mom and Dad's room from now on.

"Randy travels for work, and since I'm not working right now, we try to travel together. I bring everything—the blanket, pillow, more than one teddy bear, toys, and food," said Suzanna's mother, Sheila. "We try to get a suite—if she's in our room, it doesn't work as well." Initially, Sheila would "do anything" to get Suzanna to sleep away from home, including co-sleeping, and that set up problems when they got home. Over time, Suzanna became more adaptable, and Sheila got better at figuring out how to backslide on the road without creating longer-term disruptions at home.

Before you go, talk to the hotel about whether it has cribs, portable cribs, or pack-and-plays. Or if you are visiting relatives, think about whether enough young children will visit over the years to make it worth investing in a crib or portable crib. You'll learn quickly what your child can adjust to, and you'll then be able to pack and plan accordingly on subsequent travel.

With older children who are no longer in a crib, you may request a rollaway bed, or if the child will be in a regular hotel bed in your room, you may see if you can move it closer to the wall for safety. Put an extra pillow on the floor in case he falls out, or place the mattress on the floor so it doesn't matter if he rolls off. You may want to place the mattress next to your bed, or between your bed and another bed holding older siblings, so that the little one is reassured by being close to you.

There's a good chance he will get out of his bed and sneak into yours. Some parents return the child to his own bed; others figure it's a losing battle in the hotel. If he does end up with you, carefully explain that he can sleep with you in the hotel (or at Granny's house or wherever) but will have to go right back into his own bed when you get back home. Ilan understood this immediately, and even if he didn't sleep through the night right after a schedule disruption, he did understand that he could sleep with Mommy in a hotel or at Granny and Grandpa's house, but at his own house he'd be in his fire truck bed with his stuffed animal friends, and Mommy would be in her room with Daddy.

If possible, try to have your child sleep in one place throughout the whole vacation. You may be better off with a week at the beach than on a road trip with a different hotel (and possibly a different crib) every night. If you are visiting several relatives, it may be worth sleeping in one home for the entire trip and visiting with other family members during the day or over early dinners. For instance, one couple with a nine-month-old originally planned a five-day vacation—two nights with one set of grandparents, two with the other, and one night at an aunt's. I gently suggested they might want to reconsider, so they chose one set of grandparents as a "base camp" and arranged to have relatives visit them there or to spend part of the day at other family members' homes. They carefully explained to all concerned why their baby needed this, and to avoid bruised feelings or rivalries, they immediately let all concerned know that the other grandparents would be the "base" for the next visit.

Try very hard to make sure your children get enough rest on vacation. With all the change and stimulation, they may not nap while traveling. It's up to you how hard you press the nap; you may get a sense that if you insist and make the effort, he will nap. Alternatively, you may figure that you can spend the whole afternoon in your hotel room and he still won't sleep a wink, so you might as well go out and enjoy yourself; maybe he'll doze in the stroller. It depends on how old the child is and how long you are away. An infant absolutely still needs naps. A three-year-old can probably skip naps for a few days as long as you get him to bed at night earlier than usual.

You might also want to plan some of your travel to overlap with nap time. As you know, I normally want children to sleep in their beds, not in cars; but on vacation, a car nap might be the best you can do. Plus, if you are going to be in the car for a few hours anyway, it may be easier on everyone if he sleeps through it. Try to get back to your hotel (or relatives' home) on the early side, to have an early bedtime. A vacation isn't much of a vacation when the kids are melting down all day.

"We had trouble with naps on vacation," said Lucas's mother, Tracy. "But we found that if we had to disrupt his day, we were better off disrupting it in the morning. He'd often fall asleep and catch up later."

When you get home, make it a top priority to return to your normal routine as quickly as possible. Some families keep their activities very light for a day or two when returning home to really focus on getting napping and bedtime back in place.

TRAVELING ACROSS TIME ZONES

If you are traveling across time zones, get your child up at his usual wake-up time, both when you start your vacation and when you get back home. In other words, if he wakes up at 7:00 a.m. at home in Miami, wake him up at 7:00 a.m. Pacific time in Seattle, and then when you get back home to Miami, wake him at 7:00 a.m. eastern time. In other words, stay on local time, not home time. Do this the day you arrive on vacation, or if you all need to recover from a particularly long trip or a red-eye, do it the next day.

This means you should switch naps and sleep times to local time, too, the first full day after your arrival. So if you got in late and everyone goes to bed later than usual and then sleeps in, naps will obviously be off that first day. But don't let him nap late. Wake him from his last nap (or his only nap) early enough so you can get him to bed at his regular bedtime. In other words, if you arrived in Seattle at midnight, everyone will sleep late in the morning (you hope!). Then instead of napping from 1:00 to 3:00 p.m., he might not begin his nap until 4:00. Don't let him nap too late, though, even if he's a little cranky when you rouse him, so you can get him to bed that night at his regular bedtime, at 7:00 or 8:00 (Seattle time). Don't fret if you can't follow this exactly. A few car or stroller naps aren't a big deal on a vacation; you'll get everyone back to normal when you get home.

> ### Sleep Lady Tip
>
> Use the naps to help your child reset his clock to his new location. Exposure to sunlight, especially in the morning, helps the body adjust. And there's nothing like a hotel swimming pool to tire kids out and help them get ready to sleep.

"We went to Hawaii with two young kids, and we had to lie down with them. We knew it was a no-no, but we had to do it. They were getting up so early—1:30 a.m.," said Kathleen. "Sean had an easier adjustment than Maude, although he did want dinner at midnight. But when we got home, they readjusted in four nights. They both cried a little on the third night, but just for a couple of minutes, that's all."

ENJOY LIFE!

Although I stress routines and consistency, I don't want you to take it to such an extreme that you can't enjoy your life! I'm not sure I would have been as courageous as Kathleen, flying to Hawaii with two children under the age of four. But don't let yourself get caught in the trap Linda and Miguel experienced, either. Four months after they got Amy sleeping well, they were still too petrified even to visit out-of-town relatives for a weekend, never mind try a vacation.

"I'm afraid to get her out of her routine. I'm afraid she'd get out of whack. She would probably adapt better than I think, but I would dread going back to the way things were—it was just so awful," Linda told me when Amy was fifteen months old. Finally, after a few more months, they did venture away for a weekend with great trepidation. "She did great!" Linda said. "Nap time the first day was nearly nonexistent because of the strange environment and a new portable crib, but beyond that she did wonderfully!"

DAYLIGHT SAVING TIME CHANGES

When we change clocks in the spring and fall, switch immediately to the new time. In other words, if her bedtime was 7:00 p.m. and you moved the clock to 8:00 p.m., keep putting her to bed at 7:00 p.m. according to the new time. Make sure your child has taken a good nap so she can make it to the new time. She may wake up a little early or a little late for a few days, but then she'll adjust. Stay consistent, and don't let her start her day before 6:00 a.m. (new time). Schedule your next day's meals and activities according to the new clock time. The adjustment seldom takes even a week.

If you think your child can't make a one-hour adaptation that easily, split the difference. Using the example above, put her to bed at 7:30 p.m. (new time) for a few days, and then shift it to 7:00 p.m.

ROUTINE CHILDHOOD ILLNESSES

You have some control over when your child travels, but you don't get to choose when he gets an ear infection, a tummy ache, or bronchitis. If he gets sick during a sleep-training program, pause until he's feeling better. Don't abandon the program. If you can, freeze or maintain your Shuffle position until he feels better. If you feel he absolutely needs you closer, go back to sitting near the crib as you did on the first three nights of the Shuffle, and then move halfway across the room when he feels better. Don't draw this out; you will just make it harder for him. If he gets sick shortly after you complete his coaching, he'll probably backslide a bit, and you may have to do an abbreviated version of training to get him sleeping all night again.

When your child is sick, respond immediately to his cries at night. Do whatever you need to do—give him medicine, aspirate his nose, clean him up after a tummy attack. Go ahead and hold him and comfort him as much as you think he needs, even if it sets back sleep training a few days. My advice about not picking up crying children during sleep shaping does not apply when they are sick.

Don't totally overdo it, though. You want to take care of your child, you want to soothe your child, but there's a difference between a little backsliding and total regression. In other words, if you've recently ended co-sleeping, don't put your child back in your bed at the first sniffle. Sit by his side, hold his hand, stroke him, snuggle him, but try not to take him back into your bed. I would even rather have you sleep on a make-shift bed in his room than have him back in your bed.

But obviously, if you have been trying to get rid of his water bottle at night but he's now got a tummy ache, give him whatever fluid he needs to stay hydrated until his stomach calms down. Once you make a health-based decision to give him a drink, do it as soon as he needs it; don't make him cry for it. If age appropriate, feed him in a slightly different way during illness. In other words, if you just weaned him from night-time nursing but he needs liquids because he's sick, try a cup or a bottle instead of nursing. If he was emotionally attached to a specific sippy cup, try letting him having a few sips out of a big-boy cup.

Occasionally, we find a silver lining to an illness. I know one six-month-old who was very pacifier dependent, but he got so congested by a bad cold that he couldn't suck on it and breathe simultaneously. When he didn't use it for three nights, his parents seized the opportunity to make it disappear for good.

During and immediately after an illness, expect your child to wake up more at night and to take longer to get back to sleep. Don't assume over-the-counter cold, allergy, or pain-relief medications will help your child sleep (and don't give them without checking with your pediatrician, as many are not recommended for children under age six). These medicines do make some children sleepy, but they stimulate others, and they can get so wired that they stay awake for hours. Some parents have found dye-free medicines reduce this problem, but it's not always a solution. And even if they do induce sleep, most medications wear off in a few hours.

Vaccinations throw some children off for a night or two. Ask your pediatrician whether you should give him Tylenol or a similar analgesic before the shot, and offer the baby more reassurance at bedtime and when he gets up at night because he might not be feeling completely himself. He will usually feel better and be sleeping normally within a few days.

Ear infections are particularly brutal on sleep, because the pain intensifies when a child lies down. In fact, frequent and distraught awakenings may be one telltale sign that your child has an ear infection. If your child has chronic infections, talk to your pediatrician about consulting an ear, nose, and throat specialist on the wisdom of using a longer or different course of antibiotics, or whether he's a good candidate for surgery to insert tubes. If he gets an ear infection while you are doing the Sleep Lady Shuffle, pause where you are, and start moving ahead again after he's feeling better, usually in about two or three days (faster if he feels better after only one day).

MOVING TO A NEW HOME

A lot of families regard the move to a new home as a time to make sleep changes, but I'd be careful about this. Moving means change and stress, and you don't necessarily want to add to it if your child doesn't do well with change in the first place.

Make sure you give your children plenty of time and attention, because it's an enormous change for them. Play in their new bedrooms to promote comfort and familiarity. At night, babies, preschoolers, and even school age children might want some extra reassurance as they acclimate to new surroundings, so sit in her room or by the door at bedtime. Don't forget a night-light and a few practice runs at finding the bathroom!

You might want to let the older child, even around age three, help arrange her room. Choosing colors or decorations will help her feel in control and make the move feel more fun. Be sure to let children talk out their concerns, including questions about their new routines, babysitters, preschools, or schools.

> After Reid lost his job, he and Julia traveled by car with three young children while they tried to figure out where they wanted to resettle. They spent a lot of time in cars and hotels, and they did a lot of backsliding regarding sleep. "We gave Todd back his pacifier," said Reid. "I'm not sure whether it helped him, but I think it helped the real estate agents."

When they finally did settle in a lovely coastal city and Reid opened his own business, the kids manifested pretty typical behavior. That's when the oldest daughter became a champion bedtime negotiator, earning that "Captain Loophole" sobriquet. The second daughter, who was moving to a new state and starting kindergarten simultaneously, started showing up in her parents' bed at night. And Todd needed that pacifier again—but he would get furious at bedtime, hurling it across the room. "It's an interesting ritual, if you stop to think about it," Reid said. "He was throwing the one thing he really needed to get himself to sleep." Naturally, as the parents gave their children reassurance and everyone adapted, life calmed down or got as close to calm as any home with three children ages seven and under can be.

With a very young baby, a move to a new house or apartment is a good time to move the crib out of your room and into her own room. If she's more than six months old, you might want to start the Sleep Lady Shuffle as you make this switch (although you may not want to tackle everything at once; for example, if you move her to her own room, you might not want to try to wean her off her pacifier that same night).

If she's less than six months old and too young for the Shuffle, sit in her room and give her some extra soothing and reassurance as she acclimates. For an older child, a move is not usually a good time to switch from a crib to a bed. Let her get accustomed to the new space first, or you will be inviting more bedtime conflict. If the room configuration allows it, I like putting the crib in the same place in relation to the door as it was in your former home. As with all changes, the better your child sleeps, and the longer she's been sleeping well, the less disruptive a move is likely to be. If your child doesn't sleep well and you want to do some concerted sleep coaching, wait a few weeks after the move until she's adapted. You as a parent will also cope better with her sleep training if you've got the first wave of moving chaos under control.

We moved when Carleigh was two and a half and Gretchen was minus three weeks (I was pregnant!). Being a little hyperfocused on sleep, I had the real estate agent help me figure out which of the four bedrooms got the earliest sunlight. I then put the girls in the rooms with the least morning sun. Some people move into a new home and get the kitchen set up first, or maybe the big-screen TV. The first thing I did was put up room-darkening shades in the kids' rooms and get their furniture in place.

CHILDCARE NAP OBSTACLES

Childcare centers have their own approaches to naps, and they aren't always the approaches that are right for your individual child, even if the overall care is excellent. For instance, many childcare centers will not allow a baby to cry in the crib at nap time for fear of waking all those other babies. So the caregivers often rock or hold the babies to sleep.

You should work on nighttime sleep and weekend naps, and when you are fairly confident of your child's ability to get herself to sleep, talk to the childcare providers. Explain what you have accomplished, and ask them to work with you on getting her down drowsy but awake. Perhaps they can put your child in the sleep room or nap area a few minutes before they bring in the other babies, to give her a chance to get used to falling asleep on her own there. Maybe they can just rock or hold her for a shorter period of time and then pat and *sh-sh* her to sleep, instead of rocking her until she's totally out. Talk to them about meshing their nap schedule with your child's sleep windows. Share your knowledge of sleep science to see if you can get them to work with you. Talk to them about keeping a special lovey, blanket, or pillow at childcare or preschool. At the very least, ask that they work on filling her sleep tank any way they can so that she is not totally nap deprived when you pick her up.

One family I worked with had a very active, alert six-month-old who had difficulty napping in a bright, somewhat noisy room with other children. Her childcare center would not tolerate any nap-time crying, so the staff held her to sleep. Even that stopped working; as soon as they put her in her crib, she would wake up and cry. The baby would end up taking several short half-hour naps and be a wreck by the time her parents arrived. They then had trouble with her at dinnertime and bedtime, and she started waking up more frequently at night because she was overtired. The otherwise-excellent childcare center would not bend on their sleep rules, so the parents withdrew her and hired a nanny. It was much more expensive, but they felt they had no choice, given their daughter's temperament and sleep patterns. The childcare center did agree to reserve a slot for the little girl, and she happily returned at age two.

Some childcare centers transfer babies on their first birthdays to a new care group where all children nap once a day. Unfortunately, this is premature; most children don't transition to one nap until about fifteen to eighteen months. Talk to the center about leaving your one-year-old in the baby room for a few more months until he's ready to give up his morning nap.

In toddler classrooms, children usually nap on cots (not cribs) in a darkened room with a lot of other children. If it works, leave it alone! You can work on bedtime and weekend naps, and many children can separate what happens at childcare from home patterns.

With a three-and-a-half- or four-year-old, your challenge might be convincing the childcare staff that he no longer needs to nap, that he stays up way too late if he sleeps for two hours each afternoon. Most providers give sleep reports; if yours doesn't, ask them to fill you in.

FAMILY TRAUMA

Obviously, going through a divorce, an illness, or a death in the family is an upsetting time for everyone, and your goal should be to provide your child with maximum comfort and security. You will almost certainly see some sleep disruption—more clinginess at bedtime, more night awakenings, maybe more bad dreams.

I wouldn't attempt to embark on any major new sleep training until the trauma (your child's and yours) has diminished and new routines have been established. You can, however, try to avoid creating any new sleep crutches during a time of stress. For instance, you might be tempted to start co-sleeping to comfort your child (or yourself), but I would recommend that you do a lot of snuggling before bedtime and a lot of comforting from a chair or the doorway rather than getting into a new habit that may be difficult to break later.

SEPARATION AND DIVORCE

With separation and divorce, as always, maintaining a routine will provide your child with a great deal of security and comfort. Children may adapt better than you expect to two different sets of sleep rules and expectations. They understand, for instance, that at one house, the parent will lie down with them until they fall asleep; but that doesn't happen at their other house. What counts is consistency from each parent. In other words, if you lie down with her on Tuesday, she has every reason to expect you to lie down with her again on Friday, no matter what happened at the other parent's house on Wednesday and Thursday.

Similarly, it's fine if your kids share a room at Dad's house but have separate rooms at Mom's. If you have to sleep coach them, you may have to separate them temporarily. It's generally better to move the better sleeper to a temporary bedroom, and leave the one being coached where he is. (Appendix A, "The Sibling Factor," has more advice on sleep training more than one child.)

A parent with shared custody can do the Sleep Lady Shuffle on his or her own, no matter what the other parent is doing. It may take longer and not be perfect, but you will see improvement. For instance, if you're now a single father and don't want to co-sleep with your three-year-old daughter, you can start the Shuffle by having her sleep on a mattress on the floor of your room for a weekend or a week. Then, the next time she's at your house, you can sleep on the floor of her room while she gets into her bed. Continue the Shuffle, step by step, as best you can within the confines of your custody arrangement. Obviously, the ideal is for both parents to work this out together, but that's a tall order amid a divorce.

Don't despair of sleep improvements even without cooperation from your former spouse or partner.

LOSS OF A FAMILY MEMBER

In the sad event that your family experiences a death, follow the same advice mentioned above: Be gentle and offer extra reassurance, ideally without creating new sleep crutches. Make sure you don't tell your child that Grandpa went to sleep and won't wake up again; that only exacerbates children's evening fears. Incorporate your own beliefs in explaining death to your child. If your spouse has died, then you may want to seek grief counseling and discuss further strategies with the therapist on how to help your child. Some parents may decide to do whatever works and deal with the sleep fallout when they are feeling better themselves.

> ### Sleep Lady Tip
>
> Some parents have tremendous trouble setting any limits during the first year of divorce. They feel sad and guilty and don't want to "ruin" their time with their children by setting limits, enforcing rules, or risking arguments. Again, I must emphasize that children find routine, structure, and boundaries comforting, especially in times of stress.

SCHOOL AND WORK CHANGES

All sorts of disruptions unsettle our children's lives—new childcare providers, Mom going back to work, a parent traveling on business. Basically, you need to give extra reassurance and comfort without throwing your whole routine out the window. Keep bedtime and your child's bedtime rules consistent, but make sure you are providing the sense of security your child needs.

"When Vince travels, I stick to the plan. If I vary it for even one second, it's all over," said Beth, whose daughter, Madison, was then two and a half.

Be extra diligent about making sure your child gets enough sleep, because she will be able to handle stress and change better if she's well rested. Some parents who travel like to leave a recording of themselves singing a lullaby or reading a favorite bedtime book. Children sometimes like to mark off the days on a calendar until Mom or Dad comes home. It's very concrete, and they can actually see that the parent's homecoming is approaching. It's nice to include the missing parent in bedtime songs or prayers. Be careful, though, about talking to Mom or Dad on the phone just before bedtime. This can be upsetting to a child who doesn't understand where his parent is. If your child reacts badly, try scheduling the phone calls earlier in the day.

BABY BROTHERS AND SISTERS

Most children experience some understandable regression when a new baby comes along. They may have temper tantrums or ask for a thing they've outgrown, such as a diaper, bottle, or pacifier, or need your attention urgently every time you start to nurse the new baby.

Sleep is also affected. If the older child starts waking up more frequently at night, walk him quietly back to bed. If he's waking up because he hears the baby, explain that everything is okay, that new

> **Sleep Lady Tip**
>
> No matter how busy you get with the baby, it's essential that you spend special one-on-one time with the older child every day.

babies need to wake up and eat but that soon the baby is going to sleep all night just like his big brother or sister. Remind him during the daytime, too, if he's old enough to understand.

If he starts demanding more of your attention at bedtime, start bedtime earlier so he has longer to unwind with you. (Depending on everyone's nursing and sleeping schedules, this might only work if both parents are at home.) Or involve him in the baby's bedtime. He could "help" you read the baby a simple story, or you could read to him while nursing. (See Appendix A, "The Sibling Factor," for more advice on how to coordinate two bedtimes.)

If the baby is sleeping in your room and your child knows that he used to be there, explain that the arrangement is temporary, that the baby will go to her own room (or their shared room) in a few months. If your older child is co-sleeping with you, please don't kick him out of bed to make room for the new one! Keep the baby in a bassinet or co-sleeper, but don't add to the older child's feelings of dislocation. Sometimes one parent sleeps with the older child in that child's room while the nursing parent sleeps with the baby in the parents' room.

If you are going to transition a child to a bed before the birth of a sibling, do it at least two and up to six months before the birth. If you wait until after the baby is born, give it at least four months. Please don't rush this transition because you need a crib, particularly if your older child is under two. If your older child is still happy in his crib, leave him there and buy or borrow another crib or bassinet for the baby.

Occasionally, an older child who is already in a bed will want his crib back. He may say it, or he may show you, for instance, by climbing into his baby brother's crib. Highlight the advantages of a big-boy bed. Point out things that he gets to do with you that the baby doesn't—like going to the playground or eating cookies! Crib envy is usually his way of voicing a fear that he is being replaced, so just keep giving him all the reassurance he needs. But if he's under age two and a half and hasn't been in a bed too long, don't rule out giving him the crib back. Following big-boy stay-in-bed rules and coping with a new baby may be more than he can handle right now. But keep telling him how much you enjoy having a big boy or girl and how lucky the baby is to have such a great big brother or sister. Make sure visitors make just as big a fuss about your big guy as your little one.

Give the older child some jobs to do: Let him fetch a diaper or help wash the baby's toes. Remind him of the safety rules, too—no touching the face, no throwing things, no picking up the baby, and definitely no waking up the baby or going in when she's sleeping.

RETRAINING

When you experience a sleep disruption, address it promptly. You need to be extra consistent at the first opportunity, both in terms of scheduling and in terms of scaling back your own comforting at bedtime and at night awakenings.

Usually, the briefer and less extreme the disruption is, the easier it will be to overcome. For instance, a twenty-four-hour stomach bug is going to be a lot less difficult to cope with than a week in the hospital, and a napless weekend at a relative's house an hour's drive away will be a lot less disruptive than a two-week trip to London. But as long as the regression doesn't last months, it's usually less a matter of relearning a sleep skill than of remembering to use a skill your child already knows.

A child who has a lot of disruptions—for instance, irregular parental schedules combined with frequent illnesses—may have more trouble than a child who goes away for one week a year. You may have to go through the Sleep Lady Shuffle again, but you can probably do it quickly, just one or two nights in each position. Usually, you don't even have to do the entire Shuffle; it's enough to just do the last few nights, sitting in the hallway and then doing checks.

If the regression is significant and recurs soon after you've finished the Shuffle, say, a week or two, you may have to go back to the beginning, to sitting beside the crib or bed. But then move very quickly; change positions every night instead of every three nights. Other families just go to the sitting-in-the-doorway stage and progress from there. You may have to endure some crying because the break in the routine amounts to intermittent reinforcement, even if it was unintentional or unavoidable. In general, the longer your child has been sleeping well, the longer he's been well rested, the quicker the transition to peaceful nights. I remember getting an email from an amazed parent who had worked with me six months earlier on both her children's sleep. They had just returned from a vacation, and for the first time ever, both kids slept all night while they were away and didn't miss a beat when they came back home.

Some children conquer their sleep problems and just shake off later disruptions. Others remain highly sensitive to them—and often these are the children who were very alert as newborns and reached developmental milestones early. Babies who have reflux for more than three months often tend to have more long-term vulnerability to sleep disruption. Ilan was one of those very alert children, and Joanne certainly knew all the ins and outs of my sleep system as we worked on this book. Travel didn't disturb him too much; he usually shared her bed in a hotel but returned to his routine at home quite easily. But even a minor illness could throw his sleep off significantly.

One time, he ran a high fever for a whole week. Joanne was so tired, she kept toppling over, finding herself curled up, sleeping like a kitten at the foot of his bed. He, of course, would want her to resume her kitty-like pose at 3:00 a.m. the next night, too. She went through countless variants of star and sticker charts, including special glow-in-the-dark star bonuses. Once, she noticed that he always wanted to sign himself in and out of preschool (only adults were allowed to do that), so she started having him sign himself into bed every night! Once he signed himself in, he knew he wasn't allowed to get up and go out again. You'd be surprised how well it worked. He loved that sign-in privilege.

Chapter 17

YOGA FOR THE WHOLE FAMILY

A Natural Way to Get Some Sleep
by Mariam Gates, author of *Good Night Yoga: A Pose-by-Pose Bedtime Story*

As a yoga and mindfulness teacher, I knew after the birth of my daughter that I was going to need to put those calming practices into overdrive. My daughter was not a baby who went to sleep easily. She was usually fussy at bedtime, and I often felt stressed that I was "not doing it right." Her tiredness and mine were not a great match. As a toddler and preschooler, this continued, and she has always needed what I call a "long runway" to settle and get to bed. I started using child-centered yoga and breathing exercises at bedtime as a way to help soothe her and support a more relaxed transition to sleep.

With a few simple techniques, the body and breath can signal the parasympathetic nervous system that it is time to move into rest-and-digest mode. Gentle stretching and breathing help to reset the nervous system and actively promote the neurological relaxation response. With these tools, both of us were able to shift from the anxiety-producing task of *trying to get her to bed* to a ritual we could both enjoy. What became apparent was our mini-yoga and breathing flows were as calming for me as they were for her. As she got older, they were a way to signal that we were at the last part of the evening. These easy practices helped us to intentionally prepare for sleep together.

It is helpful to have a routine to follow so that both parent and child know what is coming next. Using a preset flow means that less attention has to be spent on adjusting to the next exercise and the focus stays on the relaxation effect. Once we had established our routines, her father was also able to mimic the flows. Of course, as a parent or caregiver, it is expected that you will make adjustments based on the specific needs and responses from your child in each set of exercises.

A note on safety: As with all things with infants and children, no movement should be forced or require undue effort. Smaller bodies need smaller movements. A key component of this practice is to be mindful while you are doing it. This means paying attention to what is happening here and now, to include your baby's or child's cues. Your little one may have some stiffness or hyper-flexibility, and in both cases, movement should be very gentle and never pushing past a moderate range of motion. The support you give is to facilitate movement rather than create it. It is also important to let go of your image of what these mini–practice sessions look like and any need to get them right. Whatever the two of you are able to do together will generate good results. If your intention is to take a little time out to focus and connect, that is what will happen. Even if it does not always look (or entirely feel) that way.

BIRTH TO FOUR MONTHS

For newborns and infants in the first months, the yoga, mindfulness practices, and breathing techniques are primarily for the parent or caregiver to use and model. Babies do, however, respond to touch. Touch supports bonding and healthy development, so a gentle massage ritual is a great place to begin.

Guided Massage: Begin by noticing your own breathing. Pay attention to the length of your next inhale and exhale and see if that shifts your awareness into the present moment. Notice the light in the room, the feeling of the bed or floor beneath you, as you keep listening to the sound of your breathing in and out.

Baby Leg Massage: Begin with your baby on her back. (Make sure she is comfortable, not too cold or in need of feeding or a diaper change.) Hold your baby's foot and gently rub the foot with your thumbs. (Try talking to your baby through this process in a soft voice, letting her know what you are doing each step of the way.) Then move to the top of the thigh; it can be helpful to lightly hold the foot in your hand and use the opposite hand to massage the leg (pay attention to what is comfortable for you and your child). Then begin to do an easy, light, caressing stroke with your fingers down the leg all the way to the heel. You can try starting back at the top again and doing a gentle pressing (like the smallest squeeze) back down to the foot, but keep checking in with your baby to see what she is enjoying. Then repeat the process on the other leg. (If you find yourself feeling distracted at any point, try noticing and lengthening your next breath in and out and seeing what you can focus on in this moment: the feel of your baby's skin, the color of her eyes, the temperature in the room.)

Baby Hands, Shoulders, and Arms Massage: Take one of your baby's hands and press lightly on the palms with your thumbs and lightly stroke her fingers. Do this on both hands. Next, place your hands on your baby's shoulders and again lightly stroke from the top of the shoulders, down the arms to the hands. You can repeat with a gentle light pressure from your fingertips all the way down.

Baby Chest Massage: Bring both of your palms to your baby's chest. Notice the warmth of your hands and her heartbeat. Next, make a light, gradual, sweeping motion to the sides. Repeat several times.

For bedtime baby massage, the idea is to keep the strokes moving away from the heart (for other massages at other times of day, the direction can go either way). Keep your touch gentle but firm and not tickly. It is important to keep noticing how you are feeling and your baby's reactions and not to overstimulate through the process. It is fine to stop at any point.

FOUR MONTHS TO ONE YEAR

There are, of course, many developmental changes in the first year, and so what works for you and your baby may be shifting quickly. The gentle massage techniques can also be continued.

YOGA MOVEMENTS
(BABY VERSION / PRE- TO EARLY WALKING)

The sun is setting, and the world is going to sleep
Hold your baby's hands in yours and bring them out to the sides and then back to the chest, elbows bent. Try extending slowly out to the sides again and back.

It's time to settle like the butterflies
Lightly bend one knee and guide it toward the baby's chest. Then slowly extend. Try again.

Then try with the other leg. Then bring both feet together to touch toe to toe and back out.

And the ladybugs on their leaves
Lightly hold your baby's feet and bend both knees together toward her chest and release.

Sweet, sweet dreams

Lightly hold both knees and rock her body slightly from side to side.

Then begin your baby massage sequence.

ONE TO TWO YEARS

As your child enters the toddler stage, she is learning so much through mirroring, which is a wonderful way for her to integrate self-soothing techniques. This next simple mini–bedtime flow can be done with parental support (holding both hands or feet and guiding the gentle stretches) or by having your child do each movement on her own while you recite the bedtime poem. If your child is moving independently, try doing the poses for the child to follow. As an additional benefit, you will also quickly feel more relaxed.

This sequence can begin standing or with your child in a seated position (cross-legged if that is comfortable) with a few simple modifications.

Begin by noticing your own breath in and out. Try lengthening the inhale and the exhale, and become aware of any sensations or places of tightness in your body. Bring that same mindfulness (awareness of the present moment) to your breathing, the room you are in, where you are sitting, and anything you can notice about your child beside you. What do you see and hear? How are you feeling? Take another deep breath in and let a long breath out.

MINI-FLOW
(USE THE IMAGES FROM THE "GOOD NIGHT YOGA FLOW" AT THE END OF THIS CHAPTER FOR REFERENCE)

Sun Breath

Both hands reach up high overhead and back down to the sides. Ideally, you are modeling taking a breath in as you reach high and letting the breath out as you bring your hands down. If seated, simply reach high overhead and then let the hands come down gently to the floor.

Star

Both hands reach out to each side. You can wiggle the fingers and add "Twinkle, twinkle" for the shining stars. If seated, follow the same instructions and let the arms extend out to each side.

Half-Moon

One hand rests at your side, and the other reaches high as you and your child bend to the side to stretch. Repeat for both sides. Again, ideally, the reach up is on an inhale and the side stretch is on the exhale, but it is not required. If seated, place one hand on the floor and let the other reach high as you and your child lean to each side to stretch.

Butterfly

Bring the feet together gently and let the knees splay out to the sides to form the wings. Children have different levels of flexibility through the hips, so keep that in mind and don't try to force any extension. It is fine if the knees are pointing upward. If your child wants to, she can also bring her hands to her ears and wave her elbows to form the second set of butterfly wings and pucker her lips to sip nectar.

Bee Breath

For this pose, have your child come onto her knees and spread her arms behind her. Note: It may be more comfortable for your child to stay sitting cross-legged and simply extend her arms back. Either one is fine.

Take a deep breath in and then buzz while bending forward. It does not matter how far down your child bends; the purpose is to lengthen the inhale and the exhale here.

Now transition your child to lying down on her back.

Final Relaxation

It's time to say sweet dreams to the world from east to west and all around.

Bring the knees to the chest and then bend both knees to one side for a gentle twist and then back up and over to the other side.

Listen to the quiet around you and let your breathing be the only sound.

THREE TO FIVE YEARS

At this age, children are able to do a longer flow combining breath and movement with great results. They are starting to build internal awareness and can describe the experience of being upset versus being relaxed and feel the difference in their bodies. Try this yoga sequence from *Good Night Yoga: A Pose-by-Pose Bedtime Story* by Mariam Gates, illustrated by Sarah Jane Hinder (Sounds True), and see the pages that follow for specific instructions for each pose.

GOOD NIGHT
YOGA FLOW

SUN BREATH

CLOUD GATHERING

TREE

LADYBUG

BUTTERFLY

425

STAR POSE

HALF-MOON

BIRD

BEE BREATH

CAT

CHILD'S POSE

Excerpt from *Good Night Yoga* © 2015 Mariam Gates, illustrated by Sarah Jane Hinder (www.sarahjanehinder.com), used with permission from the publisher, Sounds True Inc.

ADDITIONAL YOGA POSE INSTRUCTIONS

SUN BREATH

Inhale while raising your arms up over your head. Exhale while lowering your arms back down to your sides.

CLOUD GATHERING

Inhale and bend your knees and imagine you can scoop the clouds right in front of you. Exhale and straighten your legs, lifting your arms above you and letting the clouds go.

STAR POSE

Press down through your feet. Reach your arms wide.

HALF-MOON

Inhale and lengthen your spine. Exhale and bend to one side. Inhale to come up and exhale to the other side.

BIRD

Focus on one point. Spread your arms behind you, lift your foot back, and balance. Then switch feet.

TREE

Become tall in your spine. Rest your foot on your ankle or above your knee and balance. Then switch feet.

LADYBUG

Come into a gentle squat, roll your shoulders back, and press your palms together over your heart.

BUTTERFLY

From a seated position, gently bring your feet together and let your knees splay out to the sides to form the butterfly wings. You can also bring your hands to the back of your head and let your elbows form the second set of wings.

BEE BREATH

From a seated position, inhale and sit up straight with your arms back. Exhale with a buzzing sound and lower your forehead toward the ground.

CAT

Come onto all fours. Inhale and look up, letting your spine drop low. Exhale and tuck your chin, lifting your spine high.

CHILD'S POSE

Press back onto your knees and rest. Forehead is on the ground.

Try adding a gentle back massage by stroking and pressing gently on the sides of the spine, beginning at the neck.

ADDITIONAL TOOLS

BELLY BREATHING

Have your child lie on her back and place one hand on her belly (thumb on the belly button). Have her take a deep breath in and fill with air so her hand rises. Then let it out. It is fine to have your child keep one or two hands on her belly to focus on the breath moving through. You can also add one hand on the chest and help her to notice as the air moves through both places. *Breathe with Me* is a great resource for this and more breathing techniques.

Repeat slowly three times.

YOGA REST

Also known as *savasana*, this "resting without doing" is an essential component of a yoga practice and is known to reduce stress and insomnia.

Lie on your back with your hands relaxed by your sides. Take slow, natural breaths. Try closing your eyes.

GUIDED VISUALIZATION

Visualizations at bedtime can be an easy way to shift into a more peaceful state while also giving children a helpful place to focus their attention. It also develops resilience and self-soothing skills as they use their own imaginations to feel calm and safe.

You can use a resource like *Sweet Dreams: Bedtime Visualizations for Kids* (illustrated by Leigh Standley) for ideas or any print or online guided visualizations.

Resources

Good Night Yoga: A Pose-by-Pose Bedtime Story (Sounds True)
Breathe with Me: Using Breath to Feel Strong, Calm, and Happy (Sounds True)
Sweet Dreams: Bedtime Visualizations for Kids (Sounds True)

Appendix A

THE SIBLING FACTOR

*Can I Sleep Coach with Older
or Younger Siblings Around?*

For those families who have children very close in age, some of the information I shared about twins in each age-specific chapter may be useful. But here I'll answer some other questions I hear often from families with two or more children, such as:

* How do I put two kids to sleep?
* How should two parents divide responsibilities?
* What about napping?
* Will one crying child wake up or frighten the other sleeping child?
* What if they share a room? And what if one is in a crib and one in a bed?
* What if they have the same bedtime? What if they don't?

BEDTIME

The general rule of thumb is to put the youngest one to bed first. Depending on age, personality, and degree of sibling rivalry, the big brother or sister may or may not want to listen to the baby's stories and songs and be part of the baby's good-night rituals before going to bed. If not, make sure the older child keeps busy with a quiet game or activity so she won't keep interrupting the baby's bedtime in a manner that is disruptive or stimulating. You don't want the three-year-old (or any older child, for that matter) running in constantly while you are trying to get the younger one to sleep. That's what I did when my second daughter, Gretchen, was a baby and needed a nice, quiet nursing or bottle before bed and her dad wasn't home to take care of our older daughter, Carleigh. By the time Gretchen was about one and Carleigh three, I could read a "young" book to the two of them together in Gretchen's room. Then Carleigh would wait for me in her room while I put Gretchen to bed. As soon as Gretchen was down (she knew how to put herself to sleep, so I didn't have to stay there), I'd go to Carleigh and read her an "older" book and make sure she and I got some just-the-two-of-us Mom-Carleigh time. (I'll talk about shared rooms in a moment.)

If two parents are home in the evening, one may deal with the baby (often the nursing mom), and one takes care of the older child or children. But switch off some of the time so each child knows how to go through her bedtime routine with each parent. Make sure both children get a few special good-night moments with both parents. It helps if everyone makes the kids' bedtime a priority for an hour or so—take care of other household tasks a little later. Even if you aren't both routinely home by bedtime, see if you can find a time to start coaching when your work schedules will allow both of you to be home for a stretch. If not, see if you can enlist a grandparent, relative, or friend. One adult does the Shuffle with the baby, the other with the toddler. Or it might be easier for you to let the older one stay up for a little while you work on the little one's sleep. Then you can do the coaching for the older one.

"We stagger our children's bedtimes," said Kathleen, whose children, Maude and Sean, are twenty-six months apart. "That's hard as a working parent, because Maude goes down at 7:00, and I only get an hour and a half with her on the three days that I work. But I know she needs to go to bed then; kids who go to sleep at 9:00 or 10:00 have a lot more temper tantrums."

While Kathleen is busy with Maude, big brother Sean understands that it's baby sister's special time with Mom. He gets a thirty-minute video, a quiet one suitable for evening, or special playtime with his dad. Then he gets to choose if Dad puts him to bed or if he wants some Mom time of his own. The other parent comes in for a final message of sweet dreams and a good-night kiss. The family set up this basic system when Maude was an infant and Sean was two, and it was still working with just a few minor tweaks when he was four and a half.

Greta and Matt used to have both boys together for story time. Frederick would happily stand up in his crib and point at trucks while Dad read books to big brother. When that system no longer worked, when they each needed a more age-specific story, the parents split them up for bedtime.

Some children go through a stage when they only want one parent at bedtime—usually Mommy.

"First I get the baby to sleep, but I often hear Ariella clear across the house; she doesn't want her dad—she wants me. And Peg hears it, too, so then I have Ariella stalling and Peg crying. We've tried really hard to let Doyle put the girls to bed, but Ariella really wants me right now, and I have to be with Peg because I'm still nursing," said Marcy. She and Doyle have gently but persistently continued including Doyle in Ariella's bedtime. He now does baths and dinners and some evening play, although Ariella still insists on Mommy for stories and lights-out. Meanwhile, hoping to avoid a repetition of this pattern with the younger daughter, Doyle has been spending more and more time with Peggy at bedtime, and he's the one who goes in to check on her on those nights when she still wakes up.

Sometimes we worry so much about the younger child's cries waking or upsetting the older one that we rush in too quickly. Try not to fall into this trap, because you are only going to perpetuate the younger child's night awakenings by reinforcing her sleep crutches. If she cries and you come running lickety-split, she isn't going to have a lot of motivation to stop crying! Try going first, briefly, to the older child, who has been woken up, rather than the one who is bawling. For instance, if you are sleep shaping with a six-month-old and the baby is waking up your two-year-old, go to the two-year-old first and reassure her. Tell her that the baby is okay and she should go back to sleep. Then go tend to the six-month-old. If both parents are home, then divide and conquer, one of you with each child. You might also want to try a white-noise machine for the older child. There are new white-noise machines coming on the market all the time—some smaller and more portable ones—which are handy to block out unfamiliar or loud noises when traveling. Visit https://sleeplady.com/products for a list of some of my favorites.

It helps if you tell the older child what sleep training is and why her baby brother or sister sometimes cries. Most will understand this by around age two and a half. I encourage parents to start with a family meeting, to explain the expectations and find ways of getting the older child (or children) to feel like she's part of the baby's sleep education.

Depending on the age and sleep skills of the older child, you may even help her think of herself as a sleep role model for the baby. Tell her the baby needs to know how to get herself to sleep, just like her big sister does. Explain that when the baby learns, she won't cry as much, but in the meantime you have to be with her or go check on her. The older child will let you go more easily if she understands and you make her an ally. If she gets it, she may not barge in as often with demands on you just as you are finally getting the little one to drift off to sleep. Stickers or other little treats and incentives can help. Your goal, as always, is to prevent the older one from feeling displaced. Instead, you want to make her feel even more needed, more loved, and more important. (See Chapter 16, "Routine Busters," for advice on the birth of a sibling.)

Sometimes, if your children are very far apart in age, with eight or ten years between the oldest and the youngest, it seems that life should get a little easier because the big one can help with the little brother or sister, or at least take care of herself. That's true up to a point, but it's also true that the children have such different needs—logistically, academically, and emotionally—in the evenings that you may feel like you are straddling two parallel parental universes. It's tough to bathe a three-year-old upstairs while trying to pry a twelve-year-old away from his phone or tablet or to get the little one all cozy and drowsy only to have the big one noisily pop into the bedroom every five minutes with questions about sixth-grade math homework. I know some families who have enlisted the older child to help put the younger one to bed, or even to pretend that he is going to sleep at the same time, although they aren't always willing or able to go along with that gimmick all the time.

NAPS

Scheduling conflicts between your children's naps or activities also create sleep barriers. For instance, you may discover that your six-month-old's natural nap sleep window is wide open precisely when you have to pick up your older child from preschool. See if you can work out a carpool to minimize those disruptions. If you do have to drive and the baby falls asleep in the car seat, either move the car seat inside and let her finish her nap or, better, work on teaching her how to transfer into the crib: if she wakes up while you move her, stroke and soothe her back to sleep. It takes a little while to acquire that skill, but most babies do get it, so don't give up; keep working on it. Then it's lunch and afternoon naps for everyone. Playdates will work best after the afternoon naps while they are on a two-nap-a-day schedule, or in the morning once the toddler switches to one nap.

Parents often find that no matter how tears-averse they were with their first child, they have little choice once the second one arrives. For instance, if you are nap coaching an eight-month-old and your three-year-old is downstairs, it's going to be hard to stay with the baby for a solid hour and leave the preschooler on his own, unless you have a babysitter or a relative who can come over and help at nap time. Even if the preschooler doesn't mind being left on his own (and he probably will mind—an hour is a long time), you are going to be in the baby's room fretting about whether the older child is really quietly assembling that puzzle you left him—or finger painting the living room couch.

Chances are, at some point, you are going to be spending some time with the three-year-old while you leave the baby to cry for a few minutes. Try to get at least the pre-nap ritual with the baby done, putting her down drowsy but awake. And check on her every ten or fifteen minutes; you don't want her crying forever. But simply out of necessity, you may have a slightly more Ferber-like approach to naps with a second child.

Occasionally, I've run into families who thought sleep training a younger child would be too stressful on the older child. Ellen, for instance, sent the very sensitive James to his grandparents' while she trained Vanessa. Luckily, Ellen had a much easier time with Vanessa than with James, and the sleep coaching took just three days. Usually this isn't a problem; just be attuned to how the older sibling feels about the baby's sleep shaping, or have one parent stay with him and keep reassuring him that the baby won't cry forever, that he'll be sleeping soundly and dreaming sweetly in just a little while.

SHARING A ROOM

While you focus on getting the baby to sleep, try having the older one play quietly in a nearby room for a little while before coming into her own bed. (If you are all living in a one-bedroom apartment, sleep training is harder but still possible. Check out my advice in Chapter 5, "Prepping for Sleep-Coaching Success," on page 59.)

Parents often ask me for advice on whether children should share rooms or how old they should be when they are separated, particularly a boy and a girl (assuming the family has enough space for separate bedrooms). I don't think there's a right or wrong answer; do what feels right for you, and watch your children for clues to their preferences. They might be old enough to articulate what they want.

It's often helpful to sleep train the baby before you move him into the big sister's or brother's room. You can keep the baby in your room (or another room in the house or apartment) while you train him, and then move him into the shared room once he has it down. Alternatively, if they are already sharing a room, you could move the older child temporarily out of his room into your room or another room in your home. Naturally, this isn't a good idea for a child who may easily start feeling displaced, is having a tough time with sibling rivalry, or will have a hard time moving out of his makeshift bed in your room if that's where you plan on putting him. But if he is adaptable, explain to him that this is a temporary arrangement while the baby learns to sleep. You might even be able to make it sound fun.

When you do move a baby into the older child's room, teach the bigger child good sleep manners. No talking to, playing with, or waking the baby when he is asleep. Explain that it's so special to share a room and it's important to have good sleep manners.

You can sleep coach two kids or more (I have successfully coached parents of quadruplets) in one room, in cribs or beds, even if they are slightly different ages. If it's one parent flying solo at bedtime, sit between the beds or cribs and go over to first one child and then the other as needed to comfort them. If one is in a crib and the other in a bed, make sure the older one understands that once he's in bed, he needs to stay there.

Appendix B

POSTPARTUM MOOD DISORDER, BABY BLUES, AND DADDY DEPRESSION

I see postpartum mood disorder—what many are used to calling *postpartum depression*—in a lot of the families who come to me for sleep help. Exhaustion is a risk factor for depression. And depression makes it harder to sleep coach successfully, which in turn breeds more exhaustion. I'd like moms and moms-to-be to read this section. I'd like dads and dads-to-be to read it. And the grandparents and best friends, too. Women experiencing postpartum depression (and as we'll see, there is a lesser-known version that afflicts men) don't always recognize the signs or may already be too depressed to take action, so it's important for the people who are close to them to be on the lookout.

Postpartum depression is common; 10–15 percent of women experience it globally. Traditionally, postpartum depression was thought to begin in the first month after birth, but now we know it can also occur later in that first year. It's not good for the mom, and it's not good for the baby, who may have more trouble forming a secure bond with a depressed, emotionally flat, unresponsive, or anxious parent.

Postpartum depression has biological components. Pregnancy hormones plummet, affecting brain chemistry; a history of depression adds to the risk. Exhaustion, stress, and new-mom anxiety play a role. Depression does not mean you are a bad mother, an unloving mother, or a failed mother (or father). It does not mean that you will not feel better and enjoy motherhood for many years to come. It does not even mean you will experience a similar depression after every birth (although you are at higher risk).

Check out Postpartum Support International (www.postpartum.net) for resources, or call the toll-free hotline, 1-800-944-4773. Better sleep, exercise, nutrition, and social support can help. You should also have your ob-gyn or family doctor do a simple test to rule out a thyroid problem. But you may also need therapy, drugs or alternative treatments, support groups, or some combination thereof. Doctors can help you find an antidepressant, if necessary, that you can safely take while breastfeeding. If you find you need a drug that may not be as compatible with nursing, or if you refuse to consider medication while you are nursing, please consider whether the benefits of breastfeeding outweigh the benefits of treating a serious depression that may interfere with your ability to take good care of yourself, your baby, and other, older children. I'm not saying that breastfeeding isn't healthy and desirable. I'm saying that untreated depression can be very harmful, and you should not feel guilty or inadequate about stopping breastfeeding earlier than you had hoped and planned.

Depression can be very harmful, and you should not feel guilty or inadequate about stopping breastfeeding earlier than you had hoped and planned.

If you do wean early for medical reasons, do it slowly because the hormonal changes can aggravate depression. (Even if you don't have postpartum depression, rapid weaning can give you flashes of depression. I didn't have PPD, but I did experience those flashes as I weaned my first daughter, and I wish someone had warned me about that. I weaned my second daughter more gradually and avoided the problem.)

I can't "fix" postpartum depression in a few pages here, nor should I try. What I want to do is help you recognize the warning signs, understand the difference between postpartum depression and the "baby blues," and learn some techniques that you and your family can use to address the sleep and exhaustion aspects.

Getting five or six hours of uninterrupted nighttime sleep is essential—and yes, it's possible even with a breastfed newborn. For more information, I recommend the books of Dr. Shoshana Bennett (*Beyond the Blues, Postpartum Depression for Dummies, Pregnant on Prozac,* and *Children of the Depressed*). She's a psychologist who experienced two very severe undiagnosed postpartum depressions herself, and some of what I will share with you here is drawn from her work. She offers phone consultations and can be contacted through her website at www.DrShosh.com.

BABY BLUES

Baby blues—that is, brief episodes of mild mood changes—are extremely common the first few weeks after giving birth. You may feel moments of sadness or mood swings, you may cry, and you may feel vulnerable, stressed, or anxious. But the blues are transient. They go away in about two weeks. If sad feelings or anxiety are overwhelming, if you experience any thoughts of harming yourself or your baby, or if your symptoms start to interfere with your daily life, get evaluated for postpartum depression.

Parents, and especially moms, are under a lot of pressure in our society. We are bombarded with conflicting advice to do this or to do that, and sometimes we're told we're doing things "wrong" if we choose not to bed share, or if we go back to work soon, or if we don't "wear" our baby all the time. Give yourself a license to be human! If you have the time and inclination to make homemade strained baby food and you feel good about it, more power to you. But a lot of babies eat food out of a jar and grow up happy and healthy.

POSTPARTUM DEPRESSION ACTION PLAN

I've already stressed the need to get professional help. Here are some other things you can do on your own:

* **Eat healthy foods.** Avoid caffeine and definitely avoid alcohol, as it's a depressant. Drink plenty of water, and eat a healthy, balanced diet with a lot of fruits, vegetables, legumes, and whole grains. Bennett also recommends nibbling on high-protein snacks and drinking whey protein shakes. Consider a multivitamin and getting your vitamin D and folate levels checked.
* **Exercise.** It doesn't have to be superambitious—walking and stretching are good ways to start. For a severely depressed woman who may be having trouble even getting out of bed, exercise may seem overwhelming. Friends and family should encourage her to at least go outside, stand up straight, breathe deeply, and get some sunshine.
* **Take time for yourself—a few breaks a week, each an hour or two.** Take a walk. Read a book. Meet a friend. Get a manicure. New-mom playgroups, support groups, and baby-mommy yoga classes are great, but they don't count as pure mom time.
* **Sleep!** Getting at least five or six hours of uninterrupted nighttime sleep is essential to treat and potentially lower your risk of postpartum depression. Even breastfeeding moms can do this. Here are some tips:
    * If your baby is four to six months old, and the doctor gives you the okay, you and your partner can start nighttime sleep coaching now—and if it's too much for you as you deal with the depression, have your partner take the lead.

* Split nighttime baby duty so you each get at least one five-hour uninterrupted block of sleep. One of you is "on" from 8:00 p.m. to 1:00 a.m., and the other from 1:00 a.m. to 6:00 a.m. (adjust these figures to your family's schedule). When you are "off duty," sleep in a separate area and try earplugs, a fan, or a white-noise machine. The on-duty parent can sleep, too, but he or she will be the one who has to wake up to respond to and feed the baby. If you are a single parent, see if there's a friend or relative (your sister, brother, mother, or whoever) who can sometimes come and let you get a solid block of sleep.

* If you tend to obsess about when the baby will wake up or how long you've been awake, move the clock away from your bed.

* Consider pumping breast milk so your partner can feed the baby with a bottle of your milk while you get your off-duty sleep. Empty both breasts before bed so you won't wake up painfully engorged.

* If you are bottle-feeding with formula, alternate nights with your partner to get a full night's sleep. If you can afford it, hiring a night nurse or doula for even a few nights can help.

DEPRESSED DADS

We can't blame fathers' depression on reproductive hormones, but at least one in ten fathers experiences depression after the birth of a child (and not necessarily the first child). Symptoms are different. They are less likely to experience mood swings and more likely to be tense, short-tempered, fearful, angry, and frustrated. They may feel helpless, worry about finances, or have concerns about the family's new interpersonal dynamics. They often have high expectations for themselves and are confused about their new role.

Dads can develop depression even when the moms are fine, but what's the biggest risk factor for a dad to get depressed? When the mom has postpartum depression. A father whose partner is seriously depressed has between a 24 and 50 percent risk of developing depression after the baby is born. The onset is usually after the mother's depression. And when fathers have depression, the children may suffer. Sons in particular are at high risk for behavioral problems in early childhood if their fathers were depressed.

Appendix C

SAFE SLEEPING
RECOMMENDATIONS FOR BABIES

Here are some tips for baby safety. Most of the information is from the American Academy of Pediatrics and First Candle, an organization devoted to reducing the rates of sudden infant death syndrome (SIDS) and other sleep-related infant deaths. I'd like to emphasize that the following advice is primarily for healthy infants. Always talk to your doctor, particularly if your child was premature or has any health problems or unique circumstances. Recommendations have changed over the years as we have learned more about child safety and development, and they may well change again, so revisit safety issues with your doctor frequently. You may see all kinds of contradictory information on parenting and health websites. A good place to sort it all out is the American Academy of Pediatrics' parenting website (www.healthychildren.org).

1. "Back to Sleep." This motto sums up the primary rule of infant sleep safety. Always place your baby on his or her back to sleep—both at naps and at night. Side and tummy positions are not safe. This is absolutely essential to reduce the risk of sudden infant death syndrome and other sleep-related infant deaths. Once your baby

rolls over consistently backward and forward, you won't be able to keep him on his back all the time, unless that's his preferred sleeping position, so make sure he has enough room to move around and nothing in his crib. No quilts, loose blankets, pillows, soft or pillow-like bumpers, soft bedding or stuffed animals, or toys with pieces that can come off.

2. Babies should sleep on a firm surface, such as a safety-approved crib mattress, covered by a tight-fitting crib sheet. Never place your baby to sleep on pillows, quilts, sheepskins, or other soft surfaces. Infants should never sleep or nap on adult beds, waterbeds, sofas, armchairs, or soft mattresses.

3. Be careful about buying secondhand or using hand-me-down cribs, bassinets, or co-sleepers, even if they've been in the family for years. Safety standards have changed, and some products have been recalled or taken off the market, such as drop-side cribs. Contact the Consumer Product Safety Commission at 1-800-638-2772 or at www.cpsc.gov for crib standards and recalls.

4. You'll see numerous devices and gadgets on the market designed to maintain sleep positions, but they have not all been tested for safety and efficacy and are not recommended. Generally, avoid them. If you have some specific concern about your child's sleep position or movement, talk to your doctor.

5. Cribs should be placed in a warm, dark part of the room, away from windows. Blankets should not dangle from the side of the crib, and wall hangings need to be well out of the baby's reach so he can't pull them down on himself. Keep soft objects, toys, and loose bedding out of your baby's sleep area, as these all pose a risk of suffocation.

6. At six months, remove all crib mobiles or toys attached to crib sides, because once the baby can pull and grab, they become a hazard. I like keeping mobiles away from the crib all the time; hang them someplace where she's awake. Make the crib or sleep area "boring" as well as safe.

7. Do not let your baby overheat during sleep. The room temperature should be comfortable for a lightly clothed adult. Once you stop swaddling your baby, use a sleep sack or blanket sleeper. If the bedroom is cooler, use two sleep sacks or place one over the pajamas or onesies. Layer clothing in lieu of bedding.

8. Remember that the American Academy of Pediatrics strongly recommends that you do not smoke during pregnancy or around your baby. Other people should not be permitted to smoke around your baby. Smoking exposure increases the risk of SIDS and other respiratory illness. Prepare your house or car (where smoking has occurred) for a new baby's arrival. Wash down all the walls and windows. Clean carpets and curtains. Air out the house and car by opening windows. You can also place a dish of charcoal to absorb odors.

9. The American Academy of Pediatrics recommends you not let your baby sleep in an adult bed or on a couch or armchair with adults or other children. But the AAP does recommend keeping your infant close by in your room, particularly for the first six months, ideally for the first year. See my advice on room sharing in Chapter 12, "Making Choices About Co-Sleeping, Bed Sharing, and Room Sharing," for more information. If you bring your baby into bed with you to breastfeed, then put him back in a separate sleep area, such as a bassinet, crib, cradle, or a bedside co-sleeper (an infant bed that attaches to an adult bed) when finished. When baby starts to roll and move in his sleep, graduate to a standard crib for better— and safer—sleeping. Beds that are perfectly safe and comfortable for adults or older children can be very hazardous for babies. Adult beds are not made with infant sleep safety in mind. Especially dangerous are pillow top and memory foam mattresses that can conform around a baby's mouth and nose and obstruct his breathing. Soft bedding and other items in the adult bed increase the risk of SIDS and suffocation, especially for young babies. A baby or small child can also fall from the bed or get trapped between the mattress

and the structure of the bed (the headboard, footboard, side rails, and frame), between the bed and the wall or nearby furniture, or even between railings in the headboard or footboard. Fatalities have been documented.

If you do choose to have your baby in the family bed, understand all the bed-sharing safety rules and *always follow them*. Parents who do have a baby in bed with them for even part of the night must never smoke or use substances, such as alcohol or drugs (including prescription or over-the-counter drugs that make you sleep heavily), that may impair arousal, making them less aware of their baby's needs or position in the bed. Sleep is an unconscious state of mind. Babies lying right next to a sleeping adult have been known to scoot, root, and end up under another person, pillow, or blankets at the other side of the bed.

10. Pacifiers can significantly reduce the risk of SIDS (see First Candle at www.firstcandle.org). They also soothe infants and are very useful tools for those caring for a fussy baby. The AAP advises using a clean pacifier when putting the infant down to sleep, although you shouldn't force the baby to take it. If you are breastfeeding, wait about four weeks before introducing the pacifier.

11. Sleeping in unconventional beds: The AAP states that car seats, swings, infant carriers, and infant slings are not recommended for routine sleep, particularly for young infants. Parents and caregivers often use these devices, even when not traveling, because they are convenient. It is important to know the Centers for Disease Control and Prevention reported that infants sleeping in car seats are at increased risk of strangulation from straps and positional asphyxia. Injuries were also reported from falls when car seats were placed on elevated surfaces, from strangulation on unbuckled or partially buckled car seat straps, and from suffocation when car seats overturned after being placed on a bed, mattress, or couch. When infant slings and carriers are being used, it's important to ensure

that the infant's head is up and above the fabric, the face is visible, and the nose and mouth are clear of obstructions. If an infant falls asleep in a sitting device, he should be moved to a crib or other appropriate flat surface as soon as is safe and practical. Frequent stops should be made when traveling long distances with an infant sleeping in a car seat. The risk with car seats seems to be greatest in younger infants, who have the least head and neck control. While it isn't clear when the risk ends, it has been reported to wane after four to five months of age.

12. Loveys: These small blankets are often placed with infants in their sleep space to soothe the baby and encourage sleep. First Candle doesn't recommend the use of loveys by babies under the age of one year. They are considered to be soft bedding. If you use a lovey when placing your baby to sleep, remove it after she falls asleep.

13. Pillows: Well-intentioned parents and caregivers may use pillows and soft bedding to provide comfort or to cushion an area near an adult bed or couch in the event the infant falls. Pillows can obstruct a baby's nose and mouth, becoming a breathing barrier. Even as the infant gets older, a pillow could be used to stand on and could increase the risk of the baby falling out of the crib.

14. Bumpers: The design of infant cribs has come a long way. Years ago, crib slats were wider apart and allowed for a baby to fit his head and body between them. Obviously, a huge threat. Therefore, bumpers were introduced and used to keep babies positioned in the middle of the crib, safely away from the slats. Eventually, crib standards were changed and slats now should be no more than two and three-eighths inches apart. This eliminated the possibility of infants falling out between the slats and made bumpers—which turned out to have safety risks of their own—obsolete. Bumpers have been outlawed in several cities and, at this writing, in one US state.

A good rule of thumb to follow regardless of where your baby sleeps is to remember that your baby's sleep space may become a hazard because of what you put there. For infant sleep products, only use a fitted sheet. Regarding alternative sleep space like a drawer, basket, or box, you should only use a light receiving blanket under the baby and nothing else. Once you put a pillow, stuffed animal, or blanket there, you turn even safety-approved cribs into danger zones for your child.

INDEX

ABOUT THE AUTHOR

KIM WEST is the mother of two wonderful daughters and a licensed clinical social worker who has been a practicing child and family therapist for over twenty-five years. Known as the Sleep Lady by her clients, she has helped over twenty thousand tired parents all over the world get a good night's sleep *without* letting their child cry it out alone.

Kim has appeared on *Dr. Phil*, the *Today Show*, *NBC Nightly News*, *Good Morning America*, TLC's *Bringing Home Baby*, and CNN, and has been written about in a number of publications and outlets, including the *Wall Street Journal*, the *Washington Post*, Associated Press, *Baby Talk*, *Parenting*, the *Baltimore Sun*, *USA Today*, the *Telegraph*, and the *Irish Independent*.

In addition to *The Sleep Lady's Good Night, Sleep Tight*, West is also the author of *The Good Night, Sleep Tight Workbook* and *The Good Night, Sleep Tight Workbook for Children with Special Needs* with Katie Holloran.

Dedicated to providing tired parents with excellent sleep advice and coaching, she started training Gentle Sleep Coaches all over the world in 2010. You can see her directory of coaches at https://sleeplady.com/coaches/.

Visit Kim West at https://sleeplady.com/.

Follow her:

http://www.facebook.com/TheSleepLady
https://instagram.com/thesleeplady/
https://www.youtube.com/user/TheSleepLady
http://www.pinterest.com/thesleeplady/Chapter 8